The Nature and Future of the Catalog

The Nature and Future of the Catalog:

Proceedings of the ALA's Information Science and Automation Division's 1975 and 1977 Institutes on the Catalog

Edited by Maurice J. Freedman and
S. Michael Malinconico

A Neal-Schuman Professional Book

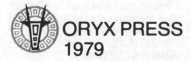 ORYX PRESS
1979

Operation Oryx, started more than 15 years ago at the Phoenix Zoo to save the rare white antelope—believed to have inspired the unicorn of mythology—has apparently succeeded. The operation was launched in 1962 when it became evident that the animals were facing extinction in their native habitat of the Arabian peninsula.

An original herd of nine, put together through *Operation Oryx* by five world organizations, now numbers 47 in Phoenix with another 38 at the San Diego Wild Game Farm, and four others which have recently been sent to live in their natural habitat in Jordan.

Also, in what has come to be known as "The Second Law of Return," rare biblical animals are being collected from many countries to roam freely at the Hai Bar Biblical Wildlife Nature Reserve in the Negev, in Israel, the most recent addition being a breeding herd of eight Arabian Oryx. With the addition of these Oryx, their collection of rare biblical animals is complete.

Copyright © 1979 The Information Science and Automation Division of the American Library Association
Published by The Oryx Press
2214 N. Central Avenue
Phoenix, AZ 85004

In association with Neal-Schuman Publishers, Inc.

Published simultaneously in Canada

Printed and Bound in the United States of America

Distributed outside North America by
Mansell Publishing
3 Bloomsbury Place
London WC1A 2QA, England
ISBN 0-7201-0908-6

Library of Congress Cataloging in Publication Data

The Nature and future of the catalog.

"A Neal-Schuman professional book."
Includes bibliographical references.
1. Cataloging--Congresses. 2. Library catalogs--Congresses. 3. Libraries--Automation--Congresses.
I. Freedman, Maurice J. II. Malinconico, S. Michael.
III. American Library Association. Information Science and Automation Division.
Z693.A15N39   025.3   79-21629
ISBN 0-912700-08-4

Contents

Contents

Preface

The Nature and Future of the Catalog presents the edited proceedings of two cataloging institutes sponsored by the American Library Association's Information Science and Automation Division (now the Library and Information Technology Association) and the Resources and Technical Services Division's Cataloging and Classification Section. The first institute, "The Catalog: Its Nature and Prospects," was held in New York City on October 9 and 10, 1975. The second institute, "The Catalog in the Age of Technological Change," was held on April 22 and 23, 1977 in New York City and repeated with some modifications on May 19 and 20, 1977 in Los Angeles.

These institutes brought together some of the most influential people in the field to discuss — and sometimes spiritedly debate from the rostrum and from the audience—the current and traditional issues involved in cataloging, the impending implementation of the second edition of the *Anglo-American Cataloging Rules*, and the technological environment created by library automation in the 1970s. Both institutes were honored by the presence of the twentieth century's greatest cataloging theorist, Seymour Lubetzky. Few who were present will forget the now classic confrontation between Professor Lubetzky, who represented over 100 years of cataloging ideology beginning with Anthony Panizzi, and Frederick Kilgour of OCLC, who propounded the perspective of new cataloging technology.

Virtually all of the proceedings of each institute are reprinted here. Because the audience interaction with the speakers at all three meetings has been painstakingly transcribed and edited, the reader of this work can relive with some degree of verisimilitude the excitement and stimulation created by these institutes and such colloquies as the Kilgour-Lubetzky exchange. Minor editorial changes have been made as necessary, and comments which were unintelligible from the tapes have been deleted. Names of speakers from the audience which were not clear from the tapes are listed as "unidentified."

The 1975 institute proceedings are presented in the first part of this work. Each speech is followed by the official reactors' statements and audience discussion. The second part of this volume combines the proceedings of the two 1977 institutes held in New York and Los Angeles. For the sake of editorial continuity, those speeches which were given at both locations (for example, Mr. Gorman's presentation) are only printed here once. The audience discussions following the presentation of each paper in New York and Los Angeles have been integrated for the purpose of eliminating duplicated remarks.

Only those who have attempted to edit the proceedings of a conference can appreciate the magnitude and scope of such an enterprise. Nonetheless, the editors and publisher agreed that the overall high level of the discussion justified the time, expense, and labor required to produce this work. As the person responsible for organizing the programs, selecting the speakers, and serving as moderator throughout the institutes, I have many people to acknowledge, beginning with my co-editor S. Michael Malinconico who offered untiring support and many useful suggestions in putting together the institutes. Donald P. Hammer, Executive Secretary of LITA, and Dorothy Butler, the Division's Administrative Secretary, handled all of the administrative details, arrangements, and logistics. I am grateful to Allen Stretton, William Myrick, and Patricia Read for their editorial assistance in the preparation of these proceedings. Finally, I wish to thank all of the speakers, reactors, and attendees who made these institutes so memorable, exciting, and rewarding.

I believe that the issues brought forth and debated in the following papers and discussions are as timely today as they were when the institutes were first held. The ideas contained herein will be central issues for consideration in the foreseeable future.

Maurice J. Freedman
Associate Professor
School of Library Service
Columbia University

Acknowledgements

ISAD appreciates the cooperation of the Cataloging and Classification Section of the Resources and Technical Services Division and the Reference and Adult Services Division of the American Library Association for cosponsoring the two institutes: one on the Catalog—Its Nature and Prospects, the other on The Catalog in the Age of Technological Change. Special thanks to the New York Technical Services librarians, who were especially helpful in promoting the institutes; and to the ISAD Program Planning Committee, in particular its chairperson, Michael Malinconico, for the conceptual organization. Further appreciation is extended to the speakers, reactors, and many participants for their ideas and support.

Biographical Notes on Contributors *

Hugh C. Atkinson, Director of the University of Illinois Libraries, has consistently been in the forefront in applying automation to traditional library problems and services. He has held a variety of positions of increasing responsibility. His first library position was as an assistant in rare books at the University of Chicago. He was the Pennsylvania Military College Reader's Services Librarian for three years. At the State University of New York at Buffalo, Mr. Atkinson was Head of the Reference Department from 1961 to 1964; Assistant Director for Technical Services from 1964 to 1967; and during the last two years at the latter position, he also served as Acting Assistant Director of the Health Sciences Libraries.

Prior to his current position, he was Director of Ohio State University Libraries for Public Services. During his tenure, OSU was recognized for the high quality Selective Dissemination of Information (SDI) program it developed in serving both students and faculty, and the aggressive approach the library staff adopted with respect to publicizing OSU's many bibliographical services and encouraging patrons' use of them.

He is probably unique among Association of Research Libraries directors in that he played a significant role in the creation of ALA's Social Responsibilities Round Table. He has published extensively and been extremely active in his profession.

Sanford Berman, Head Cataloger of the Hennepin County Library, Edina, Minnesota and Editor of the award-winning *Hennepin County Library Cataloging Bulletin,* has been an early, continuing, and outspoken advocate of user-oriented cataloging service. He received his bachelor's degree from UCLA and a master's degree in librarianship from Catholic University. In addition to his work with the the UCLA Library and the Washington, D.C. Public Library, he held successive two-year positions in Zambia and Uganda. While in Uganda he authored the Markerere Institute list of subject headings, which foreshadowed his later work at the Hennepin County Library, which he joined in 1971.

He has been well known for his voluminous writings and correspondence. Of particular note is his classic monograph *Prejudices and Antipathies,* published by Scarecrow Press, a critique of LC entry and subject heading practices. His cataloging philosophy, a prose poem, was published by *Library Journal* and was included in the *Best of Library Literature 1976.* It appeared originally in the *Hennepin County Library Cataloging Bulletin,* which received the H.W. Wilson Award as the best library periodical for 1976, and which is the only American

---

*Compiled and edited from recordings of Maurice J. Freedman's introductions at the institutes.

publication devoted exclusively to cataloging. Mr. Berman was formerly Editor of the *Social Responsibility Round Table (SRRT) Newsletter* and is still a member of SRRT, but chooses not to be a member of the American Library Association. He represents how much can be accomplished by someone who has worked from the outside. Few librarians have had both his dedication and ability to make the catalog a living tool serving all of the people.

Kenneth Bierman is the Assistant Director for Technical Services and Automation at the Tucson Public Library, Tucson, Arizona. Mr. Bierman, in his position as Data Processing Coordinator at the Oklahoma Department of Libraries, 1968-1972, was a pioneer in his use of the MARC (Machine-Readable Cataloging) records distributed by the Library of Congress. The Oklahoma Department of Libraries offered an SDI service on the MARC tapes based on ranges of classification numbers supplied by the user library. At the time, it was a startling accomplishment and gained wide recognition. From 1972-1975, Mr. Bierman was Systems Librarian and then Assistant Director for Planning and Research at the Virginia Polytechnic Institute and State University.

He has served on a wide variety of professional committees and has spoken at several workshops. He was one of the first lecturers at the early MARC institutes, at a time when automation was that great new trend that everyone wanted to know about, but about which only a few had some knowledge. It is most appropriate that Mr. Bierman's paper, presented at the 1977 Institute on The Catalog in the Age of Technological Change, focuses on the topic of alternatives to the card catalog. He completed a major study funded by a Council on Library Resources grant, the results of which have been published in "Automated Alternatives to Card Catalogs for Large Libraries" in the *Journal of Library Automation*.

Mr. Bierman received his B.A. degree from Hanover College, Hanover, Indiana and an M.L.S. from the University of Oklahoma, Norman. He is one of the new breed of librarians, a person with traditional library training enhanced by formal training in mathematics and computer science.

John D. Byrum, Jr. is presently the Chief of Descriptive Cataloging at the Library of Congress. He was awarded the bachelor's degree, magna cum laude, from Harvard University, and he attended Rutgers Library School where he graduated first in his class.

Prior to his first professional job, he was Assistant to the Periodicals Librarian at the University of Washington. He was a descriptive cataloger at Princeton and was promoted to Acting Head Cataloger, and subsequently Head Cataloger at Princeton, the position he left before assuming his present duties at LC. He's held many ALA positions and some of the more notable of them have been: Assistant to the Editor of *Library Resources and Technical Services;* chairperson of the Catalog Code Revision Committee; member of MARBI, which is an acronym for a committee with the strange but useful name ALA/RTSD/ISAD/RASD Interdivisional Committee on Representation of Bibliographic Information in Machine-Readable Form. MARBI rules on and makes decisions with respect to changes in the MARC format, so Mr. Byrum has had long and extended experience with dealing with machine-readable cataloging.

He was also chairperson of the Subcommittee on Rules for Cataloging Machine-Readable Data Files. Another important position he held was that of the ALA representative to the Joint Steering Committee for the revision of the *Anglo-American Cataloging Rules*. He was also Council on Library Resources

Fellow, and he's published several articles, the most recent with Whitney Coe, "The Anglo-American Cataloging Rules, Chapter 6, Adopted, Applied and Assessed by Research Libraries." Another honor he received is RTSD's Esther J. Piercy Award for younger members making a substantial contribution to technical services.

Maurice J. Freedman is currently Associate Professor at the Columbia University School of Library Service. Prior to his joining the faculty at Columbia, he was Coordinator of Technical Services at the New York Public Library, Branch Libraries, from 1974 to 1977. At the NYPL he was responsible for the development of a positive attitude among branch librarians toward technical services as a unit designed to facilitate public service. From 1969 to 1974 he was Director of Technical Services at the Hennepin County Library in Minnesota. From 1966 to 1968 he was an Administrative Officer of the Processing Department at the Library of Congress.

A prolific writer who is concerned with the needs of the public libraries and user-oriented technical services, he has published articles in many professional journals, including the *Library Journal, Library Trends, Hennepin County Library Cataloging Bulletin,* and *University of Illinois Clinic on Library Applications of Data Processing*.

Professor Freedman is President of the Library and Information Technology Association (formerly the Information Science and Automation Division) and a member of the ALA Council. He was one of the organizers of the 1975 and 1977 institutes on the catalog.

Michael Gorman completed his professional education at the Ealing School of Librarianship in 1966. Prior to that date he had already begun to make his mark. In 1965, he had the best results nationwide on the intermediate librarianship examination, which won him the Cawthorne Prize.

He has held a variety of positions in the library field. His involvement with library education has included the position of Research Assistant with Polytechnic of Central London Library School in 1966-1967 and one year with the University of Illinois Graduate School of Library Service. He held a number of progressively more responsible positions with the *British National Bibliography* from 1966 to 1972, the last of which was Head of Cataloging. From 1972 to 1974, he was attached to the British Library Planning Secretariat. In 1974 he assumed the positions of Associate Editor of the *Anglo-American Cataloging Rules* and Head of the British Library's Standards Office. He is currently the Director of Technical Services at the University of Illinois Library at Champaign/Urbana.

Although Mr. Gorman is relatively new to the profession, his accomplishments are many. Those who have had the occasion to hear him speak at various ALA meetings know what an excellent speaker he is. He has published in *Library Resources and Technical Services, Library Association Records, Library Trends, American Libraries,* and *Catalog & Index*. He's a member of many key IFLA (International Federation of Library Associations and Institutions) committees and has played an essential role in the drafting of the *ISBD (International Standard Bibliographic Description)*.

Frances Hinton is Chief of the Processing Division of the Free Library of Philadelphia. Ms. Hinton received her library degree from the University of North Carolina after getting her bachelor's from the Agnes Scott College in Decatur,

Georgia. Her first positions were with the New York Public Library, South Bend Public Library, and the Free Library of Philadelphia in the Reference and Young Adult Department. She also worked in the Cataloging Department at Hawaii Public Library, and was Head Cataloger at Philadelphia, where she assumed her present position.

Ms. Hinton has written several pieces on cataloging. Of particular interest are the progress and code revision series and summaries which have been appearing in *Library Resources and Technical Services (LRTS)*, the official publication of the Resources and Technical Services Division. She also wrote a review in *LRTS* entitled, "Concerning the Concept of Main Entry as Represented in the *Anglo-American Cataloging Rules*." Ms. Hinton has served on a number of ALA committees, including the Joint Steering Committee for the revision of the *Anglo-American Cataloging Rules*, the Decimal Classification Editorial Policy Committee, and RTSD Cataloging and Classification Section's Policy and Research Committee.

Bernadine E. Abbott Hoduski, presently Special Library Assistant with Congress's Joint Committee on Printing, received her bachelor's degree from St. Theresa of Avila College, Kansas City, Missouri and her master's degree in library science from the University of Denver.

In virtually all of her professional positions she has been involved with the handling of documents. She began her career at Central Missouri State University where she was Head of the Documents Depository. Her next position was Serials Cataloger at the University of Missouri. In 1969, as its first Head Librarian, she established the Region VII Environmental Protection Agency library. During her tenure as head of the EPA library, she dealt with her dissatisfaction with the national treatment of U.S. documents in a most constructive manner, by establishing the Government Documents Round Table (GODORT). GODORT has done a fantastic job of dealing with and solving documents problems. She was the GODORT liaison to the ALA Catalog Code Revision Committee.

Her contributions to the profession were recognized by her receipt of the EPA Bronze Medal for Commendable Service in 1973. She served on the EPA-wide computer committee. While at EPA she was involved in the production of COM (Computer Output Microform) catalogs for technical reports, journals, and books. In her present position, Ms. Hoduski has played a key role in LC's and GPO's (Government Printing Office) cooperative effort to include GPO-generated cataloging in the MARC services and the new GPO *Monthly Catalog of United States Government Publications*.

Joseph H. Howard began his professional library experience at the University of Colorado with several positions of increasing responsibility, the last being Associate Director for Public Services. His public service experience is both unusual and of great value for a technical services administrator. He left Colorado to become a Peace Corps volunteer from 1963 to 1965, first with the University of Malaya Library, then with the Malayan Teachers College. Upon completion of his Peace Corps commitment he served as Chief of the Catalog Department at the Washington University Library in St. Louis, Missouri.

His career at the Library of Congress began in 1967 with his appointment as Assistant Chief of the Descriptive Cataloging Division. He subsequently served as Chief of that Division, Chief of the Serial Record Division, Assistant Director for Cataloging of the Processing Department, Director of the Processing Department, and Assistant Librarian of Processing Services.

He has published *Malay Manuscripts, a Bibliographic Guide* (University of Malaya Library, 1966) and *Main Entry for Serials* in the *LC Information Bulletin*, vol. 33, no. 47 (November 22, 1974). His numerous ALA activities include his position as LC liaison between the Cataloging and Classification Section's Cataloging Policy and Research Committee and the Decimal Classification Editorial Policy Committee.

Frederick G. Kilgour is considered by many to be the father of modern networking. Under Mr. Kilgour's leadership as Executive Director of the Ohio College Library Center, OCLC has demonstrated beyond any doubt that the computer can be successfully applied to traditional library problems with the most positive results. Over 700 CRT terminals are online to Columbus and are used in a variety of ways to improve service in the local library settings from the fulfillment of catalog card orders, to cooperative acquisitions, interlibrary loan, union catalog, etc. The fruits of Mr. Kilgour's labors and creations have substantially altered the texture of contemporary American library service.

He has a bachelor's degree from Harvard College, and has done graduate work at Harvard and Columbia universities which included studies in library service. He has had positions with the Harvard College Library, culminating with his becoming Chief of its Circulation Department; he contributed substantively to the Second World War effort, for which he received the Legion of Merit; and from 1948 to 1965 he was a librarian with the staff of the Yale Medical Library. Prior to his assumption of duties in Ohio, he was Associate Librarian for Research and Development at the Yale University Library.

Mr. Kilgour's publications are truly too voluminous to list; over a period of four decades, there have been few years in which he has not published. His professional activity is equally great; among his other posts, he has been President of ISAD. In recognition of his impact on cataloging, in 1974 he was awarded the Margaret Mann Citation and, in 1978, the Melvil Dewey Medal.

Anne Grodzins Lipow received a bachelor's degree from Purdue University and a master's in library science from the University of California at Berkeley. Currently Head of the Cooperative Services Department at the University of California, she was also Campus Coordinator of Computerized Literature Searching from 1974 to 1977. She organized the library's program of in-depth seminars on how to use the library for faculty in the social sciences and humanities.

She was chairperson of the University of California Statewide Task Group on User Satisfaction and of the Task Force that in 1972 wrote a monumental report about discrimination against women in the library profession. Her ALA activity includes having been Editor of *Message from MARS*, the occasional newsletter of the new RASD discussion group MARS, which stands for Machine Assisted Reference Service. All of her work has been with public service aspects of librarianship; she's especially well qualified to talk about the reader's side of catalog use.

Seymour Lubetzky is considered by many librarians to be the greatest theoretician of descriptive cataloging in this century. He graduated from the University of California at Los Angeles in 1931. He received his certificate of librarianship from the University of California at Berkeley the following year, and then returned to UCLA where he obtained a position in the library. There he became involved in cataloging problems and participated in their public discussion.

In 1943, he was offered a three-month appointment by the Director of the Library of Congress' Processing Department, the purpose of which was to make a tentative study of the ALA rules of description. This opportunity kept him at LC until 1960 and led to his involvement in the preparation of *Studies of Descriptive Cataloging* (LC, 1946), which laid the foundation for the revision of former ALA rules of description; *Cataloging Rules and Principles* (LC, 1953), which did the same for former ALA rules of entry; *Code of Cataloging Rules* (ALA, 1960), for the Institute on Catalog Code Revision held at McGill University, Montreal, Canada in 1960; and participation in the International Conference on Cataloging Principles held in Paris, 1961.

From 1960 until his retirement in 1970, he served in the new library school at UCLA as Professor of Cataloging and Classification. Prior to his retirement he wrote a report entitled *Principles of Cataloging, Part I, Descriptive Cataloging*. In addition, he has lectured in many places and has contributed numerous articles and reviews to library literature. He is the recipient of the Margaret Mann Citation (1955), the Beta Phi Award for good teaching (1964), and the honorary Doctor of Laws from UCLA (1969).

S. Michael Malinconico is currently Coordinator of Technical Services, the Branch Libraries, the New York Public Library. Formerly Assistant Chief of the Systems Analysis and Data Processing Office of the NYPL, he is one of the few systems people who is a genuine student of the art of cataloging. His pioneering work, along with the NYPL systems staff, has resulted in the single most powerful automated bibliographical control system in libraries today.

Mr. Malinconico has a bachelor's and a master's degree in physics, and is working toward a doctorate from Columbia University in that subject. He taught physics at Brooklyn College for two years and was a systems analyst for NASA for two years, where he played an important role in the Apollo project's successful moon landing. With that accomplishment under his belt, he went to work for the NYPL in 1969 as a systems analyst.

He has published seminal papers on automated cataloging and authority control in *Library Journal, Library Quarterly, Journal of Library Automation*, and the *University of Illinois Clinic on Library Applications of Data Processing*. It also should be noted that his ideas on automated authority control have significantly influenced national automation efforts in Canada. As chairperson of the ISAD Program Planning Committee, he contributed substantially both to the content and organization of the Institute on The Catalog in the Age of Technological Change. In 1978, Mr. Malinconico was presented the Esther J. Piercy Award.

Joan K. Marshall is Chief of Technical Services at the Brooklyn College Library. Formerly Chief Cataloger at the same institution, she has played an active role in the development of national cataloging policy and practice. She was the Social Responsibilities Round Table (SRRT) representative to the Catalog Code Revision Committee (CCRC). In addition, Ms. Marshall has done a great deal of research in the area of subject control, particularly with respect to ethnically and otherwise insensitive topical and name headings. Underwritten by a Council on Library Resources grant, she compiled a thesaurus for nonsexist subject headings entitled *On Equal Terms* (New York: Neal-Schuman Publishers, 1977). In a profession which is composed largely of women, this research is most welcome and long overdue.

Ms. Marshall is active in both local and national professional organizations, including ALA's Freedom to Read Foundation. She has contributed to cataloging literature, and has been a vital and energetic voice in the movement to increase the sensitivity and responsibility of libraries to social issues, as well as a first-rate cataloger. She received a bachelor's degree from New York University, a master's in library service from Columbia University, and a master's degree in English from New York University.

Phyllis A. Richmond is Professor of Library Science at the School of Library Science, Case Western Reserve University. Dr. Richmond actually has had two careers. She achieved scholarly distinction with the attainment of the Ph.D. in history of science from the University of Pennsylvania. In her previous vocation she served as Curator of History at the Rochester Museum of Arts and Sciences and later as Assistant to the Director of Johns Hopkins University, Institute of History and Medicine.

Her transition to Library Science began with her working as a Local History Assistant at the Rochester Public Library. She received her M.S. in library science from Western Reserve University in 1956. Before assuming her present position with Case Western, she worked successively as Serials Cataloger, Supervisor of Science Libraries, and Information Systems Specialist at the University of Rochester.

Dr. Richmond's published articles number 70 and their topics range from the history of science and medicine to technical articles on libraries and information science. The title of her doctoral dissertation was *Americans and the Germ Theory of Disease*. Particularly relevant to these institutes is a recent article Dr. Richmond published in the *Journal of Academic Librarianship* on the value and need for research in the construction and application of cataloging rules. In addition to her reputation as a leading expert in information control, Phyllis Richmond is another of ISAD's official reviewers of the *AACR2*'s draft.

Marvin H. Scilken has deservedly achieved a reputation as the consumer advocate and gadfly of the profession during the 12 years of his directorship of the Orange Public Library in Orange, New Jersey. It has been to the continuing shame of the library field that his efforts toward eliminating the pricefixing of children's books have received such little note and appreciation. For the record, schools and libraries in the late 1960s recovered in excess of $10,000,000 from publishers and wholesalers as a result of unfair practices highlighted by Mr. Scilken.

As the editor, publisher, and chief contributor to *The U*N*A*B*A*S*H*E*D Librarian, the How-I-Run-My-Library-Good News Letter,* he brings to the professional literature an informative yet informal response to the problems of today's libraries, be they school, public, or academic. He chaired a committee of the Essex County (New Jersey) Library Directors Group which produced a study entitled *The Public's Attitude towards Public Library Service*. His definitive article, "Backlog to Frontlog," *Library Journal* (September 15, 1969), was indicative of his creative and simple, yet effective and economical solutions to traditional library problems. He was profiled in April, 1972 as the *Wilson Library Bulletin* frontliner.

Mr. Scilken has a B.A. from the University of Colorado and an M.L.S. from Pratt Institute Graduate School of Library and Information Science. He has participated extensively in local, regional, and national library organizations and has been in great demand as a public speaker and consultant on library service.

Jean Riddle Weihs received her B.A. from Queen's University and her B.L.S. from the University of Toronto. Further, she has received a Specialist Certificate in School Librarianship from the Ontario College of Education. She has held the following positions: Bibliographer at the University of Toronto Library, Reference Librarian at North York Public Library, School Librarian for the Scarborough Board of Education, Cataloger at the Ontario Institute for Studies in Education, and Head of Technical Services for the North York Board of Education. Her present position is Director of the Library Techniques Program at Seneca College of Applied Arts and Technology in Willowdale, Ontario, a position she has held since 1969.

Ms. Weihs is the co-author of *Nonbook Materials: the Organization of Integrated Collections*. This work has also been referred to as the "Canadian Nonprint Rules" and, until the revised nonbook chapters of *AACR* were published, it served as the best authoritative guide for cataloging these materials. She has written extensively on the problems of cataloging nonbook materials, contributing articles and book reviews. She also is Editor of the Ontario Library Association's *Newsletter*.

Ms. Weihs belongs to many organizations and is active professionally. She has served as a member of the prestigious ALA Cataloging Policy Research Committee. She's also been a member of ALA and CLA (Canadian Library Association) committees concerned with nonbook materials for the last ten years. Ms. Weihs has been chairperson of the EDP Subcommittee of the Ontario Public Library's Advisory Committee that has as its charge reporting on the possibilities of an automated cataloging network for the public libraries of Ontario. She has received the CLA's Ruby E. Wallace Traveling Fellowship and the Canadian Council Grant, both for the study of nonbook materials.

William J. Welsh is presently Deputy Librarian of Congress. Prior to this appointment he was Director of LC's Processing Department where his span of authority included a network of worldwide offices for the acquisition and cataloging of materials; the single largest publication project in history, the *National Union Catalog, Pre-1956 Imprints;* traditional library processing functions on a gargantuan scale; and the single most comprehensive bibliographical distribution service in the world today.

Mr. Welsh received a B.A. in philosophy from Notre Dame in 1940, where he also attended law school. After serving in the Army Air Force from 1941 to 1947, he joined the Library of Congress as Library Assistant on the Cooperative Acquisitions Project. After a variety of progressively more responsible positions at LC, including Associate Director of the' Administrative Department, he was promoted in 1964 to Associate Director of the Processing Department where he succeeded John Cronin as Director four years later. In addition to continuing and advancing programs begun prior to his directorship, Mr. Welsh has initiated the Cataloging in Publication program (CIP), the LC leadership role in automation, the National Serials Data project, and has actively supported current efforts toward Universal Bibliographical Control.

Among Mr. Welsh's professional activities and accomplishments are his successful efforts to foster an increased two-way communication between LC's Processing Department and his professional colleagues in the field. Lastly, he was the 1971 recipient of the Melvil Dewey Medal, which was conferred upon him for creative professional achievement of a high order.

The Nature and Future of the Catalog

I

THE CATALOG: ITS NATURE AND PROSPECTS

Introduction to Part I

by Maurice J. Freedman

The Information Science and Automation Division (ISAD) of the American Library Association (ALA) has sponsored many programs that have had technological developments and the broader aspects of automation as their primary emphasis. This Institute on The Catalog—Its Nature and Prospects, in most respects, is a departure for ISAD in that we are trying to deal with all aspects of the most complex area of librarianship: cataloging and the catalog—not merely the technology of automation.

It is clear that we can no longer discuss the catalog independently of technology's impact on it. Certainly many of the changes in such areas as entry, filing, and format have at least in part been suggested as either combinations to the computer or candidates for exploitation by the capabilities of the computer. It is also a good time to stand back and take a look at "what technology hath wrought" and some of the issues involved in our rush towards standardization on the national and international levels.

This Institute provides a discussion of cataloging and the catalog from several fundamental perspectives: the catalog as a tool, its structure, its rules for organization, and its content with respect to the world in which it exists. This is essentially the traditional enterprise of cataloging theory, but it is explored in light of current standards and developments by Seymour Lubetzky and Joan Marshall. Another perspective explored is the direct impact of automation on the catalog: How should or could the computer be used to facilitate the cataloging process, and how can it enhance the uses of the catalog? Michael Malinconico and Fred Kilgour present widely different views concerning the application of the computer to the cataloging enterprise. Hugh Atkinson discusses the totally computerized catalog.

The world's largest processing department's plans and policies are always of deep interest. When the Library of Congress (LC) sneezes, we all catch cold. It is virtually impossible to overestimate the importance of LC on bibliographic control in the nation's libraries or, for that matter, in the libraries of the world. William Welsh's discussion of the LC's processing department outlook for the future is most welcome.

Marvin Scilken offers another perspective, one of which we technical services and automation people occasionally lose sight of—that of the user. How are the cataloger and the catalog serving the contemporary library patron? There is also a review by Ken Bierman of the future of the catalog insofar as it is a physical artifact. Micrographic and computer technologies and their integration will become increasingly efficacious as agents for change with respect to the continued existence of the traditional 75 by 125 millimeter card. (We are finally in step with the age of the metric system!)

FORMAT

In addition to the eight speeches we had two official reactors: Sanford Berman and Joseph Rosenthal, as well as the ensuing discussion of the audience. Each of the reactors spoke at the conclusion of each of the papers given. However, they may have chosen not to comment at all after a given presentation. The original speaker then responded to them, following which a discussion was opened to the floor. Members of the audience were invited to ask questions, make statements, and express themselves freely. All were requested to avoid making lengthy speeches and duplicating comments already made.

Ideology of Bibliographic Cataloging: Progress and Retrogression

by Seymour Lubetzky

At the beginning of an institute on the nature and prospects of the catalog, and at a time of great preoccupation with the possibilities of computerization of library operations and services, it seems appropriate to take a retrospective look at the evolution of our catalog and the ideology which has shaped it. In our preoccupation with technology, we must not lose sight of the ideology of the catalog; in our fascination with the versatility of certain tools, we should not forget the ends to which they are to be applied. I am glad of the opportunity to discuss this subject for several reasons: firstly, I have been interested in it for some time and would like to share some of my thoughts with you; secondly, I believe that ideology is fundamental to the design, evaluation, and progressive improvement of any cataloging system—manual as well as mechanized; and thirdly and most importantly, I am concerned about some movements which I think symptomatize ideological deterioration and would have us, as someone put it, march boldly backwards into the future.

EVOLUTION OF CATALOG: FROM INVENTORY LIST TO GUIDE TO RESOURCES OF LIBRARY

To explain the evolution of our catalog, I should like to begin by telling you about an experience of Sir Thomas Bodley, the benefactor of the Oxford University library which was named after him—the Bodleian. Towards the end of the sixteenth century, about 1598, Sir Thomas Bodley was preparing to go on a book-buying expedition for the library. To avoid dissipating funds on unnecessary duplicates, he asked the librarian Thomas James to provide him with a copy of the catalog of the library. At that time the catalog consisted of a collection of inventory lists. The books of the library were divided into four general classes—theology, medicine, law, and the arts—and subdivided by size into folios, quartos, etc. Each group was then arranged alphabetically by authors' surnames on the shelves of bookcases and listed in the same order on sheets attached to these cases to show the contents of each case. These sheets were intended as inventory lists and the entries were designed to serve that purpose: they were informal and very brief. The books bound with other books were listed after the entry of the first book, as they were to be found on the shelves, and were not listed separately where they would have been if bound separately. Not surprisingly, when Bodley began to use these sheets to determine whether the books he had selected for purchase were not already in the library, he soon found that the inventory lists were not quite adequate for his purposes. He wrote to James explaining the shortcomings of his catalog. He told him that the entries were too brief and often left him uncertain as to whether the books he had selected for purchase and those he found in the catalog were of the same editions. Worse, that the failure to enter books bound with other books separately, in addition to their listing under the first book, would normally cause one to miss them. One would then assume that those books were not in the library and purchase unnecessary duplicates.

Thus Bodley discovered, and called attention to, the need of another function which the catalog should serve—that of helping one determine, in or outside of the library, whether or not the library had a certain book. This function was to grow in importance with the growth of the libraries' collections and to change the character of the catalog from that of an inventory list to that of a *finding list* or *finding catalog*, which was to mark the next stage in the evolution of our catalog. Interestingly enough, the immediate effect of Bodley's remonstrations was the inclusion in the inventory lists of additional separate entries for books bound with other books. In such cases, the additional entries were accompanied by symbols to indicate their actual location. This made the lists, transitionally, a combination of inventory and finding lists. But the next Oxford catalog, published in 1620, represented an unmixed *finding catalog*, consisting of one alphabetical listing of all the books in the library irrespective of their arrangement on the shelves. Henceforth the inventory function was no longer to be a part of the functions of the library's catalog.[1]

The ideology underlying the *finding catalog* was attractively simple. The library was regarded as a dispensary of books, and hence the catalog as an aid to the location of any desired book or books in the library. A book is normally identified by the author's name—real or assumed—and a title, and is normally so cited and referred to. Ergo, it was reasoned, an entry under the author's name and the title found on the title page or elsewhere in the book, with a symbol to indicate its location on the shelves, should readily help one find the book desired. This ideology appealed widely to the librarian as well as the library user and held sway for nearly a quarter of a millennium when, in 1841, a catalytic event in the history of cataloging took place. In that year the first volume of a long-and-expectantly-awaited catalog of the British Museum library was published.[2] The appearance of this volume aroused such a furor within and without the British Museum that further publication of the catalog was suspended. No less prestigious an authority than a Royal Commission was appointed to inquire into the charges brought against the man principally responsible for that volume, the Italian radical and political refugee Antonio Panizzi, later Sir Anthony Panizzi. The solitary volume published remains to date a memorial of that epochal event. What precipitated that furor was that Panizzi's volume represented an uncompromising rejection of the comfortable ideology of the *finding catalog*, introducing what seemed to his critics unwarranted and capricious complications calculated to make the catalog much more difficult for the librarian to prepare and the reader to use. These complications were not hidden or implicit; they were clearly set out at the beginning of the volume under "Rules for the Compilation of the Catalog"[3]—a forbiddingly elaborate and complex set of rules compared to the few simple rules required by the *finding catalog*. The faithful adherents of the ideology of the *finding catalog* were determined to combat the unwelcome intrusion of Panizzi's scheme before the Royal Commission.

The hearings before the Royal Commission, including among the witnesses some of the most prominent librarians and scholars of that day, extended from 1847 to 1849. They took on the unusual character of a great and impassioned national debate of the relative merits of the existing *finding catalog* and the alternative proposed by Panizzi and his associates. There was much in Panizzi's rules to criticize, as there is in our own *AACR (Anglo-American Cataloging Rules)*, and for similar reasons. Some of the rules were imposed on Panizzi by the Trustees of the British Museum, and Panizzi could only join his critics in denouncing those rules, such as the rules for entry of anonymous publications.[4] Other rules were based on respectable sources rather than ideological requirements, as were the rules for entry of serials and periodical publications. Ironically, the latter proved to be the most vulnerable and acutely criticized of Panizzi's rules, as, coincidentally, are the corresponding *AACR* rules, and the only defense that Panizzi was able to muster in this case was to cite the authorities instead of the reasons he followed.[5]

The main issue before the Royal Commission, however, was not the validity or adequacy of any individual rule or rules, but the ideology underlying Panizzi's catalog as a whole its meaning, function, and character—in whose light alone any particular rule or group of rules could properly be evaluated. To the critics of Panizzi accustomed to the simplicity of the *finding catalog*, "the whole volume" represented "a magnificent mistake." It was "exceedingly inconvenient" because the books were entered in it "where no person who goes to consult the catalogue would expect to find them, and the placing them where they are increases the bulk of the catalogue by occasioning a multitude of long cross-references."[6] The philosophy of these critics was enunciated by one of their most prominent spokesmen, the famous Thomas Carlyle. As an inveterate user of the British Museum library he was able to confirm that "A library is not worth anything without a catalogue—it is a Polyphemus without any eye in his head—and you must front the difficulties, whatever they may be, of making proper catalogues";[7] but as to what constituted a "proper" catalog he sharply differed from Panizzi. As Carlyle saw it, "The grand use of any catalog is to tell you, in any intelligible way, that such and such books are in the library. . . . I should expect it to be a simple thing enough to draw up a simple list of the names of the books."[8] This was the classical expression of the ideology of the *finding catalog*—the view that the catalog was *a simple list* designed to help one find a particular book in the library and nothing else. It has since been echoed repeatedly in the discussion of cataloging despite the persuasive and decisive refutation of it by Panizzi before the Royal Commission.

The ideology advanced by Panizzi gained him the support and approval of the Royal Commission and raised the catalog to a new level in its evolution. It was based on the following perceptions: that the *book* sought by a person is really, most frequently, not the object of his/her interest, but the *work* contained in it is; that that work may be found also in other editions, translations, or versions, published under different names of the author and/or different titles, some or all of which may be of equal or greater interest to that person; and that, consequently, to serve well the user of the library, the catalog must be designed not merely to tell him/her whether or not a particular book is in the library, but also to reveal to him/her at the same time what other editions, translations, or versions of the work, as well as other genetically related works, the library has. For, as Panizzi saw it, "A reader may know the *work* he requires; he cannot be expected to know all the peculiarities of different *editions*; and this information he has a right to expect from the catalogues."[9] Thus, while the *finding catalog* was concerned only with the concrete book, the catalog contemplated by Panizzi was to concern itself also with the more elusive but intrinsically more important aspects of the book: the identity of the work contained in it and of the author of that work. In effect, Panizzi's catalog was to serve as a *guide to the resources of the library*.

To accomplish this higher purpose, Panizzi argued, required a deliberately designed "system," and his much maligned rules, whatever their individual merits or demerits, were intended to embody that system. The principal features of that system were that (1) a book was to be regarded and represented in the catalog, as it was in fact, not as a separate entity, but as an edition of a particular work by a particular author; (2) all the works of an author and their editions were to be entered under one particular name, usually the author's original name, regardless of the different names under which these works or editions may have been published, so that they would all be found together in the catalog; (3) all the editions and translations of a work, regardless of their individual titles, were to be arranged, usually under the original title, in a prescribed order (the editions chronologically and the translations by language) so that a person in search of a particular book would find it, not in isolation, but in context of the other editions and translations of the work and would thus be enabled to determine which of these would best serve his/her purpose; and (4) appropriate "cross-references" were to be made from the other names of the author and from the titles in their alphabetical position to help the catalog user find the author and title sought by him/her.[10] This catalog would then present, not a list of separate books, but a bibliographically integrated picture of the resources of the library—one much more revealing, helpful, and responsive to the actual *needs* of the library user than the finding catalog.

IDEOLOGY AND TECHNOLOGY IN CATALOGING

The ideology advocated by Panizzi has since dominated not only Anglo-American but Western cataloging generally, and more recently provided the foundation for the international agreement on cataloging principles adopted in Paris in 1961 and incorporated in the so-called Paris Principles.[11] It has thus contributed to the cause of "universal bibliographic control" long before this phrase came into vogue. Significantly, however, Panizzi's rules did not prove as viable as did his ideology, and they were promptly and materially changed and recast by his most ardent admirers and followers. Thus Jewett's rules, published as early as 1852 and avowedly "founded upon those adopted for the compilation of the catalogue of the British Museum,"[12] will be found on comparison to resemble more strikingly those of the *AACR* published one and a quarter century later than those of Panizzi, published only one decade earlier. Accounting for his departures from Panizzi's rules, Jewett explained that some of them "conform more to rules advocated by Mr. Panizzi than to those finally sanctioned by the Trustees of the Museum"; others, he thought, were useful "innovations"; and still others represented "modifications and additions . . . adapted to the peculiar character of the system now proposed."[13] He was referring, of course, to his famous technological plan to reproduce the catalog from individual entries embossed on plates, a considerably more flexible and less costly method than that of printing the catalog.

There were lessons in this story which appear to have been ignored but remain valid for the future. Firstly, a well-considered ideology cognizant of the nature of the materials cataloged and their potential interests is prerequisite and fundamental to the design of any viable cataloging system, and particularly one that is to command universal acceptance. Witness the viability and influence of Panizzi's ideology despite the vulnerability of many of his rules. Secondly, the admission of rules incompatible with the general ideology adopted inevitably entails subsequent remedial revision. Witness the fate of the rules intruded on Panizzi and of those similarly intruded on the *AACR*. Thirdly, a change in the technology or the form of the catalog may have important implications for the rules or methods of cataloging. It may offer an opportunity for changes to improve the effectiveness of the catalog, but it may also require the provision of new methods to serve a function previously served by methods not applicable under the new conditions. Thus Panizzi, with an eye on the printed book catalog demanding stable entries, was led to rule that the works of an author should be entered under his earliest name and, hence, to enter the works of Voltaire under ARQUET DE VOLTAIRE—an entry that evoked the scorn of his critics;[14] while Jewett, contemplating the use of individual entries that could more easily be changed and brought up to date, found it desirable to rule that the entry should be under the latest name used by the author and cited conspicuously the entry under VOLTAIRE as an example.[15] On the other hand, the form of the book catalog made it possible for Panizzi to bring together all the editions and translations of a work by simply prescribing that they should be arranged by the editor of the catalog in a given order following the entry of the original edition, an arrangement that could be made intelligible on the pages of a book but hardly in a card catalog where the arrangement is determined by the design of each individual entry. To accomplish the same purpose in a card catalog, the original title would have to be repeated in all the editions and translations to provide for their desired arrangement. However, the rules of 1908 and 1949, on which practically all our catalogs have been based, included no such provision, save in the case of so-called *anonymous classics* where this was accomplished by the use of *uniform titles*, and in the case of other anonymous works where this was accomplished awkwardly and indirectly by the use of added entries under the original title. Thus our catalogs have largely failed our readers in the important function of revealing what editions and translations of a particular work the library had, and will continue to do so until reconstructed on the basis of the *AACR*, which has remedied the situation by providing for the consistent use of uniform titles wherever required.

TECHNOLOGICAL PROGRESS OR IDEOLOGICAL RETROGRESSION?

The advent of the computer into the library has stimulated much thought on the possibilities of its utilization in the process of cataloging; but some of the proposals brought forth in this connection represent not technological progress but rather ideological retrogression.

The first of these proposals was to abandon our traditional main entry, involving the determination of the person or corporate body principally responsible for the work, and to use instead a *title-unit entry*. The argument in support of this proposal rests on the following assertions: The main entry is a relic of the early days of the printed book catalog when, for reasons of space and cost of printing, a book was to be represented by one entry only. The subsequent use of multiple entries made the concept of the main entry an anachronism. And since the main entry is the hub and most exacting aspect of our cataloging process, its replacement by a title-unit entry would greatly simplify the problem and expedite the operation of cataloging.[16] In fact the whole cataloging process might thus be reduced to little more than a simple description of the book under its title, followed by a list of appropriate headings, from which the catalog desired could then automatically be composed and reproduced by the computer.

The argument appears sound and reasonable, but is actually erroneous and misleading. It ignores the basic function of the main entry, as conceived by Panizzi and used in the *AACR*, and the purposes which a catalog based on the main entry was intended to serve and would and could not be served by one based on a title-unit entry. As will be recalled from the foregoing discussion of Panizzi's ideology, his *main entry* was designed to represent a book not as an individual entity but as an edition of a particular work by a particular author, and one which was to be found in the catalog properly related to the other editions and translations of the work and the other works of the author. The *title-unit entry* represents a book as an individual entity under its own title, and the catalog based on it is therefore necessarily a list of books, much as was the *finding catalog* of the pre-Panizzi days. The addition of entries under author, editor, subject, and so on, would merely render it a *compound list of books*, not of the *works* of an author or editor or on a particular subject. The concept of the *work* as the principal focus of interest of the user of a library and as the entity to which other *works* in the library may be related does not seem to be a part of the idea of the title-unit-entry catalog. This is a major step backwards in the ideology of bibliographic cataloging. However, this is not to imply that the title-unit-entry idea is never applicable. It has long and effectively been used by many map librarians who felt that in their particular collections of maps the *book* and the *work*, so to speak, might be said to coincide, and that the considerations of authorship, editions, translations, and related works were largely negligible. Each map could, under the circumstances, be treated as an individual entity.[17] This may be the case in other special and limited collections. But to advocate the use of a *title-unit entry* in place of the traditional main entry in cataloging generally is to ignore the history of cataloging and its ideology.

The second proposal, since adopted, was to revise the *AACR* rules of description so as to embody the *ISBD (International Standard Bibliographic Description)*. This proposal should be seen against the background of the studies[18] on which the *AACR* rules were based. The previous ALA rules of description were based on a principle of faithful *transcription* of the title page with elaborate qualifications, which yielded as a result an entry repetitious in content, loose in organization, and confusing in its esoteric capitalization. The studies indicated what elements should be included in the entry, in what order, and in what form, so that the resulting entry would be free from the faults observed in the previous entries and would be more compact, clear, and readily comprehensible to the user of the catalog for whom ultimately the catalog was intended. And the rules of description revised on the basis of these studies were generally recognized as a distinct improvement enhancing the quality and effectiveness of the catalog. But adoption of the *ISBD* reintroduces repetition of the author's name before and after the title, which is particularly objectionable in the case of lengthy or complex corporate names whose repetition serves only to increase the bulk and hinder the comprehension of the individual entry and of the catalog as a whole, and introduces new esoteric punctuation which is bound to puzzle the catalog user. The *ISBD* presupposes that the description of a publication is a separate question independent of that of its entry, and should therefore be complete and stand on its own without the author heading—hence the resulting repetition of the author's name following the title; but this is transparently part of the ideology of the title-unit-entry catalog where the book as such is the focus of the catalog. The idea is incongruous in our general catalogs where a publication is to be represented by a main entry as an edition of a particular work by a particular author and the author heading is one of the elements of that description. There is therefore no justification for repeating the author's name except when the name in the heading differs significantly from that following the title. In fact, the *ISBD* appears as a reversion to the principle of *transcription* of the title pages which was not to be affected by the presence or absence of the author heading.

The third proposal, still in vogue, is to enter all serials uniformly under their titles. The *AACR* (North American edition) rules for serials represent a remarkable aberration in treating not only serials generally, as a special type of publication, differently from other publications, but also certain types of serials ("a . . . bibliography, index, directory, biographical dictionary, almanac, or yearbook") differently from other types of serials. These rules defy rationalization and urgently call for revision. But the proposal to enter all serials under their titles, while obviously easier to apply, is equally detrimental to the integrity of the catalog. *I. F. Stone's Weekly*, a serial, is not different in character from any other monographic report of I. F. Stone, and the *Library of Congress Information Bulletin*, also a serial, is not different in character from any monographic report issued in the name of the Library of Congress. There is a host of legislative, political, financial, consumer, and other reports of individuals and corporate bodies, and to treat these differently only because some are serial and the others are monographic in form is to play havoc with the integrity of the catalog and to confound its users. The question that must be asked first is whether there is something in the nature of a serial to require a differential treatment. This question is bound to lead one to recognize that many or most serial publications are intended to be issued indefinitely and are subject to change of authorship. These, therefore, could not satisfactorily be entered under author or the body temporarily responsible for them. Our own *Library Journal* and the British *Library*, formerly the official organs of the American Library Association and the (British) Library Association respectively, are good illustrations of this condition. They might have been entered originally under their respective bodies as their authors, but they later ceased to function as organs of these bodies and could not have continued to be treated as their products. For this reason, such serials should be entered under their titles. But this is not true of all serials. Those of personal authorship, those including in their titles the name or the initials of the name of the issuing body (as *ALA Bulletin* or *Library Association Record)*, and those serving essentially as periodical reports of the activities of their issuing bodies are inherently unsusceptible to change of authorship and should be entered under the individuals or bodies responsible for them. It should be realized, in addition, that the question involves not only serials but other works that are generally intended to be issued indefinitely in successive editions and are bound to have, in time, different editors or compilers. This is true of many directories, encyclopedias, and other reference works that need periodically to be brought up to date. The failure to recognize this special condition is strikingly illustrated in *AACR* Rule 4 where one edition of the *Directory of American Scholars* is entered under its editor and another under its title—hardly a felicitous solution to be followed in other similar cases. What is needed is not another rule for serials, because not all serials present the same problems, but a recognition of the problem of works of changing authorship in serials as well as in other publications, and a rule providing a satisfactory solution to this problem.

In summary, the proposal to abandon the main entry in favor of a title-unit entry, the adoption of the *ISBD* which suits a title-unit entry but not the author-main entry, and the advocacy of title entry for serials generally, all imply an ideology which ignores the history of cataloging, is oblivious of the aims our catalog was designed to serve, and focuses on the book or publication as the principal object of interest of the prospective library user rather than the work conveyed by the book or publication. It is the ideology which was urged against Panizzi and was cogently disproved by him before the Royal Commission in 1847-49, but whose seductive simplicity has always found friends to keep it alive. Were we to allow ourselves to be enticed by it, we should be celebrating our Bicentennial by a return to the pre-Panizzi days in cataloging.

REFERENCES

In the following notes *Royal Commission* refers to the *Report of the Commissions Appointed to Inquire into the Constitution and Government of the British Museum, with Minutes of Evidence* (London, 1850) and *Brault* refers to *The Great Debate on Panizzi's Rules in 1847-1849: the Issues Discussed*, by Nancy Brault (Los Angeles: The School of Library Service & The University Library, University of California, 1972).

1. Cf. Dorothy May Norris. *A History of Cataloguing Methods, 1100-1850* (London: Grafton, 1939), pp. 142-47.

2. *Catalogue of Printed Books in the British Museum*, vol. 1 (London: British Museum, 1841). Letter A only; no more published.

3. Ibid., p. [v]-ix; Brault, pp. 85-89.

4. Royal Commission, Questions 4122, 9693; Brault, pp. 74-75.

5. Royal Commission, Questions 4870, 5956, 6065, 8791, 9729; Brault, pp. 80-84.

6. Royal Commission, Questions 6341, 6345; Brault, pp. 82-83.

7. Royal Commission, Question 4472.

8. Royal Commission, Question 4385; Brault, p. 34.

9. Royal Commission, Question 9814; Brault, p. 50.

10. Cf. Panizzi's "Rules for the Compilation of the Catalogue," referred to above (note 3).

11. *International Conference on Cataloguing Principles, Paris 1961, Report* (London: International Federation of Library Associations and Institutions, 1963).

12. Charles C. Jewett. *On the Construction of Catalogues of Libraries, and of a General Catalogue . . . with Rules and Examples* (Washington, DC: Smithsonian Institution, 1852), p. 14.

13. Ibid., pp. 14-15.

14. Royal Commission, Questions 6373, 6385; Brault, pp. 54-55.

15. Jewett, *Construction of Catalogues*, pp. 38-39 (rule XVI).

16. Cf. J. E. Daily, "Title Entry as Unit Entry," *Library Resources and Technical Services* 16 (Fall 1972): 433-44.

17. Samuel W. Boggs and Dorothy Cornwell Lewis, *The Classification and Cataloging of Maps and Atlases* (New York: Special Libraries Association, 1945).

18. *Studies of Descriptive Cataloging* . . . (Washington, DC: Library of Congress, 1946).

DISCUSSION

Sanford Berman: My perspective, for which I make no apology, is that of someone who works daily with the nitty-gritty of cataloging, as many of you do. Furthermore, it is of someone who believes that cataloging should provide people with the materials that they want as quickly and painlessly as possible. From that perspective I should like to heartily endorse Mr. Lubetzky's comments particularly with respect to main entry—author-main entries, in particular—and *ISBD*. Both of those comments are relevant to people-oriented cataloging and to linking people with the things they want. I would suggest another intensively practical reason for author main entries over strict title entries: the establishment of a main entry—and I'm thinking particularly of public and school libraries—impacts directly on the shelf location of material, and in even further specificity, on fiction, which is a big item for children and also just for ordinary public library users. To introduce a little vulgarity, it would be absolutely hell on browsers were all the works by Agatha Christie or Dorothy Sayers or Dashiell Hammett or you name it, entered individually by their title. It's already difficult to find a lot of these things as it is, but it would be absolute irresponsibility to go to a title-main entry.

My second point may be a slightly tangential, but I hope concrete, reaction to the general tenor of Mr. Lubetzky's remarks and the general subject posed. I would like to devote a couple of moments each to what may seem strange bedfellows at first: Sholom Aleichem, *Melvil's Rib,* the CIA, and La Jolla, California. First, Sholom Aleichem. I recently spent something like twenty minutes talking over the telephone with a suitably irate and properly frustrated borrower. She repeatedly bypassed the catalog because she was an inveterate fiction reader and approached the *A* section of the fiction shelf—this relates again to my earlier comment about author entry—expecting to find Sholom Aleichem under ALEICHEM. To explain, I could only invoke rather mystical language like "bibliographic purity" (somewhat à la Panizzi) to explain why she was not finding Aleichem under ALEICHEM, but rather under Rabinowitz because Rabinowitz is Sholom Aleichem's real name. Need I say that my explanation didn't do a whole lot to relieve her, and in the course of it I became not only chagrined, but ashamed for our profession and for how, in this particular case, rules had made finding the material that this person wanted so difficult.

Next, *Melvil's Rib*: Within the past couple of months, Rutgers University Press issued a paperback volume of proceedings of a symposium that was held, I think, in the past year. The main title was *Women in Librarianship*. The subtitle was *Melvil's Rib Symposium*. What's memorable about that whole title, if you couldn't remember the editors or the main title, is *Melvil's Rib Symposium*. In fact, most reviewers and most people refer to it as *Melvil's Rib Symposium*. What I'm getting at is this: At least in the CIP (Cataloging in Publication) entry that I've seen, LC, following customary practice, made a title entry for the main title, *Women in Librarianship,* but nothing under *Melvil's Rib Symposium.* If we had not critically examined those added entry assignments and had failed to make the added subtitle entry, we would be denying access to the book to those who would approach the catalog with reasonable expectations of finding *Melvil's Rib,* the memorable subtitle. In effect, we'd be suggesting to them we don't have the book.

The *CIA.* Everybody knows the Marchetti-Marks book. If you haven't actually seen it, you've certainly heard about it. The important thing is this: Whoever cataloged it at LC, and I'm willing to bet it happened elsewhere too, probably didn't get much beyond the dust jacket where there was a big clue about something special to the book. Maybe they didn't catalog it with a dust jacket. Had they even flipped through it a little, what would they have found? There was something special about it in terms of descriptive cataloging. Pieces are missing! And there are bold-face letters deliberately inserted saying DELETED. There are other indications in bold-faced type showing that certain passages had been deleted by the government because of CIA pressure. Through litigation some statements had been reinstated, but some elements still were not there at all. A note on the dust jacket explained all this quite clearly. It was quite quotable, and at our library we quoted it. The LC cataloging made no mention of the fact that this book had been severely censored. In terms of access: Having failed to make that note, there was no futher justification for several possible subject tracings like CENSORSHIP—UNITED STATES—CASE STUDIES, SECURITY CLASSIFICATION—UNITED STATES—CASE STUDIES, and so on. That book is a source document; it's something in the hand for somebody interested in censorship and secrecy in government.

La Jolla, California. We got a book of memoirs by an ex-convict who works for the Western Behavioral Institute in La Jolla, California, which is very closely associated with publication of the work. There was tracing for the institute. However, the tracing was under (and I'm certain that there was a rule that justified it) LA JOLLA, CALIFORNIA. WESTERN BEHAVIORAL INSTITUTE. I submit that no ordinary, right-minded library user who is looking for Western Behavioral Institute is going to look under LA JOLLA, CALIFORNIA. So while that may have accorded with a rule, it violated common sense. All I wanted to underscore with these four horror stories is that descriptive cataloging, especially form of entry, provision of adequate and accurate notes, and the judicious, discretionary assignment of added entries, can either powerfully inhibit or promote access to the documents. It's that access dimension of descriptive cataloging that I suggest should get priority attention from all of us.

Seymour Lubetzky: I heartily agree in general. My objection to the use of title-unit entries is not so much that they will disperse the works of an author, because this could be brought together by means of an author added entry. The proponents do provide for an author added entry to show what the library has by an author. My point is that even if you make an author added entry, what you'll have under the author will be the *books* of an author, and not the *works.* My emphasis is on the works as distinct from the books.

Let me offer an illustration. When I was at the Library of Congress, a bibliographer used the LC catalog to try to compile a bibliography of the works and books of Ralph Waldo Emerson. He began at the beginning under *A* with *The American Scholar.* Under *American Scholar* he found editions published beginning, I believe, in the 1880s. He was surprised that he couldn't find the earlier editions, which he expected certainly must be someplace because that book was based on an oration delivered by Emerson in the 1830s. That person began to make a note to call attention to the Library of Congress to obtain from publishers the early editions of Emerson. But as he went on compiling from title to title, under *O* he came to a title *Oration Delivered before the Phi Beta Kappa,* and there were two editions under that title. One, I believe, was published in 1837, and the other in 1838. On one of them, fortuitously, there was a note entered by the cataloger which said, "Usually published under the title *American Scholar.*" The bibliographer then realized that here were the early editions that he sought. Then he complained to the reference librarian and said, "Well, you have one edition under one title and another edition under another title. Is that what you call a good catalog? Does it make sense to separate them?" By using the titles you separate the editions, and certainly translations, of a work, even if you make added entries under the author and under the subject.

Joseph Rosenthal: I agree generally with the points raised by Professor Lubetsky, although I'm less enthusiastic about this criticism of *ISBD* than I am in my endorsement of his stress on the importance of the main entry and his critique of both the *AACR* and the current code revision proposals for handling serials. I would like to look a little beyond that to the process and situation we find ourselves in now with code revision and contrast what was done, at least in the preliminary stages of *AACR*, with what is being done now. I think a great deal of this relates to the historical context that Professor Lubetzky points out in his emphasis on the ideology of catalogs.

The *AACR*, the preliminary discussions and proposals in which Professor Lubetzsky so prominently figured and which led up to the *AACR*, did start out with an attempt to fashion an ideology, a philosophical context, for those rules. In the present situation, where we are fairly well along in the process of code revision, I'm not at all sure that it's going that way. It may or may not be too late to do anything about it.

Code revision is occuring as a series of proposals which arise out of study teams. In the American case the study team is the Catalog Code Revision Committee of ALA. The work of these study teams, from the evidence that I've seen, does not stem from one consistent ideology. It stems from people in groups, subcommittees, and teams looking at particular rules, chapters, or sections of the *AACR* and trying to correct specific errors or phraseology. Whether or not these specific proposals will be brought into some kind of overall approach and ideology remains to me a very questionable point.

And yet, if we are looking at the functions of the catalog, one of the very pragmatic functions which Mr. Berman mentioned is to get bibliographic information distributed to users. It should be information that is useful and valid. It's also important, as Ben-Ami Lipetz's catalog use study at Yale University emphatically demonstrated, to get that information distributed fast. Many people working on code revision and a lot of our catalogers are well aware of the desirability of getting catalog data distributed speedily. This is reflected in attempts to simplify the rules and to make the rules more easily applicable. I suspect that the emphasis of the proposals and the Catalog Code Revision Committee's preliminary acceptance of the rules for title entry of serials reflect this desire to have a simple rule that everybody can apply and therefore get out cataloging data quickly and cheaply. The emphasis on speed is very important, but this emphasis and the more philosophical ideology of catalogs sometimes come into conflict. I am not sure which needs to prevail.

Lubetzky: There are two things which I believe underlie the *ISBD*, the design of which I was not involved in. One is to make better use of the computer. No one could possibly take exception to that. However, I do not readily see that there is an esoteric punctuation, for example, produced for the benefit of the computer that necessarily has to appear on the card. It is quite possible to provide for it without having it printed. Isn't that the case? If you can't provide for certain symbols that the computer will recognize you should use other symbols, without necessarily having it reproduced on the card where it certainly does interfere with the intelligibility and ease of reading. The catalog, after all, is an instrument of communication. The library talks to the person through this catalog, and it must be as intelligible as possible.

Second, the repetition of the name of the author before and after the title is clearly the result of that suggestion of entry under the title. There is, I believe, a provision so that it could be used without the heading. People could use it either without a heading or with a heading. Of course, as who disapproves of the use of the title as a unit heading, I don't see any justification for it. I have not said in my presentation that there is no room for entry under title. That was beyond the scope of what I was trying to cover. There are places where entry under title is in order. These are cases where the works and the books coincide. An example of this is the case of maps. You remember that in the thirties, two people, Boks and Lewis, had special rules for maps. They took the position that it is not important to bring together the editions of a map, and that authorship of maps is also diffuse. Consequently, the map itself is the important thing, and it should be entered under the title. Added entries for the area will also be applicable.

This is true also in other small collections where the need to relate editions and translations of a work does not apply. If you have a laboratory collection, the work may be regarded as the book itself. But I think when you speak about the catalog, you really have in mind the research library where there are resources that have to be related, and there it is a critical point.

Maurice Freedman: I think there's a basic point that we have to be concerned with. By making cataloging easier and saving the time of the cataloger, and by making it easier for someone who is an apprentice cataloger or a noncataloger to catalog materials, we are definitely increasing the speed through the cataloging department. We are indeed lowering the costs, but we are passing them on to our users. What we are forcing people to do is wander through long title sequences of *Journal of* or *Journal on* to find a particular organization's journal. They are in big trouble if they don't know if it's *Journal of* or *Journal on*. The excuse for this is to allow a clerk to easily make a title entry for it. It's going to take a library user who has a really precise title to find the work.

One other point: I am one of the last people in the world to be a devil's advocate for *ISBD*. I was one of the cosigners of a resolution which tried to have it repealed. The advocates of *ISBD* originally argued that it was for the sake of the computer. Ultimately, however, the position that they put forward was not that the computer was being served, but that the cataloger was being served. They argued that what you refer to as "esoteric punctuation marks" are a signal to the cataloger as to what elements they are examining, and that this will help the cataloger identify the elements even if they don't know the language or the meaning of the words. Would you want to respond to *ISBD* supposedly helping the cataloger, not just the computer?

Lubetzky: Well, I am a user of the catalog and I have been for many years. I don't believe that it would help me. I don't know how many users would be helped by the various symbols when they don't know what the symbol exactly designates or denotes.

Nabil Hamdy: I am the person who proposed the title-unit entry, and I would like to respond to what I've heard today. I don't think that the title-unit entry conflicts with the ideology of the catalog in any sense. It is just a simplification of the cataloging process, which is badly needed. If we can simplify cataloging, make it cheaper, and make the materials available to the user faster, it will be more beneficial to the use of our libraries than selecting main entries that don't serve any function with regard to the display of the author's works under his name. The author's works can be displayed by main and added entries. Mr. Lubetzky mentioned the case at the Library of Congress where the same works of Emerson appeared under two different titles, even in the case of the main entry. It is entered under his name and then the title following his name is the title of that copy I have in my hand. The difference in the title is shown usually by a note, not in the title following the name, so the title-unit-entry concept is exactly the same, or will look exactly the same as the main entry. The only difference is the cataloger doesn't have to sit down and challenge himself, select one entry over the other, and say that this person is more responsible than another person for the work. The title unit entry has been misinterpreted as the only entry that is going to be in the card catalog or any formal catalog. With regard to fiction works and how they are going to be arranged on the shelves, the title unit proposed that cataloging should be done for the first author entry, which will be one of the tracings. In this case all the works of a given author will be assembled on the shelf under his/her name as well, so it is not really in conflict and I think there is a misinterpretation.

Lubetzky: I agree with the observation that in our catalog we had not brought together the *American Scholar* and the *Oration*. That was exactly the disadvantage in our practice prior to the revision of the *AACR*. I have also pointed out that for that reason the *AACR* does provide the use of uniform titles. Under the *AACR*, if you cataloged the *Oration Delivered before the Phi Beta Kappa*, you would have the uniform title *American Scholar* which would bring together all these editions.

You say that you could accomplish by the added entries what you accomplish now by the main entries. In the first place, one of the functions which I have not specified—because it is not directly a function, but is indirectly a result of the function of the main entry—is that the underlying ideology represented by the *AACR* aims first at fixing a location for an author and then for a work. The reason for it is that there are translations of works. Normally a translation is of a work, not of an edition. It has to be related to the work. If you have the editions separated, the question will remain where you put the translations, supplements, adaptations, continuations, sequels, and works about a work. Fixing the position of a work in the catalog makes it possible to have an integrated catalog, where under the entry of the work, you have everything that relates to it. That is impossible to accomplish by means of added entries. Under added entries there are a number of problems that arise. If you have two or more authors, are you going to make added entries under each of these authors? If so, where do you put in the related works? Under the first author? Under the second author? If you are going to make it in both of these places, then of course the bulk of the catalog will very materially increase.

Leo Rift: I believe that the emphasis on abuse of title entry in the name of speeding up cataloging is not the question of a title entry versus other entries, it is the question of simplification. Simplification is cheapening the process. It does not serve any reduction of time. It does not speed up anything if the cataloging is done with the same thoroughness. We do have a computer. We do have other technologies. These should be used to speed up our processing, but the important thing is that we bring out the essential parts of a work and give all the possible entries to identify the work. That takes just as much time if we choose one entry as another. The cheapening process takes place when we just use the work at hand and don't do any additional work. Then we can do it very fast, but we are not bringing out the various characteristics. We can blame the new technologies for the abuse of the users and time, but that is not the case at all. The emphasis on title entry came from the specialized libraries, primarily the technical libraries, that were small but had the money and the power behind them to see that their view prevails. We have to see this as a political process rather than as a cataloging theory process. ALA or its subdivision have been sitting back while these powerful people get together and decide what should be good for us. It's about time that we go back to these principles and make sure that the quality of cataloging is upheld.

Rosenthal: I don't want my former remarks to be interpreted as a plug for title entry for serials. They were not that.

In connection with what Mr. Rift had to say, the opportunity is upon us to go back to principles, into an ideology of catalogs. In the development of *AACR*, one of the factors that led to a separate British and North American text was the concept—at least in North America—that catalogs of large research libraries could not be changed. This was a political and economic concept. Experience since 1967 has led us to the conclusion that that was an erroneous concept. Catalogs, even the largest catalogs, can be changed. As we will probably hear from Mr. Welsh tomorrow, we are at the point where the Library of Congress has all but committed itself to close its catalogs. Isn't this the time in this code revision to go back to ideology and do what should be done in developing a catalog code?

Pauline Atherton: Twenty years ago, I was moved by Seymour Lubetzky's document, as I was a library school student at the University of Chicago, and today I am just slightly disappointed because he has added confusion for me rather than clarity to the situation. The confusion comes partly from the use of the word *entry* in two contexts. Entry meaning *main and added entry*, and entry meaning *unit description*. I agree with Mr. Hamdy that there is confusion if you think of the title-unit-entry concept as a main entry. It is not meant to be that. The beauty of technology at this time, just as it was in the time of the British Museum catalog, is that we can look at all the data elements in our unit description and conceive of entries as they should be conceived. If there's a necessity for an author and uniform title entry, then that is done for Ralph Waldo Emerson. The cataloger with principles would never have placed some of it under *Oration* and some of it under *American Scholar*. If we had a set of rules today that helped us with all kinds of entry, not only concentration on the main entry and then one page of notes about making added entries; if we conceived of the new catalog in this age of technology, as they have conceived of it at the University of Chicago, for instance, with their quadraplaner data structure (the idea that there are four levels of data elements that we are collecting to form a catalog record), then that technology will allow us to create entries however we conceive of them and have rules for them. If there's a need for a simple author entry, it will be there. If there is a need for an author and uniform title, they will be there, because it is designated by the cataloger who has the intelligence and the ideology to set appropriate rules for the computer printing of the book catalog, card catalog, or any type of catalog. I want to see Seymour Lubetzky now concentrate on *entry*, and separately on *description*.

Lubetzky: I'm sorry to have disappointed you. If there is confusion in the term or in the use of the term *entry*, it is because we do use that term in different senses. I thought that when I said "title-unit entry," you would know what that means. It means an entry that begins with a title.

There is a difference between an online catalog and a catalog that will be used by the computer to reproduce a visual catalog. With an online catalog, the elements involved can be related by the computer to present them to the reader when s/he asks for them. We can program the computer, for example, when one asks for *American Scholar* to present all the editions under the various titles at the same time. But this will occur only if we were to revise our rules for an online catalog. There is room for important changes.

If, however, we use tape to reproduce a catalog in visual form for communication with other libraries, then the purposes that have been served before in our card catalog and printed catalog would obtain now. If the editions should be brought together, regardless of the title, then that instrument has to exist someplace. That instrument under the *AACR* is the title-unit entry. If you want a visual catalog with a title entry that's with a description of the book itself, you will have to provide an added entry that will have not only the author but the author and the uniform title. When you use that, you are first omitting the author and the uniform heading, and then supplying them later. Instead of omitting it before and supplying it later, the argument and the experience will show it's better to use it from the beginning, because you then save yourself completely unnecessary entries, entries such as SYMPHONY #1, SYMPHONY #2, SONATA IN F, or BIOGRAPHY, or LETTERS, or POEMS. Numerous titles which have to be entered under the title, as you prescribed are completely useless.

Sonia Sasuta: At the risk of sounding trite and a bit naive, I'd like to remind this group that the *ISBD* was also called, not for the cataloger's benefit, but as an international tool of bibliographic description. We have to remind ourselves that that is the ideal of the *ISBD*. In this age of financial restriction we have to see ourselves, even at the smallest unit, as an international library resource network, and unless we can deal with this concept we can't rework the *ISBD* into a viable tool.

Lubetzky: I am a great believer in international cooperation—but international cooperation involves also the United States; it involves us. We are not outside, we do not come and say, "Well, that is what international practice is, an entry of serials here under title; we've got to get along with others."

We have participated in international cooperation in Paris, but we have made a very substantial contribution to it. I think the role of the United States, of every library organization, is to improve the type of catalog that is prepared. That way we will provide for a type of catalog that will endure.

The moment we compromise, whether we compromise among ourselves to adopt rules that are incompatible with ideology, or we compromise with other countries in the interest of cooperation, then I think we are merely providing the necessity before very long to have these changes brought about. And that is not very much to the advantage of international cooperation from a long range point of view.

The Catalog in the World Around It

by Joan K. Marshall

The title, "The Catalog in the World Around It," suggests that the catalog is an abstract; I would like to refute that suggestion in the beginning. There is no such beast as *the* catalog. There are many catalogs and each of them functions in a different world—the worlds of the school child and of the college student, the worlds of the eminent scholar and of the casual reader, the worlds of the research chemist and of the adult, young adult, or child interested in chemistry. The denizens of each of these worlds have a wide variety of information needs and a wide variety of economic, social, political, and educational backgrounds. Only one fact holds true in all catalog worlds: library users—despite their great personal differences and interests—are, for the most part, expected to negotiate their own way through whatever catalog is presented to them. The catalog functioning in each user's world, therefore, should meet the information needs of the user readily and with as much ease as is possible.

But despite the many catalog worlds, and herein lies the rub—or at least a rough spot—we have been proceeding on the assumption that *the* catalog does indeed exist in the form of the bibliographic data distributed by the Library of Congress. And with the advent of computers, we have vastly accelerated the pace at which we are proceeding. The question I will address is whether our acting on what I believe to be an invalid assumption provides valid cataloging, that is, cataloging which meets the information needs of all users readily and with as much ease as is possible in all of the library worlds.

It was suggested by the organizer of this Institute that I approach my topic by considering whether the catalog is, or should be, prescriptive or descriptive. While reading linguists, as I was forced to do many years ago in college, arguing the case for or against prescriptive or descriptive grammar, I came to the conclusion that the majority opinion among linguists was that the prescriptive approach to grammar was too rigid; it established artificial barriers to communication. An oft-cited example of an artificial barrier was the unacceptability, in prescriptive terms, of a statement such as "Him and me loves Mary," even though such a statement is fully comprehensible. A reader or a listener, the descriptive grammarians would argue, would not assume, despite the singular verb and the objective case pronouns, that Mary was the subject, rather than the object, of the sentence. Although the consensus among linguists was that prescriptive grammar was too rigid, they were still appalled at the thought of thoroughly descriptive grammar. "Him and me loves Mary" never gained acceptance with grammarians.

In relation to descriptive or bibliographic cataloging, I am on the side of the linguists. The prescriptive approach is rigid—every decision is confined to rule. But a descriptive approach to bibliographic cataloging would be title page cataloging; the result of this approach in our catalogs would be appalling. I do not believe that title page cataloging is cataloging since it merely identifies the book in hand. The purpose of cataloging, as Dr. Lubetzky explained, is to both identify the book in hand and to relate the work contained in the book to other works by the author, to other editions, translations, or adaptations of the work, and to works based on or about the work. I agree with Dr. Lubetzky: the establishment of this relationship is essential in all of the catalog worlds mentioned. Descriptive cataloging, therefore, must be prescriptive.

The question that should be asked is not whether bibliographic cataloging is or should be prescriptive or descriptive, but whether, or why, the same prescriptions must be placed on all catalogs. There is only one set of rules for entry and description—that of the *Anglo-American Cataloging Rules (AACR)* (Chicago: American Library Association, 1967). The Introduction states:

> These rules have been drawn up primarily to respond to the needs of general research libraries. This represents continuation of the orientation that has characterized the rules of the American Library Association since the 1908 edition. . . . Within the framework of this research library orientation, however, an effort has been made to respond as much as possible to the needs of public libraries in which research considerations are not paramount. When the needs of research libraries and those of other libraries are irreconcilable, alternative rules have been provided for the use of the latter.

The *Catch 22* aspect of this attempt by the authors of the *AACR* to reconcile the needs of research and nonresearch libraries is that our central cataloging agency, the Library of Congress (LC), does not provide dual cataloging copy. The existence of the alternative rule, therefore, merely permits nonresearch libraries to operate within the law if they wish to do their own cataloging or alter LC's cataloging.

If, for instance, a nonresearch library acquires a work in English, issued by the Economic Research Council of the Bank of Japan, the rules *permit* the acquiring library to enter the work under the name of the institution in English, but the entry assigned by the Library of Congress will be the transliterated form of the institution's name in Japanese: NIHON GINKO. CHŌSAKYAKU. Libraries which are not dependent upon the Library of Congress for cataloging copy are free to use the alternate rule. But there are many libraries, such as the one I work in, Brooklyn College, which have rather large and varied collections of scholarly material, but which serve an undergraduate population and are not research libraries. Brooklyn College students, from my experience working with them, would be better served if Brooklyn College Library had chosen to adopt the alternative to *AACR* Rule 64. But since we, and countless similar institutions, are extremely dependent upon the Library of Congress as the only source of cataloging copy for the types of materials we acquire, and since to have chosen to use the alternative rule would have committed us to extensive and expensive recataloging of LC copy, service considerations gave way to economic considerations.

The alternative *AACR* rules, therefore, although their use would have been appropriate in many types of nonresearch libraries, have been adopted by only a few. But those institutions, and I am referring particularly to public libraries, serve a very large percentage of the nation's library users. There is a real possibility that the new edition of the *Anglo-American Cataloging Rules* will not give adequate consideration to the needs of nonresearch libraries. If the few alternative rules, which were included "when the needs of research libraries and those of other libraries are irreconcilable," are eliminated in the new edition of the *AACR*, what effect will this have on public libraries? I do not imagine, as a result, that public libraries will, for instance, begin establishing inappropriate and complex trans-literated forms of names. But how will they operate beyond the pale? How long, and to what extent, can a library operate beyond the pale and still make use of any of the Library of Congress's bibliographic data?

It is possible that we need a nonresearch library-oriented code for entry and description. The possibility that such a need exists, or will come into existence, should be explored now! And that possibility should be explored in conjunction with another: whether we should consider cataloging some titles just *twice*. The conditions that pertained in 1908 when the first rules for entry were published do not pertain in 1975, and did not in 1967 when the present *AACR* was published. In 1908, the idea of sharing bibliographic data was still an idea—the goal was to catalog a title once, and once only. In 1975, the 1908 goal is technologically possible. But the relationship between the source of most of the shared cataloging data, the Library of Congress, and nonresearch libraries—a relationship that has not always been symbiotic in the past—shows signs of deteriorating rather than improving. In the sometimes frenetic push towards international cooperation among research libraries and towards the somewhat awesome concept of Universal Bibliographic Control (UBC), the library needs of the nonscholar are easily overlooked.

Nonresearch and research libraries have, at least, one thing in common, they both operate under economic constraints. In nonresearch libraries it is becoming increasingly difficult to convince cost-conscious administrators that available cataloging copy may not meet the needs of a nonresearch library's users. The economic considerations are real. Nonresearch libraries need their share of the shared bibliographic data, but the data must meet the needs of the public the library is serving. The ideal of cataloging a title just once has been with us a long time—some may even think we have attained that ideal. But the fact is that many titles cataloged just once by the Library of Congress are recataloged many times for use in nonresearch libraries. Perhaps, in the 1970s, we should rethink this ideal and consider, instead, two codes for entry and description and the cataloging of some titles just *twice*.

Subject cataloging is much more difficult to confine to rule than descriptive cataloging. This may partially explain why, until the past few years, so little attention has been paid to it. But the lack of attention is also attributable to the oft-spoken thought that most serious library users are seeking a particular author and title in the catalog, and therefore subject cataloging is not as important as descriptive. This is an instance of a wish being father to a thought. I am convinced, from my experience in an undergraduate library, that subject cataloging is as important as descriptive, and that *all* library users are *serious* library users; they may not all be scholars—they often do not have a particular title in mind—but they do have serious information needs and they seriously need access to the library's collection.

The question is then, does the Library of Congress subject heading list and the subject cataloging provided by the Library of Congress meet the needs of all or any of the catalog world's users? I do not believe that the needs of any are being adequately met.

Written substantiation of this belief, from a wide variety of points of view, has become plentiful in the 1970s. In 1970 Jessica Harris, in her *Subject Analysis*, pointed to inconsistencies in the formation and arrangement of headings, the absence of useful cross-references, the presence of useless ones, and variations in actual practice from what is thought to be practiced. In 1971 Sanford Berman, in his *Prejudices and Antipathies*, demonstrated the subject heading list's bias toward an American/Western-European, Christian, White, male point-of-view. In 1972 Hans Wellisch, in his *Subject Retrieval in the Seventies*, discussed the inadequacy of LC's subject cataloging and the failure of LC to rectify this inadequacy by taking full advantage of the richness of the MARC (Machine-Readable Cataloging) format. Also in 1972, John Christ, in his *Concepts and Subject Headings*, concluded that there was a lack of congruence between social science terminology and the LC subject headings for materials in the social sciences.

I will add that since I have been working with the access LC provides to materials on women, a basic fault that I have found with LC subject cataloging is the absence of specificity. Under WOMEN—EMPLOYMENT, for instance, are listed works on opportunities for employment, the health and safety hazards of employment, the wages of employment, discrimination in employment, the problems of mothers, married and/or single women and employment, employment statistics, women in professional, business, trade, and home employment, the reentry of women into employment, the history of women's employment, and employment law.

Why, or how, has subject cataloging and the Library of Congress subject heading list been allowed to become so inadequate? Part of the answer lies in the Library of Congress's guidelines for subject heading establishment as set forth by David Haykin in *Subject Headings: A Practical Guide* (1951). Mr. Haykin acknowledges that we lack knowledge of the probable approach of various classes and categories of readers to the subject catalog. Although we lack this knowledge, the reader is the focus in all cataloging principles and practice, and "all other considerations, such as convenience and the desire to arrange entries in some logical order, are secondary to the basic rule that the heading . . . should be that which the reader will seek in the catalog, if we know or can presume what the reader will look under" (p. 7). If we lack knowledge of the probable approach of readers to the catalog, how can we presume to know what the reader will look for in the catalog? To continue with Haykin's guideline:

> To the extent that headings represent the predilection of the cataloger in regard to terminology and are dictated by conformity to a chosen logical pattern, as against the likely approach of the reader resting on psychological rather than logical grounds, the subject catalog will lose in effectiveness and ease of approach (p. 7).

If we consider the effect the application of this guideline would have on descriptive cataloging, perhaps we can gain some insight into the problems of subject cataloging. The guideline dictates that we abandon logic and consistency in favor of an unknown reader's psychological approach to the catalog. The basis for subject cataloging, therefore, is wholly subjective, and it is a subjectivity once removed. A subject heading is established on the basis of what a subject cataloger thinks a reader will think. This is a rather fuzzy basis for establishing subject headings, but fuzziness is not the guideline's only fault.

The application of the guideline requires the construction of a hypothetical reader. Such hypothesizing may be necessary in selecting a heading from among synonyms. The construction of the hypothesis, however, should be limited to such considerations as whether the subject heading list is designed to serve the general public or the scientific community, the adult or the juvenile user. Examination of the Library of Congress subject heading list reveals that considerations of nationality, ethnic background, religion, and sex have been factors which have entered into the construction, over the years, of LC's hypothetical reader. The reader has been identified as Western-European/American, Christian, White, and male, and this is not surprising since it merely reflects the point of view that has been dominant for so long in our society. However, that point of view no longer accurately reflects the world we live in. The points of view of non-Western Europeans/Americans, non-Christians, non-Whites, and nonmales are becoming a force in society. The subject headings we assign should reflect this.

The objection that is always raised against our subject access reflecting a multiplicity of points of view is that the reader's expectations concerning access will often not be met. For example, the Library of Congress established names of indigenous American and African peoples are very often derogatory corruptions of their real names. (KAFIRS, which LC recently changed, is the equivalent of *niggers*.) The corruptions were often established by the ancestors of LC's hypothetical reader. They are the terms with which most of us have become familiar and under which most of us would look for material, but these names are not the authentic names of these peoples. Moreover, they very often perpetuate preconceptions that reinforce prejudice.

My reply to the objection of unmet expectations is that we have been looking at one reader when, in fact, we have many readers, and so I ask, which reader's expectations? And further, that libraries as social institutions in a multicultural society have a responsibility to all elements in that society. Our effort is an educational one. We will not disserve readers by instructing them through our subject headings in nonbiased terminology; we will, in fact, be keeping all of our readers in focus.

We need new guidelines for the establishment of subject headings, and these guidelines should stress objectivity and logical arrangement of entries. As an example of such guidelines, I would like to read you the "Principles for Establishing Subject Headings Relating to People and Peoples" which was developed by the SRRT (Social Responsibilities Round Table) Task Force on Women's Sexist Subject Heading Committee. These "Principles" were presented for endorsement to ALA's Subject Analysis Committee and to the Library of Congress at the annual ALA meeting in San Francisco. They have been accepted for use by LC, and the Subject Analysis Committee recommended their use in other libraries.

The first principle:

The authentic name of ethnic, national, religious, social, or sexual groups should be established if such a name is determinable. If a group does not have an authentic name, the name preferred by the group should be established. The determination of authentic or preferred name should be based upon the literature of the people themselves (not upon outside sources or experts), upon organizational self-identification, and/or upon group member experts.

The second principle:

In establishing subdivisions for use with the names of people or peoples consider the connotation, in addition to the denotation, of the wording and structure of the subdivision. Avoid words which connote inferiority or peculiarity. In establishing subdivisions for concepts applicable to all classes of people, avoid variations in the structure of the subdivision under certain people or peoples. Avoid Western-European/American ethnocentrism. Avoid value-loaded words, aim for neutrality.

Many subdivisions now applied to minority peoples and to women (a majority with minority status) support the assumptions of the majority. Clear examples of such support were the abandoned forms SOCIAL AND MORAL CONDITIONS under Negroes and HISTORY AND CONDITION under women. Only Blacks had both a social *and* a moral condition; only women had both a history *and* a condition. Not so clear, however, is the subtle reinforcement of the majority assumptions provided by such subdivisions as CIVILIZATION OF under the names of indigenous American and African peoples, which deny the fact that many indigenous peoples had highly developed civilizations, albeit that the form of their civilization may not have been recognized by the colonizing peoples. DISCOVERY AND EXPLORATION under geographic names reinforces the popularly held notion that the world outside Western Europe had no history—and only a shaky hold on existence—before it was "discovered" by Western Europeans (which further reinforces the notion that Western Europeans "civilized" the world in the best interests of us—the majority—all). These subdivisions could be neutralized by changing CIVILIZATION OF to RELATIONS WITH [COLONIZING PEOPLE] and by changing DISCOVERY AND EXPLORATION to FIRST KNOWLEDGE OF IN [WESTERN EUROPE] or, somewhat less complex and perhaps more flexible, requiring that DISCOVERY AND EXPLORATION be further modified to specify who did the discovering; for example, AMERICA—DISCOVERY AND EXPLORATION, SPANISH.

Encounters between indigenous and colonizing peoples are described as MASSACRES when the indigenous people won and BATTLES when the colonists won. The use of the term *massacre* was defended by Eugene Frosio in the Spring 1971 *LRTS (Library Resources and Technical Services)*: "Events are not named according to what it is polite or ideal to call them, but according to what they are actually called by authorities in the field" (p. 131). The authority Frosio cites is the *Encyclopaedia Britannica.* Had he consulted an Indian history, he would have found, for instance, that what the *Britannica* called the Fort Phil Kearney *massacre* the Indians call the *Battle of the Hundred Slain* [Dee Brown, *Bury My Heart at Wounded Knee*, Bantam (1972), p. 132]. Whether an encounter between an indigenous and a colonizing people was a battle or a massacre is, more often than not, determined by who is writing the history rather than by any objective facts. *Massacre* is a value-loaded word and should be avoided. If the word *battle* does not appropriately describe an armed encounter between an indigenous and a colonizing people, the neutral word *incident* should be used. (The use of the word *incident* was suggested by Thomas Yen-Ran Yeh in the Spring 1971 *LRTS*, p. 122-128. It was Yen-Ran Yeh's suggestion that led to Frosio's response.)

The third principle:

The wording and structure of headings for minority or other groups should not differ in wording or structure from headings for the majority. Avoid all *as* and *in* constructions to describe practitioners of an activity.

The much-criticized DELINQUENT WOMEN was changed to FEMALE OFFENDERS in the 1974 *Supplement to the Library of Congress Subject Headings (LCSH)*. This is the term in current usage in the literature and it is certainly an improvement over the old heading, but it is not in line with other headings for criminals. Was FEMALE OFFENDERS established because of literary warrant or because one would not logically send *women criminals* to REFORMATORIES FOR WOMEN (the Library of Congress heading) rather than to *women's prisons?* But whether women are delinquent, offenders, or criminals aside, we are still left with the fact that only four classes of persons are singled out in the Library of Congress subject heading list as criminals. Why do only Catholics, Jews, Negroes, and women transcend their particular nationality? The other criminal elements in society are supposedly taken care of by CRIME AND CRIMINALS—[GEOGRAPHIC SUBDIVISION]. This heading is not comparable to the adjectival heading, and I would argue that the adjectival heading is valid, but it should be applied to all classes of people and to all nationalities or to none. There are Irish criminals, they are not all in Ireland; there are Chinese criminals; they are not all in China.

The *as* form, WOMEN AS LIBRARIANS, for instance, has been abandoned by the Library of Congress, but the *in* form persists although the arguments against it are the same as those against the *as* form. The use of the form connotes peculiarity (the people so described are acting out a somewhat inappropriate role) and passiveness (they are not actively participating in that role). WOMEN *in* LIBRARIANSHIP would have been just as offensive as WOMEN *as* LIBRARIANS.

The fourth principle:

Do not use subsuming terminology. Do not establish headings for certain, but not all, classes of people.

A basic rule of subject heading establishment is: "The heading should be as specific as the topic it is intended to cover. As a corollary, the heading should not be broader than the topic" (Haykin, p. 9). Subsuming terminology and the selective establishment of headings violates this rule. These headings, therefore, in addition to exhibiting a bias in favor of the majority, actively hinder access.

Headings such as SALESMEN AND SALESMANSHIP and FIREMEN, since they are assigned to works covering the activities of both men and women in these occupations, are not specific. Tradition may sanction the use of the word *man* to mean *the human race*. It does not sanction subsuming saleswomen under salesmen. SALESPEOPLE AND SELLING and FIRE FIGHTERS would be specific, and the user would not have to intuit that these headings, perhaps, covered the activities of women as well as men.

Headings such as SPORTS FOR WOMEN and SPORTS FOR CHILDREN are specific, but there is not a heading for men's sports. Hence the basic heading, SPORTS, is used both as a heading broader than the topic covered (when it is applied to works on sports for men) and as a specific heading (when it is applied to works on sports for all ages and sexes). The user interested in children's sports, therefore, is obliged, when looking under the general heading, to differentiate between those works which are general and those which are on men's sports. The user interested in men's sports has the same difficulty.

Those four principles were presented to the ALA Subject Analysis Committee and to the Library of Congress, but there is need for a fifth principle since the application of objectivity and logic alone will not resolve the related problems of lack of specificity and the timely establishment of new headings. When Ed Blume, Chief of LC's Subject Cataloging Division, was asked at a meeting of the New York Technical Services Librarians about LC's failure to have established a heading for rock music for so long, he remarked: "Today's horse may be tomorrow's carrion." This is certainly a possibility, but it is while the topic is today's horse that library users are seeking information about it. And if the topic does become tomorrow's carrion, it would not, perhaps, be inappropriate that it was buried under its own dead horse subject heading.

Subject headings should be established as the need for them arises. The existence of a number of dead headings in our catalogs is preferable to the situation created by the delay in establishing headings. All of the early works on rock music are buried under the heading for JAZZ, and the early works on linguistics are buried under the heading LANGUAGE AND LANGUAGES. Perhaps the computer could resolve the dilemma of dead headings vs. buried material. Since the Library of Congress subject heading list is to be available in machine-readable form by 1976, could not a program be written that would allow LC and other libraries to get a printout of the headings which, for example, by 1986 had not been assigned to any work during that ten-year period, and in each subsequent year, a printout of the headings that had not been used during that ten-year period. [Editor's Note: As of the publication of this book, this machine-readable list was still in the process of being compiled.] These candidates for dead heading status could be evaluated for their usefulness and examined for the possibility that a conflicting heading had been established and was in active use. Such a procedure would give us much greater control of our subject catalogs.

In conclusion, I am sure you all believe me to be either idealistic, unrealistic, radical, or just plain silly. Perhaps all four. And there is a basis for your belief: money. It is impossible to read the library press today without reading about the increasing costs of maintaining, and the decreasing budgets of, libraries, and particularly about the increasing costs of technical services. A number of the speakers at the Association of Research Libraries conference on *The Future of the Card Catalog* spoke of their fixed budgets and of the necessity of decreasing the costs of cataloging since it was cutting into their acquisitions budget.

I sometimes imagine that the first article on the high costs of cataloging was written as the first book, ever, was being cataloged. I have recently learned that even that *just once* cataloging which is done by the Library of Congress is not adequately supported. At least, in my opinion, it is not adequately supported since the catalogers at LC work under the pressure to *produce*—they actually have a weekly quota they are supposed to meet. Production quotas, I believe, are antithetical to careful, thoughtful cataloging.

I have no answers to our overall money problems, and I have no doubt that quality cataloging costs. I believe it is worth the cost, but I do not set the priorities, perhaps some of you here do. If support for quality cataloging is not going to be given, I think we should give it up entirely. A sham catalog is a disservice to the user, and participating in the creation of a sham catalog is personally degrading to a professional.

Finally, research libraries may be large, powerful, and aggressive, and, although I am not sure that their spokespersons are more articulate than others, their cataloging needs receive attention from the Library of Congress and from the American Library Association. But research library users represent a very small percentage of the total library user population of this nation. We must begin to pay attention to the cataloging needs of nonresearch library users, who comprise the larger percentage.

DISCUSSION

Sanford Berman: Lest it appear that Ms. Marshall's committee and a few others of us, notoriously associated with that kind of work, are little more than crazy, fire-breathing radicals, let me add this gloss immediately: We're an interesting "radical" company, particularly with respect to sexist subject headings. (I noticed that there seemed to be some titters when that was mentioned, as if there were still some doubt as to whether such a beast as sexist subject headings exists. I think Ms. Marshall has pinned it down.)

But let me introduce the authority of the United States Labor Department, which over the past year or more has diligently worked on removing both age and sex reference from their official occupational titles in accordance with federal law and executive directives. That's a federal agency. I believe that what they've done in this particular case represents social justice and elementary fairness. They have literally changed thousands of sexist job titles. However, in addition to the couple of examples that Ms. Marshall cited from the extant and altogether active LC subject thesaurus, there are also BUS BOYS, MAN, LUMBERMEN, LONG-SHOREMEN, FISHERMEN, etc. The list is almost literally endless if you have the patience to dig them all up. That's point number one.

Point two: Imagine that there is a graphic to project on the screen or blackboard. In your mind, divide that space into two columns, please. Consider placing the following five or six names in the left-hand column, and then tell me what you feel: Eta, Untouchables, Bushmen, Hottentots, Eskimos, and Lapps. There is not any great disquiet or discomfort. Am I correct in assuming that? Not terrible anyway. Consider now what we're going to place in the right-hand column, one for one, analogous: Krauts, Wops, Frogs, Kikes, Polacks, Micks, and Gringos. Is there a little unease about those, a little bit? Well, I surely hope so.

What is that? What's in the right-hand column? That's slanderous; they're not the names of the people. Kikes are not *Kikes,* we're *Jews.* Okay? Wops are not *Wops,* they're *Italians.* Those are their real names. The others are defamatory. These are the words that you hear every week. And two of them I heard two nights ago on "All in the Family." This is Archie Bunker crap, right? He used *Micks* and *Polacks.* It's laughable when Archie Bunker says that, because we know he's an uneducated slob. But what about when our own professional center, the Library of Congress, uses BUSHMEN and HOTTENTOTS which are analogous to *Polacks* and *Kikes* and *Wops?* ETA literally means *filthy persons.* There is an objective, neutral name for those people, and that's *Burakumin.* And similarly, for UN-TOUCHABLES there is a perfectly acceptable Ghandi-endorsed name, *Harijans.* In the case of BUSHMEN and HOTTENTOTS, the peoples' real names don't even appear as after-the-fact, last minute cross-references to the defamatory form.

San and *Khoi-Khoin,* to my knowledge, as of a check a couple of days ago, are not even yet in the list as cross-references. The others for the most part do have the right names in the catalog, but as cross-references to what I must insist are the wrong names. And what I'm trying to suggest is that there's something shameful about a profession that has allowed this kind of blatant and rank ethnocentrism, racism, chauvinism, the whole *schmier,* to persist this long.

Joan Marshall: I endorse everything Mr. Berman said. I don't have any comments.

Joseph Rosenthal: Well, you may not want to endorse everything I have to say. I'd like to respond to two main points that Ms. Marshall made. First, that there should be different rules for research and nonresearch libraries: I think that there's a fair amount of merit to this suggestion, and I do agree with her that it should be examined. I see some difficulties, and I see them in my present work—very obvious difficulties. I'd like to check this with Phil Long and the others that are active in OCLC (Ohio College Library Center): Is it not possible to change author entries if an individual library so desires? That was my impression. As a matter of fact, the record of the change is retained in at least the OCLC files and is, I am told, available to libraries.

Phil Long: It may be available online.

Rosenthal: I see. In spite of OCLC's achievements in allowing this facility, there are real difficulties in the provision of a computer-based authority file system in an online mode designed to serve multiple participants, especially in retaining different forms of entry used by different libraries for a particular heading or even particular works.

This is a difficulty of technology and design, but I would submit that a more basic difficulty lies in the implications of how we exchange bibliographical data in the ever-expanding community. We talk about the proposals that the National Commission on Library and Information Service has made for a nationwide system of networks designed to improve access to library resources for all people in the United States. Of course, that's even part of a larger network encompassing not only North America but the entire globe. So on these grounds, I would question the provision of two codes for different types of libraries. In the end, service—which I am sure Ms. Marshall and all the rest of us are very interested in—may not be served by the provision of two codes.

I'd like to applaud a great deal of the work that she and SRRT, and also Mr. Berman, have done in their criticism of LC subject headings. A lot of the work is valid and should be endorsed and accepted by the Library of Congress. I'm not sure that this applies to all the work. I think there are grounds for dispute on certain terms. I would say that the general end of objectivity in the headings that Ms. Marshall talked about is a very laudable end and should be pursued. To say, however, that the Library of Congress subject headings and the application of the subject heading list serves no users is a distortion and an exaggeration. I am frequently taken to task as someone who would try to destroy the integrity of certain catalogs on the West Coast. The reference people, at Berkeley in particular, time and time again say that the subject catalog, which is based wholeheartedly on the LC subject heading list, is one of the most important things that they use in serving their clientele. It's imperfect in many, many ways. And some of those imperfections are a result of the LC subject headings, the syndetic structure, the lack of cross-references, the lack of speed in establishing headings, the obsolescence of terminology, and all the other criticisms. Some of the deficiencies in our catalogs are the result of very practical factors in personnel resources; some are probably a fault in the way that we attack subject headings and put them in the catalog. But, a great deal of use is made of our subject catalog, and I suspect that's true of many of the catalogs that you use.

I believe that the use of the subject catalog, at least in large research libraries—and I don't think in smaller libraries and libraries that serve nonresearch publics as well—is something that we should attempt to evaluate. My tentative conclusion is that the subject catalog is used as a first approach in locating material on a given topic. It is useful for a beginner in a library or a beginner in a particular field, a scholar who comes from one field to another, a user who wants to find the latest information or a treatise which covers a topic as of a given date, or who wants to find a brief and perhaps tentative list of books on a given topic. It certainly cannot be called a conclusive or exhaustive guide to library resources. We have, on the one hand, on a more specific level, indexing and abstracting services of all kinds in many fields, and, on the other hand, the resources of libraries outside of our own, as shown in the *National Union Catalog*, catalogs of other libraries, and other bibliographies. I would submit that we cannot expect the subject catalog to cover all of these things.

Marshall: I would like to make a brief comment on what Mr. Rosenthal said. I don't think that I said the subject catalog served no users. I think that you missed a word in my talk. I said that it didn't serve any users *adequately*. There are certain things you can get out of a subject catalog. If I didn't think so, then I wouldn't be so interested in subject headings. One of the reasons a separate code is needed, or at least adequate attention be paid to the needs of nonresearch libraries in whatever code comes out in the second edition, is that unless real attention is paid to the needs of nonresearch libraries, they're going to be forgotten again.

I was sort of appalled at Mr. Welsh's comments on the future of bibliographic services that the Library of Congress is willing to provide. In a parenthetical remark he made, in terms of classification, he said—and this is not an exact quote—both the Library of Congress and Berkeley are considering closing their stacks. Therefore, the development of complex classification schemes may not be very important in the future. I would contend that the Library of Congress and Berkeley closing their stacks has nothing to do with all the rest of the libraries in the country and their need for classification.

Judith Hopkins: While you were talking, two other minor points were raised in my mind, one of which has already been covered in the discussion. The first point is the fact that with OCLC and any online system that I know about, it is very easy to change the entries to conform to the ones that you want in your catalog, no matter what the Library of Congress or any other library has provided. You can change Nihon to Japan, or Rabinowitz to Sholom Aleichem and not change the original record which is still there for those research libraries that want to use it.

The second point concerns the continual reference to Haykin's book, a sort of code of subject authority practice and its drawbacks. I will grant you all of those drawbacks, chiefly because it isn't a code. It is a rationalization of LC's practice at a certain period in time. I understand that Mr. Haykin was hoping to develop a code for subject practice, but he died and it was never done, so that today we lack a code. The need is for someone, somewhere, somehow to develop a code, so that we have something equivalent to the Paris Principles for subject cataloging. Until we have such a code the best we can do is to try to develop some logical principles, to try to rationalize the existing headings. But we are not going to get any further than that.

One other point was raised in my mind by what Mr. Rosenthal was saying about the adequacy of the subject catalog, the subject approach. I agree whole-heartedly that the subject approach is used chiefly by the beginner, the one who is working in a field new to him/her, whether it is a Ph.D. in chemistry or an historical researcher or a high school student who is looking for term paper material. But I think some indication of the inadequacies of the present subject heading structure can be shown in a study made at Wellesley College. I do not remember the exact figures, but it was found that about 16 percent of the approaches to the catalog were by way of subject headings. But when the other approaches were examined and analyzed with care, it turned out that another 16 percent were disguised subject searches. People used author and title approaches, but they were truly interested in a subject approach. This means that about a third of the users of the catalog wanted to find material on a specific subject, but only half of those were able to do so without making a somewhat indirect approach to the catalog.

Marshall: I'd like to comment on Haykin. I agree that it's not a code. However, it is used at LC. I understand from the people in LC's Subject Cataloging Division that they are given Haykin upon the day of their arrival and are expected to read the entire dull document and use it as a guideline in establishing subject headings. So that while Mr. Haykin might not have thought it a code, in the absence of anything else, it is being used as one.

Another comment concerns being able to change OCLC entries on an OCLC terminal. The objection to this is the same as the objection to changing them on a proof sheet. You have the proof sheet in hand or you have the image on the terminal. If you're trying to reduce the cost of your cataloging, you're stuck with accepting LC, particularly if you're in a library which is acquiring the kinds of materials for which LC is the only cataloging source. It's no different. Also, I'm not too sure that the other users of the OCLC data base would be particularly happy with everyone's doing input cataloging and establishing non-LC forms of names. I assume that if I were inputting something, they would want me to input it with the LC, rather than some local, form.

Mina Daniels: As head of a committee, and being recognized as such, it's perfectly all right with me if I'm called the *chairman* rather than the *chairwoman*, and I think I'd prefer that to *chairperson*.

Some of the talk that has been going on this morning has seemed to say—if we just had the right code, if we just had the right headings, if we just had the right terms, everything would be fine. The most important thing is to get most readers to most of the material they want a lot of the time. A card catalog, or any kind of catalog, is a very complex instrument at best. And nothing is going to get every person to everything s/he wants all the time with any accuracy. I would plead for more standardization, not less, because I think whatever we do is going to be imperfect. Then we have good reference librarians to assist people in using it and in getting the materials that they want.

Marshall: I disagree completely. I believe very, very firmly that librarians are educators. The collections we develop, the attempt that we make is an educational effort, and it seems to me that our subject headings are simply part of that, and they *should* be part of that. They should not reflect these kinds of biases.

I will agree that it takes quite a while to sensitize yourself to the implications of the use of *chairman*. *Chairperson* is a very awkward term to get used to. But if you have a certain feeling about language, then language ends up becoming very, very important. I will admit it takes a while to get yourself thinking this way—that language is terribly important because it does shape the way we view the world, and it is very important that we do something about our language.

Unidentified Speaker: This is a footnote on your comment about the centralization of policy in a few large libraries, in a few large policy groups. I was at a meeting last week in Illinois where one of the heads of technical services of one of the large research libraries made the announcement that he had in mind, and he had some support for the idea, that the Library of Congress and about 13 other ARL (Association of Research Libraries) libraries do all of the cataloging for the country. I wasn't sure that I should have taken him all that seriously, but he said it and I did question it. I was surprised to find that many other catalogers there sort of went along with the idea. I certainly think there are a lot of reasons why all of the other schools, academic libraries and, I presume, public libraries, too, would want to keep their hands in the cataloging business. But I can certainly imagine what would happen to cataloging policy if cataloging were limited to such a small group.

Marshall: I agree completely.

Maurice Freedman: I'd like to interject a comment at this point. The National Library of Canada in its automation development has done a remarkable and marvelous thing in terms of its interpretation and use of the MARC format. It is setting up a system of dual entries, so that the French-speaking people of Canada will have French language representation in the authorities established for Canadian catalog records. Note that it is altogether possible in a manual system to have dual entries for a given authority term, be it a subject or a name, but it would be much less practical. And as a minimum, the kind of thing that Ms. Marshall is saying, whether or not there is an alternative catalog code, is that it is in principle possible to try to have an alternative, centrally furnished heading or form which is satisfactory to the largest percentage of library users in this country, and which is not geared specifically and rigorously and absolutely to the research library user and their community. They are a very small community within the population. And that is an alternative that I hope will be considered and pursued in the planning in this country.

George Caldwell: I notice that there seems to be something of a contradiction in Ms. Marshall's approach. Early in her talk she was saying that for the Japanese bank we should use the English-language form for the convenience of the user. Later in her talk she seemed to be saying that we should use the indigenous forms of the names. Now it seems to me these are two conflicting principles. During the coffee break, someone pointed out that most of your readers will look under the term BANTU rather than the technical name. So it seems to me you should try to resolve this point of approach, whether you're going to approach it from the standpoint of the user or from the standpoint of the group being listed.

Marshall: I think that they are two very different things. The one is a direct translation into the English language of the name of the Japanese bank. The other one is a term developed by someone outside a group to name a group of people rather than that people's real name. They are two very different things. Mr. Berman can speak to this better than I.

Berman: It's so easy. *German* is the English equivalent of *Deutsche*. There is nothing imputed to the German people by the use of *German* instead of *Deutsche*. Nothing bad certainly. *Bushman* is *not* the equivalent, nor is *Hottentot* the equivalent, of those African peoples' own names. Those are, as I said in another context, monickers that were laid on them by ignorant and, I would say, mean-minded authors for their own purposes.

Unidentified Speaker: I was happy to hear that the National Library of Canada is considering two authority files that can be used to cross-reference, and we can do that with reference to entries and to other forms of names. But we can use that also for subject headings.

I thought that the discussion was on the catalog in this world. This world is not perfect. The arbitrary surnames, for instance, given Jews in the German area many years ago were often derogatory, and those remain their personal names. We now are using derogatory, sexist, biased terms for certain things. We as librarians should aim to do away with this. But we cannot carry the world on our shoulders and change the whole world. We should do our part, but we shouldn't bite off more than we can chew. And I think that we have to have some compromise there. I'm very sorry, I'm very ignorant, I didn't know until today that *Hottentot* was a derogatory term, and I wouldn't know what the proper term is. Let's by all means do our share, but we have to give the other ignorant person who uses the term *Hottentot* a chance to find this out.

Marshall: We would make a cross-reference from *Hottentot*. If you have to assign a subject heading, it might as well be an appropriate subject heading rather than an inappropriate one.

Seymour Lubetzky: A very brief comment on sexist habits and such categories. I once heard a story by Julia Pettee about the old days in cataloging when the subject heading MEN was qualified by the parenthetical EMBRACING WO-MEN. I think perhaps a return to that age of chivalry might solve many of the problems of sexist headings.

Unidentified Speaker: I am not a cataloger, I am a reference librarian. And from my own experience I would like to support the statements that Ms. Marshall made this morning. I have been extremely embarrassed at having to help people— Blacks, women, and others—through the subject heading list. I have been very embarrassed at their embarrassment at the kinds of subject headings used. So I would just like to support what you said today.

Kul Gauri: We are confusing certain aspects of the translation of Japanese terminology. I can give you an example—ISRAELI PARLIAMENT. If you make an entry for that, would you make it ISRAELI PARLIAMENT, ISRAELI GEN-ERAL ASSEMBLY, ISRAELI CONGRESS, or whatever? It has to be ISRAELI KNESSET. The same is true with Japanese. For Japan, do you make JAPANESE PARLIAMENT, JAPANESE CONGRESS, or whatever? With what kind of translation do you end up? We have to put JAPAN DIET and ISRAELI KNESSET. In certain cases you cannot make any compromise. If you establish a principle of using the national language, where do you start off? Where do you quit? It's more important to have a general principle that establishes national names. In this way, we accomplish something: The establishment of uniformity, the crux of the whole problem.

Marshall: The question that I really raised—and you do have to be uniform within a catalog—is: Is it necessary to place the same restrictions on research and nonresearch libraries? And I'm not sure that it is necessary.

Design of Online Catalogs

By Frederick G. Kilgour

The online computerized library catalog is a wholly new type of catalog having a drastically different design from the seventeenth-century bookform catalog and the nineteenth-century card catalog. The bookform catalog and the card catalog are linear arrangements of bibliographic entries, sometimes of enormous length. Online catalogs consist of a large series of miniature catalogs that may have no more than 32 entries, as is the case presently at the Ohio College Library Center (OCLC).

The computer and modern telecommunications make possible the new online catalog. The relationship of these two types of technology to librarianship is not unlike that of radio to astronomy. Radio transmission and reception was a new technology at the turn of the century. Then, in the 1930s extraterrestrial radio signals were detected, and during the last four decades a whole new intellectual area of science has developed, namely radio astronomy. Two of its devotees shared a Nobel Prize last December. I am not suggesting that any of us is going to qualify for a Nobel Prize, but the computer is in the same position with respect to librarianship that radio is to astronomy. The computer is opening up whole new areas of unknown for investigation and new ways of seeing library phenomena in the same way that radio opened up new areas of unknown for astronomical investigation.

I define a catalog as a systematic record of the holdings of a collection, its purpose being to enable a user of the collection to find the physical location of information in the collection. I will not be discussing catalogs from a viewpoint of bibliographic principles, and for simplicity's sake I am going to treat catalogs as though they contain only entries for monographs.

There are a variety of important independent variables that play a part in the design of any catalog, but particularly in the design of an online catalog. These are:

1. The catalog must be usable by users of the library. It should be designed for use by those who are trying to locate information in the collection, not for use by library staff only.

2. The catalog must be available, preferably to the user when and where s/he needs to have information.

3. Completeness and up-to-dateness are of prime importance. Up-to-dateness is particularly vital since recent and current information is in heaviest usage.

4. The catalog should be personalized for individual use; it should be designed for neither a large library nor small library, but for individual users.

5. Size of a catalog is of prime importance in design. Although size of a catalog is often referred to in discussions of cataloging, there has never been any

quantification of the growth of catalogs or studies of the impact of growth on usability. Size of a catalog is perhaps one of the major variables in that it determines how cataloging is to be done. In other words, size determines cataloging rules.

6. A catalog has flexibility. To be sure, there is not much flexibility in the classical bookform catalog. The increased flexibility of the card catalog in allowing for a more successful solution to the problem of up-to-dateness than does the bookform catalog has been the prime factor for the adoption of card catalogs. Still, both the bookform catalog and the card catalog are relatively inflexible.

7. The last variable is productivity—the productivity of those who produce the catalog.

One of the real triumphs of cataloging is that cataloging rules based on Charles Ammi Cutter's work of a century ago have been effective over such a very long time. Cutter's library possessed 105,000 volumes at the time he did his *Rules* in 1876, while Melvil Dewey's library had 30,000 volumes when his classification scheme was first published in the same year. At that time the two largest libraries in the United States were the Boston Public Library and the Library of Congress, each with approximately 300,000 volumes. There has been tremendous growth in libraries since then, but, fundamentally, it has been possible to build on the foundation that nineteenth-century heroes constructed. Those basic catalog rules have worked surprisingly well considering that 1876 was the year that Alexander Graham Bell patented the telephone; it was a half-dozen years later that the first central electric power station was built; a decade was to pass before the automobile was invented, and nearly three decades before the first airplane flew.

The development of catalogs depends on the size and growth more than on any other variable. Catalogs of the past have differed extensively in design. In the latter Middle Ages and in the Renaissance, many catalogs contained entries arranged chronologically, often by imprint date for printed books. Some were arranged by shelf number in shelf-list order. In others, entries were arranged by forename, but this arrangement gradually shifted to surname. Cross-references were added in fifteenth- and sixteenth-century catalogs. Konrad Gesner probably came closest to achieving universal bibliographic control in the sixteenth century. He arranged entries by date, but added a subject index. Later in the century (1695) Andrew Maunsell established the basic elements for bibliographic description. Present, classical catalog designs are elaborations, albeit considerable elaborations, of these sixteenth-century developments.

The principal purpose of this presentation is to describe a new catalog designed specifically for the user. In the posthumous fourth edition of his *Rules* (1904), Cutter stated, ''The convenience of the public is always to be set before the ease of the cataloger. In most cases they coincide.'' Although Cutter's remark is not a particularly strong statement, it is clear that he intended that the user should come first. A century later it seems to me to be abundantly clear that we must design catalogs for library users and not for librarians. Although I have not done a complete analytical search of library literature for discussions of the structures of catalogs, preliminary searches have turned up little except for historical discussions. Today, cataloging is discussed almost entirely in terms of the *Anglo-American Cataloging Rules (AACR)* and at the main entry level, but it is rarely discussed in terms of the number of entries making up a catalog.

It is possible to design a variety of catalog models. Essentially, an *AACR* catalog consists of an author catalog and a title catalog. The author catalog in

AACR cataloging is an incomplete model from the user's viewpoint because it does not contain entries for every work in the library, such as anonymous works and those works for which there are more than three authors. For example, I happen to be one of four coauthors (Kirby, Withington, Darling, and Kilgour) of a book on engineering history. If you wish to locate this book and can only remember that Kilgour was one of the authors, you will not find it in an *AACR* catalog.

The *AACR* title catalog is also incomplete, for there are a half-dozen exceptions, some of them pretty large exceptions, to entry under title or added title in *AACR*. There are also wide ranges of interpretation concerning title entry; for example, one of the exceptions is long titles that are involved and nondistinctive—a thoroughly subjective judgment must be made here.

It is not possible to tell a user that s/he can find a book by looking under author or the author s/he knows, or that s/he can find a book by looking under title in an *AACR* catalog. Neither one of these models of an *AACR* catalog is complete and, obviously, a subject catalog cannot be complete either.

The model of an online catalog that I am going to discuss is designed from the user's point of view, and I am going to exclude from the model access by ISBN (International Standard Book Number), ISSN (International Standard Serial Number), wrong ISSN, coden, or Library of Congress card number for the obvious reason that users do not know these number codes. The model of the title catalog in an online catalog is complete in the sense that every book has at least one entry under title, and often more than one. A book is always entered under the title on the title page, and sometimes under an original title, a uniform title, a supplied title, or a collective title.

The model of an online catalog can be viewed abstractly as a long string of title entries, although this is not the actual arrangement, with every title in the collection being in the string. In addition to the string there are headings: author headings, subject headings, uniform title headings, and so forth under which title entries are also entered if appropriate. The user of an online catalog can be sure that s/he will always find an entry under the title of the book for which s/he is searching; unlike the *AACR* title catalog, the online title catalog is complete.

Online cataloging will involve extensive changes and simplification in rules, unlike the changes that occurred when card catalogs replaced bookform catalogs. I once intended to write a paper on the differences between cataloging rules in the third and fourth editions of Cutter's *Rules*. The fourth edition has rules designed for a card catalog, whereas the first three editions were designed for printed catalogs. I thought it would be interesting to write a paper on how those rules were changed in order to do cataloging for a card catalog. However, a detailed comparison of the fourth with the third edition turned up only 13 differences that pertained to card catalogs, and these differences were minute. In short, there were no data that would justify a paper. However, the evolution from bookform catalogs and card catalogs to online catalogs will involve considerable and extensive changes in cataloging rules.

An online subject retrieval catalog has a far greater potential for retrieving information than does a bookform catalog or a card catalog. Unhappily, an online subject retrieval catalog also has the potential for heavy burden on the computer. OCLC is currently working on a subject retrieval system wherein subject headings will be indexed with the substantive words in subject headings being truncated, as well as with words in the title entry and author entry. In addition, elements such as date of imprint and language will be indexed. In searching, a user will post-coordinate truncated keys derived from words in various elements of the entries, thereby making possible an extremely powerful retrieval tool even though his/her information about an item or a subject may be incomplete and inaccurate.

Another type of online catalog is an author-title catalog, which in no way resembles a listing of titles under an author name in *AACR* bookform catalogs and card catalogs. The author-title catalog actually combines the author and title into a single entry or access. Such single entries, however, are not arranged linearly as in classical catalogs, but in a bidimensional matrix. Placement in the matrix is by a search key derived and truncated from the author and title (actually in the OCLC system the search key and pointer to the catalog record are in the matrix); the basic search key in the OCLC system consists of the first three letters of the author entry and the first three letters of the first word of the title not an article.

Figure 1 depicts the placement in a matrix of William R. Smith's *History as Argument*. Of course, all other entries having the truncated derived search key SMI,HIS are placed in the same position. With more than two million entries in OCLC's online catalog, there were 225 with the search key SMI,HIS. A user searching for Smith's *History as Argument* who was not sure under which subject it would be entered, would have to prowl through a huge number of cards in a card catalog to find the entry under SMITH. However, online interaction beginning with only 225 entries makes it possible for a user to locate the entry far more rapidly than would be possible in a card catalog.

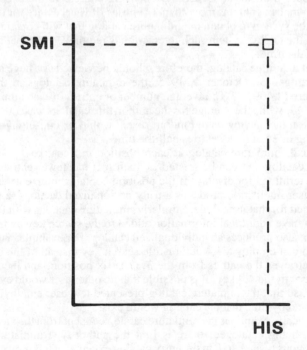

FIGURE 1

Logical Matrix for Placement of Author-Title Search Keys

A moment's reflection on the characteristics of a matrix-type catalog as shown in Figure 1 reveals the retrieval power of such a catalog. If one assumes that each axis in Figure 1 has a thousand positions on it, and that the author segment of the author-title entry is on one axis and title on the other, there are 1,000,000 positions in the matrix for the placement of entries. In contrast, a bookform catalog or card catalog has only a thousand positions for such entries. There is, of course, no need to limit the dimensions of the matrix to two; indeed, the truncated derived search keys for titles in the OCLC system are derived from up to four words, so that the matrix in this case is four dimensional, albeit skewed because not the same number of letters is derived from each word. The retrieval power of an *n*-dimensional matrix catalog is so much greater than that of classical linear catalogs that the user needs to have only a relatively small amount of information about a book to retrieve the entry swiftly and accurately.

MINIATURE CATALOG CONCEPT

Logically, each position in a catalog matrix contains entries that serve as the basis for the construction of a miniature catalog to be presented to the user. The catalog system designer can set the upper limit of the number of entries to be presented on the basis of such variables as the number of lines on a terminal screen, and the number of screens that a user can manipulate readily. As already mentioned, the upper limit in the OCLC system is 32 entries. In the event that the position in the matrix contains more than 32 entries, it is necessary for the user to interact with the system to obtain the miniature catalog that will contain the entry s/he seeks. In the OCLC system such interaction is required somewhat more than ten percent of the time.

Design of an online catalog, therefore, should be viewed as a huge number of miniature catalogs. On October 4, 1975, the miniature catalogs in the OCLC system numbered 1,409,577. The average number of entries in each miniature title catalog was 2.43, while the average for the author-title catalogs was 3.0. If the use of the OCLC online catalog were random, users would be consulting miniature catalogs having three or fewer entries half the time.

The logical, miniature catalog at each position in a matrix is in essence a prestructured catalog and can be treated as such if it has fewer entries than the upper limit determined for display. If the position contains more entries than the upper limit, user interaction produces a truly personalized catalog—a miniature catalog designed for that user alone. Similarly, miniature catalogs with fewer than 32 entries can have additional information added to the search key by the user so that the system also produces an individualized catalog. For example, a user of the OCLC system can employ a 4,4 author-title search key instead of the basic 3,3. The system retrieves the entries from the 3,3 matrix position, and then discards those that do not fit the 4,4 key. It is possible that no other user would ever use the same 4,4 key, so that the miniature catalog presented to a user employing such a key may be the only time that the catalog would exist.

If one logically examines the miniature catalog concept from the viewpoint of the collection being cataloged, there is first the author-type miniature catalog which is analogous to an *AACR* main-entry catalog except that it is more complete. Second, there is the online title catalog, also similar to *AACR*, except that the online catalog is complete; it contains every title in the collection. Third, there is an author-title catalog for which there is no comparable *AACR* catalog.

The question of which entry is preferable as *main entry* is not a useful question for the design of an online catalog. It has to be a useful question for design of classical catalogs and particularly for single-entry catalogs, as is the case with most union catalogs. Indeed, for classical bookform and card catalogs it is an absolutely necessary question requiring resolution with the most unique and specific of answers. But with the multiple retrieval power of an online catalog, the concept of *main entry* is not useful.

Does an online catalog conform to the Paris Principles? The answer is yes. It must be remembered that *AACR* does not follow the Paris Principles completely, as Mr. Lubetzky quite rightfully and disappointedly pointed out. The function of a catalog is to inform a library user whether or not the library contains a particular book specified by author and title. An online catalog achieves this function and more. If an author is not named in the book, a user can identify the book by title alone. The online catalog also shows which works by a particular author and which editions of a particular work are in the library. Much more important, however, is the fact that an online catalog contains many more retrieval accesses than a catalog based on the Paris Principles, and is therefore a far more effective tool from the user's point of view.

ASSESSMENT

In general an online catalog possesses high usability, indeed far greater usability than does a bookform or card catalog. The online catalog provides more extensive physical access, greater numbers of accesses to information in the catalog, and it is faster and more accurate to use than a bookform or card catalog. Moreover, rough estimates show that an online catalog servicing a computerized library network costs far less per unit of use than do classical bookform and card catalogs. In addition, it costs each network library less than do its classical catalogs.

Evaluation of design of online catalogs can best be done employing the aforementioned seven variables:

1. *Usability*. As already stated, an online catalog is a highly usable type of catalog, more readily usable than is the bookform or card catalog. It can be and is more extensively designed for library users to locate information in collections than are designs based on bibliographic principles.

2. *Availability*. A card catalog has the capability of being kept up to date, but it is a wretched way to make information available. The user has to go to the library to consult the catalog. As Hugh Atkinson describes in his paper, "The Electronic Catalog," the Ohio State University Libraries' remote catalog access and circulation system makes it unnecessary for the user to go to the library to discover whether or not the library possesses the item s/he desires and whether or not it is available to him/her. The OSU (Ohio State University) system employs telephone access to an online catalog via terminal operators. As for the future, the technology already exists for interfacing head-end computers on cable television systems with online catalog computers so that television sets can be employed to access catalogs, thereby greatly increasing the availability of catalog information.

3. *Completeness and Up-to-Dateness*. An online catalog is certainly more complete in its accesses and more up to date than is possible with a card catalog since the entries are available within seconds after completion of cataloging. Of course, a bookform catalog is always considerably out of date, e.g., the New York

Public Library averages six months out of date.

4. *Personalization*. Online catalogs can be and are personalized in a way in which classical catalogs cannot be. Classical bookform and card catalogs are monolithic arrangements of entries, completely dehumanized in the sense that they cannot respond to individual persons as individuals.

5. *Size*. Moreover, an online catalog can be personalized even though it is huge. The OCLC online catalog is equivalent in size to the catalog of a library for over seven million volumes. It should be emphasized, however, that from the user's point of view, the OCLC catalog is a small, highly usable catalog.

6. *Flexibility*. An online catalog has the flexibility required for transition from classical hardcopy catalogs to electronic display. In any technical development it is necessary to begin with current technology and to evolve from that position. Systems like OCLC are going from classical catalogs in the direction of online catalogs, and at least one institution on the OCLC system has discontinued adding cards to its catalog. The present OCLC system does not produce catalog cards in sets, but if it did it could produce over 6,000 different sets for one title. Its capabilities are highly flexible and need to be so in order to produce a product acceptable to a large number of libraries. Moreover, OCLC and other systems can and do restructure their online catalogs with little effort compared with the effort that would be required to restructure a card catalog. Hardcopy formats and display formats are not uniform; they comply with standards without having to force the formats into uniformity, as is the case with manual procedures.

7. *Productivity*. Experience shows that use of online catalogs for cataloging increases productivity of library staff, and similar uses for serials control, acquisitions, circulation, and particularly by users will surely further increase productivity.

MECHANIZED DESCRIPTIVE CATALOGING

It must be pointed out, however, that the potential for online catalogs to increase library staff productivity has hardly been tapped. An online catalog when it is complete has the potential for highly mechanized cataloging. If a miniature catalog never contains more than 32 entries, it is not necessary to have the 400 pages of descriptive cataloging rules that are in *AACR*. When using a 32-entry miniature catalog it is not necessary to know that my middle name is Gridley (although one OCLC-participating library thought so in cataloging a book I edited), or to know that I was born in 1914 to differentiate me from 31 other entries (actually the search key KILG,F, produces a miniature catalog of four entries, each of which I authored or edited).

The miniature catalog concept, therefore, leads to the conclusion that mechanized descriptive cataloging with minimal human intervention for cross-references will be possible employing only the string of text on a title page. After all, everyone except bibliographers and librarians have found the text on the title page adequate for the past 500 years. Human intervention may also be necessary to mark off the area in the string on the title page that should be indexed, and possibly to add an imprint date if not present.

It will also be necessary for humans to add call number and subject indexing, although a considerable amount of work has already been done on mechanized subject classification and subject indexing, which is at least as good as human indexing. Such mechanized cataloging could not possibly work in classical catalogs, but at the present time there is every reason to believe that mechanized descriptive cataloging will work for online catalogs and thereby greatly increase productivity of library staff.

SUMMARY

All of the seven variables affecting cataloging design have a higher value for online catalogs than for classical catalogs. Some models of *AACR* catalogs and others that are helpful in thinking about catalogs have been presented. It must be remembered, however, that cataloging has been discussed from the user's viewpoint and not from the librarian's viewpoint. A logical design for an online catalog, of which the fundamental aspect is that the online catalog is complete for title entries, has been included. A concept of miniature catalogs that is highly effective for an online catalog is also presented. Assessment of the online catalog shows that it works. It conforms with the Paris Principles and also has additional retrieval power. Finally, it should be emphasized that although online catalogs are operational, much more development must occur to approach the potential of such technology.

DISCUSSION

Joseph Rosenthal: I'd like, instead of commenting on Mr. Kilgour's speech, to ask him a question. To what extent do you visualize the online catalog as the replacement for traditional catalogs and as the interface with other machine data bases that are maintained by abstracting and indexing services?

Frederick Kilgour: I think this is going to be an extremely important development. At the last meeting of the Board of Trustees of OCLC the staff was empowered to initiate scheduling the development of an interface between the OCLC network and these other nonmonographic data bases. There are two types of interfaces. One is the type at Systems Development Corporation (SDC), and the other is the large group at Lockheed. Both are accessible via TYMNET. There are other important data bases such as the *New York Times* data base that is not, so it's a matter of interfacing with TYMNET and some of these other data bases. When this occurs, and when there is the same kind of indexing done in the monographic data bases such as the LIBCON technique that SDC's ORBIT uses, then the power of the librarian to serve the patron with information will be enormously increased.

Seymour Lubetzky: I can readily visualize how an online catalog will make a particular book more readily available and findable. I recognize the importance of this in view of the fact that people who come to look for a book quite frequently do not have an accurate citation. Because the online catalog can manipulate different works, it can locate the book by specific parts of the name or title. But is it also that your catalog will meet the requirements of the Paris Principles? The Paris Principles state what is desired, but they do not give the reasons for those desiderata. That was not the objective. Instead, one might raise the question: "Why do we need all the works of an author together?" One might also ask, "Why do we need all the editions and translations in the catalog?" I will not discuss these questions at this point, although I would be willing to, if necessary. Let me further specify the requirements of the catalog envisioned by the Paris Principles. What is envisioned, if one takes the functions of the entry together with the purposes and objectives of the catalog, is a catalog in which an author has one particular place. Under the author each work has a particular niche where all the editions, translations, and related works are listed together. This is the objective of the principles. The result anticipated is the assumption made originally by Panizzi, that a person who looks for a book really does not necessarily have as his objective the book, *but the work in it.* The person may know what work s/he is interested in, but s/he may not know all the peculiarities of the different editions. It is that information which s/he is entitled to expect from the catalog.

Now, if these are the objectives that your catalog is going to fulfill, I have a specific question to ask you. There are two books published under the titles *Denmark's Day of Doom* and *Rats in the Larder*. They are the same work. Not only are they the same work, they were run off from the same plates. And if you examine a certain page where you will find a broken letter in one, then you will also find it in the other one. That is how identical they are. When this was published in Great Britain, there was a propensity for alliteration. The British used the title *Denmark's Day of Doom* to convey the sentiment expressed in the book. In the United States it was thought that to most people alliteration was not worth very much, hence, *Rats in the Larder*. (Incidentally, it was about the invasion of Denmark.) So they ran off the same copies, except with a different title. Now people who come to the catalog may have a reference to *Rats in the Larder* or to *Denmark's Day of Doom*. If a person came to your catalog to look for *Denmark's Day of Doom*, will s/he find only that or will there be more than that?

Again, to make clear the meaning of my question, I would like to add this. Under the objective of the Paris Principles—and again I say that not everything was brought out; there's a great deal behind the Principles which we must find elsewhere—if s/he comes to look for *Denmark's Day of Doom*, s/he should be led to a place where s/he will find *Denmark's Day of Doom, Rats in the Larder*, translations of this work, possibly dramatizations, and possibly books about it. That is, that niche will tell him/her what is available. S/he does not come to look for other things, but that does not mean that they are not of potential interest. That was the objective of the classical catalog. What I'm asking again is what will a person find in your catalog when s/he comes to look for *Denmark's Day of Doom?*

Kilgour: S/he can find exactly what you would put in it, if you were doing the catalog.

Lubetzky: Am I right to assume that s/he will find not only *Rats in the Larder*, but also all the other editions, and in the context of the other works of the author?

Kilgour: Yes.

Lubetzky: Fine, then I'm completely satisfied and I say, "Amen." I would like to ask, how would that be accomplished?

Kilgour: Well, it can be accomplished in the same way that it's accomplished now. However, it can be made more powerful, because now you're confronted with the question: "What is the preferred entry?"

But you know if you have it equally under both entries, then you don't have to have a preferred entry. That's the one difference, but it achieves what you want to achieve.

Lubetzky: Well, then I'm completely satisfied. When I spoke earlier, I mentioned that there could be a difference in implications for cataloging in an online catalog. Now I can visualize how that would be done, and if that is what you have in mind, very well. In a computerized catalog, the cataloger will have the same work that s/he has now. The cataloger will have to know that *Denmark's Day of Doom* and *Rats in the Larder* are editions of the same work. S/he will also have to enable the user of the online catalog to find other translations and other works of the author in the same place.

Kilgour: Yes. Remember what I said: It is a combination of mechanization and human addition. The human addition can be as extensive as you wish to have it. In some cases it will have to be very extensive, and in some cases zero.

Lubetzky: Then really there is no difference. What you are saying is that we do the same cataloging, only the result will be obtained by the other means.

Kilgour: Incidentally, you published an article with Bob Hayes in which you use an example of Newton's *Principia* in a variety of languages.[1] The intriguing thing about that is (and this perhaps isn't a very fair comment, but it will show you what can happen, even with the rudimentary techniques that we are using at OCLC) those entries all come in exactly the same place by using the OCLC truncated search keys.

Lubetzky: I have no objection as long as the results are satisfactory.

Rosenthal: Aren't you both saying that someplace a human act must link those two titles together?

Kilgour: Exactly, exactly! At least once.

Lubetzky: My point is only that there is sometimes an assumption that in a computerized catalog you can *simplify* the rules; that word has been used often and I think you also used *simplification*. There is no simplification involved here; you do the same work except you impose something else upon it. The online catalog which Mr. Kilgour has just described would be all right if it is also consulted only online. If this is to be used to reproduce a hard copy catalog, then you have to come back to exactly what you are doing now.

Kilgour: No, it can't be used to do that. It's a different type of catalog entirely. It's the twentieth century catalog.

Kul Gauri: When Lockheed and SDC were designed, they had never heard about *AACR*. They had never heard that librarians want the main entry, or author entry, or added title entry. They went ahead and designed it. But now when we have this kind of online computer technology accessible to us, I think that the *AACR* has become sort of redundant.

Kilgour: I am not sure *redundant* is the correct word.

Leo Rift: I come back to one major difference. We have just stated that the linkage of varying titles and varying forms of entry have to be done on the same basis in an automated situation as in a manual situation. The value judgments need not be the same. It can be substantiated that in switching over to new technologies we often have not done this kind of linkage. Let me give you an example. I am more familiar with changes of titles of serials. When you enter the successive title, all that is required of the cataloger is to link it to the one title before and the one title after—no further. Before, when we had the latest title, earliest title, or anything else, or even before that, when we had to determine what the main entry was, we were forced to go through all this work to determine all the linkages. The moment we relax on it—we are no longer forced to do it, and it often is not done, and the connection is not made—then we are in trouble.

Tom Stafford: I'm not a catalog person, I'm a computer person, and I'm very excited about this concept. The question I have regards natural concerns about the computer going down, and the situation that may exist when the library is cut off for an extended period of time from the online catalog. Are we back in the situation where you have concerns about how to produce a microfiche catalog, or whatever product would be required to take care of that kind of situation?

Kilgour: No, you have to have sufficient redundancy in your system so that your computer system doesn't go down. You may lose one out of four or one out of three, but you've got another one that you can put in to take over. There are some other major problems: We weren't able to do it because we couldn't get the money. We designed a secure—and we will build it eventually—computer room that was fireproof, tornado proof, and would take a hit from a single engine craft. But this is much more of a problem than losing a machine and going down for two days or something like that. There are some major problems in online networking of which we are acutely aware in Columbus, Ohio.

Elizabeth Chambers: You've talked about the point of availability, and I realize you've said that we're back where the Wright Brothers were. But on the availability basis, it seems to me that access to the terminals is limited to one or two people at a time. I've been in our University catalog room when 50 to 60 people were looking up things simultaneously. Can you really say now that the availability of the online is so much greater than the card catalog?

Kilgour: It certainly doesn't have to be limited to the catalog room; that's the point of the availability.

Chambers: Yes, but even now if somebody would answer, you could call up on the telephone and ask somebody to look it up for you.

Kilgour: The technique of using a computerized system at the end of the telephone line works. This never worked with a card catalog. You know many libraries have had telephone jacks at the end of the catalog cases and reference people were running around, except they didn't do it very much. They had plugs to use after they looked in the catalog, but this didn't work. It does work when you have an integrated system.

Let's assume though, that we only have terminals in the catalog room instead of the catalog. We don't know how much faster and more accurate the terminal is, or if it could enable 50 people to use five terminals instead of 50 drawers in a catalog. We don't know the answers to that question. This is one of the many, many questions in which investigation has to be done before we can really design these systems.

Rosenthal: I hope we do hear more about the design of online catalog systems as replacements for traditional catalogs, because I think many of us are concerned about the accessibility and the cost implications of terminals right now.

Pauline Atherton: Mr. Kilgour, can you answer Ms. Chambers' question, at least in terms of your own experience? At OCLC you have 700 terminals connected to OCLC, right?

Kilgour: The last figure I saw was 828, but you're in the right realm.

Atherton: At any one moment in the day when you're up, how many people can get on at that same instant? I think that's what she's interested in. When we all walk into the catalog room because the drawers to the catalog are there, 50 or 1,000 or maybe 2,000 people can possibly use it if they don't all want the same catalog drawer. The point is, given your experience at OCLC, how many people at any moment in the day can come up and use it?

Kilgour: One per terminal.

Atherton: I understand that.

Kilgour: Well then, I don't understand your question.

Atherton: At ten o'clock in the morning, how many people are using OCLC? One per second?

Kilgour: At the end of June, 1975, the messages were being received at the rate of 6.9 a second.

Atherton: So at that second, an average of 7 people could have their questions answered.

Kilgour: Yes, that's correct, 7 a second. Actually it's up to 9 a second now.

Hugh Atkinson: The answer is really only one. Mr. Kilgour's answer to how many people at a time can do it, really, is usually only one, maybe two. The thing is that one takes such a small amount of time that it's virtually a very large number of people. But the real question of how many terminals is not answerable in a finite number. The expandability of a terminal system is not dependent on the system but simply on the availability of terminals, and those which can be ordered. That is, you can round up terminals if you have to very rapidly. You cannot expand the catalog, a card catalog, without restructuring. I think that's the fundamental answer regarding the numbers of access.

Atherton: To reiterate and to give you another example, we had 100 terminals at Syracuse University spread around the campus. We offered a service where every one could get to that terminal and make a request for service. Our system allowed us to accept four messages and queue them so that the person sitting at a terminal thought s/he was the only person on. It was that quick. Now that was a very limited system. Only four could feel that they were all online at the same time. The others had to be told, sorry, busy, try again soon. That was a very limited kind of service, and, as you can see from what Mr. Kilgour says, OCLC is much better than our limited system was.

Now my question has to do with this very important interface between abstracting and indexing services and our catalogs. Our experience in this country is in a way too limited because of the split exactly at the time when the *AACR* came out. The people who were doing the cataloging of reports and journal articles and abstracting and indexing services followed their own rules. These data bases are based on rules. Now how different those rules are from the *AACR* was a subject of study at that time. Ted Brandhorst and others were actually comparing the differences between the *AACR* and their own rules, so that I truly don't see any serious problem of interfacing. It's a mess on our side as well as their side in terms of the way we've handled names inconsistently, but I don't think it poses any serious problems. In Sweden, for quite a while now, the cataloging of the National Library and the tapes of abstracting and indexing services have been merged into one system for searching and for selective dissemination of information notices. They then go back to libraries for interlibrary loan use or fulfillment of photocopying request. So, I think that the merger, the interface, is already there.

Kilgour: Ohio State University does that now.

REFERENCE

1. Seymour Lubetzky and Robert Hayes, "Bibliographic Dimensions of Information Control," *American Documentation*, vol. 3, no. 3 (July 1969): 247-52.

The Library Catalog in a Computerized Environment

by S. Michael Malinconico

Before embarking on a discussion of the nature and future of the library catalog in the context of computer technology, we should quickly review the forces which have carried us to this threshold of the future. As a point of departure we should remind ourselves that the genesis of this brave new world of solid state logic, in which bibliographic data are reduced to phantasmagoria on the faces of cathode-ray tubes, extends at most only three-quarters of a decade into the dim past.

There were several important library automation projects initiated in the early sixties. Most of these experiments resulted in badly deformed still-births. Of those that proceeded beyond the fetal stage, few survived the close of the decade in their original form. Automated cataloging support systems, with any pretense to sophistication, did not begin to appear until the inception of the LC/MARC II (Library of Congress/Machine-Readable Cataloging) project in late 1967.[1]

Library automation was in its ascendancy at precisely the same time that the nation's economy was firmly embarked on its present calamitous decline, a situation severely aggravated by the sudden withdrawal of nearly a decade of federal largesse toward education and education-related activities. We might next note the unprecedented success of the Library of Congress' MARC Distribution Service, which provides authoritative, quality cataloging data in machine-readable, and hence, machine-manipulatable, form at approximately 2.5¢/record. Such liberal terms would tax one's imagination to create an automated system that could not demonstrate some sort of economy. Finally, add the mass confusion wrought by the sudden appearance of a new technology in the library, with its practitioners chanting acronymic prayers, seemingly derived from a mushroom ritual. And we have all of the ingredients for the creation of an atmosphere in which the proponents of expediency could couch their arguments in terms of *cost effectiveness*, coupled with sage assurances that the flexibilities possible with machine processing would, at some time in the undefined future, obviate most of the problems not addressed. Those objections not amenable to such solution were disposed of with the canonical assurance that such *wasteful* practices are only engaged in for the benefit of a certain, arbitrarily small, class of Bohemian scholars, who are probably anarchists anyway.

The formative period of library automation, if we restrict this discussion to automated cataloging systems, was characterized by an initiation ritual in which librarians were asked to explain and/or justify principles in terms of a linear, sequential, and statistical logic with which they were not entirely conversant. Principles developed over a century and a quarter of thought and experience (extending from Panizzi's defense in London, in 1849, to the Paris conference, in 1961) were poorly defended by professional catalogers, and even less so by administrators harried by increasing personnel budgets. Administrators all too easily fall prey to the siren song of cost reduction, especially if phrases like *innovation* are employed as harmonic accompaniment. The net result has been, to the largest extent, the automation of certain clerical activities ancillary to cataloging, without actual inclusion of the entire cataloging process, or the catalog itself, as part of the total system. The activities selected for automation were generally those whose costs could be easily ascertained and shown to be decreased by the new system. If the resultant machine-readable file bore no relation to a coherent catalog, that was of no serious concern, as the record of-record was still the three by five card created more economically, but, nonetheless, filed in an offline, manual catalog.

However, it doesn't take very long before the supporting machine file attains greater importance than the manual catalog. This is especially so if the machine file is the product of cooperative input, in which case it becomes an easily accessed union catalog of a consortium's holdings. It is at this point that the serious problems begin to occur; when the apotheosis is effected from *file* to *catalog*. A file, it should be recalled, in normal data-processing terms is nothing more than a collection of related physical records. A catalog, on the other hand, should manifest the attributes of a *data base*. That is, it is a file upon which a coherent, logically consistent structure has been imposed. Such a structure must be imposed from the outset, and control over it exercised during any activity against the data base. *Ad hoc* attempts to impose a rigorous structure will prove either impossible, or so expensive as to render the exercise impossible.

The questions raised by these developments and possible alternatives form the subject of this discussion, specifically: (1) the need to impose a rigidly controlled structure on a machine-readable catalog; (2) the capabilities and limitations of machine processing in achieving this end; (3) some of the possibilities the machine might offer for control of the catalog; and (4) their extension permitting a degree of control not possible in a manual system.

We have already been impelled toward a definition of the future catalog by forces not especially conducive to its development into a more effective instrument. Indeed, the direction we seem to be embarked on may result in the negation of a century of well-established principles in favor of a machine-negotiated, stochastic access to individual items in the collection. That is, a probabilistic access in which discrete, known items will, with good likelihood, be found.

I should like briefly to review the functions we expect a library catalog to perform, and how these might relate to an automated system. Ninety-nine years ago Charles Cutter began his exposition of a set of cataloging rules with the following objectives:

1. To enable a person to find a book of which either (A) the author, (B) the title [or] (C) the subject is known.
2. To show what the library has (D) by a given author, (E) on a given subject [or] (F) in a given kind of literature.[2]

These aims were reiterated in working paper no. 2 presented to the International Conference on Cataloging Principles: "the catalogue of a library must be designed not only (1) to show whether or not the library has a particular item or publication, issued under a certain name of the author or under a certain title, but also (2) to identify the author and the work represented by the item or publication and to relate the various works of the author and the various editions and translations of the work."[3] These are, of course, Dr. Lubetzky's words. His definition apparently found consensus among the participants at the conference, as the following statement was adopted regarding functions of the catalog:

> The catalogue should be an efficient instrument for ascertaining
> 2.1   whether the library contains a particular book specified by
>   (a) its author and title, [etc.] ... ; and
> 2.2   (a) which works by a particular author and
>   (b) which editions of a particular work are in the library.[4]

We can see that the basic functions expected to be served by the catalog have not altered, and indeed have been reendorsed after a century of experience. In simple terms the catalog should (1) provide access to a predefined item in the collection; (2) organize the collection; (3) attribute authorship responsibility, when possible, to a work; and (4) assist the user with information regarding its own organization.

The first function is obvious. When the reader is seeking a precisely defined item, which s/he can unambiguously name, s/he is provided with a location identifier by which to obtain the item. Even in this mode a certain organizational assistance is provided when the collection is shelved according to some classification scheme. This is due to the fact that the material is itself organized as a form of subject added entry. For the purposes of this discussion we shall ignore such a mode of collection access.

The second function is perhaps the most important, difficult to achieve, and least addressed by automated systems. We should realize that a library is not simply an aggregation of discrete recorded materials; rather, it represents a *collection*, or more precisely *collections* of works. A research library's value is in direct proportion to the comprehensiveness of its collections, and the degree to which a rational collection policy is developed and carried out. The catalog, if it is to serve an institution so defined, must be capable of reflecting, and assisting in the maintenance of, these collections.

The catalog entry, as we all know, is a surrogate for the item described. Therefore, as a logical corollary, the catalog is itself a surrogate of the collection, more importantly, as a result of the added entry structure, several simultaneous surrogates. The alternate access points created by an added entry structure do provide assistance in locating a specific item. However, this structure represents much more than simply an alternate route to a specific item. It permits the collocation, in one sequence, of all items which partake of a particular organizational attribute, e.g., all editions of an author's works, all works for which an author has primary responsibility, those for which s/he has secondary or tertiary responsibility, those works derived from his/her works, etc. It also permits the same item to take its proper place in several such sequences. Alternate sequences could not, naturally, be created by physical organization of the material. From the point of view of the catalog's utility, the ability to present a comprehensive sequence under a given heading, or headings, is at least as important as its ability to provide the location of a precisely specified item.

This idea of drawing entries together is quite independent of the medium supporting the catalog. Whether the sequences are created by filing multiple copies of a unit card in a card catalog, or by having a computer draw together various unit records in response to a query, is really quite irrelevant. The only difference is that in the case of the card catalog complete sequences exist whether or not someone is actually viewing them, while on a CRT (cathode-ray tube) screen they exist only so long as the phosphors continue to glow.

The point is that the catalog is not simply an index to the collection. In a sense, by its ability to create the collocation of entries, it assists in defining the collection. By an examination of its various sequences the catalog permits us to determine what has been written about a particular subject, how a particular idea evolved, how a particular author's thinking evolved, how a particular author's works affected others, what manifestations of an author's works the library owns, etc. The importance of this idea of collocation appears even when we try to define what is an author's work. Dr. Lubetzky has noted "that the materials of a library . . . are representations of the works of authors, *not the works themselves;* . . . a given work may be represented in a library in different forms or editions, under different names . . . or under different titles."[5] I would be inclined to go one step further and treat the entire corpus of an author's writings as his/her *work*. T.S. Eliot offers an interesting observation in his attempt to explore the difference between a major and a minor poet: "whatever a minor poet may be, a major poet is one the whole of whose work we ought to read, in order to fully appreciate any part of it."[6] One can only wonder what Mr. Eliot's reaction would have been to the suggestion that some of Dante's works could be found under DANTE, while others might be found under ALIGHIERI. And the works by F.H. Bradley, the subject of Eliot's doctoral dissertation, could be found by looking under F.H., FRANCIS H., and FRANCIS HERBERT BRADLEY; or that he should examine all of the Bradleys in the Harvard University library catalog in order to determine what other works by that philosopher the library holds. I would venture to guess that he would have characterized these suggestions as the "eructation of unhealthy souls."

If the catalog is to fulfill any of the requirements just enumerated, then it must be capable of responding to a user's query in a manner which is complete in terms of the collection and which at the same time does not result in extraneous citations. It must also be capable of displaying the relationship among items in the collection. Creating and maintaining these relationships is, after all, the function the acquisitions librarian attempts to perform when defining, and carrying out, a collection development policy. And the function of the cataloger, who attempts to integrate each new item into the catalog in the context of what already exists.

How does this relate to an automated system? The answer lies in an examination of the capabilities of the machine, made without losing sight of its limitations. The machine is indeed quite adept at creating alternate access points and customized sequences. But it performs these feats within the rigid discipline of Boolean logic, and then only on data in the form in which it receives it. That is, the machine can provide very rapid and novel accesses to information, but it cannot impose an order which is not already there. It has no capacity, for example, to make the intellectual decisions which would attribute publications by Puschkin, Puskin, and Puszkin to the noted poor marksman Aleksandr Sergeevich Pushkin.

There is one fundamental attribute of the machine which should be borne in mind; *machine logic is of the most literal variety*. By way of illustration: it is the machine's habit, in its rush to complete bit by bit compares, to perform remarkable feats, such as augmenting western musical heritage with the discovery that the eighteenth century gave birth to two contemporary composers—one named MOZART, W.A. and the other MOZART, WOLFGANG AMADEUS. If we instruct it to ponder this question more leisurely, it will quickly try the user's patience with digressions concerning the less illustrious senior MOZART, LEOPOLD. A rather simple solution could be found to this particular problem. The search key could be formed from the last name, plus the initials of the first two names. However, Mozart did sometimes identify himself as Johann Chrysostom Wolfgang Amadeus Mozart, yielding a key of MOZART, J.C.

It might be argued that we are dealing with a rather unique example: a classical, voluminous author. This may be so, but we might consider an author whose first published volume appeared only 23 years ago: Evgeniĭ Evtushenko. A perusal of the 1967-1972 quinquennial of the *National Union Catalog (NUC)* would discover the following variants of his name used by publishers of his works:

EVTOUCHENKO, EUGÈNE De la cité de oui à la cité de non. Paris, B. Grasset [1970]	LC 78-515993
EVTUSHENKO, EVGENIĬ ALEKSANDROVICH Bratskaia GÉS [Chicago, Russian Language Specialties, 1965]	NUC 68-25850
JEWTUSCHENKO, JEWGENI Das dritte Gedächtnis Berlin, Volk und Welt, 1970	LC 72-561931
YEVTUSHENKO, YEVGENY Flowers and Bullets and Freedom to Kill. [San Francisco, Calif] City Lights Books [C 1970]	LC 74-19894

This should illustrate rather dramatically how failure to adopt a single well-defined form of name could spread entries throughout the alphabet. In this simple case of four entries, we could have two sequences under *E*, one under *J* and another *Y*.

The same arguments, of course, also apply to subject access. Failure, for example, to observe the distinction between HORSE and HORSES creates the possibility of having to consider HORSE-CHESTNUT; HORSE SHOE, BATTLE OF THE; and HORSEPOWER (MECHANICS) while attempting to connect the two sequences. In fact, the seventh edition of the LC Subject Heading Guide shows 33 primary headings and 7 cross-references separating these two terms.[7]

We might all easily agree that LITERATURE, IMMORAL is not particularly descriptive of, and an anachronistic euphemism for, PORNOGRAPHY. Nonetheless, the indiscriminate use of both terms in a data base creates a situation in which the serious scholar is either deprived of access to half of the material in the collection, or must consult two sequences. This might, perhaps, be considered a facetious example; however, consider the effect of the indiscriminate use of LATIN AMERICA and SPANISH AMERICA.[8] This not only creates split sequences for anything listed under the heading or any of its subdivisions, but it can appear itself as a subdivision of other headings, thereby proliferating such split sequences throughout the alphabet, e.g., PRESS—SPANISH AMERICA and PRESS—LATIN AMERICA.

The machine cannot by any of its logical processes draw together such variants into single coherent sequences. *The order must be imposed by the cataloger.* It is only by human intervention at the time of data creation that sufficient normalization can be effected to make innovative machine access meaningful.

Note the distinction between organization of the data and methods of access. The machine is indeed capable of providing very rapid access based on combinations of data elements; combinations which a human could scarcely keep in mind while reviewing entries in a static, manual file. Interactive online systems do permit the user to renegotiate his/her search as s/he proceeds. CRT displays, which produce their replies out of pure light, do provide rapid response. These factors, when combined with the computer's ability to select all, and only those, items meeting a bewilderingly complex set of conditions, do provide an access capability unimagined with the book or card catalogs of Mr. Cutter. But, keep clearly in mind that we are describing only access. The more important question is access to what? We have already noted that the machine, by advances in the sophistication of its methods of access, cannot create an order that is not already intrinsic to the data. This is an immutable axiom, which can be assumed to hold true for the forseeable generations of computing systems and systems analysts. Access techniques and data base organization are logically separable facets of a system. They contribute as mutually independent parameters in determining the quality of a system's response.

Sufficiently sophisticated techniques already exist which will determine whether or not a single well-defined record exists in a data base of arbitrary quality. Computers are quite adroit at such simple yes/no response without much prodding. In fact such levels of sophistication were attained at least ten years ago. But this is not the sole function of the library catalog. By conscious or unconscious fixation on this single, already *passé*, facet of data processing technology we risk totally ignoring the other functions of a catalog; namely, to show in some efficient manner "which works by a particular author, and which editions of a given work are in the library," or "what the library has on a given subject." The user is ill-served by a system which conceals a significant number of items that might be useful, or which force the user to make a choice from a selection containing a great deal of background noise in the form of irrelevant citations. Likewise, a library or consortium—and ultimately the user—is ill-served by a system which inhibits the realization of a rational collection policy by permitting the duplication of expensive items because there is no straightforward way of determining that the item is already held either in that library or elsewhere in the network, as a result of the caprices of data entry.

Let's consider one further aspect of the human/machine interface before discussing the alternatives the computer might offer. There is a rather simple and obvious fact concerning computing systems whose significance, nonetheless, is all too often ignored: namely, when data are encoded into machine-readable form they can only be retrieved again by machine logic. This results in an imbalance of error tolerance. Any transcription process, as we all know, is susceptible to error. The graphs in Figure 1 show the fraction of records that can be expected to contain no errors as a function of record length, and keyboarding accuracy. The plot for 99.9 percent represents about the norm for good master typists. The implication here is that in the course of keying 400 character records, 30 percent will contain at least one error. Parenthetically we might also note how with small decreases in accuracy at the key stroke level the overall accuracy rate can dramatically decrease. The shift from 99.9 to 99.8 percent can result from fatigue or any of a number of other factors. The point is that errors are inevitable. An examination of the MARC file will show that the fields which can form headings—main entry, uniform and series titles, added entries and subjects—comprise, on the average, 116 characters of data.[9] This would imply, given a 99.9 percent accuracy rate, that approximately 11 percent of all records would have at least one faulty access point!

FIGURE 1
EFFECT OF KEYBOARDING ACCURACY ON KEYED RECORDS

Each graph is for a given keyboarding accuracy. The resultant plots show the fraction of records which might be expected to be keyed without error as a function of characters/record.

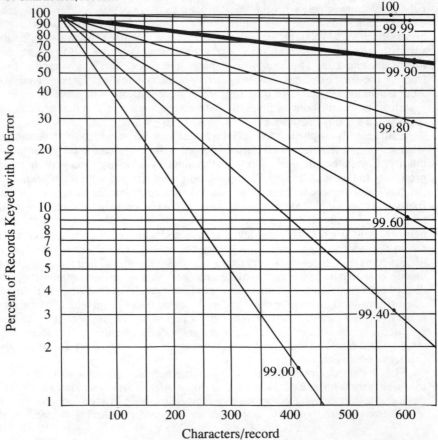

Let us perform a simple thought experiment. Assume that a cataloger has committed a simple transposition error and transcribed YEATS, WILLIAM BUTLER as YEATS, WILLIAM BULTER. It is highly likely that this might escape the notice of the cataloging revisor. It is even more likely that a filing clerk, whose imagination is given license by all of the other cards reading BUTLER, would file the card correctly. Under these conditions the user would, without doubt, find the card. At worst, if s/he even noticed it, s/he would be amused by the error. The moral of this little story is that at each of the critical steps in the cycle—the creation of the data, its placement into the data base, and its retrieval—the error tolerances were compatible, hence, the system functioned despite the error. This is not so with an automated system, as a similar error would result in the parthenogenesis of a totally new author in the file. Since BULTER sequences ahead of BUTLER, and given the limited scan range of a CRT display (approximately 25 lines of 80 characters each), this record could easily become lost. It is not difficult to imagine a slightly more serious error which would place the record completely out of reach. It should be realized that the nature of machine retrieval and the limitations of display devices make *any* computer-based catalog equivalent to a large catalog. This is true even when a Ruecking algorithm $(3,3 \text{ key})$[10] has reduced the search to a seemingly manageable set of ambiguous choices, as it is still the same inexorably literal logic which must ultimately glance into the chaos, and small differences create infinite displacements between records.

Clearly the only solution to the problems posed is to use the machine itself to control the data. The techniques for accomplishing this are neither new to computing systems nor to libraries. Under manual systems libraries have traditionally maintained *authority files*, either as separate files or embedded in an official catalog. Authority files are just that: the authority for all personal, corporate, conference and place names; uniform and series titles; and subject headings. By the use of these files one could be reasonably assured that all headings used in the catalog were in conformity with an existing structure. Any new heading would be established in this file in a logically consistent manner, thereby guaranteeing the continuing integrity of the catalog.

The computer allows us to extend this concept in several important directions. For instance, were we to render this file machine manipulatable:

1. It could be used to mechanically verify all headings used in bibliographic records. We would then have a system in which human data entry is verified with the same logic which will subsequently be used to retrieve it. Thus, we will have established the sought-for balance of error tolerance.

2. The heading data need only be created and stored once. Only a single copy of the name, subject heading, etc., would be maintained in the system and referenced by every bibliographic record using that heading. Thus, having entered the authority datum correctly once, we could be sure that no matter how many bibliographic records used it they would all do so with mechanical consistency.

3. The machine can be programmed to control the internal structure of this file, hence guaranteeing a degree of internal consistency within the authority file itself not feasible in a manual system.

The incorporation of such features into a system would permit us to create a *machine-based catalog* rather than a reference file of bibliographic records. This should be our first concern, not the gadgetry which allows us to peer into it. Only such a controlled data base, when combined with sophisticated access techniques, permits us simultaneously to address both major functions of the catalog: *access* and *collocation*. Virtually any system can satisfy the former requirement, but only by addressing the question of integrity of the data base can we hope to satisfy the latter.

Mechanically, this can be accomplished in a rather straightforward manner. First, whenever a new bibliographic record is entered into the system all elements susceptible to authority control are identified. In simplest terms these can be identified as all elements which are potentially common access points for a group of records (for example, author main and added entries, series titles, subject headings, linking entries for serials, etc.). The bibliographic title for a monograph (unless analyzed) pertains only to that single item, hence it would not be controlled by an authority file. Figure 2 gives a list of fields derived from the published MARC formats which are of this nature. These elements could then be alphabetically compared with valid headings already in the authority file. If no valid match is found, the system would signal the cataloger of this fact. This would imply that either an invalid form is being used, a keying error has occurred, or that the heading still needs to be established. The cataloger may then take the appropriate action. If a valid match is found, the system would automatically replace the text for that field with an identification number for the appropriate heading. Figure 3 shows a record entering the system with an error; consequently, no valid match is found. When the error is corrected, a valid match is found and the text replaced by the heading's control number.

FIGURE 2
AUTHORITY FIELDS—MARC FORMATS
(Books, Serials, Maps, Films)

Tag	Field	Remarks
022	ISSN	Attached to serial title.
030	Coden	Attached to serial title.
090	Local classification number	Without volume designator. Attached to series title when kept 'together as a series.'
1xx	Main entry	Includes first indicator and tag suffix. Excludes relator data.
222	Key title	Attached to serial title.
240	Uniform title	May require combination with main entry.
245	Title statement	Only for serials and series main entry records. May require combination with author main entry.
4xx	Series statement	Without volume designator. May require combination with main entry. Includes first indicator and tag suffix.
6xx	Subject added entry	Excludes relator data.
7xx	Added entry series linking entries	Excludes 740. Excludes medium qualifiers. 700-730 includes first indicator and tag suffix.
8xx	Series added entry	Excludes volume designation. 800-840 includes first indicator and tag suffix.

FIGURE 3

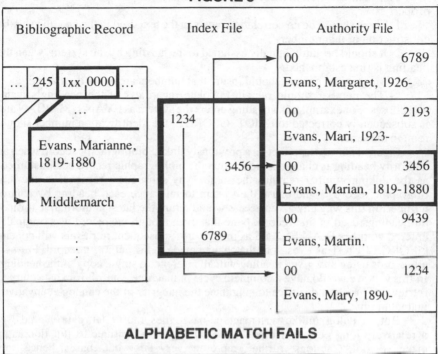

ALPHABETIC MATCH FAILS

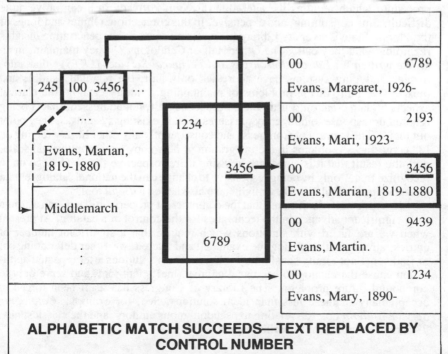

ALPHABETIC MATCH SUCCEEDS—TEXT REPLACED BY CONTROL NUMBER

This identification number (or control number) should possess the following properties:

1. There should be no correlation between the text used in the heading and the construction of that number.

2. It should be automatically assigned to the heading by the system, when the heading is first established.

3. Mechanical control should insure that numbers are never duplicated.

4. The number should remain inviolate regardless of the heading's metamorphoses. For example, if a heading enters the system as EVANS, MARIAN and is subsequently corrected to ELIOT, GEORGE, the identification number should remain the same.

Figure 4 shows the effect on a previously linked bibliographic record when an authority heading is changed. Notice that the bibliographic record is undisturbed, as the linking number remains the same. Any subsequent retrieval of the bibliographic record would cause the system to reference each heading by control number. In this way any given access would return the latest authoritative form of all headings used in that record. Note that even though the record was originally entered with MARIAN EVANS as main entry, subsequent retrievals will contain GEORGE ELIOT as a result of the change made to the authority record. Further, all records using any given heading will all reference a single copy of the heading. In this way we would have a complete cycle of machine control from data entry to retrieval. This should suffice to guarantee the integrity of the catalog at any given instant in time.

But, a catalog, unlike most machine-based files, must relate data entered over a relatively long period of time, if the catalog is to continue to function as an effective tool. Catalogs, further, represent very large data bases; hence, any procedure which requires the alteration of records already in it can prove quite difficult, time consuming, and expensive. In this connection, Ohmes and Jones of the Florida State University Library have offered some rather penetrating insights regarding what they call "The Other Half of Cataloging." They maintain, in an article written for *Library Resources and Technical Services (LRTS)* "that automated cataloging systems have addressed only half, the relatively simple and inexpensive half, of the problems of maintaining a library catalog: the clerical aspects of data creation. Further it is the second half, not addressed, that is being ignored in response to budgetary pressures even in existing systems." They point out that, "The Library of Congress [and consequently any other library relying on LC copy] faces problems in the integration of new copy on a monumental scale, with the result that it is constantly revising its retrospective file." They go on to recognize that, "only by being responsive to change can the national catalog remain an authoritative tool."[11] They might have also added a *useful* tool.

It is especially in this area that the computer, if properly utilized, can afford a truly significant advance in the techniques for the control of a catalog. At present when we are faced with situations which require that a significant number of entries, already in the catalog, be examined and altered, we either defer doing so, or find some not totally satisfactory solution. Such solutions after repeated application cause the catalog to become a clumsy, inefficient tool, and serve only to compound future problems. The Library of Congress has itself been forced to accept many of these less than ideal solutions. See, for example, *Cataloging Service Bulletin* no. 106 relating to pseudonymous authors, and the classics, nos. 79 and 80, announcing superimposition.

FIGURE 4

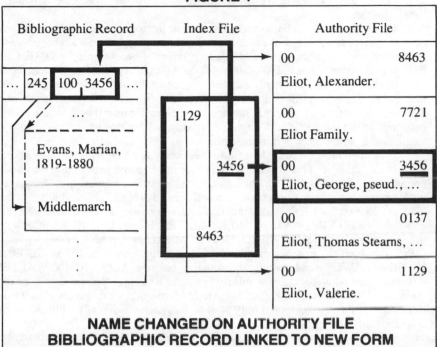

**NAME CHANGED ON AUTHORITY FILE
BIBLIOGRAPHIC RECORD LINKED TO NEW FORM**

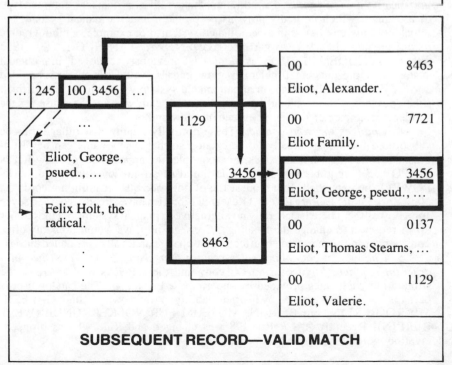

SUBSEQUENT RECORD—VALID MATCH

Let us consider some typical examples and how they might be handled in local catalogs.

1. *Subject heading changes*. As usage of the language causes terms to become anachronistic, or as increases in our level of awareness reveal undesirable connotations, we seek to change subject heading terms. For example, WOMEN AS POLICE becomes POLICEWOMEN, or SPANISH AMERICA is changed to LATIN AMERICA.[12] In many catalogs these would be handled by a *see also* reference. The net result is a heavily overburdened cross-reference structure.[13] The *see also* reference was only intended to inform the user that there are related headings in the catalog which might be considered, not that the search should be continued in some other part of the alphabet.

2. *Name changes*. We often find it necessary to change the form of a name used in the catalog. This is because an author has become better known by some pseudonym, or variant of his/her name; names of women authors frequently undergo transformations as a result of marriage and divorce; political jurisdictions also are annexed or gain independence and sometimes a new name; etc. For example, GORDON DAVIS, ROBERT DIETRICH, and DAVID ST. JOHN are all discovered to be HOWARD HUNT. MARIAN EVANS, who wrote as GEORGE ELIOT, was at times fond of identifying herself as MRS. GEORGE HENRY LEWES, and eventually actually became MRS. JOHN WALTER CROSS. *The New York Times* informs us, one morning, that in all subsequent issues the CONGO will be known as ZAIRE. Here again we might resort to the old expedient of the *see also*, or simply pretend that each version of an author's name implies a different person.

3. *New information causes a heading to change*. These changes actually fall into the previous categories. I would, nonetheless, like to consider a common type of a change, which normally presents no problem under a manual system, but which could wreak havoc in an automated system. For example, a bibliographic record created after 1973 would use AUDEN, WYSTAN HUGH, 1907-1973 rather than AUDEN . . . 1907- as in material previously cataloged. In a manual system this presents no problem as new entries would nonetheless be filed correctly. On the other hand, in an automated system we would have a difficult time convincing the machine that Mr. Auden's death was not the cause for the sudden appearance on the literary scene of a new author.

4. *Changes to avoid conflict*. These normally require that fuller forms be substituted for names already in the catalog so that a new name can be distinguished from other similar names. For example, the appearance of a new JOHN M. POWELL requires that the middle initial of an already established JOHN POWELL be expanded. In a modest file of only one quarter million records the New York Public Library (NYPL) Research Libraries have already recorded seven John Powells.[14] There is generally no alternative in manual systems but the tedious effort required to change the headings. Consequently, we would probably often consider cutting corners and not effecting the change under all of the added entries.

5. *Changes in cataloging rules require that headings be established in a different manner*. Anyone using LC copy and the *AACR* is well aware of the stimulating challenges provided by superimposed headings. The catalog user is perhaps not quite so amused by his/her inability to divine why it's not GALERIE MIKRO BERLIN, but BERLIN, MUSEUM FÜR VÖLKERKUNDE (WEST BERLIN). Recently *AACR* Rule 98 was changed and Rule 99 was dropped, creating more of these fine conundrums.

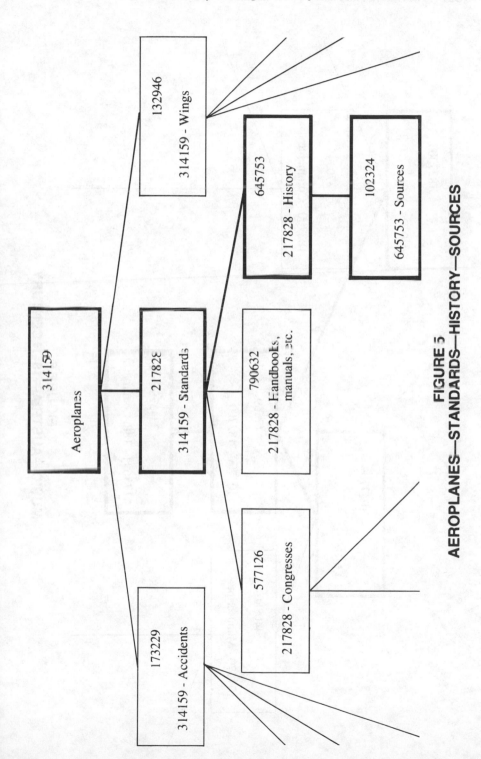

FIGURE 5

AEROPLANES—STANDARDS—HISTORY—SOURCES

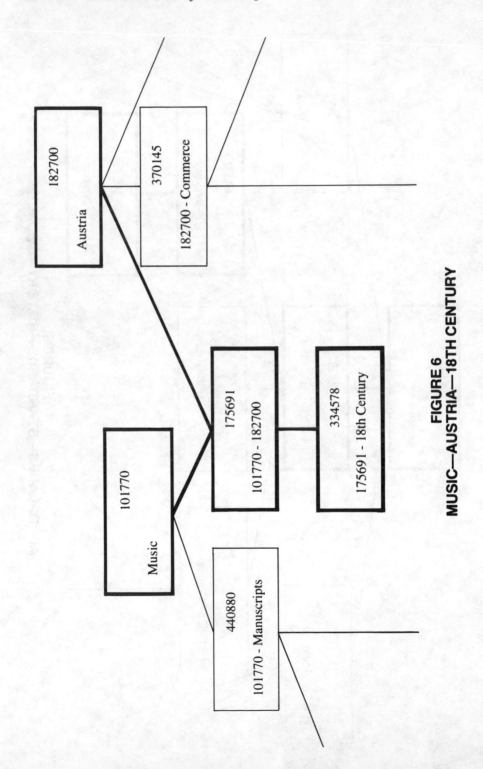

FIGURE 6
MUSIC—AUSTRIA—18TH CENTURY

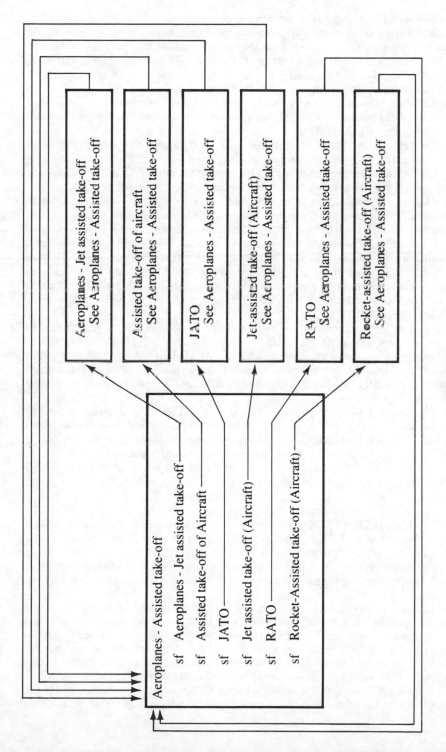

FIGURE 7

Each of these changes, if we were to deal with them in an adequate manner, create severe workload problems for the cataloging department. If ignored, the problems are only passed on to *all* the users of the catalog: the public, the reference department, the acquisitions department, and naturally the cataloging department. If, on the other hand, we had a system in which each heading was represented by a link to a single authority record, then by the application of a single maintenance transaction we could change the form of that heading throughout the catalog. And because of the nature of that link we could be certain that the change had been effected uniformly throughout.

We can extend these two concepts—(1) neutral links to a single copy of an accepted form, and (2) mechanical verification of the validity of data—one step further, and use them to guarantee the integrity of the authority file itself as well as to provide a very simple mechanism for restructuring the catalog.

Let us first consider interlinked records. It is clearly quite useful to be able to change all occurrences of a heading with only a single transaction. Nonetheless, we would still not wish to hunt through the file in order to maintain all subdivisions of that heading. If we set up our system in such a way that any subdivision of a heading always mechanically referred to the next higher level heading (see Figure 5), then any change made to a primary heading could be made to have a global effect on the entire authority file and hence the catalog. In this way we could change AEROPLANES to AIRPLANES, and at the same time change every subdivision of AEROPLANES.

Figure 5 demonstrates how this technique could be applied repetitively to create the heading, AEROPLANES—STANDARDS—HISTORY—SOURCES. Note how all headings which are subdivisions of the primary heading AERO-PLANES ultimately reference that record. Thus, it should be obvious that a single transaction changing AEROPLANES to AIRPLANES could be made to alter the entire catalog.

Likewise if all place names, either subdivided for direct regionalization, or used as subdivisions of other headings in indirect regionalization, were maintained as links to a single record (see Figure 6) defining the authorized version of that name, we could affect all subject headings which used it with a single action. In this way, for example, all occurrences of CEYLON could be changed to SRI LANKA, both in headings of a direct form as in CEYLON—POETRY— . . . and those of an indirect form such as ART—CEYLON— . . . .

Figure 6 demonstrates this technique with the heading MUSIC—AUSTRIA—18TH CENTURY. Note that all subdivisions of AUSTRIA and the first subdivision of MUSIC both reference a single record for the place name AUSTRIA. Note also, that the subdivided heading MUSIC—AUSTRIA consists only of two pointers. It should be obvious that under this scheme any changes made to the single place name record will automatically reflect itself throughout the file.

Similar considerations could be extended to the cross-reference structure. If the cross-reference structure of the file was treated as a network of mechanical links between proper headings and their associated cross-references (see Figure 7), then we could always insure that there would be no blind references, and that any change of a heading would be automatically reflected in all reciprocal records. For example, with such a system a change of the heading AEROPLANES—ASSIST-ED TAKE-OFF in Figure 7 would without further effort be reflected in the six associated cross-reference records; or a change made to AEROPLANES—JET-

ASSISTED TAKE-OFF would be automatically reflected in the *see from* notes associated with AEROPLANES—ASSISTED TAKE-OFF.

The ability to perform these operations with such relative ease affords the cataloger the freedom to make decisions to restructure the catalog whenever it becomes necessary. The number of bibliographic records, entries, or other headings are of no concern, as the effort will generally require no more than a single manual action. The cataloger, by being relieved of the onerous clerical burden of reorganizing the catalog, is free to devote professional attention to making the catalog a more responsive and useful tool. Equally important, the cataloger can be assured that changes will be applied with mechanical consistency, without any possibility of clerical error or oversights.

The maintenance of complex networks of uncorruptible links among disparate records is one of the fundamental attributes of any computing system. We are simply using it to make *explicit* those relations already intellectually *implicit* in the catalog. There is yet the other capability inherent in data processing systems— literal verification of data—that we can employ to guarantee the integrity of an authority file. Within an authority file we wish to maintain rigorous consistency of headings. For the most part this is still a human responsibility. Only a human can decide if two names actually represent different individuals, or if different subject terms represent distinct concepts, or are synonymous. However, once these human decisions have been entered into the system we should be able to use its magnetic memory to assist us in guaranteeing that we don't, in the future, create logical inconsistencies. For example, the system, once informed that GORDON ASHE is in fact JOHN CREASEY, should, on its own limited initiative, be capable of correcting the error if an unauthorized form of name is used as a form of entry. Similarly, it should be capable of either correcting, or refusing to accept, headings constructed illogically within the context of the rest of the file. For example, if we inform the system that MUSIC DRAMA is in fact OPERA, it should treat MUSIC DRAMA—COSTUMES as at least suspect; or, the commandment KÖLN see COLOGNE should be sufficient cause for the rejection of the illicit proposal to establish OPERA—KÖLN.

Rigorous mechanical control of the machine-based catalog of a single institution is indisputably desirable. However, if we are to attempt to collect a coherent national bibliographic data base in machine-readable form, it must be made an essential feature of the collection vehicle. This is especially so if input is to come from disparate sources. The problem of consistency of data has always plagued attempts to create a national union catalog. They exist in manual systems, and as we have already pointed out, they are only exacerbated by automated systems. John Cronin, former director of the LC processing department, in discussing plans for publication of the pre-1952 *NUC* noted the enormous benefits to be derived from such a catalog. But, then went on to state that, "the editing of the catalog is essential and presents the chief problem." He included among the necessary editing steps:

1. [to] combine multiple reports for the same title and edition . . . ;
2. [to] eliminate conflicts between main entries and added entries serving as entries for the same work and change entries conflicting with straight cross references;
3. [to] adopt one form of name for authors entered under variants of the name. [15]

Edwin Buchinski, of the National Library of Canada, has extended these considerations one step further by noting that a machine-readable data base, collected from disparate sources, would also require that the coding structure be upgraded to conform with format conventions for content designation, i.e., delimiting, tagging, etc.[16] The National Library of Canada is intending to accomplish this by applying the techniques of linked authority files to contributed records. It intends to do this in the following manner: After a valid alphabetic match is found, the text for that field including correct delimiters and tag suffixes will be retrieved from an authority file. These data would then replace the access point data found in the contributed records.

Cronin, of course, was only addressing the problems of editing and creating a static national data base. The data having already been collected, attempts to impose consistency as part of the collection process were moot, as were questions of its continued maintenance once it was published in book form. The printed catalog could only represent a frozen moment in time. A machine-readable national data base, or for that matter any catalog, should be capable of existing in time; it must be capable of responding to a dynamic reality in which terms, "strain, crack and sometimes break under the burden, under the tension, slip, slide, perish, decay with imprecision, will not stay in place, will not stay still."[17]

The techniques presented in this discussion are neither new, nor purely theoretical. Henderson and Rosenthal, in 1968, in a study undertaken to determine the future of the NYPL card catalogs proposed a very similar system.[18] Most of the features described have been included in the Automated Bibliographic Control system[19] developed as a result. Those not implemented were excluded only because of the hardware limitations of the NYPL computer configuration in 1969, when the system was still under development. They have been made a part of the design for conversion of the system to an online mode of operation. The National Library of Canada, early in 1975, implemented a similar system of linked authority and bibliographic files.[20] The Library of Congress, too, has included similar considerations in the design of their automated system.[21]

The effective application of a new technology to an existing procedure requires that we thoroughly understand the unique properties of the medium and relate them to the basic tasks to be performed. In the case of the computer, data are reduced to machine-readable form for two major reasons: (1) to provide efficient, instantaneous, decentralized access; and (2) to manipulate their elements. The latter reasons may be further subdivided into those operations (a) which synthesize, from existing data, new data, and (b) those in which we wish to alter and restructure existing data for whatever reason (simply stated: when we expect that we shall have reasonable provocation to change our minds). It is the great expense and difficulty involved in changing a record, once filed into a manual catalog, which has proven an anathema to the framers of cataloging codes, and created a schism of interests between technical and public service librarians. Catalogers are in general sympathetic to the needs of the users of the catalog, if only because they themselves are very frequent users. However, they are also subject to pressure to refrain from altering existing records, as well as to adopt rules which can be interpreted consistently by all. The reference librarian, on the other hand, wants a tool which is reflective of the approach that a user might take at that moment, not the approach of a user who might have flourished at the time when the record was made. Cataloging codes, and the principles espoused for their development, have had a tendency to attempt to recognize the user's needs. These laudable sentiments are all too often couched as exceptions with phrases like: "use unless better known as." The intent is to create a mechanism which recognizes the needs of the reader, in contradistinction to simplifying clerical procedures within the cataloging department. The problem, in general, is at the time when the record is created, being unaware of the sign-on procedure which would put him online to Delphi, the cataloger cannot realistically make such decisions. Then due to the difficulty of altering a manual file and the pressure to catalog more new books faster, s/he is administratively enjoined from attending to such details when the situation does resolve itself, but the record has already been created and filed.

The *ALA 1941,* despite its deficiencies, did attempt such a practical approach to the user's needs. For example, *ALA* 5A counsels that collections should be "enter[ed] under the compiler or editor, individual or corporate. . . ." But provides the following exceptions: 5A (1b), "enter under title . . . when they are generally referred to by title"; or 5A (1a), "enter . . . collections under title . . . if there are frequent changes of editor." Series according to 5F(1), are to be entered under editor or publisher when, "familiarly known by the name of editor or publisher." Note the practical, but predictive nature of these rules: "when generally referred to . . . ," "when there are frequent changes . . . ," and "when familiarly known. . . ." The Paris conference put forth similar exceptions in its statement of principles, e.g.,

> 11.3 *The uniform heading* . . . for works entered under title should be the original title or the title most frequently used in editions of the work, *except that*
> > 11.31 if the work is generally known by a conventional title, the uniform heading should be the conventional title.[22]

Here we have a double set of predictive exceptions: "most frequently used . . . ," and "generally known by. . . ."

Finally, the *1967 AACR* Rule 40 requires that a person be entered, "under the name by which he [or she] is *commonly* [author's italics] identified."

The principles are excellent. Unfortunately under a manual system they are difficult to apply. The cataloger is often the first to see a new title. S/He is, nonetheless, asked to make decisions which require that its future behavior be predicted. In general, the cataloger is asked to create a structure which is consistent, *permanent*, and responsive to the user's needs. However, the inertia of an existing structure tends to make these requirements incompatible. Further, changes in the external world serve to render judgments, valid at the moment, wrong at best, and detrimental to the effectiveness of the catalog at worst.

It is in this area that the computer can provide the greatest potential for a truly innovative advance in the maintenance of a catalog. The framers of cataloging codes, rather than concerning themselves solely with the limitations or requirements of the computer, could instead utilize its capabilities to create a code which is more responsive to the user's needs. The potential is enormous, but so are the problems. It is easy to predict that a majority of either large or affluent libraries in this country will employ some form of catalog under machine control in the forseeable future. Thus, they might be able to respond to a dynamic environment. But, how are the libraries with more modest resources to be accommodated in this scheme? What, for example, will be the impact on the library community as a whole if LC closes its existing catalogs and replaces them with an automated system employing linked authority control? How will the rest of the community keep up with the relatively complex changes LC will be able to make in its own catalog? Will LC, after becoming the *de facto* national library as a result of the technological innovation of the standard, printed catalog card, be forced to abdicate its role? Or will LC, in order to continue in its role, be forced to forego the opportunities presented to it by this new technology? We cannot address these questions in this discussion, as they would lead us far from our topic. However, they are important questions, which will need to be answered soon.

Technology certainly exists which will permit us to create machine-based catalogs without giving up any of the quality and integrity traditionally striven for in manual catalogs. Indeed, as I hope we have demonstrated, the technology is actually capable of creating an even more precise level of bibliographic control than was feasible, other than in principle, in manual systems. The technology can, at the same time, be used to make its single greatest contribution by serving as the medium by which the incompatible requirements imposed on the catalog are resolved. That is, from the point of view of the cataloging department's productivity, a cataloging record and the catalog's structure should be as permanent as possible; while from the point of view of the reader, the catalog should be consistent, accurate, and reflective of his/her thought processes. Resolution of these conflicting requirements can be accomplished by utilizing the computer's sophisticated access techniques with a rigorously controlled, and easily reorganized, data base.

Data bases required by libraries, whether controlled or created according to standards based on caprice, are expensive to create and maintain. It is, in general, quite difficult to motivate an administrator to divert the resources necessary to upgrade an existing file of poor quality. An annual report showing the number of records upgraded is not nearly as impressive as one showing a large number of new titles *cataloged*. The natural tendency is to accept the evolving practice as the norm for expected quality. Thus, data bases, by their sheer size and inertia, are quite capable of creating *de facto standards* in their own image. A recitation of the best thought out principles for a cataloging code is easily drowned out by the clatter of a bank of direct access devices vainly searching for misplaced records. As American industry has conclusively proven, the most direct way to cut costs is to debase the quality of the product. The real cost of an inferior product does not appear until it is put into use and found not to provide the service expected. In the case of the library catalog the costs are simply passed on to its users, both the public and the library staff.

Mitch Freedman observed that the success of a product is often inversely proportional to its quality. He then went on to note sardonically that, "this may not be a major drawback . . . , because of the increasingly uncritical acceptance of less authoritative cataloging data and of cataloging data which probably conflicts with previous practice at a given library."[23] While another colleague of mine at the NYPL, who has been intimately involved in the development of automated library systems since the early sixties, offered the wry comment that "as the computer's capabilities have increased our expectations of what it can do have proportionally diminished."

I have, it is hoped, demonstrated that the computer by its intrinsic nature has not yet negated any of the principles upon which cataloging codes have been based. Not only are the principles still valid, but the computer can actually provide us with the means to apply them in a far more consistent manner. Desiderata contained or implied in cataloging codes, abandoned because of the expense or difficulty of application, can be implemented with relative ease by properly employing the computer's capabilities. Further, rules can be framed with greater regard for the convenience of the user without imposing undue burdens on the cataloging department. The alternative is to limit the computer to addressing only the simple clerical aspects of bibliographic control, with the expectation that control would be imposed by existing, awkward manual methods, or ignored in response to economic pressure. We can permit ourselves to be hypnotized by the gadgetry for access and by illusory cost reductions, or we can use the computer effectively to transform the catalog into a truly responsive instrument. Finally, we can use the century and a quarter of experience in conjunction with the fundamental properties of the machine to implement and extend the principles developed, or we can turn our backs on them with fatuous arguments, which posit their anachronism and the nonexistent intelligence of computing machinery.

Library automation has become a multimillion dollar industry. We can no longer treat automation projects as interesting experiments, which are disposable if they fail. We have too much invested, and the new systems too intimately integrated into the everyday operation of the library, for us to assume any longer that we can, by sheer force of will, temper their influence on emerging standards. The only realistic approach is to establish the standards for quality as part of the system's design. We can program the computer to insure adherence to intelligently established principles, or we can permit it, in the absence of such guidance, to establish its own. We could then simply alter our expectations accordingly, and exult in the progress we have made.

REFERENCES

1. Henriette D. Avram, "MARC: The First Two Years," *Library Resources and Technical Services* 12 (Summer 1968): 245-50.

2. Charles A. Cutter, *Rules for a Dictionary Catalog*, 4th ed. (Washington, DC: Government Printing Office, 1907). The first edition appeared as: U.S. Bureau of Education, *Public Libraries in the United States of America: Their History, Condition and Management*, pt II (Washington, DC: Government Printing Office, 1876).

3. Seymour Lubetzky, "The Function of the Main Entry in the Alphabetical Catalog—One Approach," in *International Conference on Cataloguing Principles, Paris, 9-18 October 1961, Report* (London: International Federation of Library Associations and Institutions (IFLA), 1963), pp. 193-43.

4. *Statement of Principles Adopted at the International Conference on Cataloguing Principles, Paris, October, 1961* (London: IFLA, 1971), p. xiii.

5. Lubetzky, "Function of the Main Entry."

6. T.S. Eliot, "What is Minor Poetry," in his *On Poetry and Poets* (New York: The Noonday Press, 1961), p. 44.

7. *Subject Headings Used in the Dictionary Catalog of The Library of Congress*, 7th ed. (Washington, DC: U.S. Library of Congress, 1966), p. 600.

8. *Cataloging Service Bulletin*, no. 65 (Washington, DC: U.S. Library of Congress, 1965).

9. Statistics derived from the LC/MARC file in July 1973 by the NYPL Systems Office (unpublished). The file contained, at that time, 329,354 records. It was found that there were an average of 3.39 authority fields/bibliographic record. The mean length of these fields was determined to be 34 characters. Thus, with a

keyboarding accuracy rate of 99.9 percent one could expect 36,229 records to have at least one faulty authority access point.

10. Frederick Ruecking, Jr, "Bibliographic Retrieval," MARC Pilot Project Progress Report no. 3 (Rice University, Fondren Library, Advanced Library Systems Project, 10 August 1967).

11. Frances Ohmes and J.F. Jones, "The Other Half of Cataloging," *Library Resources and Technical Services*, vol. 17, no. 3: 320-29.

12. *Supplement to LC Subject Headings: Quarterly Cumulative Supplement to the 8th edition* (Washington, DC: U.S. Library of Congress, March, 1975), p. 368.

13. Maurice F. Tauber, *Technical Services in Libraries* (New York: Columbia University Press, 1953), p. 172.

14. *Dictionary Catalog of the Research Libraries*, PHO-Q (New York: New York Public Library, September 1975), p. 362.

15. John Cronin, "The National Union and Library of Congress Catalogs: Problems and Prospects," *Library Quarterly*, vol. 34, no. 1: 77-96.

16. Edwin Buchinski, "Authority Files at the National Library: Plans and Developments," in *Automation in Libraries: Papers Presented at the CACUL [Canadian Association of College and University Libraries] Workshop on Library Automation, Winnipeg, June 22-23, 1974* (Ottawa: Canadian Library Association, 1975).

17. Cronin, "National Union and Library of Congress Catalogs."

18. James W. Henderson and Joseph A. Rosenthal, eds., *Library Catalogs: Their Preservation and Maintenance by Photographic and Automated Techniques* (Cambridge, MA: MIT Press, 1968).

19. S. Michael Malinconico, "Role of a Machine-Based Authority File in an Automated Bibliographic System," in *Automation in Libraries: Papers Presented at the CACUL Workshop on Library Automation, Winnipeg, June 22-23, 1974* (Ottawa: Canadian Library Association, 1975); S. Michael Malinconico and James A. Rizzolo, "The New York Public Library Automated Book Catalog Subsystem," *Journal of Library Automation*, vol. 6, no. 1 (March 1973): 3-36.

20. National Library of Canada, *Accessible*, vol. 3, no. 3 (November 1975).

21. Henriette D. Avram, et al., "Automation Activities in the Processing Department of The Library of Congress," *Library Resources and Technical Services*, vol. 16, no. 2 (Spring 1972): 195-239.

22. *Statement of Principles Adopted at the International Conference on Cataloguing Principles, Paris, October, 1961*, pp. xvii-xviii.

23. Maurice J. Freedman, "What Do Libraries Really Need?" *Library Journal* 15 (October 1974): 2570-71.

DISCUSSION

Joseph Rosenthal: It seems to me that Mr. Malinconico has strongly emphasized what he considers to be the importance of computer-based catalogs and cataloging systems, the importance of authority file and authority file control; whereas Mr. Kilgour de-emphasized the role of this feature. I would like to ask each of them to tell us whether in fact there is a clear difference of opinion and direct opposition or whether there is no real inconsistency.

Michael Malinconico: Well, it's difficult to be first and answer the question as to whether there is a difference of opinion or not. It seemed to me, from the discussion and description of the mini-cat, that what was being attempted was the provision of enough alternate access points to provide access to a single well-defined item. However, the function I think the catalog ought to serve is what I like to call the collocation function: the drawing together in a single sequence of entries, the bringing together of works under a single author's name, or bringing it all together under a single subject heading. You do not do the users a lot of good when you send them jumping all over the catalog simply to draw together material. And you do them less good by concealing a fraction of the collection from them simply because they are unaware of the capricious form under which the materials were entered.

Frederick Kilgour: Many years ago I went to a meeting at the Boston Medical History Club, and an emeritus professor of what was then called bacteriology gave a paper that involved the great German pathologist, Rudolph Fairchild, an emeritus professor at Harvard. He began by pointing out that one of his predecessors in anatomy, namely, Oliver Wendell Holmes, had once said that it was a great shame that all of the great discoveries in anatomy had already been made. And it turned out that in the same year that Holmes made that remark, Fairchild said that all you have to do is scrape an organ with the back of a scalpel to make a discovery. Then he peered over his glasses at us and said, "Different points of view." Well, you've heard that same thing happen this afternoon—different points of view. I'm talking about an online catalog and Mr. Malinconico is talking about a classical catalog. What he has to say is more important for a bookform catalog than it is for a card catalog. It is a matter of different points of view, and Mr. Rosenthal is correct: I did de-emphasize it, because authority information is not nearly as important in an online catalog as it is in a bookform catalog, where it is absolutely imperative to have it.

Malinconico: In response, authority control is not important if one is looking for a single well-defined item. If one is asking the catalog to draw together so that one can peruse a coherent sequence, then the concept of authority control is valid regardless of the medium of the catalog. The only difference I see between an online catalog and a card catalog is that the sequences exist in the card drawer whether or not someone is viewing them, whereas on the screen they only exist in response to a user's query. I assume that that is a difference of opinion which relates to what function the catalog should serve. Should it serve as the index to a collection when one is seeking a very precisely defined item—an item which one can name unambiguously? This can be satisfied by most systems. But what is traditionally been striven for in a catalog is something that would organize the material, and this requirement is independent of the catalog medium.

Philip Long: Mr. Malinconico, is it possible that the issue is not whether you and Mr. Kilgour disagree about the *onlineness* of it all or whether you use 3,3, or 5,4, or twice the square root of pi as the key; but rather, what might be the content of the mini-cat as the consequence of the form and manner of the original entry of data into the system?

Malinconico: Precisely. I think I stated twice that the medium supporting the catalog—*onlineness* or *offlineness*—is not a very relevant issue. It's the function that the catalog is to perform which is really at issue.

Unidentified Speaker: About two or three years ago seven people in the South Central Research Council Region in the State of New York came to New York City to investigate what the New York Public Library was doing. We were impressed with the approach that was discussed today, namely, that we have to keep the controls alive, even for an automated catalog. At that time OCLC was already going strong, and we tried to find some backing from the State of New York and possibly from the federal government to marry those two systems—one that has a proven capability of communication and of interfacing many libraries, the other system that is based on traditional values of authority files. We had no response, either from the State or from any other sources. But I am again calling for attention to these two systems and hope that we can bring about some reconciliation of these two approaches and then have a valuable authoritative automated online cataloging system.

James Schoenung: Let's assume, Mr. Malinconico, that you are right. What is going to happen with the investment that we already have in OCLC? Is the data going into this sytem going to prevent us from achieving the type of integrity that you are talking about? Is it too late?

Malinconico: Well, that's a difficult question to answer. First, 45 or 50 percent of that file consists of Library of Congress MARC records, the integrity of which is laboriously insured by manual methods. So there is at least that big chunk of a file which is already a rather coherent catalog. For the remainder of the file the questions are: (a) what function should a catalog serve, and (b) how much effort are you willing to invest in it?

An authority file can also be used to clean up an inconsistent, dirty data base. We actually did this with my good friend Maurice Freedman when he was at the Hennepin County Public Library. Hennepin had been collecting a file over about two years, consisting of 77,000 records. They were converting a shelflist. The shelflist itself had problems, since it consisted of cataloging practices that spanned some fifty years. Now, there were those problems inherent in data, and there were also the normal keyboarding problems. We took that file of 77,000 records and matched it against an authority file. In cases where we could find a valid match, we did what the National Library of Canada was intending to do—we supplied delimiting and tag suffixes. In the cases where there was no match, we intentionally created a dirty authority file. In other words, when we got through with that first pass, there was a file that consisted of TRILLING, LIONEL; TRILLING, L.; TRILLING, LIONEL, ED.; and so on. The next step was a rather painful, laborious manual effort. I believe Mr. Freedman hired about 11 student assistants to go through this intentionally dirty file and clean it up. We implemented a transaction with the authority system called a *transfer transaction*. By keying two nine-digit numbers one can transfer all occurrences of a given heading to another given heading. After several weeks, these 11 student assistants did manage to clean up a good chunk of that file. Actually, there were something like 11,000 maintenance transactions against this dirty authority file—6,000 of which were the transfer variety—to bring HORSE and HORSES together or TRILLING, L. together with TRILLING, LIONEL, etc.

The basic answer to your question is: yes, it can be done. It's a matter of motivating an administrator to divert the resources to do it. It's a lot easier if you start at the beginning, but that's something that I hadn't intended to get into. I haven't done the arithmetic so I could be wrong, but if you wait until you've acquired a significant number of records the effort is probably geometrically greater than if you had done it from the beginning. This is because each record in a full file of end records has to be compared to all end records; whereas, the other way around you are doing it as they are entered. The basic answer is a willingness to divert the resources to do it, and the ability to find the resources.

David Weisbrod: I would like to present a question and a statement. In the clean-up operation that you just described you recalled a figure of approximately 11,000 transactions. Would you have some ideas as to what the multiplication ratio of bibliographic records affected by those transactions was against the authority file?

Malinconico: That would have been a very valuable piece of data to have collected. Unfortunately, the basic problem was to get the file cleaned up in a hurry, and nobody was particularly concerned with research.

Seymour Lubetzky: I have just two very minor points, but since people can go away with certain impressions about certain things, I would like to make certain corrections. I am an incurable teacher of cataloging. It is because of this that I am making these observations.

One is the reference to the objects stated by Cutter. Many people have traced the function of the catalog as included in the Paris Principles to Cutter's objectives. *Objects*, as he called them—are not quite the same. Cutter was concerned with bringing together the works of an author and works on a subject, but not in the *Objects*. The *Objects* do not include bringing together the editions of a work. Cutter has under *Objects* the reference to the work, to an edition; but if you read the section that is called *Means*, you will find that what he is concerned with is the description of the book—that is, second or third edition—and that should not be omitted.

That does not mean, however, that Cutter was not concerned with the work. He did provide for editions in his rules. But in Cutter's *Rules*, there was a distinction between the rules of entry and the rules of arrangement. There was a second part called *Arrangement* that he was writing for printed book catalogs.

Now in a book catalog the assumption was that you don't have to make a special provision for editions. You merely inform the user that editions and translations are to be arranged following the original edition in the following order. So when the *1908 ALA* rules superseded Cutter's rules, the whole provision for bringing together editions fell out, and we didn't have them until the *AACR*. I am making this merely as a correction: the *Objects* stated by Cutter should not be equated to the Paris Principles.

Another point is that you have referred favorably to a rule in the *1949 ALA* that collections should be entered under the editor or compiler, except when better known under title. This happens to be a very important issue in cataloging. Throughout the history of cataloging, some people have held, and Cutter was one of them, that the way a work or rather a book is best remembered is the way it should be entered.

We cannot base an organized catalog on a speculation of how it should best be remembered. It may be remembered by some people in one way, by others in another way. This is something that we have actually not followed. A very striking example of this is the fact that in all our rules there is the provision that anonymous publications should be entered under the author when known. Now certainly anonymous works are not best known under the author. The reason that rule was made is the system requires it. The fact that an anonymous work would be better known by the title is a reason for making an entry under the title. That could be accomplished, however, by a title-added entry; it does not control the main entry.

The main entry has a different function, as I've tried to explain before. You will get a more organized catalog if you enter all works uniformly under the author when you have this information.

The Continuing Role of the Library of Congress in National Bibliographic Control

by William J. Welsh

It seems appropriate that an institute on the nature and prospects of the catalog should include a statement on the continuing role of the Library of Congress (LC) in the future of American library catalogs. As you know, the Library of Congress has been contributing bibliographic information to the American library community for more than three-quarters of a century in the form of catalog cards, book catalogs, and allied services. The standard of LC cataloging has been generally recognized to be of a high order and so its records have gained wide acceptance. Thus, as we stand on the threshold of what is undoubtedly a new era in catalog control, it is worth considering to what extent the traditional services of the Library will continue in the forms now available and to what extent they will be modified and expanded.

As a starting point, let me give you an overview of present LC cataloging services. Since 1898 the Library has printed its catalog cards and since 1901 it has offered them for sale. During this period, the Library has produced an aggregate of nearly 6 million catalog records, and it has sold more than 1.613 billion cards while distributing millions more as depository sets.

In the 1940s the Library began using these cards to produce the book catalogs that eventually became the *National Union Catalog (NUC)* in book form. This catalog combines LC cards with outside library reports of items that the Library has not yet cataloged or that it may never catalog. These records represent the current cataloging output of the American libraries participating in the *NUC* effort. Another contribution to national bibliographic control is the Library's publication *New Serial Titles*, which has performed a similar function for newly cataloged serial publications since 1950. Mention should be made also of the *Monthly Checklist of State Publications* which performs an important bibliographic service for the library community.

Distribution of cataloging information is by no means limited to cards and book catalogs. For many years regular cataloging data has been available also in the form of proof sheets. These have the advantages of economy, and (if the subscriber desires) selectivity because the records on the proof sheets are divided into broad categories which can be obtained separately.

Of course, one of the most important developments in the distribution of catalog records are the Machine-Readable Cataloging (MARC) tapes which have been available on a regular basis since 1968. Although there are only a small number of direct subscriptions, hundreds of libraries benefit from this service through secondary distributors such as the OCLC (Ohio College Library Center), Stanford's BALLOTS (Bibliographic Automation of Large Library Operations Using a Time-Sharing System) system, and commercial services like BIBNET. MARC records have also been used in book catalogs produced by the New York Public Library (NYPL), the Washington State Library, and others. As of now, more than 634,000 LC records for monographs, serials, films, and maps are in MARC form and the data base is increasing at a rate of about 140,000 records per year. Over the next five years, the coverage of the MARC Distribution Service will be systematically expanded until it takes in all of the 230,000 titles cataloged by the Library each year. Inclusion of records for nonroman alphabet languages assumes a satisfactory resolution of the treatment of the great diversity of scripts and characters. An LC working group is now engaged in studying this problem.

The most recent advance in the distribution of cataloging information is provided by the Cataloging in Publication (CIP) program which involves supplying the essential data in advance of the publication of a book so that it can be put on the verso of the title page. By copying this information, libraries can sharply cut the costs of producing their own catalog records. CIP data are made available also through the MARC Distribution Service as an aid to acquisitions before the books are issued.

In addition to the catalog records themselves, the Library furnishes many aids to cataloging. Of these, the best known is *Library of Congress Subject Headings*, which is now in its 8th edition. This list and the Library of Congress classification schedules have been published since the early years of the century and have been subject to constant revision since that time. The Library, in cooperation with Forest Press, also maintains and develops the *Dewey Decimal Classification* by preparing new editions and applying decimal numbers to a substantial proportion of its cataloging output. The most recent publications of value to catalogers are *Name Headings with References* and *Monographic Series*. These tools, which began appearing early in 1975, fill a long-felt need for information that was not previously available outside the Library.

To support its bibliographic activities, the Library has engaged in various programs designed to obtain publications at the earliest possible moment. The All-the-Books program for American publications, the P.L. 480 program for Middle East and South Asian countries, and the worldwide National Program for Acquisitions and Cataloging are prime examples of this kind of effort to speed the cataloging of newly published materials.

In another field, the developmental work on the MARC system and the formats to input various types of records into MARC have had a major worldwide impact on library automation. Working with the library community both in this country and abroad, the Library has taken a leadership role in encouraging standardization of the structure and content designators of machine-readable bibliographic records as well as the character sets they require.

A new program that combines automation and cooperation in the service of libraries is the CONSER (Conversion of Serials) project. This is a truly collaborative effort involving the Council on Library Resources (CLR) as the management and funding agency, the Library of Congress, the National Library of Canada, the Ohio College Library Center, and 12 participants from the research library community. Records for serials will be input online to the OCLC data base so that users of the OCLC system will have access to a far larger body of serial records in machine-readable form than any of them could have produced on its own. The records will be validated by the Library of Congress and the National Library of Canada and regularly included in the MARC Distribution Service for the benefit of libraries that are not members of OCLC. This project should soon become operational after a somewhat protracted developmental period. Closely related to this effort is the National Serials Data Program (NSDP), which is jointly funded by CLR, the National Endowment for the Humanities (NEH), and the National Science Foundation (NSF). NSDP is responsible for assigning International Standard Serial Numbers (ISSN) and key titles to serials published in the United States.

Another aspect of cooperative effort is COMARC (Cooperative MARC), a pilot study being conducted with a grant from the CLR to expand the LC/MARC services to the nation's libraries. Since the MARC Distribution Service for books is still limited in coverage in terms of language and imprint date, libraries with automated cataloging systems are converting records locally and using LC cataloging copy from printed cards, proof sheets, or *NUC* pages for much of this activity. COMARC participants have been asked to submit monograph records in the MARC communications format for those titles converted based on LC cataloging copy. The Library of Congress will process these records to remove duplicate titles, check the remaining titles in its Official Catalog, update access points when necessary, and distribute the records without charge to COMARC participants. Other libraries will be able to purchase these records as a separate service. The Library of Congress expects to add these records to a national data base and have access to them for online retrieval and other products. While not a condition for participation, COMARC participants are also asked to provide location reports which could then be added to the *NUC Register of Additional Locations (RAL)*.

Part of the CLR grant is being used to fund a study to develop a format for machine-readable reports to the *National Union Catalog*. Based on the premise that it is feasible to define the characteristics of a machine-readable *NUC* report at a lower level than the full MARC format, the study will attempt to define the level of MARC encoding necessary and to determine how this lower level record could be upgraded to the full MARC encoding. This study has many implications for an ongoing COMARC effort beyond the present pilot project because it is evident that a very small number of libraries can furnish machine-readable records with full LC/MARC encoding. The reporting format will be instrumental in building the national data base, not only for gathering cataloging data but also in conjunction with gathering location information.

Concurrent with these activities, the Library of Congress has also been engaged in building the RAL file from location reports received in machine-readable form from outside libraries. Previously, these libraries had been producing printed cards to send to LC as their location reports, which in turn were rekeyed into machine-readable form by an LC contractor for addition to the RAL data base. The New York Public Library is at present the only contributor sending machine-readable location reports for the RAL data base. Work is also proceeding on providing online access to the RAL file. Additional funds are being sought for further study of expansion of RAL data using machine-readable records and for a survey of the utility of a microform edition of RAL.

Now, having heard about the products and services that the Library has been providing, you may well wonder whether they will be offered in the future. Since it

The Continuing Role of LC 75

seems clear that many libraries will not be automating, they will have to depend on traditional sources of cataloging data such as cards, proof slips, and book catalogs. *Therefore, I want to assure you that the Library will continue to provide these products as long as there is a need for them.* Regardless of whether automation emancipates the Library itself from reliance on cataloging data in these forms, we recognize our responsibility as a national bibliographic center to meet the needs of libraries that cannot take advantage of the new technology.

What about new products and services that the Library may be able to provide because of automation? I think that the most important advance that we can look forward to is a great increase in the amount of authority data in MARC form.

The Library will disseminate name authority records containing not only the established form of heading and its associated *see* and *see-also* references but also the citations of sources and the information used to determine these forms. Some of this information is now provided by the Library's book catalogs and by the new publication, *Library of Congress Name Headings with References*, but the coverage is not comprehensive and the data are incomplete even for the headings given. In 1976, the Library will begin to put into machine-readable form complete authority records for all name headings used in current MARC records along with all new and changed records for nonMARC headings. The authority records will be used to produce an enlarged version of *Name Headings* in book and microform. In due course, these records will be available online through the MARC Distribution Service. Gradually, authority records will be provided for all name headings in the retrospective MARC data base. By 1980, the MARC names file should contain about 1 million headings.

The Library will expand the coverage of *Library of Congress Subject Headings* to include categories of headings previously excluded from this publication. Among the types of headings that will appear in the expanded list are: places and regions, structures such as bridges and buildings, chemical compounds, and systematic names in botany and zoology. The eighth edition, prepared according to the older guidelines, has been issued in book form and on microfiche. [The data became available in machine-readable form in 1976.] The list will be kept up to date by regular supplements which will be cumulated frequently. In the face of present priorities and staff commitments, the Library feels that it cannot undertake a comprehensive study of the subject heading system that would pave the way for a major restructuring of the system. Such a study might be conducted outside the Library if a highly qualified specialist were available to undertake it. Meanwhile, the list will continue to evolve dynamically in a way that is responsive to contemporary needs.

The Library will apply *Dewey Decimal Classification (DDC)* numbers to all MARC records. This will entail a substantial increase in the output of decimal numbers as MARC encompasses more and more languages and forms of material. It seems unlikely, however, that the Library will provide universal decimal classification numbers or that it will undertake to develop a new system to replace the present LC classification.

[In 1976 the Library began converting its preliminary catalog records to MARC form so as to build an automated Process Information File (PIF).] This file controls items that have entered the technical processing flow until they are represented by regular LC catalog records. The automated file will have several advantages over the present manual file: the information it contains will be more up to date and it will be possible to search the file in more than one way. Because the PIF data are incomplete and the choice and form of main entry are subject to change, a subset of the MARC format will be used.

Input will begin with English language materials and then expand to other languages. In building this file we plan to use records created by other national centers. Agreements have been reached with the National Library of Canada and the Bibliothèque Nationale not only to use their records this way but also to redistribute them in an unaltered form. It is hoped that similar agreements can be made with the British Library and other producers of national bibliographic data. Since the preliminary cataloging data and the redistributed national records will be available sooner than full LC cataloging data, they will be offered through the MARC Distribution Service as an aid to acquisitions work.

A major modification in the Library's traditional bibliographic services will lie in the formats in which they will be offered. Many more publications will be available in microform resulting in faster, cheaper, and more easily updateable publications. Several studies are currently in progress to analyze the needs of libraries to determine the best kinds of microform and the most useful cumulation patterns. As mentioned before, the LC subject heading list is already available in microform and it is expected that the *National Union Catalog Register of Additional Locations* will be soon available in the same way.

We also plan to make most of our bibliographic services available in machine-readable form—some through the traditional tape services and some online.

While continuing to provide these services to individual libraries, the Library will cooperate in the development of regional networks so that, whenever possible, they can take on the role of secondary distributors of LC bibliographic data online. In assisting in network development, the Library will encourage building on present systems in preference to the creation of new ones.

Along these lines, the Library is undertaking a network study funded by the National Commission on Libraries and Information Science. The objectives are to produce the following items:

1) A statement of the role of the Library in the evolving national information program over the next five to seven years, showing in priority order the steps the Library will need to take to fulfill that role;

2) A summary of the status and plans of major US library and network systems, including their basic characteristics and network experiences to date;

3) Based on the above, a statement of what appear to be the major missing components requiring implementation to assure progress in network development;

4) A statement of the Library's role in international developments;

5) A statement of the requirements for a national system of bibliographic network, including necessary products and services, with a statement showing the responsibilities of the Library of Congress in relation to the rest of the information community.

In a related activity, I serve on the Advisory Group on National Bibliographic Control which was established by the National Science Foundation, the National Commission on Libraries and Information Science, and the Council on Library Resources. Its mission is to advise the three sponsoring agencies on how best to coordinate their programs in this area and to recommend priorities for action. The six persons on the group represent libraries, abstracting and indexing services, publishing, and information delivery services. As requirements for specific projects to enhance national bibliographic control are agreed on, working groups will be set up to undertake each task. Such working groups are already studying the requirements for a national bibliographic name authority file and formats for journal articles and technical reports.

The great significance of a fully developed network will be that it will relieve libraries of the necessity of maintaining their own copies of the master data base. It is likely that a single master data base can be maintained in one location with each of the regional subsystems keeping only the portions that they actually need. Individual records will be available online on demand from the central system to the regional subsystems.

To test this possibility, the Research Libraries Group (RLG) and the Library of Congress are proposing a joint pilot project to investigate methods of allowing RLG direct online access to the MARC Master File to build their own machine-readable data base. In Phase I, RLG will use the computer at NYPL to request records from the LC/MARC file online and the desired record will be transmitted directly to the NYPL computer. Initially these records will be used to support the cataloging activities at NYPL and Columbia University. In due course Yale and Harvard will participate in the Pilot Project. In Phase II, a minicomputer communications controller will be added at NYPL to improve the communications technology on which the online access is based and an identical minicomputer will be added at LC to handle traffic loads. This controller will permit LC to access files at RLG which could set the stage for interesting experiments in cooperative cataloging. Phase I will begin as soon as possible; RLG is now writing a funding proposal. LC will supply computer services and staff from the MARC Development and Information Systems Offices, all to be reimbursed by RLG. This project will benefit LC by supplying raw data relating to transaction loads and costs. The project will also benefit all libraries by providing early experience in network design, communications protocol, and data base access.

We anticipate that eventually bibliographic information will flow in both directions in such a system. It is a recognized fact that the Library of Congress cannot possibly catalog all the books needed by all libraries in a timely fashion. We hope that the national network system will be developed to allow for decentralized input of both bibliographic and name authority records. Such records would be made available to other libraries in other systems and to some extent will be reviewed or authenticated by the Library as time permits.

The Library will continue to take initiative in providing packaged data such as the book forms of the *National Union Catalog, Films and Other Materials for Projection, Chinese Cooperative Catalog,* and *Monographic Series*. Recognizing its responsibility for ensuring the continuity and integrity of such services at a reasonable price, the Library will consider relinquishing them only when there is strong assurance that their transfer would not adversely affect the library community. At the same time, the Library acknowledges its obligation to cooperate with major abstracting and indexing services to build a comprehensive national bibliographic data base.

What are the prospects for an automated Library of Congress catalog?

By 1980 when all of current LC cataloging is in MARC form, users will consult the data primarily through online terminals. The transition to this new system will be evolutionary, not revolutionary. That is, components of the system will be implemented, tested, and evaluated in stages. For example, the Library already has access to nearly 600,000 monographic records online so that they can be searched by title key and name-title key as well as by LC card number. The compression keys are built for all main- and added-entry combinations appropriate to a record. When the response to a search query is too large, the system offers a powerful technique that permits a search to be narrowed by specifying virtually any data element or word in the desired record. Several divisions are already taking advantage of these capabilities in their daily work and their experience has pointed the way to refinements in the system.

Once this new system is fully developed, what will become of the Library's card catalogs?

When the automated system has a proven capability to meet the Library's needs, new cards will no longer be added to the Main and Official Catalogs. Of course, these catalogs will still remain indispensable guides to LC holdings not represented by MARC records. Eventually, the better of the catalogs will be published in book or microform after errors in filing arrangement have been corrected. Meanwhile, the MARC data base will be considered to be complete for cataloging purposes and new entries will be tailored only to its requirements.

By treating the MARC data base as self-contained, the Library will be free to undertake many desirable projects to enhance its quality: alteration of older name headings that are incompatible with the current rules, adoption of international standards for romanization, and more vigorous improvement of subject headings. Even more important, reliance on the MARC data base will enable the Library to make complete name and subject authority information readily available. This, in turn, will promote truly efficient decentralized input to the national bibliographic data base.

Naturally, changes stemming from these actions will affect all users of LC cataloging data, but it seems unlikely that the consequences will be catastrophic. Over the years the Library has routinely made changes in its name and subject headings and its classification numbers, and libraries have generally been able to accommodate to them. Nevertheless, each library will have to consider whether it will continue to accommodate to changes in the same way that it has in the past. The larger libraries may well wish to consider the possibility of closing their catalogs and indeed, if they plan to automate, they will almost certainly elect to do so. Smaller libraries will make other adjustments that are appropriate to their size. One possibility would be to set up parallel headings linking the old and new forms by *see-also* references.

Although the volume of changes will be significantly greater when we begin to rely on the MARC data base, their effects should not be severe. Whatever the immediate difficulties may be, they will be more than compensated for by the long-term benefits of automated bibliographic control and the vastly increased potential for collaborative effort on a national scale.

It would be a mistake to cling to the seeming comforts of the old ways at the cost of being unable to get the full advantages of the new ones. Only an incurable pessimist would refuse to concede that the future will be longer than the past.

DISCUSSION

Unidentified Speaker: Mr. Rosenthal, Mr. Berman, and many others of you can speak far more authoritatively than I about how LC copy is distributed nationally in the form of MARC records, cards, and so forth, and about networking.

I am concerned, however—and I hope some of you are, too—with *what* it is that's distributed. The human intervention, that we were assured earlier is still so necessary to the cataloging process, in fact takes place largely at the Library of Congress. That may not be altogether healthy. I think it somewhat bespeaks a professional abdication by a lot of us. Like it or not, that's how it is. Perhaps Mr. Rosenthal and Mr. Berman can comment on the quality and value of the products distributed by LC.

Sanford Berman: As a consumer of LC's human intervention, particularly in the key area of subject cataloging, I submit that the product is not what it should be and that very often it's just plain shoddy. So, in the bicentennial spirit here's a three-point bill of particulars or grievances (in addition to what was mentioned previously with respect to offensive or inauthentic terms):

(1) Failure to assign descriptors, either at all or often enough, that are already in the LC thesaurus. There are plenty of omission failures of this sort, and they litter most of the Hennepin County Library *Cataloging Bulletins*. However, fiction—from a public library standpoint, but not from a research or academic standpoint—is a terrific example of under-cataloging. It would be useful to have at least optional, bracketed, supplied, possible subject tracings with the FICTION subhead, whereas now these are almost never, or at least most sparsely, supplied.

The following two examples illustrate the point. *The Final Fires* is a recent novel by Dennis Smith and was reviewed last Sunday in *The Minneapolis Tribune*. It's clear from the dust jacket and from the review that it deals with some topics that are particularly interesting now, such as firefighters in New York City, specifically the effect of a firefighter's strike upon the City. It was assigned no subject tracings by LC. Only the title was traced. Similarly, Nicholas Meyer's best-selling *Seven Percent Solution* includes interesting characters. Protagonists such as Dr. Watson and Sherlock Holmes have become pseudopersonalities. There is a terrific interest in Holmesiana nowadays. I needn't belabor that to anyone. Sigmund Freud also appears as a character. Again, no subject tracings were assigned by LC. But I think these would have certainly been *people-responsive* tracings, and we had to add them at Hennepin. It cost us time and trouble. LC could have, I submit, done this work once for the entire country.

(2) Failure to recognize new topics, or a failure to recognize them until it's almost ridiculously too late, that is, after there has been abundant literary warrant for them. For instance, ROCK MUSIC was only recognized ten years after the fact. There is now an even better (or worse) example that supplants rock music as the classical example of, not cultural lag, but musical lag, and that's GOSPEL MUSIC or GOSPEL SONGS, which has just now been established.

A corollary of this is the failure to promptly create headings for genuinely new and relevant topics. For instance, we find that children's literature, alternative culture, radical movements, and ethnic themes don't get adequate treatment. At our library in Minnesota, which is not a huge collection with the resources of an academic library or LC, we have clearly identified material that deals with affirmative action, alternative energy sources, homesteading, Chinese-American boys, androgyny, food co-ops, many types of business and consumer frauds, national liberation movements, bedtime, Kwanza, the Afro-American holiday, mudpies, leprechauns, senior power, red power, the Chinese New Year, prisoners' rights, and workers' control. None of these, to my knowledge, has been appropriately subject cataloged by the Library of Congress.

(3) Failure of LC cataloging exhibits to contemporize archaic, or just simply awkward, forms that impair both access and credibility. They make us look like the stereotype of old fogies. For instance: *rhyme* is still RIME; *gypsy* is spelled

G-I-P—most of us are instructed to spell it "g-y-p." We're not English. MOTOR TRUCKS: The freeway signs in the country don't say *motor trucks*, they say *trucks*. And that's what most of our people say. CRUELTY TO CHILDREN is quite clearly *child abuse*. That's what everybody is talking and writing about. DEFORMITIES—GENETIC ASPECTS is an aspect of *birth defects*, and that has not yet become a standard LC heading.

These kinds of changes, incidentally, are relatively easy to effect through the sort of authority control system that, may I say, was so brilliantly described yesterday afternoon by Mr. Malinconico. And may I say parenthetically that at least two publishers out of the enormous number that are so often touted as belonging to the CIP program have themselves become so distressed at how their books are being mislabelled by LC subject cataloging through CIP that they're now printing their own homemade and superior cataloging in publication data.

William Welsh: Fortunately for all of us in this room and for the nation's library, Mr. Berman and Mr. Blume, chief of our Subject Cataloging Division, are in communication. I just recently talked to Mr. Blume. He has a very high regard for the communication, and I think that he is responsive to your suggestions, and will make changes. We fortunately do have forums for bringing changes to our attention. One is the written word, letters to LC, and no one is particularly shy on that score nor should be. There's also the Subject Analysis Committee of ALA, which I think has been very useful. For example, the most recent meeting of that group endorsed the recommendation of the Black Caucus that we change BLACKS and NEGROES to AFRO-AMERICANS. We announced that change in the *Cataloging Service Bulletin* which is at press. We happen to have a consultant in the library who heard about this change and recommended that we do a little more surveying on this. But we are trying to be responsive. There are two sides to a number of these issues.

I don't pretend to defend what we are doing at any gathering such as this. I expect that somebody will get up and make some very constructive suggestions. I welcome those suggestions. I think that we have established a communication which we have lacked in the past. The automated system will enable us to make the changes without reference to the old catalog, and that's been one of our great handicaps. The greatest handicap was the fact that we weren't as receptive to change as we should have been and I think we're now on a different track.

Joseph Rosenthal: I've been somewhat familiar with what Mr. Welsh has been talking about. I think we've all had our chance to read in the *Information Bulletin* his June statement about the Library of Congress as the National Bibliographical Center, the current activities, and the projected future activities. It's a staggering list of accomplishments, and considering bureaucracy and some of the internal problems of the Library of Congress, I think that the Library deserves a great deal of credit and commendation. I'll take the opportunity later in the day to talk about some of the changes and perhaps you all will want to raise questions.

I do have a few particular questions though. One regards the Process Information File. I realize that the availability of this information online internally at LC is extremely important. I would ask Mr. Welsh, is it important to distribute this information to other libraries? Do we really need it that badly? We found that CIP information on tape causes us certain problems and we're questioning whether it's really worth it in terms of finality of data and in terms of revision that we find we have to make sometimes after we've used the CIP data. But if LC is going to use a subset of MARC as a record format for Process Information File data, we would be very interested in being able to have an outline of the format for that subset. Will it be available?

Welsh: Yes.

Rosenthal: Good. A second question. From what you said about the quantity of data, can we assume that you are anticipating that LC cataloging output will remain stable for the next half dozen years and perhaps even further? And if so, would you say that the stability in terms of quantity will allow for attention to improved quality control in cataloging, in subject heading and consistency of authority information?

Joan Marshall raised a point I'd like to reiterate, and that is the suggestion that a separate cataloging code be developed for research libraries on the one hand, and another for smaller libraries—and I'm not sure what the exact parameters of the community were that she meant—that would include public libraries and probably smaller academic libraries. Do you think that that is a viable suggestion, and have you considered this at all in the Library of Congress?

Welsh: Let me take the last question first. Mr. Scilken has mentioned that in the past. I'm not sure that we need two separate cataloging codes. We can have some discussion on that subject. I think that Mr. Scilken's point was that there's so much material on the traditional three-by-five record that it's less useful, that it's distracting, in fact, and does a disservice to the public library. There's no technical reason why we can't eliminate such material. We haven't developed any plans as yet for that, but I think that it can be done, if that would meet the objective.

Regarding LC's Process Information File (PIF) distribution, let me go over this in just a bit of detail. I don't know the answer to your question of whether you need it or not. We were simply going to make it available if you want it. Let me explain how I think this can benefit you. The PIF will include, as I said, international MARC records. We are getting MARC tapes from the British Library and the National Library of Canada. We can hang these tapes on our system and we can extract from them those records that we need for our cataloging output. It will also be a record that could be available to you on the assumption that you're going to do some cataloging that we're not going to do in the same timely way. Now, this is precisely what is done in the shared cataloging program. We get a complete record of the output of the major national bibliographies. That record is maintained in three-by-five card form for a period of three years. If your library, for example, acquires an item that we haven't acquired, you search the depository file; and if you haven't gotten the catalog data for it, you notify us. We go to that record, pull it out, change the item's priority and upgrade it so it gets out to you quickly. This is what I envision that we can do, not only with the total record of the national bibliographical agencies, but also with Automated Process Information File (APIF). If in the shared cataloging program, you identify an item that you are about to catalog, we can upgrade the priority for that item. As something you may or may not know, every item going into the processing stream is assigned a priority, and our judgment will in many cases be different from yours, as our needs will be different from yours. The reason we're maintaining and developing this elaborate control is so that we can be responsive not only to LC but to the rest of the library community. So that if you find the APIF record has been assigned priority seven—which is our lowest priority—you would know that, and you could communicate with us. As part of the shared cataloging program we will upgrade that priority and get that record to you much more quickly than we would have otherwise.

The whole concept of this APIF approach is that we will maintain a management record of what is in the stream, to be able to identify an item as quickly as possible, change the priority for any customer that's part of the system today. That's the intent. Whether you will want to get the full PIF record or not remains to be seen. Whether you will need to get it remains to be seen. Given the regional network concept I would assume you wouldn't. We would maintain the complete record. In your particular region you would inquire of the region possibly through an index. Not finding a particular item in the region, the search would be switched over to the national data base, and the record could be supplied. Whether the record needs to be distributed or not I think remains to be seen.

With respect to the output of cataloging remaining stable: I would hope not. We will continue to go to Congress and ask for additional funds to acquire materials on a more comprehensive basis. Because of the Edith Green sponsored investigation of several years ago, Congress has not given us monies to expand the National Program for Acquisitions and Cataloging (NPAC). It has given us monies to maintain NPAC at the present level. We need, for example, at least another acquisition center in Latin America. We need at least another one in Africa. We certainly need another one to cover mainland Chinese publications. We need another one in South Asia. Those are just the bare beginnings. We would like to be able to cover materials published throughout the country comprehensively. There is a large number of government document publications that we are not covering now. I'm not sure how we're going to solve that problem. We are working to try to get more agencies into the Cataloging in Publication (CIP) program. It's very difficult. It's interesting that publications in this country are far more difficult to find out about than they are in some foreign countries. Quality control is something we certainly try to improve. As the system grows larger it's more difficult to maintain that control. It's a question of the price we pay for it. We would suppose that we would like to do the best we can and get comment and input from you about the mistakes that are made. With the MARC service we ought to be able to make the changes that are brought to our attention when a mistake occurs. We have just recently made an internal change in the system. We've eliminated the editorial proof section and consolidated that operation—the editorial work—in the MARC verification group, so we're hoping that's going to improve the quality.

Lorene Pouncey: I'm not an administrator, I'm a senior cataloger. I want to thank Mr. Welsh publicly rather than writing him a private letter for providing the means for communication at the ALA San Francisco Conference this July (1975) between the people in the Processing Department at the Library of Congress and the ordinary individual librarian who goes to the ALA conferences. I would like very much for Mr. Welsh to continue to provide travel funds for the people who are under his supervision to attend future ALA conferences.

Welsh: This is a very difficult problem. Obviously it would have been most desirable to have at least Ed Blume here yesterday to respond to some of Joan Marshall's particular criticisms, and more importantly, to have visibility. This type of meeting occurs many, many times throughout the year, and unfortunately we do have a limitation on the travel funds that allow us to be present here today. As a matter of fact, half of the cost of my coming here today was borne not by ISAD or RTSD but by the Research Library Group that paid for my travel to New York. This really is a problem. We've got a sum that compared to your budget is probably magnificent. I think we spent $82,000 last year, but it's not really enough to meet the needs. We now have a new Librarian of Congress who seems to understand the necessity of our getting out and traveling, and hopefully we can improve this. One other recommendation that I made to the National Commission on Library and Information Science was for additional resources to send staff out and, of equal importance, to bring some of you in to see what we are doing.

Judith Hopkins: I would like to wholeheartedly agree with what the previous speaker said and to express my thanks to the Library of Congress and its staff members. I've always found them very, very helpful. Any time I have written to ask a question or make a comment, it seems the answers come back in the very next mail. And since I myself am not so prompt in answering letters, I appreciate other people being better than I am.

One point was not clear in your presentation about the full online cataloging that would be completely MARC: What is going to happen to those records that have been produced up to now under superimposition and therefore have headings that were created according to the *ALA 1949* or even according to earlier codes? Will they be changed and updated into *AACR* headings, or will these old *ALA 1949* headings still exist in the new online MARC data base?

Welsh: I did mention that. I probably didn't stress it though. They will be updated in due course. We're beginning that effort with the CONSER Project. We're inputting for the CONSER effort only those records according to the new rules, and we will plan to do that retrospectively. Fortunately the data base is not that great. The number of records is not that great either. So it's possible and it will be done.

Sidney Forman: I thought that the record should be clear, if I'm correct, that we were witnesses to what was probably an historic confrontation between Professor Lubetzky and Mr. Kilgour. I felt that Dr. Lubetzky represented some of the historic values in the philosophy and ideology of cataloging as it has evolved to the present period. And he carefully articulated certain questions which were surely in his mind, and I think in the minds of many librarians, about whether technological developments and computerization would allow the preservation and retention of these values. And coupled with it, the simple answer, yes, I think made for a rather historic exchange, and it surely was worth the price of admission.

Edith Spencer: I was disturbed before coming here. I am really frightened now. For two reasons: One is that the need for the kind of service that OCLC and others are providing certainly exists; but what frightens me about OCLC is the fact that I am disturbed by the integrity of their kind of cataloging. I am also disturbed by the point of view that Mr. Kilgour presented yesterday. I represent a very small library, and we have had some interest in OCLC, and though I am not involved in making administrative decisions, I had the feeling that we should not proceed with participation in OCLC. I endorse completely what Dr. Lubetzky and Mr. Malinconico said in their talks yesterday afternoon, and I am certain there are other librarians who feel the same way I do. I don't see that we're going to stand a chance unless there is something very definite coming out of this conference and similar conferences where these ideas are advanced and where this point of view has some impact on the technology and expression in the technology. I am disturbed by the fact that this seems to be a problem, and that it is not being addressed.

My second reason for concern stems from Joan Marshall's talk yesterday, and the question she raised about alternative rules that would satisfy the needs of public libraries more than the present cataloging rules do. The trend toward cataloging, both in the MARC record and the way the rules seem to be evolving at this point, ignores this point of view and does not make this kind of record available.

Maurice Freedman: Thank you very much. Mr. Welsh, would you try and relate the first part of Ms. Spencer's statement to the program you talked about, in terms of the distribution of name authorities as developed by LC?

Welsh: You couldn't keep me from it. The reason I stress and give such a high priority to our provision of authority information is because I think this is of critical importance in network development. I think that each network should have access to that data so that the integrity of the record can be maintained at the same high level that we have tried to maintain it in the past. There is no question in my mind of the value of such a record. I know that there ought to be someone to speak on behalf of Mr. Kilgour's point of view if it's at variance. It's our position that the integrity of the catalog, whether it be on three-by-five cards or a machine-readable record, is terribly important; there must be a consistent application of the rules. This is what we're trying to do, to enable this to be done by distributing both the subject and authority information. We will do what we can. We're going to take an energetic role in the development of networks with this expectation in mind.

May I speak again to the question of alternative rules. I think all of you have an opportunity to make your feelings known to the descriptive cataloging committee and to its parent body in the development of the rules. And if this, from your point of view, is a very real issue, then it's your responsibility to communicate that, so that the new rules can reflect that need.

Freedman: I think that Ms. Marshall wasn't necessarily calling for new rules, but for the implementation and use of the rules—if the principles are broad enough—so that at least basically diverse needs will be met.

Helen Druley: I will defend Mr. Kilgour. At the time OCLC started, there was no prospect for a national authority file. We tried. And you must all remember that an OCLC record is no better than the library that inputs it. If they don't care, the record will reflect that fact. You have to develop some feel for such a library. You simply note that it does lousy cataloging. Having used it for four years, we feel that way about certain members in the system. There are libraries that do very good cataloging, which we'll accept without questioning. So the authority is each individual library and what you feel about it, not what LC feels about it, because there was no way at that time to know what LC felt about it.

Freedman: For the record, at the same time that OCLC was being developed, the New York Public Library was developing an automated authority control system. I think it was a question of what was desired by the OCLC system designers. In principle, authority control was possible and being developed at the time. I don't want people to get the impression that there was a reason why it wasn't implemented.

Druley: No computer reason. The reason was the desire of the membership.

Freedman: Correct, fine.

Druley: So I feel, in Mr. Kilgour's behalf, that everybody should understand that OCLC is a bunch of individuals. And if you don't care, the system is going to reveal that.

Freedman: In fairness to Mr. Kilgour, too, I think he feels strongly that the system itself should not impose rigid requirements.

Druley: That's right.

Welsh: I want to react, though, to your description of lousy catalogers. Because I think that's not really the problem. I think there are no more dedicated group of people than the catalogers of this country. The problem is that we have a situation like form and choice of heading, and there are differences. Cataloging is of a very high standard throughout the country. There are different interpretations. The reason that we established the *National Union Catalog* seemed to be so that disparate records could be brought together and made consistent at the national level, a consistent interpretation where necessary. The Mansell pre-1956 imprint catalog, in 604 volumes, is being edited at the rate of 20,000 entries a week, and is costing $1 million per year to edit. This is not because the cataloging is lousy, but because there are different people interpreting the rules differently. It's very difficult to establish a set of rules, especially when a set of rules is to meet the needs of all people. It's our role to do the editing. So I think that's the problem, and the fact that there hasn't been a readily available authority list in machine-readable form. The *NUC* is in effect an authority file if you choose to use it that way. But you've still got to have a staff that's going to edit the resulting records to insure a consistent data base, even if you have the best group of people—and we do—inputting.

Susan Park: As a public librarian, I applaud much of the subject heading work that Mr. Berman is doing. I would, nonetheless, like to endorse what the Library of Congress is doing with respect to holding back a little on English subject headings. From this conference I gather that the Library of Congress is becoming somewhat of an international bibliographic authority. If our data are going to be used in other countries, we have to remember that English users would prefer standard English. Perhaps a little waiting on the part of the Library of Congress is good if we're going in the direction of international cooperation.

Freedman: Mr. Berman, since you were referred to, would you like to respond?

Berman: I don't like to personalize matters, but I hope, as a result of having worked in Europe for four years and Africa for four more, that I am as committed as anyone to international cooperation and amity. There's no question about that. I am also committed, however—and this is what our taxpayers are paying us for—to serving our library users, the people who are paying our salaries. That's enough said. The United States Library of Congress is precisely that, a *United States* library of the *United States* Congress. While this may sound like a contradictory and reactionary sort of chauvinism coming from an iconoclast, our people have got to come first. That's number one.

Number two is this, and it has nothing to do with subject cataloging: I believe that what Ms. Marshall mooted yesterday and what has since re-arisen in discussion is a very real, and perhaps unbridgeable, difference of interest. I'm not saying that it is bad, but it is a real difference of interest between the needs and purposes of research libraries and the public libraries, and I would also throw in the school and almost certainly junior college libraries. I would like to demonstrate with one example the importance of the alternative rules that Ms. Marshall mentioned. There is an alternative rule in the *AACR* in very fine print that we're now using. It's obviously not the one used regularly by LC. It's on the use of pseudonyms, and it allows one to use—if they are used in the books themselves—the names of Eleanor Hibbert or Victoria Holt and/or Jean Plaidy. Now these are very popular pseudonyms for one person, of course. The LC form, following the major heavy-printed rule, is Eleanor Hibbert with *see* references from the other two variations. Our people, however, who use public and school and junior college libraries, don't make such fine distinctions, nor should we insist that they do. That is a kind of, I would submit, bibliothecal arrogance on our part, a kind of intellectual elitism, if you will. If people want a book by Victoria Holt, that's what they should be able to find on the shelf and in the catalog, linked with *see also* references to other pseudonyms used by that author, as the alternative rule provides. But of course we don't get this in the cataloging copy we receive from LC.

Welsh: Being all things to all people is a difficult problem. But I think a bridge is possible. I think the annotated card program for children's literature—sometimes known as *kiddy lit*—demonstrates that we can be responsive and that the problem is akin to getting the radio audience to communicate. Make your wishes known. And if we could do this through ALA, through some of the committees that are established to meet this need, we ought to be able to be responsive or to tell you that we can't be. Because I think what you need is an answer and I think that it's our responsibility to give it to you.

Esther Greenberg: I don't know how to describe my relationship to OCLC. It started at the beginning. I first want to comment on what Helen Druley said about the way we use and select records in the data base. And I want to point out that we aren't doing anything different than we did when we used the *National Union Catalog* for contributed cataloging. When we looked at those symbols we knew which cataloging we wanted to use and which we didn't. And we're doing precisely the same thing now. For those of you who are not familiar with OCLC and the way we work, or maybe are not in close contact with your networks, the data base is not a vast receptacle into which we throw any kind of record that anybody wants to put in. The cataloging advisory committee spent a full year writing standards. We thought we were doing this for our own convenience. It turns out to be one of the most important things we have now. Any library coming into OCLC has to agree to abide by those standards. Not only are the standards written, but there is a body called the Peer Council which works very hard at enforcing the standards. We monitor the data base. We know the percentage of error; we know the percentage of allowable error. If we find that a library is exceeding that allowable percentage, we go to the library and we find out what the problem is, and if they can be helped. As a matter of fact, there are four libraries that are no longer with us for a variety of reasons. We are very concerned with the integrity of this data base. Please accept this from the person who was probably the biggest skeptic in the State of Ohio at the beginning—if we had waited for this from the start, I think we never would have started. But we have started, and I think it's to our advantage to be in OCLC. We know what our problems are, and we can attack them from that point of view.

Freedman: For the record, I doublechecked this with Mr. Welsh. Having worked there, I used to be somewhat familiar with the procedures at the Library of Congress. Any entry sent from an outside library and going into the *National Union Catalog* is searched by LC staff. So I think that there is a difference, in principle anyway, between the entries you'll find in the *NUC* and the entries going into the OCLC file. I don't mean that judgmentally either, but every record is searched before it goes into the *NUC* to insure consistency of form and eliminate duplicates. There is no central authority at OCLC nor mechanism in the OCLC system which does this searching or insures uniformity.

Joseph Leiter: Like others, I've been wondering when I'd get my money's worth out of this meeting, and I was beginning to despair. But I think that the discussion we've been having today has really identified what I think is a critical issue, and ought to be highlighted even more. The issue is not ''should we have authority'' or ''shouldn't we have authority.'' The whole issue that has been raised is the fact that we're going to have a computerized authority and also a network with online access as a critical aspect of it. An authority file that is not accessible to anybody is only a limited authority file. One of the great virtues of networking is that it democratizes access to information and access to authority. Everybody in the country becomes as big an authority as the Library of Congress when there is online access to an authority file in a network. It makes authority accessible to everyone. It isn't a question of whether somebody is a lousy cataloger. It's the fact that the rules and the regulations which are establishing authority do not exist in 4,000 places, but exist only in a limited number of places. The solution is to make it accessible to them. I think the plans to develop networking and an online authority file will do much to resolve the issue. There will be acceptance of common language and common authorities. That's the important message. It's not a question of whether the good old way is good, and the new way is trying to do something to the established principles, but that the new way is going to make it possible to realize the principles which have been established but which had not been worked on. It isn't a question of whether you're lousy; that's the result. If you don't get authoritative information, it isn't worth anything.

David Weisbrod: I think it is important to recall a point that Paul Kebabian made much better than I possibly could in his appendix to *National Aspects of Using and Creating MARC Records*, an LC publication which I recommend as being very insightful and very relevant to today's discussions. It is useful to remember that contributed or shared cataloging, or the interchange of cataloging among libraries, does not of itself make a common catalog with the kind of consistency with which Mr. Lubetzky and Mr. Malinconico are concerned. Standards, as Mr. Kebabian points out, are not enough. It is important, as Mr. Leiter said, to have tools accessible with which to apply the standards, so as to get consistent results, if consistent results are what we are interested in. If, for example, you are using the OCLC system to produce cards, you are confronted with the problem not only of what is in the OCLC data base, but also with the problem of producing cards from OCLC that are going to interfile into your existing catalog. The only way to solve these problems is either to revise your catalog in its totality or to cut it off. This is very important to remember in assessing the true significance of the potential of the LC catalog cutoff, to which Mr. Welsh refers.

Seymour Lubetzky: I'd like to submit two comments on the questions which have been raised here, because they were also raised in the course of the past revision of the code. One is raised by the special code. The question during the revision that was carried out in the fifties and sixties was to recognize that there is a difference between the diverse needs of the catalogs of public libraries and of research libraries. The question was raised whether we should not have two codes of cataloging rules. The position at the time, as I remember (I was for it), was that it is better to have one code with footnotes permitting differences. The differences are not in very many areas. If you have only one code, that code can be kept up to date more easily than two different codes. If you have one code with footnotes, then those footnotes denote an adaptation of a certain principle which is equally applied in both cases but under different circumstances. It also prevents the development of two types of catalogers, who see things differently, which they should not see because they work with the same problem. And so for all these reasons, the position taken at the time was that a code, the fullest code which is for the research libraries, footnoted with adaptations as in the case of the uniform title, would be more desirable and helpful than having two different catalog codes.

Another point is about the international considerations which have also emerged here. At the 1961 International Conference in Paris this very point arose. The representative from Italy at the time argued that the entries have to be of a kind that can be used as they are in all countries, if we are to have an international code. For example, Germany should be entered under DEUTSCHLAND, Japan under NIPPON, and so on, because they are in the international form. Now that would militate against the point that Mr. Berman has raised. We must acknowledge various other languages in international cooperation. They, unfortunately, cannot be eliminated. As long as the languages exist, they have their value. The catalog is no different from any other book. It is an instrument of communication between the library and the people who come to use it. And for that reason this is one area where the variety cannot be eliminated. To adopt terms or names in various languages, which are probably unfamiliar in a certain other language, would be to nullify the usefulness of that catalog to all of these users in the interest of cooperation. That is, in international cooperation there are limits. We can have international cooperation, but at certain points we can also have such adaptations as we have for research libraries and public libraries between one country and another.

Freedman: I would like to make a brief statement at this point. Mr. Welsh made reference to there being several of these kinds of conferences. And I think there's one difference between this conference and at least all the other conferences to which I've gone and been associated with ISAD: This one has been blessed with the presence of the brilliant mind of Seymour Lubetzky.

Suzine Nicolescu: I would like to ask Mr. Welsh about the separate coding system mentioned by Ms. Marshall yesterday for research and nonresearch library users. I would like to imagine a happy medium. Would it be feasible to construct a coding system with such flexibility that a research library could use a more expanded coding system, while nonresearch libraries can use a shortened coding system—however effected—in the same code? My second question is: Is there any office or person in the Library of Congress that responds to all the suggestions that come in from each library?

Welsh: I'll take the last item up first. It's a rather large department that you're talking about, over 1,700 employees, highly specialized, all attempting to meet your needs. So I suppose all the mail could be addressed to me, and I feel at times that's the way it comes in. But if it's a descriptive cataloging matter, it ought to go to the Descriptive Cataloging Division, if a subject analysis matter it ought to go to the Subject Cataloging Division, questions on Dewey to the Decimal Classification Division. That's what would be preferable. If that doesn't serve the need or if you don't know the addresses, we can probably do something to correct that. But any letter that comes in addressed to me will be sent to the proper place for response.

Since I wasn't here yesterday, I'm not sure about the encoding system. The list of subject headings, now known as the eighth edition and soon to be the ninth edition, theoretically takes care of that problem. It's a matter of application. And when I referred earlier to the Children's Annotated Card Program, in fact the application supposedly does that. There's a separate community that deals with the feedback to us. I suppose what I ought to do now is to request a copy of Ms. Marshall's remarks and see how we could address ourselves to that question. It deserves a response, and we'll try to give it.

The Catalog as a Public Service Tool

by Marvin H. Scilken

I would like to contrast the libraries for which the rules spoken of by Dr. Lubetzky were developed and the present day American small- to medium-sized public library.

Libraries such as that of the British Museum acquired everything and discarded hardly anything. They were used by only the small portion of the population that could gain admittance. Comparatively few people could read and write. Very few books were published. A library in the early 1800s might envision actually gathering most or much of the world's printed knowledge. Books were not usually loaned so there was an almost perfect congruence between what was in the catalog and what was on the shelf. There would be a high degree of confidence in finding that which was cataloged and what was to be found.

Can rules developed from that background hope to fit today's American typical *public* library? Collections are limited to a fraction, and in most cases a very small fraction, of each *year's* vast outpouring of America's *trade* book industry (which apparently consisted of some 40,000 titles last year). (It is recommended by the American Library Association that public libraries discard at least five percent of their collections every year in order to keep the library "fresh.") In today's economic situation we are seeing the actualization of the nongrowth library. We have libraries that contain a tiny, *constantly changing* segment of the country's printed matter. Public libraries have much of their collection *out* at all times (hopefully in circulation). Consequently, there is far less congruence between the catalog and what is to be found on the shelf. The typical user may have, from experience, developed a low degree of confidence in finding on the shelf things listed in the catalog.

Public libraries hope to include rather than exclude every possible user. Do rules descended from Panizzi's 91 rules of 1839 help or hinder public library users find the material they are seeking?

I came to the conclusion some time ago that the public libraries of this country should have their own cataloging center. I suggested this first in 1969 to offer speed in card service. ("Backlog to Frontlog," *Library Journal*, Sept. 15, 1969.)

A study done at the Burnaby (Vancouver, B.C.) Public Library in 1973 indicates that a substantial percentage of users (especially older users) never use the catalog. So we know that of those few people in the community who use public libraries, a substantial portion do not (at least in Burnaby) use the catalog. My findings, and those of my colleagues in New Jersey, though less scientific, agree with the view that less than half of the users use the catalog. The Burnaby study notes that there is remarkably little information on catalog use in small- and medium-sized *public* libraries. The Burnaby study concludes, as did a similar study in Great Britain, that public library users do not use much of the bibliographic information on the entries.

There are four, not mutually exclusive, groups of public library users, three of which use the catalog. I believe that every part of our national cataloging data has serious deficiencies for the three basic groups of public library catalog users.

One group of public library users is the *browsers*. They hardly, if ever, use the catalog. The browsers are willing to select from what the library happens to have available, much as they would if they were in a book store. Our catalogs are not necessary to this group but classification may be important.

Another group of users is the *something-on-a-subject* group. Typically they may need to fix a faucet. Any book that will supply them with that information will do. Unless the library has a whole book devoted to the repair of faucets they will have to, and do, look under one of the less specific headings, find the number(s) assigned to the subject they are seeking, and proceed to examine likely looking candidates from the array presented to them on the shelf.

There is another group of public library users that are seeking specific titles. The most important group (for they usually have no other public institution to supply them) is the *adult nonstudent* group. This group is usually seeking new titles that have just been reviewed in the newspaper or whose author has just happened to appear on T.V. For many libraries this is a very large group.

The other group seeking specific titles is *students*. They represent the *failures* of their home institution's library to have, to have in sufficient quantity, or to loan items that they need (or to otherwise discourage borrowing).

Each of these groups has different needs. Browsers don't need the catalog. The subject hunters may need only a subject to number(s) classification list. Charles Joyce, in a *Library Journal* article some years ago, suggested that perhaps we don't need to file all the subject cards that have the same classification number. He suggested a guide card that read something to the effect that—most of the books dealing with this subject will be found under the "following number." The reader was further instructed to look behind "this card" for the books bearing on this subject that don't carry this number. To find what the library owns on this specific subject the user was directed to ask to see the shelflist. Perhaps Joyce's system would serve this subject hunting group better than the present system does.

The Yale catalog-use study suggestion for more title and title-like entries would also help this group of subject-approach users. These title and title-like entries are valuable to the user in finding *newest* subjects, subjects that never developed enough of a literature to be recognized by the Library of Congress (LC), subjects that developed a literature that is not recognized by LC, or have terms that are more familiar than those currently being used as subject headings by LC.

This may be considered an argument for the dictionary catalog. Many public library users in this group do not know and do not need to know the difference between a subject head and title entry. This group will also be helped if subject cards are filed by date with the most recent filed first. Filing cards by date has several advantages. With all the changes in Dewey numbers, readers are led to the newest books. The library demonstrates that it does indeed have *new* books on a particular subject. It is a help to most users using the subject approach. (It is presumed that if one knows the author or title, one of the latter approaches is used.) And finally, it saves filers' time.

What of the two groups looking for specific books? The group looking by title or author should find *in the catalog* some listing for books on order or received. Scilken's User Loss Law states that a percentage of potential users disappears between every file. The number of *lost* potential users is geometric to the number of files to be consulted. That is, a library that has three places to look loses nine times as many potential users as a library that has only one place to look.

New books and books on order should be listed in the public catalog to at least theoretically satisfy the *catalog* requirements of the group seeking new books. (Actually having the books would be of great help too.)

The group of users seeking less recent books, usually students, are a greater difficulty. Because of buying and discarding policies of public libraries, this group frequently does not find their books listed or, if listed, do not find the book on the shelf.

How does all this fit in with the subject we are here to enlighten? Public libraries not burdened with huge collections need catalogs and a cataloging code that reflect their situation.

Let me call once again for public libraries to establish their own cataloging centers with their own codes so that the greatest number of library users can be best served. A public library cataloging code for small- and medium-sized public libraries might include the following (the list is not exhaustive):

AUTHOR ENTRIES

Authors should be entered by their names (in English) as they appear on title pages (PAYNE, ROBERT not PAYNE, PIERRE STEPHEN ROBERT) with appropriate authority files to take care of variations that would scatter these entries. Libraries may or may not establish references to other pseudonymous names. (What good does it do a reader to know that Victoria Holt's real name is Burford, Eleanor, according to the Cumulative Book Index (CBI), or Hibbert, Eleanor, according to LC.) A reader *might* like to know that Hibbert-Burford also writes under CARR, PHILLIPPA and PLAIDY, JEAN. Since books by these authors are in different styles, should public libraries spend the amount of time getting them together that we do? I am fairly certain that this amazes and confuses many users.

Small- and medium-sized public libraries have comparatively few books by corporate bodies. In any case, a book by a body or several authors should be entered as it is likely to be cited by the uninitiated in composing bibliographies. Cataloging in Publication (CIP) may help in the compilation of bibliographies and result in a better fit between bibliographies and our catalogs.

The cataloger should feel free to enter or delete any or all authors on the title page. The question should always be, will this entry be used by enough users to justify its cost? Author entries that will not be missed should not be entered (for instance, authors of booklets in the Monarch and similar series. We may be doing the author a service by *not* entering his/her name.)

TITLE ENTRIES

Titles should usually be entered. Subtitles should usually be entered. As discussed later under Subject Entries, *catch words* and *synthetic titles* (title-like entries) should be made when the cataloger feels they will be used. Movie titles should be added if the title of a movie differs from that of the book.

SUBJECT HEADING ENTRIES

Subject headings should be established as soon as a *single* trade book is produced on a *new* subject. We should have a dynamic subject heading list, constantly changing, with *live* headings replacing *dead* ones to reflect the currency of our small collections. (I understand that the Library of Congress recatalogs appropriate books after it establishes a new heading entry but the average public library has no way of knowing what books have been recataloged.)

Use title and title-like entries to cover gaps in the subject approach. It makes no difference to a reader who is led to the appropriate location on the shelf whether the lead was from a title or a subject entry.

We might indicate through *grades* (such as those used in some LC Science Tracer Bullets and perhaps elsewhere) whether the subject heading for a book is *highly relevant, relevant,* etc.

Genre subject headings for types of works (Mysteries, Science Fiction, Gothic, Regency, Plantation, Adventure, etc.) might be added. Perhaps there could even be more finely defined headings such as Future Life-Fiction, Famous Detectives, Puzzle Mysteries, etc.

Subject head fiction more heavily, such as is done in Wilson's *Fiction Catalog* and the British *Fiction Index*. Add lists of books by and/or about various ethnic groups arranged by classification numbers. Names in common use, if not pejorative, should be used as subject headings.

Public librarians need their own subject headings list which will be dynamic —something more than *Sears* and LC's annotated card subject heading list and something much less complex than LC's subject heading list. Libraries that aren't burdened by millions of volumes do not need subject heading lists prepared for million-volume libraries.

FORMAT

Our entry format should delete, or at least separate, items that are not of use to most users. The format of every item in the entry should be tagged to be not only machine readable, but tagged so that people can read it too. It is ironic, is it not, that we are willing to apply tags so that machines but not people can read the data. We in public libraries need *people-readable* cards. Public library cards should be simple—have no abbreviations, no unusual punctuation or symbols, and be written in English. (The Orange, NJ fiction card has a legend across the top, "Look for under author's last name in fiction section.")

CROSS-REFERENCES

Cross-references should be made extensively. Cross-references to be made should be indicated somewhere on the entry as a guide to libraries without professional catalogers.

MISCELLANEOUS

Add entries for publishers where appropriate (as is done at the Hennepin County Library). Famous fictional characters might be entered. Enter common misspellings. Any possible way that a work could reasonably be approached should be considered. Subject headings should be nationalistic, i.e., —U.S. should be dropped whenever possible. It should be assumed that most public library users are looking for things that concern them.

OMISSIONS

Omit most joint authors, illustrators, editors, etc. For fiction, omit title entries that most likely will not be used if "author to genre location" will suffice. Not every book in a genre needs to be subject headed. Suggested alternatives: "Mysteries will be found. . . . ", "Regency novels have been written by the following authors." Books that the cataloger believes will only be approached through browsing need not be cataloged at all.

The central concern of a public library catalog must be *retrievability* by the largest possible number of users. *Authorship* should *not* be the central concern of a public library catalog. Not who created the work, not international consideration (*ISBD*), but how this work may most easily be found by our publics must be our concern. (Our economic future seems to indicate there won't be many librarians, friendly or otherwise, to help users.)

A number of studies indicate that many users are seeking *new* works. New works presently take time to be entered in printed catalogs. Perhaps a weekly updated COM (Computer Output Microform) roll film catalog or an online catalog will answer this problem. At the present time online catalogs seem to be prohibitively expensive for public libraries.

If some or all of the suggested entries are made, many more entries will be made than heretofore. With the high cost of labor in acquiring items, the additional costs involved in finding more users for the material should be justified. The use of the catalog may be more successful to more users thereby encouraging catalog use, helping to justify the catalog's cost. It may also make the library more responsive to more users. Librarians should give less thought to overburdening the catalog than to overburdening the user.

We have *excellent traditional* cataloging for works desired by comparatively few people, and *poor or no* cataloging for works sought by others. (CIP may be a help if we are willing to go back to typing our own cards.) We must study how people actually approach libraries and their catalogs for the material they desire. It was Lipetz, I believe, who suggested that the very way we catalog our materials may influence the users' approach. Perhaps we could do something better, something more, something less. People should need to know as much to use our catalogs as they do to use the telephone book or Sear's and Ward's general catalogs. Public library catalogs must be considered primarily as *merchandising* tools rather than as scholarly ones.

Retrievability should be our watchword and people should be our concern.

APPENDIX

FIGURE 1

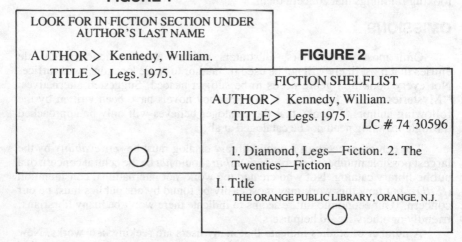

LOOK FOR IN FICTION SECTION UNDER
AUTHOR'S LAST NAME

AUTHOR > Kennedy, William.
TITLE > Legs. 1975.

FIGURE 2

FICTION SHELFLIST
AUTHOR> Kennedy, William.
TITLE> Legs. 1975.
LC # 74 30596

1. Diamond, Legs—Fiction. 2. The
Twenties—Fiction
I. Title
THE ORANGE PUBLIC LIBRARY, ORANGE, N.J.

AUTHOR AND FICTION SHELFLIST CARDS

Shows format and subject headings used at the Orange Public Library.
Diamond's real name is Jack but he is entered as we and the author believe he is
best known to users. (The LC catalog card number is recorded for a possible *union
numerical register*.) This is a sample shelflist card. The actual card would have
book identification number(s) (accession number) for most hardback copies
owned by the library.

FIGURE 3

Title. . . . Three Days of the Condor.
Movie based on Six Days of the Condor.

Author: Grady, James.

Title: Six days of the condor.
copyright 1974.

SAMPLE CARD SHOWING MOVIE TITLE ENTRY

FIGURE 4

> Wrong title: Experimental religion.
>
> 234.2   Author: Niebuhr, Richard R.
>
> Ni   Title: Experiential religion.
>   Harper & Row [c1972]

SAMPLE CARD SHOWING MISSPELLED TITLE ENTRY

FIGURE 5

> 658.85*
> SUBJECT: MARKETING RESEARCH
> You may also be interested in books listed in
> this catalog under:
>   SUBJECT: MARKET SURVEYS
>   SUBJECT: MOTIVATION RESEARCH
>   (MARKETING)
>   *Numbers indicate where most of the books on
> this subject may be found on the shelves.
>   If you have any difficulty the librarian at the
> reference desk will be glad to help you.

**SAMPLE "SEE ALSO" CARD BASED ON A
CHARLES JOYCE READING**

FIGURE 6

> SUBJECT: THE BICENTENNIAL, BOOKS
>   OF INTEREST ON
>
> 325.26   Author: Franklin, John Hope.
> Fr
>   Title: From slavery to freedom. Knopf,
> copyright 1956.

SAMPLE CARD SHOWING AN UNUSUAL SUBJECT ENTRY

A sample card showing a catalog subject entry not usually found in most
libraries. (The Bicentennial Subject Heading and its scope was suggested by

Katherine Gaines.) Cards with this particular subject heading are filed in shelflist order to help librarians cope with questions such as "I need a book on slavery during the Colonial Period." Subject heading entries for books by or about various ethnic groups in the community are also maintained in shelflist order.

FIGURE 7

> THIS BOOK IS ABOUT:
> BERLE, ADOLF AUGUSTUS, 1895-1971
> 973.9   Author: Berle, Adolf Augustus.
> Be   Title: Navigating the rapids, 1918-1971;
> Publisher: Harcourt. Year of publication: 1973.
>
> For other items on the subjects discussed in this book, look in the card catalog under the following headings:
> 1. Berle, Adolf Augustus, 1895-1971. 2. United States —Politics and government—20th century. 3. United States —Foreign relations—20th century. 4. United States— Economic conditions.

A "SCILKEN SUPER CARD"

A "Scilken Super Card" on which most items are identified. For full discussion and possibly better alternatives, see *The Unabashed Librarian*.

FIGURE 8

> Title: The electric kool-aid acid test.
> Title: The electric cool-aid acid test.
> Title: . . . kool-aid acid test.
> Title: . . . cool-aid acid test.
>
> 301.431   Author: Wolfe, Tom.
> Wo   Title: The electric kool-aid acid test.
> New York, Farrar, Straus and Giroux, copyright 1968.

SAMPLE CARD OF VARIANT TITLES

Sample of card showing variant titles that have been found useful. The tracings are at the top so that the reproduced card need not be returned to the typist for retyping of the heading after printing. A highlighter is used to indicate the filing position.

DISCUSSION

Sanford Berman: First, I would like to make a minor point. The difficulty in rendering an instant judgment, as Mr. Scilken invited, on a particular piece of cataloging illustrates something that I think is a general difficulty. It illustrates something that is increasingly not done, but which I still regard as essential. If you're going to make a judgment as to how good you think the cataloging was, you really ought to examine the material that is being cataloged, beyond just examining the title page. Mr. Scilken's remarks underscore what has become at least something of a leitmotif in these past couple of days. They are most significant to me from the perspective of public library service. The issue is the research and nonresearch library dichotomy. I believe that the reality is that the chasm between these two interests can't be bridged simply by including, as I think Dr. Lubetzky was suggesting, an alternative rule as a footnote at the bottom of a page in a code. However nice a gesture that might be—and it's appreciated, certainly, because most data are now centrally supplied even to smaller libraries—the central suppliers and producers such as the Library of Congress do not follow the alternative rule found in the footnote at the bottom of the page. They are not likely to provide—in fact, they have said in essence that they will not provide—the simplified format, whatever form it might take, that Mr. Scilken and others have suggested. Such a format would be far more appropriate to nonresearch libraries. It would exclude, for instance, not only abbreviations but also some particular collation data that are utterly, I believe, irrelevant to our users. No public library user has benefited much, to my knowledge, from information expressing centimeter sizes for spines.

My wrap-up point is this: If, in terms of the content and format, what we require and want is something very different from what LC and the other central suppliers are providing for their research library oriented clients, and we want it to be relatively economical, we probably need a nonresearch oriented cataloging center. Let me add that I am not even completely sanguine about such a solution.

Marvin Scilken: Mr. Berman, that was the part I didn't get to. I suggest that it be done at a public library with branches. It might be New York Public, Hennepin County, or some other public library that is as interested in cataloging as in feedback from its users, and it should concentrate on the books we buy most. Mr. Welsh told us this morning that LC processes 250,000 titles a year. We buy from a universe of 40,000 trade books a year. Consequently, we are not concerned about the other 210,000 records that are produced. In fact, they hurt us because it slows everything down for us. And I think this could be done economically

Joseph Rosenthal: I share Mr. Berman's feeling that a thread has run through this past day and a half. I think it's a false thread. I'm somewhat sad to hear the dichotomy between research libraries and nonresearch libraries regarded as unbridgeable. I think a lot of the things that were well said this morning pointed in the opposite direction. The comment made by Mr. Leiter was in that direction as well. I know that confrontation and conflict sell newspapers, but I don't think that this conference is the place for confrontation and conflict. There are a lot of things that can be done for all segments of the library community, the information community, and the community that serves library and information users. Things that can be done by the Library of Congress, the American Library Association, and other associations in the library and information field.

I was very interested to hear what Mr. Scilken had to say about the techniques that are used in his library and other public libraries. But I would submit that those techniques, while the particular ones may be novel, represent some of the many examples of similar techniques used by lots of different types of libraries. I think special libraries deserve a great deal of credit in this area, and their innovations have not been acknowledged widely enough. But that's not the only place. Some of the largest research libraries use many techniques which are similar to what Mr. Scilken was talking about. I know that in the branch libraries at Berkeley the librarians who have many of the same problems in getting books of immediate interest to users do all sorts of things for their public in the way of fast accessibility, and of highlighting subject interest, using many innovative techniques. As a matter of fact, in some of our libraries, in some of your libraries I'm sure, there are things that we might point out to some of the public libraries—ways to "do things good" for users. I'd like to see some serious attempts made to do that rather than to make the gap more complete and more unbridgeable.

Scilken: I'm glad to hear that we're all doing the same thing or similar things. It's a shame we all have to do it separately. We have to toy and play with cards to make them accessible to our readers. But it seems like a waste of money. If it could be done economically, as Mr. Berman points out, we would get our data in usable form, and not have to play with it after we get it.

The National Library of Medicine has its own subject headings which LC prints on its medicine related cards. Mr. Berman and I are not asking for the same treatment as the National Library of Medicine. Let us have our subject headings and perhaps our entries. If they can do it for them and if they can do it for the *kiddies*, perhaps they can do it for the adults too, maybe on the same card, maybe with the same code, but it's not there now. I'm sure that we would be happy to find somebody to submit our data to LC for us, if LC would print it on the card. But the card, the three-by-five card, may have to be reduced somewhat. Look at all the type on it.

Maurice Freedman: I'd like to make a point as the moderator of this conference, in regard to what the purposes of this conference were. There was no attempt or effort to engender conflict. As my favorite ex-president used to say, I want to make perfectly clear that I wanted to see the different points of view and issues in the cataloging world today openly discussed in a meeting that is open to all the people who have demonstrated their interest in it. I'm not particularly happy about the fact that most of the ALA and Washington meetings where the decisions are made are small meetings of committees, and this is one place where the issues could be openly brought out, discussed, and debated.

Judith Hopkins: This question is not really addressed to Mr. Scilken; it is addressed to the audience as a whole. I was wondering if there was anything that would be useful to us from the German experience. I know very little about the cataloging in Germany, and I trust that there is somebody in this audience who knows more than I do. It has been my understanding that in the past they have had two cataloging codes, the Prussian Instructions for the use of the research libraries and another code for public libraries. I also have the impression, and it is no more than an impression, that the two are coming closer and closer together. I do know that the Germans have brought out a new cataloging code. Does anybody know whether this is a code for all German libraries? Or is this just for the research-oriented libraries? In short, are the Germans going in the direction we have gone towards one code or have they had success with two codes for two different types of libraries? If so, can we learn from their experience?

Scilken: May I make one point? The other part I left out is that I don't see any computer use other than what is going on now for staff use at our library and our type of library. We have people who can't use a copying machine, and I would hate to sit them down at a terminal and say this is how you find books or records or what have you. It's just not in the cards for us at this time, both in terms of users and money.

Seymour Lubetzky: In answer to Ms. Hopkins' question with regard to general practice: The Prussian rules, which have been translated into English, are more strictly structured than ours have ever been. They are very strict in terms of bringing together the editions and works of an author. The Germans have participated very actively at international conferences on cataloging principles, and they have adopted the Paris Principles. I am not quite aware of what is going on right now in their development of a new code based on the Paris Principles, but they have been adopted.

I do not mean to imply that all cataloging codes that are based on the Paris Principles will be identical. I'll give you just one illustration. Under the Paris Principles, the Germans have taken the Cartwright option. That was one concept which separated most strikingly the Anglo-American rules and the Prussian rules. They have adopted it, but their method of implementation may be different. There is a strong opinion among some—I don't know whether or not they are a majority —that they should make an added entry under the corporate body, but for them the concept of authorship is still one that does not quite encompass a corporate body. For them the concept of an author is a person who sits and writes. A corporate body doesn't sit down and write a work. They can accept the idea of responsibility by corporate body, but that will be expressed by means of an added entry. This may not be a complete answer to you, but it illustrates the fact that codes based on the same principles are not necessarily alike in every respect.

Karin Begg: I send a lot of students to our public libraries to get a variety of books, because our collections are not meant to be the same, and I should hope they would be treated as more than nonpersons when they get to the public library. I'm a little disturbed by the dichotomy that's being stressed between the public library and the research library. Undergraduates in particular have many of the same needs as the users of the public library. They, too, need more up-to-date, more popularly structured subject headings. The research population of the library is relatively small. Part of my job is to act as an interface between the user and the catalog. Most people come to me with problems and can't make their way around because the library catalog is structured for the research worker. So I don't see that we need two different codes.

Scilken: Perhaps you might adopt our code.

Begg: Mostly for reasons of economics, I don't think we can do that much work on our own. We have to go with OCLC for better or for worse.

Scilken: I think that's my main point. You're stuck with it.

Begg: I'd like to see more of an incorporation of a popular approach in what we are stuck with.

Scilken: Right. But that's the main point. You're stuck with it: It's been foisted on us, and we can't operate well because we have to sell our service. We can't afford to have a lot of unsatisfied people around because they won't pay us. We have to sell everything we do. If it doesn't elicit a response, we have to try to get rid of it.

Begg: I should hope that we would be motivated by higher reasons to provide the same sort of service.

Margaret Wright: I'd like to ask whatever happened to the "People's University." I still want it. I use a college library and a public library. I also use the Central Reference Library of the City of London when I'm there. I find that other libraries are more and more often failing me, and now the catalog is too.

Scilken: How so?

Wright: They will buy more books about Tarzan, but they won't buy the complete works of Trollope.

Scilken: Well, I think you're looking in the wrong place.

Wright: Oh, yes. But there are many people who aren't college graduates.

Scilken: Well, I happened to inherit a full set of Trollope, and I had the guts to throw it out. I threw it out because you're not living in our town where nobody else seems to be interested in Trollope. Well, the point is that we cannot exist looking down our noses at people and saying, "You should like Trollope instead of Tarzan." And if they want Tarzan, we have to buy and catalog it so they can find it. If people want Trollope, we can get it for them, but we won't necessarily own it. We can borrow it from Princeton.

Jack Kent: I was struck by some of the techniques that you have presented just now on the screen. And it seems to me that it's not entirely a problem of the data that you're getting from the Library of Congress, so much, perhaps, as what's done with it by the processing agencies that produce the cards. What struck me particularly was the line you have at the top of the card "This book is about." And since the data on the MARC tapes have tags, it seems to me theoretically . . .

Scilken: Wait, wait! May I just cut you short, because I've discussed this problem with Peter Jacobs just this week.

Freedman: Peter Jacobs is with Brodart, Incorporated, a commercial processor.

Scilken: He said they can't do it unless a lot of people want it, because it's a very expensive program to print out, in English language, the kind of things I want printed out. I can't blame him; he was going to lose money. Now we could do it for ourselves, perhaps, we could have Brodart or Josten's do it. There have to be a lot of us who would want to buy it. The sad truth of the matter is a lot of public libraries don't give a damn about cataloging.

Hugh Atkinson: This time I'm going to speak as a library administrator. We have brought out a lot of differences that are no differences at all. You are telling us that the public library has to sell its services to the public. Now what do you think we are doing in the college libraries? I wouldn't last a year in my position if I didn't spend at least 50 percent of my time, and much of the time of many of my librarians and my staff, in public relations. We have to sell our services; we have the same problems that you have. We have a public too. It may be a little bit different. But, you know, our students read Tarzan, too, and if they want it we have to give it to them. We have to give it to them whether we own it or not. It's about time that we worked together. We have to listen to your needs. It may be that some of the subjects and pseudonyms are valid and that we need them. My children come home with new ideas. And I'll look at the new terms. My junior high school boy uses my college library more efficiently than some of our juniors and seniors, too. So it goes all across the line.

I live in a community where there are a large university and a college, and the demand on the public library is quite different from that in some other area. Now it's about time that we got together. We can use the same principles. We can interpret them differently. If your people do not come and ask more questions, then ask yourself if there is something wrong, and if you should be selling your services better. The catalog isn't used as much as it should be; it isn't a simple tool. So are many other things. Some people cannot even use a telephone book so we have to help them. We should be available to help them. So let's work together on this.

Lubetzky: This gentleman just said something about which I feel strongly. A library—I think it was recognized a long time ago—is a complex instrument. The catalog is of necessity a complex instrument. We cannot simplify everything. By simply reducing it to the lowest level, efficiency suffers. From the point of view of a university library—it applies also to a public library—libraries are institutions that have a very important function, an educational function, to fulfill. As the lady asked before, what happened to the people's university? The library is the people's university. It is another educational institution. I think education, from the public school to the high school and through college and the university, should make provision to teach people how to use a library, how to use that institution. In buying an automobile, do not ask people: "How would you prefer to drive the automobile? Would you like the clutch in the back or in the front? Would you like the brakes as something you pull from behind?" This is an engineering problem. If things are wrong, this too is an engineering problem. People have to make the decision that a system can be designed. This is perfectly obvious, and there is no question about it. But once this decision has been made, the objective is for the system to work properly. That is, for example, the car should stop when you want it to stop; it should go exactly where you want it to go. That will not be accomplished by asking: "How many people are for having the steering wheel in a round form or some other form?" You can't do that.

Your library will never be reduced to an efficient instrument—and it is of necessity an instrument, just as the catalog is an instrument—by asking people: "How would you like to find it?" Because there is an assumption there which I think is misleading. You think that the people who go to the catalog know exactly what they want, but they do not know. They grasp for something that they know. They have heard about a work and they will ask for it by author, by title. It is misleading to think that the idea is to provide them with the author or the title as fast as possible. You will not provide it for them if they do not know exactly what they want. You heard everything I said yesterday, and I apologize for saying the same thing again. When you think that providing a book for a person as fast as possible has served that individual's purpose, you will fail very often, because you have exactly what s/he wants, but you have it under another name or another title, and thus cannot find it. In short, I think that what librarians have to recognize and what schools have to recognize is that language is an instrument by means of which we communicate. Librarianship has a language that is very difficult to learn, but unless you learn it and know the grammar that allows you to operate the language, you will have nothing with which to communicate. The catalog is an instrument of communication; we can never get away from that. A person who is going to use that instrument must learn how to use it. The answer is not by trying to reduce it to the lowest possible level, because efficiency is the price that you will pay for such a reduction.

Scilken: I disagree. I think we can make the catalog easier to use without dropping its efficiency, and that's been our object. We want as many people to use the catalog and the library and the books as possible. But we don't do it by scaring them. The study at the Burnaby Public Library (Canada) showed that the more education people had, the more they used the catalog. But I'm not sure what that buys us. I see very few teachers in the public library. We are very rarely visited by teachers or librarians from the schools, and I'm not optimistic about people learning to use the card catalog in school.

The Electronic Catalog

by Hugh C. Atkinson

I suppose there is no more difficult topic to speak about than that of an item which doesn't exist or exists only in the imagination. That is the case with the electronic catalog at the moment, at least the electronic catalog for Ohio State.

This is not to say that there are not things now in existence which are very similar to catalogs, that is, tools which now serve as guides to a body of literature, and which are electronic or based on machine-readable or machine-accessible data and are online. Some of the most obvious of these are the three general text-searching programs now widely available throughout the country which are, in effect, searching techniques that are not dependent on any particular set of data. These are DIALOG from Lockheed, BASIS from Battelle, and Systems Development Corporation's (SDC) ORBIT. *The New York Times* Information Bank is another example of such a device, although it is more closely wedded to the text itself than the other three systems.

The electronic catalog that we plan for Ohio State University (OSU) is, in fact, BASIS, as installed in the Ohio College Library Center (OCLC) computer. We are already dealing with a large portion of the catalog online and have been doing so for the past four years. An abbreviated record of each of the titles in the Ohio State University Libraries—a record approximately 103 characters long, drawn from the shelflist—has been used as a remote catalog access and circulation system since 1971. The system does allow for known-item searching. Ben-Ami Lipetz's study at Yale indicated that the biggest bulk of academic library use (or at least catalog use) is for known items. The results at Yale, which seem to be applicable throughout the country, indicated that approximately 80 percent of the people entering the library were searching for a particular item. (Why is another question.) It is that kind of search that our present system provides. Over 3 million such searches were made last year and, with searching at that level, it is clear that some serious inroads on catalog use have already been made. The catalog is still there, and one has the option of using either it or the Library Control System (LCS) for known-item searching. As far as we can tell, patrons are choosing the auto- mated system. After all of the catalog-use studies of attitude, measurement, effectiveness, and the like, we still know so very little about why people use the catalog and how they use it. We have some inklings though. The Lipetz study confirms our suspicions that much of the complexity is not needed by most of the patrons; that is, the most complex portions of the catalog are, of course, the subject, series, and other added entries, and the structure of cross-referencing to provide linkage. It is precisely these portions which are least used by our users.

We also know that large catalogs are not only incredibly expensive to maintain, but are increasingly impossible to use. The practical experience of any librarian at a catalog information desk will confirm this over and over again. So we are now at a stage where the Library of Congress (LC) has made a clear decision to close its catalogs in 1979 or early 1980 [now 1981], and when the costs of any labor-intensive activity—and maintenance of a card catalog is certainly labor-intensive—are rising astronomically. It is a time when the tool being maintained is becoming less and less useful on a per-item-contained basis and the demands for speed, accuracy and at least rudimentary Boolean search capability are growing greater. It is a time when technology is available and when the basic data—that is, the catalog information itself—are already produced in machine-readable form.

It seems that it is time to close the card catalog and to continue the analysis of the collections and the guides to them with an electronic information retrieval system rather than a manual one. We do not propose to make a complete substitution of an electronic system for the card catalog. We now have well over a million titles which account for approximately 3 million volumes. We also know that a very small percentage (somewhere around 20 percent) of these items account for a large portion (approximately 80 percent) of the total circulation each year. Thus, it does not seem at all feasible or worthwhile, no matter how cheaply one might be able to store data electronically these days, to add any further cost to that system, especially if that cost is incurred by the addition of data that will not be used.

Since approximately 1970, we have been producing the cards that go into our catalogs through OCLC. Such production has entailed the production of bibliographic records in the Machine Readable Catalog (MARC) format. This is true for all items in the western languages. The decision has become more and more clear that nationally we will transliterate from the nonwestern languages, and by the end of the decade, we will be producing all bibliographic records in MARC format. We can use a data base with a five-year overlap for all western language items and can begin to transliterate items in the nonwestern languages in preparation for the switchover at LC. Having already available to us machine-readable records of our cataloging enables us at least to have solved the data preparation issue.

OCLC is installing BASIS in its machine; thus, we will be able to search by subject and by full text processing the records stored in that system, the records that have made up our catalog for the last five years. The serious problems are not the cross-reference problems, the syndetic structures, or the technical complications of authority files, that is, the continuation of items in the newer catalog in the same form as the older one, and the like. These are all problems which are inexplicable now to the users and are not likely to be major deterrents in the future to the users of the electronic catalog. Rather, the two most obvious problems are the number of terminals one has available and the speed with which interactive systems are able to provide data. These factors are, of course, connected and are in some ways interdependent.

We have had great success using an algorithm or a code technique of searching the rather slim records we use with the LCS system. The application of four characters of the author's last name and five characters of the first word of the title for author/title searching, and of four characters of the first word of the title and five characters of the second word of the title for title-only searching have proved to be extremely fast. The lack of precision has not proved to be a detriment at all, but rather, in many cases, an advantage. For instance, the code for Betty Smith's *A Tree Grows in Booklyn,* which is SMIT TREE space, produces not only the three or four editions of that American novel owned by OSU, but also two editions of Smith's *Tree Crops.* Since the shortened or truncated search code demands far less accuracy than the longer or more complete ones—and as we all know the library patron is not a model of accuracy—one does not have to spell very well at all to retrieve data in this way. Our patrons do not seem to be confused by noticing both *Tree Crops* and *Tree Grows in Brooklyn.*

Furthermore, when systems are very fast, and by very fast I am referring to response times in the nature of three seconds or so, one can repeat and vary the searches when the first pass is unsuccessful. In fact, in the same amount of time it takes to look up an item in a traditional large card catalog, one can perform seven or eight searches on LCS. Even if one or two searches are wrong, LCS can still satisfy the search far more quickly. Therefore, the worry about an adequate number of terminals has to be understood in terms of how fast a simple and direct searching system can be. At the same time we are using the LCS system, we are also using OCLC's shared cataloging programs and have placed a terminal in the lobby for public use. Although the searches are much faster than catalog searches, even on records which average between 300 and 400 characters as opposed to the 103 in the local system, we have discovered a significant difference in response time. When our experience with *The New York Times* Information Bank (which we have just started and is truly an interactive system) is added to that, we must conclude that subject searching will be much slower than author/title searching or title searching. Known-item searching can be programmed very quickly. One must segregate, if at all possible, a series of terminals for known-item searching from terminals used for the much slower, somewhat cumbersome and, in fact, necessarily self-instructing interactive systems for subject searching. When we realize that 80 percent of the traffic will be on known-item terminals and only 20 percent or less will be on the other terminals, however, the problems diminish somewhat.

Among the things that will affect the electronic catalog are such things as whether that 20 percent is all subject searching. All of us have some experience in observing our patrons when they do what they call a subject search, or at least some kind of a search that is not a known-item search. They are often looking for a call number so that they can go into the stacks and grub around in the materials near that call number. So the catalog may well be used as much to serve as a substitute for the LC classification schedules or the Dewey schedules as it is for true subject searching. Such an activity certainly changes the prediction of the amount of time needed or the number of terminals needed for full subject searching.

The other things that we have learned through the use of our telephone center and the like is that it is often much better, faster, more efficient to provide a staff member to operate a computer system than to expect the patrons to do it themselves. However, it does seem to us that both services must be provided. The most useful terminal in our whole system is the public access terminal situated right next to the main catalog, and people seem to love to use it. In fact, even with only two terminals available to the public, the terminals seem to be used as the first pass at the catalog. Only when the patron's need is not satisfied with the terminal does s/he turn to the card catalog. The segregation of terminals by type of search can therefore be by a fail/succeed system whereby a patron would transfer to another terminal if failure occurs.

An easy-to-use direct access system seems to be able to provide for most of our patrons' needs. Watching *The New York Times* Information Bank in operation, I have observed that a fair amount of skill is necessary to operate the system efficiently. Such skill can be taught right from the terminal as you go along, but it is an expensive and slow way of doing it. It may not be any slower than the use of the card catalog, but it is still too slow.

With machine systems which employ a Boolean statement or some other logical combination of descriptors, the searching power is much greater than the traditional single point filing and retrieval systems found in the card catalogs. Therefore, to use an electronic catalog well, one has to formulate the search in a much more explicit and precise way than one has to formulate the search of a card catalog. Some patrons are obviously able to do so since we have had so many complaints of how "I looked in the catalog for a criticism of Eliot's *Four Quartets*, and did not find anything," and upon investigation discover that the query made of the catalog was for the topic of a term paper and not in the more general language of the LC subject heading. I have all too often heard "I'm supposed to write a term paper on the architecture of the Cathedral of Florence and I looked in the catalog and couldn't find anything"; users find it hard to believe such precision would not be used.

The technology is available and it is available now cheaply enough to be able to use quite widely. A terminal is available for less than $100 per month. Storage costs have dropped enormously, and it looks like they will continue to drop.

Perhaps the greatest potential advantage of the electronic catalog is its ability to deal more efficiently with serial literature. Sometime around the turn of the century the American library community decided against continuing its analysis of the periodical literature that we find so well explicated in the printed catalogs of Enoch Pratt and other major libraries at that time. The analytics now provided in most of the library catalogs simply apply to items in series and no longer attempt to provide subject access to the individual periodical literature.

As a profession we seem to have assigned such tasks of indexing the primary medium of scholarship to the professional societies and to the commercial index ers. These same societies and commercial indexers are now providing in electronic form subject access to individual periodical articles. Now available are a whole range of such services as Science Citation Indexes' Tape Service, Chemical Abstracts Service, and the Educational Resources Information Center (ERIC) Tape Service, and more will continue. Such data can be matched against the library's general title holdings and, if such a match occurs, the analysis of materials for such titles can be added to the catalog with little effort on the part of the library staff.

Such a huge file is only useful, given what we know about the cumbersomeness of the present card catalog, when one has an electronic means of sorting and searching. But if such systems can be provided and they are available, it would provide for the first time in some three-quarters of a century access to those library materials of primary interest to scholars in the same tool as the analysis of the monographic literature.

Since the programs which do text searching are often combined with those doing searching by label such as subject heading, descriptor, or MARC tag, one is no longer limited in an electronic catalog to a thesaurus of terms such as the *List of Headings Used in the Dictionary Catalogs of the Library of Congress*, the *ERIC Thesaurus*, or any other set series of standard searching points. Any word in the descriptive cataloging or in the body of the record can be searched. The more cumbersome the search, the slower it will be: that is, the letter-by-letter or word-by-word searches of large files are much slower than searches of indexed words such as subject headings or descriptors.

In summary, the advantages of the electronic catalog are 1) remote access, 2) the ability to provide at least some Boolean capability, 3) the ability to use previously prepared catalog copy in indexing material especially for the periodical literature, 4) the ability to segregate the fast searches from the slowest, and 5) the distance *independence* of any electronic device.

Since we have yet to see in operation a library's electronic catalog I am somewhat hesitant to make a judgment about its future, but I will nevertheless. It seems to me that the electronic catalog provides the ability to build a file large enough to contain the most necessary data—a file that can, in fact, be easily weeded. By *weeded* I mean the transference of data being stored in such a way to enable quick access to a medium which should provide a much slower searching routine. I suggest that somewhere between 10 to 25 years' worth of material be stored online and that the catalog be weeded or purged yearly; those items older than 10 to 25 years be transferred to microfiche in accumulating single file. The result that I envision would resemble the old card catalog, a microfiche file of those items that were added to the catalog after 1976, but are older than 25 years; the online catalog would be used for the most used in the newer items.

With such a system, very, very few people would be using the accesses to the older literature. You must remember, I am arguing for continuing the known-item searching file, for keeping the author/title and title indexes for the complete collection online. Although I cannot prove it, nor do I propose it, it is my secret belief that, in fact, almost no one would use the older two files since one can reasonably assume that almost all of the use of the materials which are older than 25 years is by direct citation and not through the subject searching ability. It seems to me that is a step that we do not need to take now, that there is no reason not to follow the path I have outlined. If it is proved that older files are not at all used, some disposition may be made of them at that time.

DISCUSSION

Sanford Berman: Just a short question, Mr. Atkinson. To what extent is it possible in this imagined electronic catalog to make analytical searches? For instance, if one of our borrowers in the Twin Cities area in Minnesota sought material on the "Minnesota Iceman" and it happens that the only available material is a chapter in a book on big-foot monsters, would that borrower, as you foresee the electronic catalog, be able to find that subject material analyzed?

Hugh Atkinson: The first question is—and I have to respond to you with a question—was that item analyzed by any of the geologic or other professionally prepared indexes, the *Science Citation Index* or the history index or any of the . . .

Berman: For purposes of this question I am positing—and you'll have to accept the posit—the only data in our whole collection that it's possible to reach would be this one chapter in the one book.

Atkinson: No, but to be able to answer you, you have to find out if it was cataloged or indexed by anybody. The fact is that I don't know. It will depend also on whether you can purchase that analysis or not, whether you're willing to purchase it or not. Probably you're not. When I talked about how you allocate resources, one of the reasons that we all quit indexing the periodical literature—obviously the wrong choice, we should have quit indexing the monographic literature—was probably economics. I don't know why H. W. Wilson did that in 1900. But if we won't catalog it, it won't be accessible.

Berman: I accept the answer. That was the intent.

Atkinson: Unless there is some clue in the title of the book.

Berman: There isn't any clue as a matter of fact. What I wanted to establish is to what degree would local human intervention still be possible. I'm going to generalize now. In the kind of automated electronic catalogs that we have been discussing for the last couple of days, it would have been possible for a cataloger sensitive to local needs in Minnesota—and this would apply to any area with similar material—to have made a suitable note, a partial contents note if that were necessary, and then what amounts to an analytic subject tracing. In fact, as it happens, we did that at Hennepin, because in Minnesota it then brings out the "Minnesota Iceman" as a subject heading in cross-references, etc. It would seem to me that that is necessary, to be more responsive, to serve your own local clientele through, in effect, customized library cataloging. This is frankly something I wouldn't expect LC, through its MARC record, to do for us. I really don't think LC should. I don't expect a reference for "Minnesota Iceman" and the five other possible creatures that are covered in the book. But it is, I think, our responsibility still. And we can't do it if we're again slavishly and uncritically, for reasons of imagined cost savings, accepting every damn thing that comes out of the tube or out of the machine.

Atkinson: Remember that I said that one of the reasons I wanted an electronic catalog was to decentralize it. What that means is that the chemistry library or the physics library or the geology library or the browsing room can in fact add to that catalog those items quickly and easily without having to worry about the authority files, for instance. As far as I am concerned, since it is a perishable document, it doesn't have to stay there forever. Furthermore, the machine can overcome the complexity of the file itself so that the natural language probably is far more easily used in a large file than it would be anywhere else. Yes is the answer. Yes, you can modify it. But administratively you're going to have to say, "Some folks can do it and others can't," although I'm not absolutely sure of that. That's the reason I want to see the catalog department become completely decentralized, so that the question is not as a cataloger, but as a librarian: what is needed and in what proportion by each of your patrons?

Joseph Rosenthal: It seems to me that Mr. Berman is tilting against windmills. There has always been, at least in the history of modern libraries, a good number of local analytics. Many, many libraries make them. I imagine that most of the libraries represented in this room make some kind of local analytics, some for pamphlet materials, some for fugitive material, some for chapters in books, and some for articles in periodicals and journals. We've known how to do it for a long time. The New York Public Library, in addition to Enoch Pratt, has done it at the rate of about 5,000 analytics a year since the turn of the century. I don't see this as a very real problem. I would think that we would encourage libraries on the local scene to make some kind of local analytics, especially for material of particular geographic interest. We do it in Berkeley for material of California interest, and it's done widely elsewhere.

I'd like to ask Mr. Atkinson a couple of questions about cost. Since you've been on the OCLC system, I assume that cataloging costs have altered, and I would hope for the better. In other words, is your unit cost for cataloging lower than it was, with inflationary factors accounted, before you became part of OCLC? But I'm also interested in the effect of the online shelflist. I would suspect that this has a very beneficial effect on cataloging speed and productivity and efficacy. I wonder if you've done any studies on that. The second question relating to costs is: can you give us any hint of how you are planning to build in the costs of the terminals and increased costs of the total online catalog?

Atkinson: First, yes, the cost has changed with OCLC. There are some figures that I could keep secret—not from you but from our faculty—that is, the cost to catalog an item, counting fringe benefits. To catalog, not to acquire and to process, but to catalog (including fringe benefits and overhead) is about $3.23 a title with OCLC. For original cataloging it's about $10.25. If our community knew it costs ten dollars just to catalog the average book, it wouldn't let us. It would say, put that money into the serial or reference budgets because for ten dollars you can give a helluva lot better service. It may be wrong, but it would say that. So I don't go around saying that very often. The community control of an academic library is enormous, and that kind of thing would be imposed on us. The community is probably right, but I don't really want to engage in that fight now; that is, it's not worth seven more dollars for what you get out of it rather than accepting someone else's cataloging. It's not worth seven more dollars from our community to have full cataloging rather than to have simple author-title entries, i.e., no cataloging at all. If there was a vote on our campus, it would be 99 to 1 for putting the seven dollars almost anywhere else, including toward maintaining buildings and grounds.

Has the online shelflist lowered the per unit cost of circulation? I'm not sure what it does to the per unit cost of cataloging, since the only people who use it online are the people using OCLC. There is a terminal for our system right next to each OCLC terminal. The response time is less than three seconds on one system, and 12 to 14 seconds when it's good on the other system. I'm not sure what kind of saving one is making, except that the LCS terminal is not being tied up because the OCLC system is so fast. But it has resulted in some change in the cost of cataloging. We have a command that permits the entry of a real or imaginary call number, which we implemented so one could do shelflisting. The LCS system displays the 15 items that precede and the 15 items that follow the call number in the query. It turns out that the public, the students, have figured out that that's a way of doing some kind of subject searching, and they do it all the time. Likewise, they figured out that the title words facilitate some kind of subject searching, and they use that all the time throughout the system. But as to costs, how am I going to get the costs? Those costs, by and large, are people. In our case we have a turnover of around 25 percent per year of our clerical staff. What we will do is to transfer the people that are now working on maintaining the catalog to the vacancies occurring throughout the system, to recover some $80,000 to $120,000 in maintenance costs, and use that money to buy terminals.

Marvin Scilken: What percentage of your potential users use the library?

Atkinson: Well, I wish it were as high as at Berkeley and at Chicago and so forth, but I'm pretty sure it isn't. I would guess that of the 50,000 students on the campus something like 70 percent use the library during the year. They borrow, though, only on the average of about 20 books per student. That's derived by just taking the raw number of student circulations and dividing it by the number of students. That also counts reserves and all others. We do a lot of advertising but for many people, at least in our kind of funny place, you don't have to use a library all the time. That is, if you're getting a degree in chicken culture or whatever you call it—and we do give a Ph.D. in chicken raising—I guess you don't have to use the library very often. So I say, we're just a bunch of poor, old, midwestern pig farmers shuffling along trying to do what we can.

Michael Malinconico: I'd just like to offer two comments. First, I'd like to clarify a point that I made yesterday, and I'm sorry if I perhaps spoke too fast and the point didn't get across. I never suggested that horseradish would make horse meat any more or less palatable, or that the user was unaware of the fact that Trilling, L. is in fact Trilling, Lionel. The point was that by creating such double files, you do the user very little good, because you either end up hiding half, or some fraction, of the material from the user or you send him/her scurrying after two or more sequences to complete the search.

The second is something of a general comment. If my comments yesterday managed to evoke the landscape of the State of Ohio, I offer no apologies. But the basic thrust of my paper was not a concern with any single system. It was a concern with the direction in which automation and expediency seem to be taking bibliographical control and the catalog.

Atkinson: I recognize that, but as I said, I am not committed to the authority file concept of bibliographic retrieval for our purposes. I think LC has to, because that's their job; but for us, the costs are too great. If you can provide a cheap system, that's fine, if that system works. But the costs that I've seen so far aren't worth it for what it gets for our patrons, that is, the number of misses we can afford compared to the costs of making sure people don't miss.

Malinconico: It's still not very clear just to what extent the cost of not providing a service is passed on to the user and to the rest of the library.

Atkinson: Correct. We have to take their judgment as well as ours.

Seymour Lubetzky: I would really like to follow up on what Mr. Malinconico said. I fully agreed with him yesterday when he made that point, namely, we have two problems. One, what kind of a catalog do we wish to have, or do we recognize we need? And the other, how can we produce that kind of a catalog? The first one is concerned with the form of the catalog, whether we are using an electronic catalog, or any other catalog.

There are one or two points that you made and to which I referred yesterday and today, but I think that I ought to comment on them again. You began by questioning the importance of identifying an author by one particular name, which is also the means by which we bring together the works of an author. You asked who would be interested in access to all of the works of Linus Pauling, as he has written on different subjects. Well, for one, the *Science Citation Index* considers this as an approach by subject. Subject cannot be simply identified because of the interrelated nature of the different subject fields. When you have the works of an author together, you may not necessarily want all of them from *A* to *Z*. But the chances are, if an author has written one book, then others, that what he writes will also be related by subject. So bringing together the works of an author is of importance even from the perspective of subject access.

However, that is not my justification for bringing together the works of an author. This benefit is just incidental. The point that you made is that 80 percent of all users ask for particular items. I will agree with you. How else could they find a work? The work does not exist except in the form of an item. But the question is, what is that item? Is that item the one that carries the name *X* or the name *Y*? The first edition came out under the name *X* and the second edition was published under the name *Y*, but it is still the very same item. Assume that a change has been made between editions. Assume also that the work has been brought up to date. One cannot assume that the person who seeks title *X* is not interested in the later edition—which might be more interesting because it is the latest edition. Consistent author entry provides for bringing together the works of that author that might not otherwise be found. Identification of the author is therefore needed not simply to show all of the works of that author held by the library. We could even agree that no one in our experience is terribly interested in knowing about all of the works of an author, and this would not gainsay the value of consistent author entry. But you must recognize that the works are important. You will recognize readily that you need that, even if only to bring together the editions of a work that may appear under different names.

You will find in your catalog—perhaps not in your catalog if you did not bring together the different editions, but at least in the Library of Congress catalog—many works that have appeared in their first edition under one name and later under another name. That entity is not the artifact that carries name *A*; it's not the artifact that carries the name *B*. It is what is inside of them that is important, and it is the identification of that with which I am concerned. Now, there are other ways of bringing together all the works of an author. They are concerned still with what you said, the particular item. I have already mentioned that the bringing together of the various editions is the real problem.

I want to depart for a moment to something that has been discussed earlier, which is also relevant here. Some are interested in entering a book under the name of the author as it appears on the title page. I argue that this does expedite finding the book right away for the reader. If you do not enter it exactly under that name, you are creating a hurdle the reader has to jump over. When you want to provide for the reader a means of finding any other edition or another work by this author, the proponents of title page entry will say, "Well, we will tell that reader 'See also *A;* see also *B;* see also *C'* and so on." Now, why are you sending the reader to three places, from *A* to *B* to *C?* This too is a hurdle, a hurdle much more difficult to negotiate. By saying at the begginning *B* and *C*—see *A*, then no matter which name a reader looks under he or she will be led to a single name and find all of those works, and editions for that matter, which may have appeared under different names.

There are other complications, but it would take too much time to go into them. You should recognize the importance of bringing to the attention of a reader who is interested in an author or a work the fact that there is a work about that author or work. If you do not bring together the editions of the work, the works of an author, how then do you identify this work when you need to relate another work to it? You have only works—and I am repeating myself, but it doesn't seem that I made the point yesterday—you have not only editions, you also have translations. A translation is not a translation of edition *A* or of edition *B* or of edition *C*. It is a translation of the work. You cannot relate a translation to any edition or to the work if the work does not exist in your catalog or if the work is divided under various forms in separate places in the catalog.

Another point. Librarians or catalogers have been aware that few people ask for a particular item, that is, they do not always have the precise citation. Somebody will read something, let's say, John Doe in his *Introduction to the Study of Librarianship*. Now what was the title? The title could have been *Introduction to the Study of Librarianship, The Study of Librarianship*, or just *Librarianship*. You are not always quite clear where the title begins and where it ends. People are not always precise in citing the title, particularly when the title begins with a word that does not describe the character or the subject of the book. If you bring together all of the works of an author, a person with an imprecise citation can find it by looking through the sequence of entries under an author even without an accurate citation. If you do not bring the works together, the reader will not find that work.

There is a third point to consider. There are books that are not even cataloged separately. They are cataloged as part of one larger work or of a collection of works. A person who has a reference to that work may be misled by not finding it in the catalog, if it is placed separately. When you have them together and you have the opportunity of looking through all that the library has, then one has the only sure guide to determine whether the library has the item he or she is really seeking. What I discussed yesterday does not deny the fact that people come to look for particular items. What I did try to explain is that they have to understand what they mean by that item. The item is really not the package or the label under which it is packaged, it is the contents of the package. You also mentioned the fact that we really do not bring together the works of an author anyway, because most of the author's works, perhaps the most important from the point of view of timeliness, are in the form of articles. We could if we wanted to, of course, include articles in the catalog. Our catalog would then be increased a hundred times. We do not do this because of the cost of cataloging. You say there is a place where this service already exists. If it does not exist, that is where the cataloging profession should be concerned, because this concerns every library. Indexing, once it is done, serves all libraries. This is a service that should be used. Consequently, your catalog should have a guide card which says, "Here are entered only separately published works" or "the collected works of an author—for original articles, see the indexes." But that has no bearing on the validity of bringing together the works of an author.

One more point. You seem to recognize the importance of decentralization. When I came to the Library of Congress my first assignment was to look over the various catalogs which the Library of Congress maintained. I wrote a paper about this. I remember, I found a separate catalog in the music department. There was one thing wrong with it: There was no single place where you could find what the Library of Congress held. I made that point. I said, the Library of Congress maintains a union catalog to help one find books that are held by various libraries. It does not have a union catalog for those catalogs maintained by its various divisions. If you are interested in decentralization, you certainly realize that no departmental catalog can be quite complete. It will have to draw on the publications held by other departments and the library in general. If you are going to integrate these catalogs, you must have a system. This is the value of a systematic record. It is more important in the case of a decentralized service than it is in a centralized service.

One more point. The cost of cataloging in 1876 was published in a large volume called *Public Libraries in the United States*. It was on the occasion of this country's centenary. One of those articles, as I remember, discussed the problem of the correlation between the cost of cataloging and the value of the collections. The issue was, how do we allocate our money? Is it more important to have a larger collection and a poorer catalog, that is, to spend less money to catalog, or is it more important to spend more money on the catalog, to have a perfect catalog and a smaller collection? Neither extreme could be justified, and certainly there has to be a balance. But the point made in that article that has to be recognized is this: If the function of the library is a return on the investment in its lighting, the maintenance of the building and grounds, the purchase of books, if all of these costs are to render returns, the returns come only in terms of the use of the collection. The better the catalog, the better the library will be used. If the catalog is limited in its functions because of the cost, you will have a large mass of materials in the library which will never be used. And your return on the investment will be slow.

Atkinson: I have some comments. The easy ones first. With respect to *See also* references: It is in fact the electronic catalog that can bring the *See also* reference to the patron and not send the patron to the *See also*.

With respect to the question of decentralization: One of the properties of a decentralized electronic catalog is that it has no place. Remember, *locus* is not a function of electronic devices; that place is anywhere there is a terminal. So the catalog of the physics library is the same catalog as the general catalog, as the catalog in the chemistry library, in the classics library, and so forth. They all have access to the same general catalog.

With respect to costs: I wish it were so, but every time one tries to do the kind of cost study to which you refer, it just shows over and over again that the high usage does not come from the complex and detailed cataloging. It comes from the cheap. Indexing services are valuable because the periodical indexing is already done by the other services. Therefore, if you want unity of entry, go there. I could say the same about bibliographies. Go to the bibliography of Hemingway if you want to keep Hemingway together. Go to the bibliography of Shakespeare. That same argument can be turned against you because there are printed bibliographic unities of authors.

With respect to the last point: I simply disagree that the author is the unity. I'll give you an example. In Ohio State, plain old people that we are, we've been trying to develop for the last fifteen years a grape that will still survive the grape blight that wiped out the vineyards in southern Ohio in the 1920s. We have produced some five or six dissertations on the subject. The unity is not in the author. It is the professor who is directing that work. Each of those dissertations builds one upon the other. Here is a clear case where it is not the authorship of each of those dissertations that creates the fundamental unity, but, in fact, the steadily increasing stream of scientific experimentation. If a serious student were to come in, that student should be led through each of those dissertations which are building a new varietal grape that will be worthwhile to support vineyards once again. That is important. The concept of authorship as unity is still fundamentally a view of belles-lettres or an historical view rather than a scientific one. I think that is the kind of philosophic difference between the scientific kind of building block of one piece of data on another, which is independent in some sense of the author and more dependent on the director of the science, the professor in this case.

Robert McGee: Listening to Mr. Kilgour and to you describe your files—something like what I'm familiar with as a coordinate index using *uniterms*—I just wonder if it's possible that our subject approach to both serial and monographic literature will evolve into a type of *uniterm* system which will do away with the need for authority files for one thing and a subject authority file in particular, and will also make the catalog much more easy for our customers to use.

Atkinson: I think that this will change discipline by discipline, not in general. I really dislike consistency, quite obviously. I think that what is valid for chemistry or for agriculture is not necessarily valid for English literature or German history. Each uses a different language. The language of chemistry is one of form as well as one of language, and the language for the social sciences is conceptual language. I think you'll see that once we can free ourselves from having to do it all the same way we will see, discipline by discipline, a growing change in how we describe and how we provide access.

Unidentified Speaker: One question I have has to do with nonroman alphabet titles, which you brought out, but which I somehow missed in Mr. Welsh's talk.

Atkinson: He slid over it. Remember, he was saying that by 1977 he was going to get Cyrillic into MARC, but he didn't say that the only way was to romanize. I think you are referring to his comments about international agreements on romanization. He wasn't as explicit as he might have been.

Unidentified Speaker: So those of us who are cataloging in nonroman alphabets should expect at some time or other that a Tibetan Lama is going to have to read a record in romanized form.

Atkinson: If he's at Stony Brook he probably will.

Unidentified Speaker: Okay. The point is that even our most adamant, conservative faculty members, those in Near East and Middle Eastern studies, are slowly dribbling in and saying, "You know, would it be any faster if you transliterated?" I say usually, "It might be if LC did." And, in fact, I think that there is a change in the hearts of our patrons, and that they are coming more and more—they're not there yet—toward the acceptance of romanization.

Next question. You brought out something that I've been on the verge of asking for two days. As of this time on OCLC we can't call up our own class number. At what point can we search by class number, because it is a way of bringing together that which is separated by our subject heading?

Atkinson: I realize that, but I don't know. I'm just one old plain member of OCLC, and Mr. Kilgour doesn't tell me any more than he tells you. But I assume soon.

David Wakefield: We've heard a lot of talk here during the conference about the future of the catalog, and specifically that of online catalogs and electronic catalogs. I'm more concerned about the immediate future for public libraries though. I have no doubt that your online catalog can do everything that you say it can and probably more. But to give an example: We went to a book catalog about two years ago and right now it would cost us about $180,000 to produce a total cumulation of that catalog. We get about $90,000 a year for the purpose of producing a catalog that the people can use, and we found that microform catalogs would cost about half that much, so that's what we're going to do. Yet I feel a little paranoid when I hear statements such as "We've got terminals that are only $100 a month." We're buying 130 microform readers. If we had enough money for that many cheap $100 a month terminals, we'd have more money than we've had in years for the catalog.

Atkinson: "How many" may be two, two plus a telephone. If in fact in Fairfax County you have evolved some sort of regional network where you can pick up a three-dollar-a-month telephone and get your cataloging access through that, you can afford it. I suspect that will be the salvation for the smallest libraries, that is, one or two cheap terminals and a telephone for the more complex searching. It could be complicated, though. They don't talk about that. Of course you have the use charges, the line charges, and other things.

The Future of Catalogs in North American Libraries

by Kenneth Bierman

INTRODUCTION

You have heard distinguished experts speak eloquently about the ideology and philosophy of cataloging and the catalog, discuss the inadequacy of current subject analysis and the importance of authority control to maintain the integrity of the library catalog, and talk about the online electric catalog of the future. You are about to hear an undistinguished nonexpert speak prosaically about the library catalog as it currently is and the library catalog of the near future in terms of the majority of libraries. In other words, my job is to attempt to put what you have heard into perspective in terms of today and the future.

First, a few ground rules:

1. I will not be speaking about cataloging or cataloging principles, philosophies, or even practices. Rather, I will be speaking about the physical form, the physical carrier if you will, of the catalog. In terms of Mr. Kilgour's eight factors outlined yesterday, I will be speaking about number seven—format.

2. I will focus on North American libraries and will try to provide some perspective on the present and near future for all types and sizes of libraries, excluding school libraries about which I will make no comments.

3. In discussing library catalogs in terms of size, I will be referring to size in terms of titles in the catalog, not volumes represented, as the number of titles is the key factor in determining catalog size. Arbitrarily, I will use large library or large catalog to mean greater than 200,000 titles and small to intermediate to mean less than 200,000 titles.

4. In terms of my comments about the present, I am talking about living, ongoing active library catalogs that indeed attempt to provide a systematic record of the holdings of a collection. I am not talking about automated onetime catalogs, such as the University of California Catalog Supplement and I am not talking about automated catalogs that supplement card catalogs. Further, in talking about automated catalogs, I do not mean card catalogs wherein the cards are produced by computer.

5. I have been asked to summarize what is and what I think will be in terms of the next ten years. I have not been asked to summarize what I wish was, nor to predict what I think, wish, or hope will happen. Rather, I am to predict what I think will happen. My comments today are wholly my own and are based on reading and, more importantly, on a study on the current state of planning and implementation for automated alternatives to card catalogs in which over 80 libraries of all sizes and types were contacted. I wish to acknowledge the financial

support of the Council on Library Resources and the paid leave time support of the Virginia Polytechnic Institute and State University Libraries.

WHAT IS THE CURRENT SITUATION WITH REGARD TO THE PHYSICAL FORM OF THE LIBRARY CATALOG?

Over 99 percent of the total number of current library catalogs are card catalogs. It is, I think, important to remember and keep this fact in perspective. The card catalog is currently very much alive and very much dominating the scene. Whether it is in good or poor health depends on the particular library situation and the particular person with whom you are talking, but I suspect that for a significant number of libraries, probably a majority, the card catalog continues to serve the library reasonably well.

Having said this, it is equally important to note that because of perceived deficiencies in card catalogs there is currently much interest in studying, planning for, and experimenting with automated alternatives to manually maintained card catalogs. This is witnessed by the fact that 400 of you came from throughout the United States to New York City in these bleak financial times to pay $75.00 to attend a conference exclusively on this topic! This interest runs throughout large and small academic, public, and special libraries. There are many reasons for interest in automated alternatives given by libraries, the most popular being:

1. To provide access to the complete and most up-to-date catalog from multiple locations—remote catalog access.
2. To provide more and improved access points and search capabilities.
3. To expand the availability of increased resources through sharing via union catalogs.
4. To eliminate or at least reduce the inconsistencies and inaccuracies of card catalogs and their inhospitality to change (change in headings, filing rules, etc.).
5. To reduce the increasing problems and costs of maintaining card catalogs as they grow in number, in size, in age, and in complexity.
6. To deal with influences and pressures for change which come from both internal and external sources.

In addition, two reasons not mentioned by a majority of libraries, but vehemently stated when mentioned, are to reduce the floor space occupied by the catalog and to arrest the physical deterioration of old and heavily used card catalogs.

The importance of the reason for interest in automated catalogs, and the corresponding perceived inadequacies of the present card catalogs, vary with the individual library situation. Large central research libraries want improved access or searching capabilities most, while multilocationed libraries (public, academic, or special) want remote catalog access the most. Whatever the reasons, many librarians are very interested in alternatives to their present card catalogs.

If 99 percent of the libraries in North America have card catalogs, the remaining one percent must have something else. Of the alternatives, computer-produced hard-copy printed book catalogs are currently the most numerous. This is the oldest form of automated catalog. It is difficult to know for sure just how many libraries have exclusively printed book catalogs of their collections, but I would guess somewhere between 25 and 50 libraries or library systems. The majority of the printed book catalogs are located in public libraries with many branch locations; the book catalog is economically justified in this type of situation where maintaining many copies of one union catalog is more feasible than maintaining single copies of many individual catalogs. This is interesting in terms of the registration at this meeting: Of the 400 registrants, 12 percent are from public libraries, 12 percent from all other types excluding academic, and 75 percent are from academic. I think this is not so indicative of where the interest lies as where the travel money is available!

Of the printed book catalogs that include more than 100,000 titles, the majority hover around 150,000 titles and include Fairfax County, Virginia; Orange County, California; Baltimore County, Maryland; Enoch Pratt, Maryland; King County, Washington; Prince Georges County, Maryland; and Bell Telephone Labs, New Jersey. Also, the majority of these computer-produced printed book catalogs are products of commercial firms.

To my knowledge, four printed book catalogs representing more than 200,000 titles exist: Los Angeles County, California with 325,000; UC/Santa Cruz with 250,000; New York Public Library Research Libraries with 250,000; and the New York Public Library Branch Libraries with 200,000. Only one of these is produced by a commercial firm, the remaining three are primarily done locally in terms of computer manipulation.

If the majority of the one perent of libraries that now has automated alternatives to card catalogs has printed book catalogs, the minority must have microimage catalogs. In a sense, microimage catalogs are no different from printed book catalogs in that fixed *pages* are displayed, but in microform rather than hard-copy form. Computer-produced microimage catalogs are more recent than book catalogs; most have been in existence less than three years. Existing microimage catalogs are smaller than most of the book catalogs with the majority being less than 100,000 titles. Examples of libraries that have microimage catalogs include the Lockheed Missiles Library, California 175,000 titles; Boeing Library, Washington 150,000; UT/San Antonio 130,000; UT/Permian Basin 90,000; UT/Dallas 50,000; Georgia Institute of Technology 75,000; and the Tulsa City-County Library 50,000 titles. The majority of these are fiche catalogs rather than roll film. Of the examples just cited, only UT/San Antonio is roll film. Finally, there is currently much interest in microform catalogs, particularly on the part of those libraries that now have printed book catalogs. They see microform catalogs as a means to reduce the cost and time lag and to increase the recumulation frequency of their present book catalog system.

What of the online catalog of which we have heard so much at this meeting? Well, they must be in the future because I do not know of a library of any significant size that relies exclusively on an online catalog. Some libraries have partial online catalogs; these include the Rochester Institute of Technology, Syracuse University, Stanford University, University of Chicago, Northwestern University, National Library of Medicine, National Agricultural Library, Aerospace Corporation Library, National Aeronautics and Space Administration (NASA), International Business Machines (IBM), and, of course, all of the Ohio College Library Center (OCLC) participants have a partial online catalog. But, as of right now, despite all of the interest, I do not know of a library relying exclusively on an online catalog.

In summary, the vast majority of libraries have card catalogs. Those few libraries that have an automated alternative are primarily less than 200,000 titles. Interest in automated alternatives to the card catalog is high in all types and sizes of libraries but certainly not in all libraries.

Before proceeding to predictions about the future, I would like to make a few general, and perhaps parenthetical, comments about the current situation. First, as noted yesterday, there is no clear generally agreed upon definition of the library catalog. Extremes range from those that emphasize the finding concept and those that emphasize the collocating and syndetic functions of the catalog. These two extreme views may well result in different contents of library catalogs. Second, many of the libraries currently interested in automated catalogs are thinking in terms of automated card catalogs rather than new types of access/description that may be more appropriate for online catalogs of the future. Third, not only is there no clear and generally accepted agreement on the definition and purposes of library catalogs, there is little knowledge of how the existing card catalogs are actually used, much less knowledge of how a restructured catalog might be used. This is a severe hindrance in planning *new* catalogs for the future.

WHAT IS THE FUTURE FOR FORMS OF LIBRARY CATALOGS?

No one knows what the future of library catalogs will be. What follows are some predictions about the future of library catalogs through the middle to late 1980s:

1. There will be considerable and continually growing interest in automated alternative forms for library catalogs and this interest will be exemplified by the creation of an increasing number of formal committees, task forces, etc., which will write an increasing number of reports. In addition, there will likely be an increasing number of meetings held on the subject!

2. There will be a slow but steady increase in the number of small- and intermediate-sized libraries and library systems (particularly public libraries) which will close their card catalogs and implement an automated alternative in the next ten years.

3. Very few large libraries will close their card catalogs and implement automated alternatives before 1985. Possible exceptions include Ohio State University, Northwestern University, University of British Columbia, and one or more of the national libraries of the United States.

4. Printed book catalogs will cease to be the most popular automated alternative to the card catalog and will be replaced by microimage catalogs in the near future. Further, as film reading equipment becomes more reliable and less costly per unit of information stored and displayed, microfilm catalogs will become more popular than microfiche catalogs because of their increased ease of use.

5. When large numbers of libraries implement automated alternatives to card catalogs, they will be developed, implemented, and operated cooperatively through regional-nationl networks. They will not be done by individual librearies, as is often currently the case.

6. Small- and intermediate-sized libraries will be able to do complete retrospective conversion and many of these libraries that implement an automated catalog will do so. Large libraries, however, will not attempt retrospective conversion before the year 2000 but rather will first close their card catalogs, and then within five to ten years freeze their card catalogs and commit them to microimage through photographic processes. Large libraries that choose an automated catalog will thus have two catalogs: a frozen retrospective catalog and an ongoing automated catalog.

7. By 1985, a significant number of the automated alternatives to card catalogs that are in operation will be online catalogs supplemented (in the sense of

being in addition to) with hard-copy catalogs in card or microimage or printed book form with great variations of experimental options. Exclusively printed book catalogs will not be acceptable because of the time delays in appearance and the extreme cost. Exclusively microimage catalogs will not be generally acceptable because of lack of user acceptance and because they offer no significant improvement over card catalogs. Because automated catalogs can be responsive to change, those libraries that have implemented automated catalogs will be in a constant state of alternative *mixes* of online, hard-copy, and microimage catalogs to meet changing situations, needs, and financial conditions.

8. Although many more libraries will have automated catalogs by 1985, the vast majority of libraries will still rely exclusively or nearly exclusively on card catalogs.

9. Beyond 1985, online catalogs containing authority-quality control systems will increasingly become the single form of catalog in use by an increasing number of libraries of all types and sizes through regional-national-international interconnected networks.

In conclusion, in terms of the future of automated catalogs, the Wright brothers have just flown and it will be many years before the supersonic transport catalog is generally available for the majority of libraries. As always appears to be the case, the best is yet to come.

DISCUSSION

Unidentified Speaker: What impact do you think it's going to have on the user, Mr. Bierman, three, five, eight, ten years from now, when a user goes into a library and is told to look either in the microfiche, the online, or the old card catalog? You said all three would be present and would have their own uses.

Kenneth Bierman: Yes, and it'll be different from library to library. Also remember I said that at least for the next ten years the vast majority of libraries will continue to have card catalogs. So, for the vast majority of users who walk into the library, it will be what they basically find now. I don't think the change is going to come that fast. In terms of what it's going to be for the users, it will be the same thing as we have now. We have libraries now—not a large of number of them—but we have libraries with various mixes of catalogs. For example, the New York Public Library has a closed—I believe now frozen—card catalog and an ongoing printed book catalog.

By the way, I didn't say anything about the problems of closing card catalogs, and we haven't talked about that at the Institute at all. There are many such problems, and it's not as easy as it might sound. It might be well at some ALA meeting, perhaps an annual meeting, to have somebody sponsor a meeting of speakers who have actually gone through closing card catalogs, perhaps the National Agricultural Library and the New York Public Library.

Marvin Scilken: I just wondered why Mr. Bierman felt that users wouldn't accept roll film microform format.

Bierman: I'm sorry, I didn't mean to imply that. I think the user would accept roll film microform for the catalog much better than s/he would accept fiche form.

Scilken: I agree with you, but you implied that we were going to abandon that for something else.

Bierman: No, I meant that right now the vast majority of microform catalogs are fiche catalogs, not roll film. I think in the very near future this will change simply because readers will be available economically. I didn't mean to imply that in terms of the near future they would be abandoning the microfiche catalogs. I think in terms of automated alternatives, as I said, microfilm catalogs, as compared to the printed book, will become the most common certainly within the next five years, perhaps as quickly as two or three.

Scilken: But you spoke of a more distant future.

Bierman: Meaning sometime beyond 1980, sometime over the great blue yonder. I have no idea when, obviously, but I think the advantages of the online catalog, if properly constructed, are tremendous. At some point this is going to become common in many, many libraries. It's not to say that those libraries that have online access might not also have some form of microimage catalog. In essence, the user would have a choice, depending on the library, of what was available at that library, and of what he or she wanted to use. I do agree with the majority tenor of this meeting that at some time in the future online catalogs are going to be readily available, because I think their advantages are going to be significant. The other point I'm trying to make is that it might be a mistake to plan a library building now that was going to be built in the next two or three years that didn't provide for a card catalog. It's not going to be in that time frame.

Joseph Rosenthal: I don't want to go out on a limb and argue with Mr. Bierman's predictions. I think they're a fascinating set, but I thought it might be of some interest to this group to talk for a couple of minutes on what Berkeley is doing in studying the future of the catalogs. Most of you probably know that the initial study resulted in a phase one report entitled *To Close or Not to Close.* Following that report, there are a couple of teams of librarians working on phase two, which consists of studies with differing assumptions. The first assumption is that we would plan for a catalog that would still have author-title information in one alphabet. It might be a continuation in card form or it might not be. There would be, for author-title information at least, only one file in which to look. The other plan would be to close the catalog concurrently with the Library of Congress (LC) closing and begin a new catalog in 1980 or thereabouts, with substantially all information going into the new catalog in machine-readable form. The teams are supposed to find the cost of these alternatives and describe the specific catalog systems. We are assuming that bibliographic access would not decrease, and we are paying attention to such things as collaborative efforts within California as well as nationwide. Finally, we are assuming that our annual cataloging output would rise to about 90,000 titles from its present level of about 60,000. We also assumed that online authority information would be available for cataloging purposes at a specific cost from the Library of Congress. The deadline for these second phase reports is, I believe, October 30, 1975. I can't say definitely that they would be available, but we will probably make them available at a nominal cost.

Concluding Remarks*

by Maurice J. Freedman

This Institute on The Catalog: Its Nature and Prospects proved that the interest in cataloging and catalogs is an ever-present reality. The greatest living theoretician of descriptive cataloging, Professor Seymour Lubetzky, graced the Institute with his brilliance, insight, and fierce dedication to the integrity of the catalog and stressed the importance of this integrity in making the catalog a useful tool for the user. Joe Rosenthal of the University of California, Berkeley and Sanford Berman, Hennepin County Library (Minnesota) served as official reactors to each presentation. They both did a commendable job of reflecting a sense of unity in the program and providing a perspective for audience discussion, which at times became quite lively. Highlights were presentations by Joan Marshall, who called for an alternative catalog code designed to serve the needs of the nonresearch libraries of the country; Bill Welsh, who expounded on LC's current and future plans and its dedication to service and who felt that LC could be sufficiently responsive to eliminate the need for an alternative service; and Mr. Kilgour and Mr. Malinconico, who presented diametrically opposed views regarding the role and impact of the computer on the catalog. Fred Kilgour, Director of the Ohio College Library Center, the modern father of networking, made a speech which described the inutility of traditional rules of cataloging which focused on bringing together all of the works of an author under the same heading. OCLC's data base does not include this traditional value as an essential ingredient, but it does provide, through its online service, a multitude of minicatalogs which bring together everything which fits the OCLC 3,3 search key. This, in addition to the virtually unlimited access points possible with a computer-based catalog, obviates the need for rigorous control over the heading data used in a cataloging record, according to Mr. Kilgour. Mike Malinconico, a solid-state disciple of Professor Lubetzky, who contributed significantly to the New York Public Library's book catalog and automated bibliographic control system, made a vigorous argument for the integrity of the catalog and for the importance of the computer being an integral component in controlling cataloging data. He noted that sophisticated access techniques and the computer's intrinsic properties cannot compensate for a lack of rigorous control over bibliographic data. He made a strong case for the need for such control if the catalog is to remain a truly useful library tool.

Professor Lubetzky, in his keynote speech and in his responses to all of the speakers who espoused a tolerance for the degradation of the catalog's integrity,

---

*This conclusion appeared in a slightly different version in *Library Journal* 101 (February 15, 1976):594-95.

demonstrated how essential it is to ordinary library service to have the catalog properly organize the works of an author, not to be unnecessarily redundant, and to avoid doing anything which would confuse the catalog user. Tracing a history of the ideology of cataloging, he viewed current events as essentially an ideological retrogression. For example, he pointed out that universal title entry for serials, advocated by many of the code revision people, would create severe problems for the user trying to find the work of a corporate body where the authorship was constant but the title changed each year (e.g., the annual reports of many public libraries); *ISBD (International Standard Bibliographical Description)* is a step backwards because it introduces confusing punctuation, unnecessarily repeats the author's name in the title statement (for long corporate authors this is especially painful), and it is an example of cooperation for its own sake. Professor Lubetzky felt that meaningful participation in international standards and practices should include at least something useful for each participant.

The other speakers all made important points and gave much food for thought: Marvin Scilken with his totally user-oriented catalog cards; Hugh Atkinson with his Ohio State University Library electronic catalogs, which were concerned less with cataloging and more with library use; and Ken Bierman, the only noncontroversial speaker, who reviewed the present and future alternative formats to the card catalog.

There were three themes that were almost continuously present in the Institute:

1. The dissatisfaction with LC's subject cataloging, particularly its lack of sensitivity and contemporaneity and its seeming dedication to the service of research libraries to the exclusion of other libraries.

2. The catalog's loss of integrity; and, through recent and anticipated changes in cataloging rules and the absence of rigorous authority control in automated systems such as OCLC's, the catalog's deterioration as leading us down the road to lesser quality library service.

3. The catalog as a luxury no longer affordable, and the online computer through automated search keys providing even better access and lending all of the integrity a user really requires; present cataloging rules as deficient and possibly outmoded anachronisms.

The Institute on The Catalog was probably the single biggest ALA institute not associated with an annual or midwinter conference. The Institute drew over 400 people.

Regardless of the differing and conflicting views of the participants, the underlying view which most came across was that serving the library's users should be our paramount concern. With that message, the Institute on The Catalog: Its Nature and Prospects is concluded.

THE CATALOG
IN THE AGE OF
TECHNOLOGICAL
CHANGE

Introduction to Part II

by Maurice J. Freedman
and S. Michael Malinconico

We are all aware of the nature of the threshold on which the catalog—that often maligned instrument that spells the difference between the library as a chaotic warehouse of recorded artifacts and a coherent collection of information organized for efficient access—is poised. A library collection is only capable of fulfilling its intended function of supporting scholarly research and providing ready answers to practical questions or a treasure of freely accessible materials for leisure reading if it is adequately organized for access. That is the crux of the matter—access. Modern computer technology is uniquely able to enhance this function. The importance of the library catalog and the significant threshold to which technology has brought us is perhaps attested to by the number of participants who have attended these programs. The previous program held in 1975 in New York City drew an audience of 400 librarians. This 1977 edition, which is being held on both coasts of the United States, has attracted over 700 participants. The participants represent three-quarters of the Anglo-American library community: Britain, Canada, and the United States.

We are now experiencing the second and undoubtedly the most dramatic revolution which the library catalog and perhaps the library service have undergone in this century. Both the medium in which it is maintained and its very nature are being critically reexamined. We are all aware of the current frenetic activities surrounding the revision of the *AACR*. In addition, most of us have felt the impact of the introduction of the computer and microform technology into our own libraries. The current ambience is such that we are facing a new crisis in cataloging. Crisis is not necessarily a bad thing. The Chinese character for crisis consists of a combination of two ideograms, one signifying danger and the other opportunity. Hopefully, an important start will be made toward establishing a dialog concerning these two aspects of the unprecedented, rapid development of the most recent decade. Let me now introduce to you your moderator, and the organizer of both this and the 1975 program, Maurice Freedman.

The Institute on The Catalog in the Age of Technological Change could not have been planned for a more propitious time. Cataloging tradition, rules, and practices are receiving the most careful scrutiny that they have received since the debates of the early sixties preceding the publication of the *Anglo-American Cataloging Rules* of 1967. The late 1970s, unlike the early 1960s, have a totally new component tempering the framework within which this new code has developed. The solid state computer has put tremendous pressure on all of us to be more aware of each of the many facets comprising our personal and professional existence. From having computer-controlled signals regulating highway traffic, to computer production of most of the bills and checks we receive, to the cathode-ray tube terminal phosphorescently glowing LC's latest catalog output before our eyes, the computer's entrenchment in our lives is a brute fact and not a debatable or negotiable point, which brings us to this Institute. The new code of cataloging rules is presently being drawn up in this day of data processing. One of the most fundamental issues that will be addressed concerns the impact of this new machinery on the theory, values, and practices which have prevailed from Panizzi and Cutter through the time of the Paris Principles, probably the last work on the foundations of cataloging prior to the impact of automation. Are the notions we learned in library school sacrosanct? Are they of permanent significance? That is, do the basic notions of cataloging embodied in the Paris Principles still pertain as stated independently, or might we say, despite the effects of the computer? Or must the notions governing the organization of library collections be changed because of the power of automation? Michael Gorman and Seymour Lubetzky discuss the basic issue of the impact of technology on the cataloging enterprise. They present their views on the notions of entry and description, giving a theoretical framework for the following papers.

John Byrum, Phyllis Richmond, Frances Hinton, and Bernadine Hoduski discuss the *AACR2*—the background concerning the new code, the issues with which the drafters have been dealing, the basis for the changes being suggested and future rules. The point and counterpoint nature of the talks specifically concerned with *AACR* reflects the official roles the speakers have with respect to that draft. Sanford Berman and Anne Lipow discuss the application of these rules, as well as the other functions regarding the total catalog record and the instrument of which it becomes a part—the catalog. Its effects on the user: Do these discussions pertain to the person passing through the library's portals? Is the catalog a tool which actively promotes access to the materials found in public and research libraries? Is it a barrier, and how can the data processing technology play a facilitative role in providing access? In sum, what are the users' needs?

Jean Weihs is concerned with what has been a specialized category of materials, specialized in the sense that general libraries, both public and academic, have long neglected, hidden away, or scrupulously avoided nonprint materials as part of their basic collection and services. Are the problems of nonprint unique with respect to print materials? Does the nature of nonprint material require special rules for entry? These materials are different from books, but they are also similar in that they convey information and they must be entered and described in our catalogs if the user is to gain access to this vital and valuable material.

Finally, Joe Howard discusses the Library of Congress as the National Bibliographic Service.

FORMAT

Following each paper, a transcript of the discussion which followed is reproduced. In New York, the two official reactors were Paul Fasana and Edwin Buchinski, who both made comments before the discussion was opened to the audience. Paul Fasana was joined by Eleanor Crarey and their reactions instigated the audience discussion in Los Angeles.

Cataloging and the New Technologies

by Michael Gorman

My interest in the new technologies in technical services in libraries arises from the simple belief that technology, if intelligently applied, can bring three important benefits. It can improve the efficiency of our service to library users; it can enable us to spend our limited resources more sensibly; and it can improve the nature of the work of all employed in the library. The last of these advantages is too often ignored. In our precomputer systems much library work consists of mindless drudgery which is an insult to the intelligence of those who carry it out. Who would willingly spend their days filing cards in a card catalog? The ideal of a technically improved library system can be found in the words of William Morris written nearly one hundred years ago: "[W]ork in a duly ordered community should be made attractive by the consciousness of usefulness, by its being carried on with intelligent interest, by variety, and by its being exercised amidst pleasurable surroundings." (William Morris, *Useful Work versus Useless Toil*, 1885) I believe that that ideal is as valid now as then, and that it constitutes a primary factor in the appeal of the new technologies. Efficiency is not the only criterion, we must also pursue the improvement of the lot of the library worker.

An interesting aspect of the new technology is the widespread fear of change and cynicism about change among many people who might expect to benefit from it. This is, of course, due in great part to an entirely understandable reaction to the ills, real and imagined, that can be seen as resulting from many modern technical advances. I strongly believe that we must cultivate a more positive attitude towards change in the field of library work, and that this attitude must pervade all levels of librarianship. It is evident that library administrators and library educators have a great responsibility in this respect. Only when this more positive attitude is widespread can we begin to achieve the real benefits of the new technology, because only when new systems are enthusiastically applied by people who believe in what they are doing will a new era in librarianship be achieved.

A common attitude to the mechanization of library technical services is that the machine can be used to accomplish many of our current practices more quickly. In my opinion this approach is incorrect, and the use of computers to speed up and perpetuate outdated systems is a perversion of technology. I wish to show that the best use of mechanization will be founded on a complete reconsideration of all of our systems, an examination of what we are doing and why we are doing it. If this process leads to radical change, so be it. If it means the abandonment of cherished ideas of the past, then let us abandon those ideas. I must emphasize that this does not mean a supine acceptance of temporary technical and financial limitations of the present stage of automation. In this country it is scarcely necessary to point out that what human beings can imagine, human beings can do. We should think of the eventual possibilities of machine systems and what they can achieve, and not be diverted by short- or medium-term problems.

I intend to examine a number of the changes that the computer has made, is making, or will make to cataloging. I hope that these will demonstrate the extent and nature of those changes and show the direction in which we should be moving.

First, let us look at the physical nature of the end product of our work: the catalog. Too often the prevalent attitude towards the physical form of the catalog is that expressed by a student of mine in an essay which began "As well as normal catalogues there are book and microfilm catalogues." I will divide these forms into what I call the *old* forms (that is, the card and the book catalogs) and the *new* forms (that is, the microform catalog produced from machine-readable records and the online computer catalog). If we contrast these two categories, certain qualitative and quantitative differences become apparent. The old forms are either unique (that is, located in one place) or, in the case of the book catalog, expensive to duplicate and heavy to transport. The new forms can be made available in many places, both inside and outside the library. The old forms are perpetually and inescapably out of date. The new forms are capable of speedy updating and near complete currency. The old forms are inflexible in that they allow limited and highly structured access to information. The new forms, either because of their nature (as with the online computer catalog) or because of the cheapness of the material on which they are produced (as with microform catalogs) allow the possibility of many more points of access to information. The old forms arise out of previous technologies, and have the restrictions and limitations of those technologies. The new forms arise out of our current and emerging technologies, and do not suffer from those restrictions and limitations.

These changes in the physical form of the catalog have implications which go far beyond changes in form or even in improvements in speed and convenience to the catalog user. They should be seen as changing the nature of what we are doing, or, at least, as forcing a reconsideration of our cataloging practices. To take an obvious example, in a new catalog how does our old friend the main entry fare? To attempt to answer this question I must go beyond the physical form of the catalog and delineate the machine-readable catalog record of the future.

As with all emerging technologies, the computerization of catalog records has had to develop both technically and conceptually. It has had to go through various stages, each of which is both a prerequisite of, and paradoxically a hindrance to, the next stage. It is only now, after 15 years, that we can see the shape of computer records of the future. Those records will be true products of their technology, as opposed to what we have now—a computer record which amounts to little more than an electronic version of a familiar and much-loved artifact measuring approximately three inches by five inches. The developed catalog record that is emerging is multilayered and multidimensional. It uses computer technology to achieve far more than the mere mechanization of catalog entry production. (See Diagram 1.) You will see from this diagram that information relating to a particular item, which is at present contained in machine records as a single unitary set of information, is presented in the developed machine system in a number of *linked packages* of information. So, there are individual packages relating to the names of a person, to the names of a corporate body, to the titles of a work, to a subject, and to the description of a particular physical item. These are, as is shown in the diagram, linked to each other when they apply to an item or

DIAGRAM 1

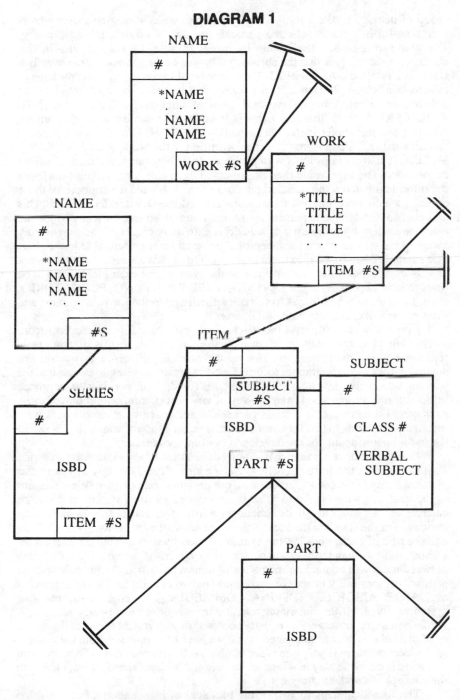

THE DEVELOPED MACHINE RECORD

group of items. To take a fairly simple example, we can imagine a user who is searching for information about a particular edition of Dante's *Divine Comedy*. The user can approach the system by name, by title, by subject, etc. In this instance, let us imagine that the approach is by one of the forms of name by which Dante is identified—ALIGHIERI. This name would give access to the package of information relating to Dante. This package will include two important pieces of information. First, that the standard form of citation for Dante is DANTE ALIGHIERI. Second, that that name is linked with a number of works, among which is one sometimes identified as the DIVINE COMEDY. The work package contains the information that the standard title for the work is DIVINA COM-MEDIA. It also contains links with packages describing particular manifestations of the work. The user would then be presented, on a screen or in a print-out, with the information about the standard citations of the work and descriptions of those editions which were English translations entitled the DIVINE COMEDY. This process of assembling and presenting information is done automatically within the machine system by program and it is done extremely quickly. The user is only aware of the way in which the assembled information is presented to him or her. The example I have used is extremely simple. Other packages relating to the work and its manifestations are also present in the system. For example, there will be links to individual parts of the DIVINE COMEDY (INFERNO, PURGATORIO, etc.); to series in which items have been issued; and to the subjects, names, and titles of the work, its parts, and of the series.

I do not wish to discuss the mechanisms by which this developed record works, but to concentrate on it conceptually. In looking at this diagrammatic representation of the system, we can see the essential difference between it and catalog entries or bibliographic records found in previous systems. Because of the way in which the developed record is structured, it is possible to approach information from any level, and by way of any access point within one of those packages. For example, if a series package is associated with subject packages, information relating to that series will be retrieved in a subject search. It is here that the multidimensionality of the developed machine system lies.

I embarked on this somewhat lengthy description of a system with a question about the main entry. In fact, I believe that the idea of the main entry as a particular physical entity in the catalog arose out of our previous technologies. What remains of the main-entry idea is the fact that the developed machine system, if it is to be capable of carrying out all its functions, allows for, and indeed demands, an indication of the standard manner of citing the name of each person and each body and the title of each work. In the example I used there is a standard citation for Dante and a standard citation for the *Divine Comedy*. As the link between them will contain an indication of their relationship (in this case, that of primary responsibility or *authorship*), the standard citation for the work emerges as DANTE ALIGHIERI. DIVINA COMMEDIA. This enables the machine system to fulfill all the remaining useful purposes of the main-entry idea. Individual items can, however, be equally accessed by any variant forms of that name or of that title. What has happened is that we have been released from the tyranny of the idea that there is only one place in which full information is to be found, and that there is only one way in which an item should be approached. We are left with the concept of standard citation.

The likely contents of two of the packages of information are: (1) a name package and (2) a work package. (See Diagram 2.) The replacement of the main-entry idea by that of a standard citation can readily be seen. In the name package there is a place for the preferred form of the name. In the work package there is a place for the preferred form of the title. Each package will contain links which not only connect one package to another but also define precisely the nature of the relationship between them.

DIAGRAM 2

NAME PACKAGE	WORK PACKAGE
Control number	Control number
Preferred form of name	Preferred title
Other forms	Other titles
Different spelling	. . .
Romanization	Additions
Standard	Language
Others	Date
Pseudonyms	Etc.
Real name	Linking numbers
Dates	
Full forenames	
Cutter number	
Linking numbers	

It is evident that the work of the cataloger in preparing these packages is very different from the work involved in preparing conventional catalog entries. (See Diagram 3.) Diagram 3 illustrates a different symbolic representation of the developed machine record. In this diagram a complete aggregation of related information is presented, rather simplistically, as a set of building blocks. Using this analogy, the task of the cataloger can be seen as that of constructing new building blocks and fitting them into an existing structure. These new modules will be standard descriptions of items newly acquired, new subject packages, new name packages, and new work packages. Once these are created, the cataloger must perceive the links between new and existing packages, and build them into the system. Familiar injunctions such as "Enter under . . ." seem to have been lost. In fact, in many applications the choice of main entry (or standard citation) is unimportant. A standard description will be accessible by a number of characteristics, each of which has equal validity. As far as the user is concerned, all access points are main access points because they all provide an equal amount of information. In other applications the choice of standard forms is very important, so this task remains when constructing multipurpose records.

Diagram 3 also demonstrates the multidimensional nature of the developed machine record. The subjects of a series, an item, or a part are equally accessible, as are the names associated with a series, an item, or a part. The user can approach information either (in the terms of this diagram) horizontally, that is, at one level containing subject, name, and descriptive information; or vertically, that is, by category of information irrespective of level. The catalog no longer has to concentrate on one level of information to the complete or partial exclusion of all others.

DIAGRAM 3

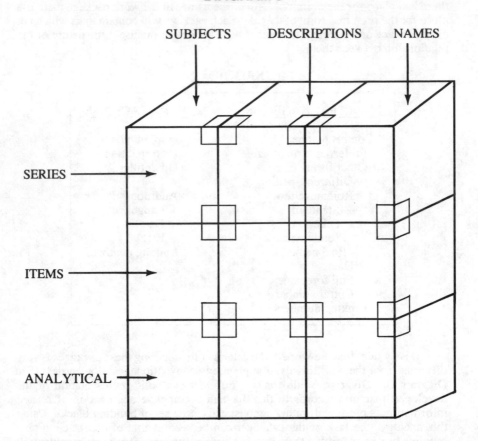

SUBJECTS   DESCRIPTIONS   NAMES

SERIES

ITEMS

ANALYTICAL

MODULAR NATURE OF THE DEVELOPED MACHINE RECORD

We have seen that the work of the cataloger is different in that these packages of information are prepared individually, but it is the same in that such work demands as much, if not more, professionalism and commitment to standardization as before. There is one further important difference between such work and conventional cataloging; this lies in the fact that the element of repetition that our present system demands is all but eliminated. Once a package of information is established and its links to other packages are made, it remains as the package for that name, subject, item, etc., and subsequent work connected with the same data consists simply of citing the control number for that package in the appropriate field. Thus the machine system can be used to eliminate busywork and to leave the cataloger with the task of establishing new information in a standard manner, that is, the truly professional task. To return briefly to the quotation from Morris, I believe that this aspect of technological change goes a long way towards the realization of the ideal of "useful" work.

Another change that technology can bring to cataloging is the possibility of resolving what have hitherto been considered irreconcilable problems. Take, for example, Russian names. (See Diagram 4.) No one has yet come up with a satisfactory solution to the problem of whether one should use a romanized form of name or the *popular* English form of name. Another instance is the difference between the English and North American practices in adding dates to personal names. In English practice they are added only when there is a conflict; in North American practice they are added, when available, in anticipation of conflict. Another instance is that of the choice between pseudonyms and *real* names of persons. Other instances of unresolved or partially resolved conflicts of this type abound in our precomputer cataloging codes. Using a developed machine-readable record these problems can be resolved. First, the question of whether one uses the systematic or *popular* form of name for a Russian: In the developed machine system, each of these forms will be present, and each will be accompanied by an indication of the type of name. A particular printed catalog using that record could select, by program, the form which is preferred for that catalog. Even within one library one could use the systematic form for a general catalog and the *popular* form for a reading list. The other example, that of dates added to personal names, is resolved by the fact that, in the name package I showed you, the dates are held separately. These dates are recorded when the package is created (or subsequently) and remain in the package only to be printed when conflict occurs. In that way, the irreconcilable problem in our premachine systems—the necessity to record dates and use them or not to record them at all—is overcome. They are recorded in all instances, but only used in instances where they are relevant and necessary. Again we see that the impact of technology is to alter the cataloging task and to alter the nature of the decisions that the catalogers have to make.

DIAGRAM 4

Romanization
> EVTUSHENKO, Evgenii Aleksandrovich
> or
> YEVTUSHENKO, Yevgeny Alexandrovitch

Dates
> FUTZENHAMMER, Shamus
> or
> FUTZENHAMMER, Shamus, 1871-1970

Entry element
> GOGH, Vincent van
> or
> VAN GOGH, Vincent
> or
> ?

An impact of computer technology which has already occurred is the systematization of the description of library materials. This was brought about by the introduction of *International Standard Bibliographic Description (ISBD)*. I do not wish to discuss the merits or demerits of this particular way of systematizing description, but to make some deductions from its occurrence. The *ISBD* has been through a lengthy process of development. It will be seen that the second edition of *AACR* contains a complete scheme for the description of library materials based on *ISBD*. A fundamental aspect of *ISBD* is that the description is formalized in two ways. First, in the standard order in which the elements of the description are presented. Second, in the formalized punctuation that is used to separate one element of the description from another. This formalization was intended to have two purposes. The first was to enable the automatic translation of human-readable data into machine-readable data. Fairly simple programs can be used to recognize the various elements of the description. The second, and to my mind, much more important, purpose was to aid the human comprehension of descriptive data. Here we can see the interaction of machine systems and cataloging standards: The desire to make information more understandable to the user meets the necessity in the machine system for pieces of information (in this case elements of descriptive data) to be clearly delimited. Some people have said that this implies some kind of sacrifice of standards and the imposition of alien conventions on cataloging. I would reject both of these assertions as it seems to me that the systematization arises from an increased desire to communicate and from an enhanced understanding of the interaction of cataloging and machine- and human-readable systems. This interaction is entirely desirable and furnishes a good example of the sort of cooperation and growth that should take place in the future.

The *ISBD* system is widely used throughout the world and in our own English-speaking cataloging community. No such universal system exists for the formulation of headings and uniform titles, though there has been much discussion of the possibilities of such a system. There are a number of reasons why this universal system does not exist. The most important reasons are that the differences between different codes are far greater as far as access points are concerned than they were as far as description was concerned; and the fact that the question of the choice and form of headings is perceived to be far more important in its implications than the question of description.

We have, I would suggest, arrived at a point where many of the differences regarding access points are either resolved or on the point of resolution because of the introduction of machine systems. In a developed machine system a name package can carry a number of preferred forms of name, each of which is accompanied by an indication of the environment in which it is preferred. For example, the name package for the government of the U.S.A. can include the forms *United States; Etats-Unis;* and *Estados Unidos* with an indication that these are the preferred forms in an English language, French language, and Spanish language environment, respectively. Thus the machine can be used to resolve a fundamental problem in international standardization. There still remain certain problems that cannot be resolved by the manipulation of name packages. One problem which is representative of these is the question of standard entry element for persons with family names that include a prefix. Some codes enter all such names under the part following the prefix, others (as in the case of *AACR*) base the decision on the language of the person bearing the name, and others base the decision on the nationality of the person. There are two ways to solve this problem.

We can either aim at complete international agreement on entry elements or we can use the computer to arrive at a solution acceptable to all. This second solution presupposes that there is no one way to enter such a name. The cataloger's task is to recognize and code each element of the name, and to add other necessary indications. Programs can then be used to cite the name in the form appropriate to a particular output. (See Diagram 4.) If we take the example of the name VINCENT VAN GOGH, we find that it consists of three elements: a forename VINCENT, a prefix VAN, and a main element of surname GOGH. The cataloger would add codes to each of these and an indication of the language of the person, the nationality, etc. An *AACR* program would use the indication that the person's language was Dutch to assemble the name for printing in the form GOGH, VINCENT VAN. Other systems would use different programs to achieve different results.

The implication of all this is that we no longer need an international code of cataloging rules, whether based on the Paris Principles or not, because of the introduction of machine systems. We no longer need a single solution to each problem. The machine allows us to choose between a range of options, in a standard and controlled manner, and permits these options to be selected by program depending on the purpose for which a particular record is used. To return to a prevailing theme of this paper—the impact of technology on the work of the cataloger—the cataloger is then entrusted with the task of analyzing data and ensuring that alternative treatments are possible. He or she is no longer required to decide on one solution, and is therefore no longer presented with the kind of invidious choice that our present rules demand

My last instance of the changes being brought about by technology is that which is commonly, though inaccurately, known as alphabetical filing. Modern filing rules, such as those developed by John Rather for the Library of Congress and those being developed by the American Library Association and by the British Library Filing Rules Committee, are much simpler than their predecessors. This simplicity depends, to a great extent, on a principle which states that one should file a character as it is and not as if it were something else (Diagram 5). For example, the number 3 occurring in a title is filed as a number, in with other numbers, and in an order dictated by its numerical significance. One does not file it as if it were *t-h-r-e-e* or *d-r-e-i* or *t-r-o-i-s*. This change has resulted from a reconsideration of all our filing practices which itself resulted from the use of the computer in filing. This does not mean that it would be impossible to file 3 as if it were a word, in fact such a thing is perfectly simple. What it does mean is that the use of the computer in filing has made it necessary to look at our filing practices and to ask ourselves why we file one thing as if it were something else. The conclusion that most of us have come to is that such a practice may have had some validity in the past but has no validity now. It now seems a manifest absurdity to say that if this elephant were an orange, it would file in such-and-such a place. This is an illogical premise upon which to base an agreement. An elephant is not an orange, it belongs with the elephants and not with the oranges. Why, again, have we chosen to file names beginning with *Mc* as if they began with *Mac*? The answer is that they (almost) sound the same. Why base an aberration in arrangement on sound? These are the awkward questions which the process of mechanizing filing poses. I do not wish to argue for one filing arrangement or another, though I do believe that the simpler the arrangement and the fewer the rules, the more chance users have of finding information speedily. I wish merely to point out that the reconsideration of filing practices which was necessitated by the introduction of computer filing has been a healthy and fruitful process. It has made us examine every aspect of the process, to stop doing things out of habit, to retain those principles which are logical and comprehensible and to discard those which are simply the accretions of the years. I strongly urge that the type of reconsideration we have given to filing practices should be applied throughout the whole range of cataloging practices.

DIAGRAM 5

Filing

1 man . . .
2 femmes . . .
3 groschenoper. . .

or

dreadnought . . .
3 groschenoper . . .
Drell, Heinrich

and

trespasser . . .
3 femmes . . .
Trondheim . . .

Technology can bring three important benefits. The first of these is an improvement of the efficiency of our service to library users; for example, the user of a developed machine system can approach information at many levels and from many access points. The second benefit is that we are able to use our limited resources more sensibly; for instance, using a machine to arrange entries is more efficient and more cost-effective than using people to carry out that task, also the elimination of redundant and repetitive work of all kinds is something that tends towards efficiency and cost-effectiveness. The third benefit is the improvement of the nature of the work of those engaged in cataloging and other technical services. I hope I have demonstrated that the advent of the computer does not imply the abolition or the lessening of standards, that it does not imply the reduction of cataloging as a professional task, and that there is as much room for standards and for expertise in a computerized system as there ever has been. Furthermore, that the computer can be used, and is already being used, to eliminate drudgery, busywork, and useless toil in library systems.

I would like to close now with another quotation from William Morris in a vision that he had of the future : "All work which would be irksome to do by hand is done by immensely improved machinery; and in all work which it is a pleasure to do by hand machinery is done without." (That was, alas, from Chapter 15 of William Morris's *News from Nowhere*, 1890.)

DISCUSSION

Paul Fasana: I am impressed with Mr. Gorman's bold, confident, intellectually tight, and, perhaps, satisfying view of the future. There are many things that I agree with. There are three things I would like to query him about. He places emphasis on the long-range future and says that we shouldn't be concerned with the immediate future. Unfortunately, practical librarians have to be concerned with what we have now in terms of card catalogs; we have to be concerned with rules that are of the past. In effect there is a transitional period that has to be addressed. I can agree with many of the points that Mr. Gorman has made about the future, but how do we develop a strategy to achieve that future? There are card catalogs, there are retrospective collections to be concerned with. And then there's the important aspect of continuity with the past.

A second point that I would mention, one that he makes very ably, is about the factors that are affecting us. His view, however, of how they are affecting us is slightly different than mine. Change and technology are having an impact on libraries today; one cannot deny it. The issues, it seems to me, are in technology; for example, too often being too close to the operation, one tends to confuse the means with the end. The end here is not a clever use of computers; it's, I think, to prepare recorded knowledge for use by a general public. I'm not accusing Mr. Gorman of this sin; however, I think that if one becomes overly intellectual or overly mechanistic towards problems or operations of this sort this is a possible result. Another factor was change. I think that Mr. Gorman characterized librarians as being afraid of change. I would suggest that they have a concern with change because too often change can come to control. The objective is to control change, not to be controlled by change.

One last comment and that is that Mr. Gorman's paper seems to assume that change and the use of new and innovative technology will automatically result in progress and beneficial results. This is not necessarily the case. I would submit that we have to guarantee and insure in advance through empirical research, among other tools, that what we are implementing or replacing is better than what we presently have. This I find more satisfying than simple blind faith in change and technology.

Edwin Buchinski: I was very pleased to hear Mr. Gorman's remarks and his positive statements, and his request that we approach technology with a positive attitude. I think he should have emphasized that this attitude must be very critical. I think he is critical and his presentation dealt with primarily the cataloging rules. What the conference, as outlined by Mr. Freedman, lacks is someone who would look critically at technology and try to relate that to the catalog code. Some areas of technology that need to be examined and understood are things like data-base management systems. Mr. Gorman directed his comments at data-base management systems without identifying them. This is a new type of software just being developed and made commercially available. It is going to take some time before we all know what data-base systems can do and how they can be used in the library. Mr. Gorman definitely has anticipated these systems in his analysis of what the cataloging record will look like.

Librarians on the North American continent are not used to looking at a series statement and thinking of it as a serial record related to other items. Another point that Mr. Gorman made very strongly that I endorse is that the computer does not reduce the need for standards. In my present position, and in some of the work we're doing in the National Library of Canada, I must say that this point is being emphasized and reemphasized. Our authority system design at the National Library follows very closely the concepts that Mr. Gorman has outlined. Various packets of information are linked to others in our system; thus far in our development I think we've done a fairly complete job of personal names and corporate names; we are gradually getting to subject headings. At the National Library our need to take this kind of approach was highlighted by the requirement that we should provide access to bibliographic data in both of Canada's official languages. By taking the approach that Mr. Gorman has outlined it is possible to concentrate on the description and provide two sets of access points: one in English, one in French. Thus far the results are very encouraging and we definitely will be proceeding along this way.

Michael Gorman: Just a couple of points on Mr. Fasana's comments. I was aware of the fact that I did not address the transition period between now and then, because I felt this was an issue that would have taken much more time than I have. I'm not, however, unaware of this; I do believe that we need a radical solution to this problem. I would say that if I were the director of a large library with a card catalog, I would swiftly and as expeditiously as possible move to close it down. Now this may sound somewhat Draconian as an approach to the problem, but I really do believe, and I have studied this and thought about it very carefully for many years, that this is the only answer, that anything else is just an amelioration of the problem and is building up problems for the future.

The only other thing I would like to react to about Mr. Fasana's comment is that I am aware that there's always a danger of confusing the means and the ends, and I was attempting to point out that the end of getting information to your readers is the paramount thing. I have written somewhere that the catalog can only be judged by how efficiently it does that, and that is the only criterion by which you should judge catalogs.

Just in passing, I didn't actually say that librarians are afraid of change; I just said that I found it curious that among many people you find this fear of change, this cynicism about change. I don't think that librarians en masse have any one set of characteristics; I just found it interesting that one does come across such a large number of people who seem to feel this way. My own personal feeling is that one should be as optimistic as possible, and as positive as possible, because that is the only way to achieve results.

S. Michael Malinconico: You raised some questions regarding computer filing; if I might, I would like to offer perhaps a tentative answer to some of them, and to listen to your reaction. You asked if sound should inflict aberrations on filing arrangements. Well, if we start with the assumption that a computer is a tool, and if we make a rather benighted assumption that tools should be extensions of our human faculties, and if we make a further assumption that human sensory input is not limited to the visual, are we not perhaps then amputating our human faculties by limiting ourselves to the kind of meaningless cacaphonation of symbols with which computers deal, for the sake of trying to mimic the efficiency of computer logic?

Gorman: I understand the drift of your question. I think that large "alphabetical files" are very, very difficult things for people to follow. They're much more difficult than most library users realize. I think that we have to have two trends in filing; one is towards objectivity, the other towards simplicity. By *simplicity* I mean the fewer the exceptions, the more of a sporting chance the user has of understanding the arrangement. By *objectivity* I mean filing by criteria which we all know; we know for instance that 3 follows 2 and that *C* follows *B*. We have in the past, I think, tried to make guesses about how people will approach information; the classic example being the book about James Bond, which was called *The .007 Dossier*. Anyone of us could think of five places to file that by sound: *P* for point, *D* for double, *O* for o, etc. The only way we can come near to having a filing arrangement which people will understand is to have as few and as objective rules as possible. All right, it does mean that you rely on arbitrary characteristics, but I think that is the only way we are ever going to find things; I have had intimate acquaintance with very large files, and I know the enormous difficulty that people have, and, even more, the fact that they don't understand the difficulty they're having. They don't find something, and they assume it's not there. It is there; it's just that it's been carefully hidden away.

Malinconico: Agreed, a simple filing arrangement is probably easier to decipher. But, on he other hand, don't we provide more clues by creating a collocation and an arrangement of materials? Some people come into a library with a precise citation; many are unaware of the orthography of a title page. Does it really serve a user to ask to look for Mark Twain's *£1,000,000 Bank Note Robbery*? It turns out in that case, that it appears on the title page as pound sign, *1,000,000 bank note*. The only significant words in that case are going to be *bank note*. So does it really make sense to insist that the user be aware of the typographical caprices of that particular title page for the sake of a consistent set of rules?

Gorman: No, it doesn't, but I don't know of any filing rules by which the title would be found under BANK NOTE. I suspect that what you really want is some kind of retrieval system which allows you to pick out keywords in the title, and I would agree with that; but if you're going to find one place to file a title, the simplest place is dictated by the characters in that title. You know, the Burkhoff filing system many years ago said that there are four ways to spell Kaufmann and since nobody is going to come up with an exact means of spelling, the Burkhoff system filed them all together. That's a very different approach to what we've always done. It's not logical, but it has some merit to it. But I don't think it finds much support these days.

Dorothy Puryear: I couldn't agree with you more, Mr. Gorman; I couldn't be more for you, because you are talking about the people I deal with every day—the users. Simplifying the filing rules and adding more points of access are exactly what we need. As librarians we have continued to develop complicated rules for main entry; our users don't know about that; our users only want to find what they are looking for.

Ruth Tighe: I agree with Mr. Fasana, particularly in his concern with the fact that Mr. Gorman has ignored the transition period. You have talked about the fact that in the developed machine record concept the main entry becomes less significant. You are assuming, I think, that online access is ubiquitous, but in the interim what do you do with things like citations in journal articles or other footnotes which should lead you to a record? If there is no identification or acceptance or widespread use of a standard main entry, it makes it very difficult to reach that particular item itself; in other words, I think access has problems in that kind of a situation. Given that there will always be—or I am assuming there will always be—printed files, printed catalogs, how do you print out a catalog? What form of entry do you use in your catalog that will accommodate the different points of departure from which users are coming? Some people know that DANTE should be DANTE ALIGHIERI, and that the title is in a foreign language, and others do not. You can't assume that the same type or level of user will always use that one catalog.

Gorman: Yes, the first point, I think, arose out of a misunderstanding. I tried to convey the idea that in the developed machine system each package would contain an indication of the standard way to cite that person, that title, that body. If you were printing out bibliographic citations, that is, one citation alone for a work, it would be that preferred form of name, that preferred title. I wasn't advocating abandoning that; far from it, I was advocating retaining that idea. What I would do about printing out catalogs is to move as speedily as possible towards computer-produced microform catalogs. I don't mind if they're fiche or film, but they give far more access points simply because less material is used, and they are very much cheaper than printed paper catalogs. It seems to me that microform catalogs are the transitional medium. If you want my answer to the transitional period, it will be to close down the card catalogs as soon as possible and to move toward microform catalogs, which are very speedily updated.

I would predict an enormous change in microform technology and microform availability in the next few years. I personally believe that something akin to what happened to pocket calculators is going to happen to microform readers, that they're going to become ubiquitous and cheap. After all, they're considerably less complex than the television set; and when somebody is intelligent enough to realize that a $20 textbook printed on paper can be gotten out in a quarter of the time for $3 printed on microform, and when every student is carrying around a briefcase-sized microform reader, then we won't need to postulate or to argue for microform catalogs in libraries. They take up less room; they're more sound ecologically (they're not chopping down half of Canada everytime you make a large catalog); I can see nothing against them except the idea that many librarians have that people don't like them. I've never seen any evidence of this, and, in fact, such evidence as there is seems to prove the opposite. I'm old enough to remember when we first got televisions at home; my mother said you mustn't watch television more than a quarter of an hour because you'll go blind. And I think that kind of attitude is still around with microform.

Anne Lipow: You may yet go blind! I didn't even dare think about something that you raised as a goal and a hope about this new technology, that is, that somehow it will liberate us from the drudge work. I wonder if that's true. So far, the introduction of technology and online cataloging is evoking a lot of complaints from catalogers who say, "I'm now tied to a keyboard. I used to get up and walk around a lot and now I'm an extension of this terminal." I don't think that that is a very liberating experience, especially a terminal that's hooked to a large thing that almost no one understands, no one but a very few people. If I disapprove of something in my card catalog I understand completely how it got there; I could conceivably steal into the library in the middle of the night and change it all around, if I wanted to. I have no control over this computer, I don't understand it, although I support it. I don't understand a car either, but I use one, and I get places with it. But I'm not sure about the liberating experience that this is supposed to be in terms of one more thing: jobs. I think I'd rather see 5,000 filers than a machine put 5,000 people out of work. I think that we must not push the progressive nature of this too far.

Gorman: You covered several points. I really don't know what it means to be tied to a terminal as opposed to being a manual cataloger tied to a desk. Is it more difficult to get up from a terminal and go look at something than it is from a desk? I can give you a specific instance of the elimination of drudgery. In the *British National Bibliography* machine system—I'm talking about a primitive machine system as all of our systems now are—there is a British Government publication which is represented by about 370 cards. Each issue is cataloged individually for the *British National Bibliography*. That means that 370 times a year somebody sits down or writes out substantially the same information, the information about the new part being the only thing that's different. Now that is drudgery; it is also utterly inefficient because no matter how good your catalogers or your key-boarders are, there's a margin of error. The best typist in the world is going to miss a key every 2,000 characters. If you're going to write something out 370 times or type it out 370 times there will be at least two or three errors. In the developed machine system you would set up a record for that whole thing; then when the parts came in you would describe only the information relating to the parts and cite the number relating to the whole thing. That is a specific instance of elimination of drudgery.

As for putting people out of work, I have never seen any evidence of this. What I would like to see would be the redeployment of staffs of libraries. I think that librarianship as a whole, and I'm not talking about technical services, has had its priorities wrong. I've been working in libraries for over 20 years and throughout that entire period, you can very, very frequently go into a large library in search of information and have extreme difficulty finding somebody to help you because there are about 40 people sitting out in back doing something which somebody else is doing down the road. I think it's not a question of putting people out of work; it's redeploying people. I don't think that card filing is a job for a human being; I think it's a revolting job. Believe me, I started working in libraries when I was 15, and filed cards for what seems like a century, and it is absolutely appalling. It is also extremely inefficient. I remember that someone from the Library of Congress said that LC only had a 4% error rate in their filing in the card catalog. Can you imagine what that percentage represents?

Robert Meade: Mr. Gorman, would you comment a little more, please, on nonroman script and data bases like Russian, Hebrew, Arabic. You mentioned one possible solution; I was curious if you have some other ideas on the subject.

Gorman: This is something we've been considering for sometime in the British Library. The British Library, as you may or may not know, incorporates what was the British Museum Library with its extensive oriental collection, Slavic collection and so forth, so this has been a matter of considerable importance to us. There are three possibilities with nonroman names; you can take them in the form in which they appear in English language items, which is a kind of arbitrary form. (It can pop up in one form one week and in another form another week.) You can systematically romanize them, that is, turn them into a standard English form; the only drawback to that form is that nobody recognizes it. (If you want to read a polemic about this, read Wilson Follett's *Modern American Usage* where he fulminates for two pages about librarians imposing these ridiculous distorted names on the public.) The other thing you can do is to hold the names in their original form and have separate language catalogs. This is substantially what C. Sumner Spalding is arguing for in his *LRTS (Library Resources and Technical Services)* article. The problem with this is that it is relatively easy now in the present state of machine systems to deal with alphabetical languages, that is, to hold the Greek character set, the Russian character set, etc.; in fact, they're easier than the extended roman alphabet, which is rather complicated. The problem comes with ideographic languages. There's a great deal of work being done in Japan but I think it's fair to say that for many of these nonalphabetical languages, it is very difficult. What I was proposing was that for English language users the machine could hold the romanized form. I'm talking now about people who want to read a book by Tolstoy, say *War and Peace;* they don't want to read it in Russian, they want to read it in English, and they want to find it presumably in with all the other books in their catalog. You can have it in your standardized romanized form or you can take it as it appears very commonly on title pages. All I'm saying is that you can use the machine system to give you either option. No matter which form you ask for, you find the books by Tolstoy. Or you can print out one form in one catalog and another form in another catalog. This resolves the old public library vs. research library problem. The only country I know where this is being dealt with is in Denmark where they do set up different fields in their machine records saying, "This is a public library field, and this is the academic library field." As I work for a national library I don't feel partial either way but if I were a public librarian I think I would take exception to the idea that there was some kind of common plebian form which I could use. I mean, the New York Public Library is, after all, a fairly large library.

Ritvars Bregzis: I'd like to make two points. The first is an entirely technical one, and the second is a comment on the brilliant analysis by Mr. Gorman on bibliographic conceptualization. The technical point first: Indeed, the micro-readers and the microtechnology are here, and it is quite correct to say that just around the corner are some further breakthroughs. However, they probably should not yet be completely equated with the electronic calculator in that the electronic calculator has multiple magnitudes of analytic power. In optics there is really no comparable development to the large-scale micro-electronic integration. I suppose the closest they are really looking for in optics is a 72 times reduction in a pocket-sized reader, and they really are around the corner. Of course, that would put the holdings of large libraries on small microfiche in one's shirt pocket.

The more important point I want to make concerns bibliographic conceptualization. The analysis of a multilayer, multidimensional concept—getting away from the mandatory employment of some of the present conceptual constructs such as main entry—holds out a promise of integrating what we know as catalogers with what we know as indexers. In other words, we are getting away from the mandatory and exclusive use of authorized forms, and can handle these together with what I call *free form*. I suppose we are very close to indexing technology being married to cataloging technology, and I think this is a real breakthrough which we should be examining much more closely than we have thus far.

Gorman: The only comment I have to make is on your first point. The parallel I was trying to draw between the calculator and the microform reader was not a technical one, although the saying was that pocket calculators became cheap when they were manufactured in the millions. The only reason microform readers are expensive and not highly developed is that they're manufactured in the thousands. When you hit certain levels, prices go down sort of exponentially.

Barbara Coe Johnson: I represent probably the smallest type of library, a hospital medical library. We are technologically advanced in medicine, and many of us are able to have access to the medicine data base and catline of the National Library of Medicine (NLM). However, there is a lack of equality among equals that has to do with the way small libraries can get access to the data base. We're probably customers for your calculator output kind of microform reader, but for a while there won't be these microforms, and at sometime LC will close down its catalog—at this point where are we going to get the cards?

Gorman: I have no knowledge of or influence over the Library of Congress' plans for the future. I think the way ahead for small libraries will be that the larger libraries in a small country like Britain (in our case our national library) will custom-make printed catalogs and probably a microform catalog for them. We already do this in Britain for a couple of public libraries. What we do is to draw up certain records that smaller libraries ask for. If it isn't on the data base, the libraries create the records themselves in standard form and send them to us, but we create their catalogs. I think the advantage of technological change is that the user of the small library will get the kind of service which the user of a large library has had in the past. In other words, there'll be much more uniformity in cataloging service throughout all kinds of libraries, irrespective of their financial muscle. I think it's always been a mistake to assume that small libraries aren't important libraries. I think they're extremely important, in fact, but there is a problem there certainly. My local public library at home has a computer-produced microform catalog which is an extremely unsuccessful catalog. I was in there trying to use it and the bulb in the reader burned out. I went to the desk and said, "You know, there's something wrong with your microform machine," and she said, "Oh, that computer; it's always breaking down." So I think it's a problem of education there, too.

David Remington: LC is tentatively planning to close its catalogs in 1980. What we also are dealing with is the transition that's been discussed this morning, and we recognize that there will be a significant transition period for many of the 103,000 libraries in this and other countries using our products. So we definitely intend to continue to produce catalog type card records for a long time to come, for as long as they're needed and it's a significant need. I just wanted to assure you that that's in our thinking and not just in a dying way but in a more dynamic way than we've been doing it in the recent past.

Bertha Stone: As you know, the Smithsonian Library is quite an octopus and our catalog is varied and deals with many disciplines. I would like to make two comments: one to Ms. Lipow and I can surely sympathize with her predicament. I think she was subliminally, perhaps, touching on a point that has not been brought up, namely, quality control in cooperative cataloging, which we're all for. We sometimes get a record on the screen and look aghast at it, and say, "Has somebody really cataloged this?" This is something that somebody has done for me, and I am to accept it at the moment. Until there is more quality control, correcting a record is a very time-consuming part of this time-saving procedure. Secondly, one of the other virtues that was promised us when we went into automated cataloging was that filing would be a thing of the past. But, unfortunately, we have not closed down our card catalog and all these cards still have to be manually filed. I don't see those cards when they come from Ohio walking themselves into the catalog, so there is still manual work.

One more comment. When we close down the catalog and we're at the Utopia where everyone, curators, old scientists, etc., is walking around with these microform readers, you say it'll be far less costly. Have any studies been made as to what the national resources are of wood and petroleum, which, I believe, are the basic elements used to make these microform readers?

Gorman: I'm all for quality control and I think there isn't enough of it. In your first few comments I think you were making the point I was trying to make, namely, automating what you're doing already is always a fatal mistake. What you have to do is to think it out again. Very briefly, about the other point, microforms are petroleum based, but they use a very, very small amount of it. A microform catalog is a very tiny amount of material as opposed to a big book catalog.

Unidentified Speaker: Assume that one has a COM (Computer Output Microform) catalog in fiche form. What about the problem of theft? Someone could easily pocket the fiche catalog and take it home for his/her personal use as a subject bibliography of the library's holdings.

Gorman: I think you should eliminate theft by giving catalogs away. In other words, give a copy of the catalog to anyone who wants it. The whole point about having such a catalog is that it is freely available outside the library. You should guard against its destruction or theft by having duplicate copies. Another advantage to microform is that it's so cheap to have multiple copies once you've made the master.

Unidentified Speaker: I'd like to know Mr. Gorman's opinion. On two different occasions I heard a specialist in the field of information science say, "OCLC will kill catalogers." In the last issue of *Journal of Academic Librarianship*, someone wrote that graduates from library schools are not now required to take a cataloging course, they can get or receive their degree without cataloging.

Gorman: I may be English but I know enough not to comment about OCLC. Concerning the other comment, I think it should be a mandatory requirement for all library school students to take cataloging. In fact, the error in catalog education is teaching people to be catalogers when in fact they should be taught how to understand and to use a catalog.

Maurice Freedman: I'm very surprised that no one has commented on the following. I wondered, in your description of the removal of the main entry, if you were talking about a change in manifestation rather than in identification. It seemed that in your example of Dante Alighieri's work that you still had a basic identification upon which you were hanging all of these new or added access points, which seems to be very much within keeping with the notion propounded by Lubetzky in the Paris Principles. It seems that, conceptually, what you're proposing isn't really a radical change. What I've heard you suggesting is a far greater and more intelligent exploitation of the computer to generate many, many more access points and to provide many more manifestations of authors' names and the names of their works. The particular name and title employed would be determined by reference to individual user needs or individual collections of users' needs. But underneath all of that you still have Lubetzky's basic notion of *work and main entry,* the only way the various manifestations of authors' names and works can be related to each other, or organized.

In relation to Ritvars Bregzis's point: Without the basic notion of main entry, or what you call standard citation, to organize or relate these added access points, I would think that trying to integrate these records with any other indexing services would result in a chaotic situation. There would be no way to link or relate the various manifestations of an author's name or the variety of ways by which the author's works are known.

Gorman: The answer is that you replace the main entry with the idea of a standard citation, which does not preclude access by all the other things. The idea of the main entry or the preferred sort of name is in our current cataloging rules, and by current I mean the one that's not yet been published. I've just written a large number of pages which contain a large number of instructions saying, "enter under this," and "enter under that," so you are literally going to make an entry under this one thing. This is not a reality and hasn't been a reality for years. What "enter under" means translated in this environment is "standard way of citing this work is," or "the standard form of name for this person is." It does not preclude all the variant forms. I agree that the proposal about integrating indexing systems with the gothic systems is brought nearer but still is replete with problems.

Freedman: It would be oversimplifying things to substitute the notion of standard citation for "enter under," but it seems there's a tremendous similarity, and from that standpoint . . .

Gorman: If I were entirely in charge of *AACR2*, I would have a rule that said "when you have this problem, make the following entries; regard one of these as the standard entry if you wish to," instead of having a rule that says "enter under" with some kind of afterthought tucked away at the end of the chapter saying "also make the following entry." I think the order of priorities is wrong. By this, of course, I do not mean that *AACR2* is less than perfect, or that it's incapable of being used in modern systems.

Fasana: I'd like to make a comment and pose a question to Mr. Gorman. My comment isn't involved with the theoretical model that he has described and presented to you, except to note in passing that the information scientists of the early sixties had blind faith in the future of the use of computers, and what we have of that era is sort of a glorious failure. The computer cannot be used to synthesize new knowledge. My comment, though, really doesn't involve what the information scientists did in the past; rather, I'd like to comment on the message Mr. Gorman has presented that I feel is rather dangerous or pernicious. The underlying theme was change; change, however, which he characterized as something that had to be fostered. If a positive attitude towards technological change has to be fostered, I find this rather unnerving. Mr. Gorman goes on to threaten us with the fact that unless we learn to enthusiastically apply the new technology, the new era of computerized cataloging will never be realized. To me, I'd rather have mature judgment based on experience brought to bear. Let me quote three truisms or caveats that are popular now in systems analysis relative to change, and which I think are pertinent to Mr. Gorman's comments: *First,* change is something to be controlled rather than to be controlled by. *Second,* change should not be equated with progress; they are different. *Third,* we should not confuse the means with the end. Too often in Mr. Gorman's presentation I had the feeling that the means actually became the end in his mind.

Let me now ask Mr. Gorman a question; perhaps it's a plea. As a practical administrator of a large technical services operation, I'd like to know what he sees for the short-range future. We have a bold, mechanistic view of the long-range future, but we're told that we should sacrifice everything. We're told that we should be radical in order to realize the long-range potential of computers, but again being an administrator, let me ask, what will we do with existing card catalogs? Do we simply walk away and abandon them? Is this a reasonable, rational, responsible attitude towards our public? How will we relate the past with the future? This is a technological question of great import, one, though, that Mr. Gorman has avoided in his talk. And third, what advice can he give us towards being able to control change so that what we will have will be progress rather than simple, meaningless change?

Gorman: I'd like to make a very brief rejoinder to Mr. Fasana's comments: If the opinions and the sentences which he attributed to me came over in my talk, then my talk was a complete failure. I had no intention of conveying any such message and I sincerely trust that if these things get published and people read them that they would try to see that I was specifically not advocating change for change's sake. I was saying that we shouldn't have a supine acceptance for temporary limitations, etc. Beyond that I really don't wish to comment. It is evident that there is a complete divergence of views, and if one's arguing from such different premises, one is never going to reach agreement.

As for the question about what to do with the large card catalog: I would (if I were in the fortunate position of being able to control such a thing) close it down. I would close it down immediately, or with all due dispatch for several reasons, some of which I have discussed in my talk. I don't think that it's the kind of work that people ought to be engaged in, and I don't think that it is any longer an efficient tool because it absorbs an enormous amount of money in a totally sterile way, and it is an encumbrance to the library system. In fact, it becomes the end rather than the means. So I would close it down. If you wish my views on how you ought to close it down, I think the best way to close catalogs down is by the publication date of the material contained in them. In other words, not to close it down arbitrarily on the 31st December and just say anything acquired by the library after this point will be in the new catalog. I think there are several positive advantages to maintaining the old system. These advantages are advantages to the users because they know which catalog to look in for given items, and there are advantages to personnel because such work absorbs the work of people trained in maintaining the old catalog and who may not wish or, for some reason or another, are not suitable for being retrained in the new catalog. I hope that's my answer to your question: close it down.

Eleanor Crarey: I've long admired and been fascinated by Michael Gorman's concept that we could have a totally new and flexible approach to our information that did not have to be limited by a physical format. I think this is a very exciting and very relevant point of view. I do have a couple of questions, though. First of all, I've worked as an administrator also and I have to say I can't accept the fact that financial considerations are only temporary. They seem to be becoming increasingly more serious for all of us, and there's no way to say that an online catalog is a cheap investment. I think we can demonstrate that sooner or later it does pay its way, but it's a very heavy thing to start out with.

I also would like to point out the difference between an online situation and a microform type of catalog. Microform, unfortunately by its nature, is still static, and an online format, of course, is an absolutely dynamic form, one that lends itself most readily to everything that Mr. Gorman has described. An online catalog is accessible by any element that you choose to program, tag, locate, and manipulate, and I think that is a very fine concept. However, the microform catalog, once you've set it, there it is. There's a distinction that has to be kept in mind, but one can easily lead to the other. Certainly an online catalog can lead to a dynamically formatted microform catalog and I'm thinking of many of our small libraries in remote locations for whom an online catalog would be financially out of consideration. Line costs in this country are pretty important. Mr. Gorman comes from a country where line costs probably are not as major an item as they are for us in a vast geographical set-up, and until we have some sort of satellite arrangement that's something we have to think about.

I also had a question about something that I don't know whether he'd care to go into now. I'm not certain that I fully understand, in something that becomes a static catalog, such as the microform, what the difference really is between the standard citation that would be accessible by various forms versus an entry that is a totally full entry to which you'd have multitudinous added entries, and at each point of your added entry you again get your total citation?

Regarding discs or storage space, one of the points Mr. Gorman has made is certainly marvelous, that is the concept of linking numbers, because sooner or later that's going to save you a lot of space when you don't have to keep repeating and repeating and repeating data, such as forms of names or forms of titles.

Gorman: If I could just take the points in the order in which they were made. I'd like to make one observation about costs. It was estimated to me recently that a large university library in this country spent over $200,000 a year on filing card catalogs. Now that is an awful lot of money. If you're thinking in terms of a capital investment that will abolish this huge expenditure, then I think one should weigh that kind of sum against what you're talking about.

I may have somehow given the impression that I don't work in a kind of real-world situation; I do work for the British Library, a newly formed library which includes one of the largest catalogs in the world, and which also has one of the most technologically backward catalogs in the world. We are working on the system I have described with the express notion of replacing it—so it is not an idle hobby of mine, to sit there and devise impractical, immature, and expensive systems.

Microforms interest me because I think they are different from the other alternatives precisely because of the speed with which they can be produced and the relative cheapness of the material from which they are produced. I can give you one instance of that: The British Library uses something called "Books in English," an ultramicrofiche which has a reduction of 250x, i.e., 1/250th the size of the original. It contains all the English language items from the U.K. MARC data bases. Something upwards of 70,000-80,000 records, producing 300,000 entries or thereabouts, are on a very small number of these ultrafiche. You could put them in an envelope and post them if you wish. It's produced in a tenth of the time it takes us to produce the printed *British National Bibliography Annual Cumulation*. It takes ten times as long to produce the paper pages, and it costs an enormous amount of money for each copy; whereas once you've made the master of the ultrafiche, duplicate copies get progressively less and less expensive. The idea is of a kind of throwaway catalog that you can afford to update speedily and often alters the nature of the thing.

Regarding your other point, what I was saying was that because the microform is so cheap, it is possible to duplicate full entries over and over again, something you can't do in a book catalog. Therefore, for practical uses in a library environment there would be a number of full entries with a number of different access points, none of which would necessarily be distinguished as the standard form. In other words, any access point would be equally valid and give a user the same amount of information.

Communication with an online catalog is what I meant when I referred to these short limitations. An extensive international MARC network study is being done which has a special paper on the telecommunications aspects. The prognosis on this for Western Europe, which is a pretty large area, is that it will be possible to bring this kind of online access almost instantaneously throughout that region.

Already in the United States you have networks of telecommunication, computer interactive networks, which are not necessarily used for library purposes but which can be so used. I have a feeling, you see, that all our old technologies are getting progressively more expensive and more inefficient, and that all our new technologies are getting progressively cheaper and more efficient because of questions of scale. For example, a terminal is now a very expensive item, but when terminals are produced in the millions rather than in the thousands, these then become considerably cheaper. You can see that kind of progression in the development of television, for example, and a terminal is perhaps less complicated than a color television.

Hugh Kirkendall: In Mr. Gorman's talk he delineates the fact that there could be multiple full entries. However, with a massive catalog such as the British Library Catalog, wouldn't it be much more economical to have multiple-entry access points which are cross-references rather than full entries? Even on the fiche you are required to use the data processing equipment to sort each of the variable entries. Whether you sort for printing purposes or for COM output purposes, or give an individual's name in a variety of ways, depending upon the country for which you are producing the catalog, that manipulation still has to be done by the machine for each entry.

Gorman: The obvious answer is yes, of course. In the present state it would be necessary; you wouldn't be able to duplicate every entry under every form of an author's name. You would be left with the problem of the reference which is inherently, to my mind, an undesirable form. The more one can do away with references, the better, because references are frequently obscure to people; to us it's very obvious what is intended if something says GOGH, VINCENT VAN see VAN GOGH, VINCENT or the other way around. We've done some observations of people using the British Museum catalog, who are by definition not the lowest grade of intelligence in the country, and we found that people simply do not understand the instruction we're providing. So anything they look up that doesn't give them the information is inherently undesirable. I do accept that there are economic constraints at the moment. Where they will not exist, of course, is in the online system. You will, in fact, have a reference. It's just that the machine will take the instruction, not the person, and it will take you to the information and present the information as if it were a full entry. But I accept the fact that there presently are economic constraints.

Unidentified Speaker: I have several questions. I'd like to speak about online cataloging because that's what I'm connected with. We've been on OCLC for over a year now, and I'd like to say that some of the problems with online cataloging have not been brought up. I think that you are talking about a highly advanced computer; at least, OCLC can't do some of the things that you mention. You cannot, at the moment, search via the subject entry. The computer is only as good as the original input and a very good example is the initial article in the title entry. I am the original music inputter; I do a lot of music scores and a lot of the nonbook cataloging as well. You cannot find the material; you can't get to it. It may be in OCLC, but you can't get it. Try looking up Beethoven's *Fifth*. You also neglected to mention downtime on a computer. We took a survey and over the year we have been on OCLC we average about 18 hours a month downtime; the computer is asleep. Also, you were talking about closing the card catalog at a certain date. Well, if I were the person using the card catalog, this would bother me because our patrons many times don't know when the item is published. They want some information by subject or author or title; why not put everything into the computer, that is, why not input the shelflist? Right now with OCLC updating is free. We're starting to input our shelflist. I know that Wright State University in Ohio and many other large institutions have input their shelflist. This is something to consider.

Finally, going back to financial aspects, both the hardware and personnel costs are expensive. I find that we are so linked to the computer that when the computer takes a nap we just sit there staring into space. Fortunately, we still have a card catalog. Can you imagine what would happen if we had terminals in a public service area? Then what?

Gorman: I intended to speak about what I saw as the machine record and machine system of the future. What you said about your problems with the online catalog is summed up in your own quotation; it's only as good as the original input, to which I would add that it's only as good as the system into which you're inputting. The particular system of which you speak is not a good system in my eyes insofar as it is not a developed machine system. OCLC is simply what I refer to as a mechanization of the card catalog. I am aware of the downtime problem with computer systems. It is very difficult to measure a breakdown in the card catalog, but I think you will find that almost all very large card catalogs have, in fact, broken down by one criterion or another. Take your point about the conversion of existing records. I would urge you most sincerely and strongly to think twice or three times before putting your shelflist into an undeveloped system. It will be necessary in the future to convert one's existing records. Mr. Fasana asked me the question of what I would do now, and what I would do now is to close the catalog. What I would do in the future is to transfer the information in the catalog in a kind of orderly manner into a developed system. I would certainly not transfer it into an undeveloped system such as OCLC's.

The problems that you refer to are not inherent computer system problems; they are problems in the misapplication of the technology. As far as the terminals are concerned, I would guess that you will have times even in the future when they will break down, but technology does improve. One doesn't have to be particularly old to go back to the analogy I used in answering the last question, to remember what televisions looked like 25 years ago and how inefficient and costly they were, and how it's now possible to get one that is nearly 100 percent perfect. Nothing in the world is ever going to be 100 percent perfect, but computer problems are more immediate and more tangible. I would urge you not to confuse what can be accomplished using the computer with the misapplications.

Alice Drake: The articles that I read say that the computer is changing. I read articles about voice transmission being preferable to the old inefficient number-crunching system that we have now. Do you feel that we should stay with our old number-crunching, inefficient system or switch to voice transmission, which seems to be coming up fairly fast? At least, shouldn't we be thinking in these terms?

Gorman: I would use whatever is the most expeditious way of getting data into the system at the time that one's doing it. As far as voice transmission is concerned, I understand that the problem is one which I encountered yesterday afternoon when I asked somebody directions in this city and he said, "What did you say?"

Mary Blackburn: It seems to me that with a real computer system of the future, once you've described the material and put it in, there may be even more capabilities than you describe. You could program it to rethink your subject headings. I'm a serials cataloger, and I just have accepted that there's going to be change. Not only is the material I have constantly changing but the way people think about it is constantly changing. If you have the microprint catalog or the online catalog, you have the capability of going ahead and changing it according to the latest thought. Such changes with a card catalog are absolutely impossible; you're stuck with the past and with past ways of thinking. This is one of the things the future kind of catalog can do for us. It will really be the best; our product will represent the latest thoughts—the way people are thinking about things right now, rather than something 20 years, 10 years, 50 years old.

Gorman: I agree with you. The reason I didn't bring this up in my paper is that I've learned from bitter experience that it's well to be radical about one thing at a time. I think the flexibility of the machine system will allow all kinds of different ways of getting access to information.

Bill Pease: We recently started on OCLC, but my question is not particular or peculiar to OCLC; it has to do with any online system, in fact, any remote cataloging system. It is in regard to local authentication. This seems to be our big hangup: the time and the level of review we feel we should go to in verifying the data in OCLC. I would like that problem of local authentication to be commented on by Mr. Gorman.

Lynn Smith: I don't pretend to speak for the library community, but I think I do speak for the concerns of a great many people. It seems that just as the computer was ignored in the 1967 *AACR*, it now seems to be driving the current standards. I wonder if I could get you to comment a little on what is happening now, which seems to be throwing people into perhaps the twenty-first century before we are truly out of the nineteenth. I think that there are too many libraries in this country and around the world which will not be able to embrace the computer immediately; that the demise of the main entry is going to prove a real problem for single entry catalogs, such as serial union lists and check-in records; that many of us who have had to deal with the card catalog, will still have to deal with the card catalog. Perhaps you can talk about the form of the cataloging rules as they are shaping up now, and what it will do to those of us who will still remain in the end of the nineteenth and the beginning of the twentieth century.

Gorman: I think it's inappropriate for me at this point in the Institute to answer questions of that nature. I'd be very happy to do so after people have spoken about *AACR*; I don't want to anticipate what they're going to speak about. I agree with you on your general point: I don't want to dodge the issue but I think we should listen to the papers on *AACR* first. There is a definite problem in that the cataloging rules we've had have been firmly rooted in a bygone era. I'm not sure that these new rules are going to be rooted in the present. I think we might have got up to the 1940s, but I would probably really find that my fears go in the opposite direction.

Dianna Shepler: I was disappointed to hear Mr. Gorman dismiss the problem of filing rules so quickly. We have a microform catalog. Because of economic constraints, we do not reproduce the complete entry at each point, so I see the problem of the *Mac's* and *Mc's* as a more difficult one. They have been interfiled in the past to make the catalog more usable by the public, and obviously machine filing is unacceptable to the public. However, to program the computer to file according to our usual rules is far too expensive. To come up with a happy medium is not an easy thing.

Gorman: I'm sorry; I didn't wish to skate over that. I just wanted to point to one development in filing rules. I'm actually one of the very few people in the world who's interested in these things. I'm the chairman of the British committee that has just developed a set of filing rules. I've had discussions with ALA's filing rules committee. You say things like the unacceptability of machine filing, but it all depends on what you mean by acceptable. To take a very broad stand: Large catalogs, irrespective of their form, are very complex to use because of the way in which they're arranged. Now, I know a large library catalog in this country where the person in charge of filing has to adjudicate on the average four times a day on where a particular card should go. Now, if you have to fetch this person from an office at the other end of the building in order for her to say where the card is going to go in the catalog, what hope do you or I have of ever finding that card? Therefore, I would advocate that we need rules that are based on simple, comprehensible principles, and one of the principles is to file something as it is. That you don't file *Dr.* as *doctor*, you file it as *Dr.*; that you don't file *Mc* as *Mac*, but you file it as *Mc*; and so on. But what do you mean by machine filing? You can get the machine to file it upside down in mile-high purple letters. The question is whether it is worth spending money on something that is inherently complex or that makes what is already a complex tool, more complex.

Unidentified Speaker: In converting catalog records to machine-readable form, would your advice be to make the record as complete as possible? How would you reconcile the difference between the public library, which feels it needs the minimum amount of information and has a pre-MARC system, and a research library which wants a more complete record? Do you have any advice on that subject?

Gorman: I gave a paper at the University of Illinois Clinic on Data Processing (1976), which was about the conversion of catalog files because I had been involved in a reasonably extensive conversion in Britain. I think that there is really an irreconcilable conflict; there are the problems of the cost of upgrading full information and putting it into machine-readable form, the editing costs, the keyboarding costs, and so on. On the other hand, what you don't put in, you'll never be able to use in the future. Now, what I see as the ideal of a machine system is to produce an all-purpose tool, a single tool which is no longer a catalog. If you're going to a library seeking information, there's a sporting chance that there may be seven or eight different files where this information may be found; it may be in an order file; it may be in the bindery; it may be in a circulation file; it may be in the catalog; or it may be in any of a number of other files. The ideal use of the machine would be to create one file that would give you the reference status of a given item, to say that it exists; that we've ordered it or we haven't got it yet; that it exists but it is at the bindery; or that it exists, but it was borrowed by professor so-and-so three-and-one-half years ago.

Now if you want to create that multipurpose tool, you can't do it on the basis of limited records. So that's something I have to think about very, very carefully. I think the big danger is converting something just for one use, rather than converting it to act as the basis for all your activities in the future. These particular chickens do come home to roost. We've already had this problem in Britain. We've converted some particular files in the British Library. The British Library is a conglomeration of already existing libraries and many catalogs, so we've had a vast range of experience in the last five years. We converted a particular file simply to get it in machine-readable form as a catalog; but then we wanted to tie it in with the circulation list and found that we didn't have enough information. The reverse often happens; circulation lists are very abbreviated; there's not enough information for cataloging purposes. One needs to think very carefully about it. It may be that the answer is to postpone action. I think very often we change things too quickly. We should think about change, weigh the implications, see what other people are doing, see what kinds of things can be done. After all, maybe it doesn't matter if you convert your catalog in 1983 as opposed to 1981, especially if you're going to get a better result.

Freedman: The big problem is what you're going to produce for the user to see, and the public library user may not need to see all that information. But it's a separate issue from what goes in. If you have it all in the machine, then someone who needs that extra information would be able to have access to it.

George Richardson: If you don't include all of the record at the time of conversion, what's omitted is permanently unavailable. A person who spoke earlier indicated that perhaps a system such as Michael Gorman has described could only exist in the future. I just wanted to point out to those of you who don't know that a system very like the one he described exists in the State of Washington within the Washington Library Network. It has a data base with a structure similar to what he has described, and it is searchable by subject, series, title, keyword and author, etc.

Gorman: Most of my ideas were based on work we've done in the British Library, which is published in *Program*, the library automation journal in England. The system we developed is called the Merlin system. The journal has at least two articles in the last year by colleagues of mine describing the system from the machine side.

Barbara Lamson: Do you foresee your computer idea requiring each library to develop its own computer base, or do you see it on a regional or national computer base?

Gorman: This kind of work can only go ahead on a cooperative basis, whether it be based on economic circumstances, the size of one's country, for example, or various other extraneous factors. I also firmly believe, as an employee of a national library, that the system should be at least coordinated, though not dominated, by the national library.

The Traditional Ideals of Cataloging and the New Revision

by Seymour Lubetzky

As a veteran member of the cataloging profession who witnessed the miscarriage of one revision and the compromise of another, progressively principled and promising one which followed it, I should like first of all to express my appreciation to the enterprising and energetic partnership of Mitch (Freedman) and Mike (Malinconico) for their indefatigable efforts to focus attention and foster discussion on current developments and issues in cataloging, both by their own contributions as well as the organization of such forums as the present Institute. As one who was deeply involved in the revision now being superseded barely a decade after its conclusion, I am glad of the opportunity to comment on two basic aspects of that and the current revision. I feel particularly happy to be associated on this occasion with Mr. Gorman whose writings I have admired for some time not only for their thoughtfulness and perspicuity but for the style and wit they have brought to the literature of cataloging. If I do not seem to agree fully with Mr. Gorman on the new revision, it is not because of any failure on my part to recognize fully the prospective role or importance of the computer in cataloging—apparently the dominant factor in the current revision—or the real improvements made in certain aspects of the revision, but because I think that the basic, traditional ideals regarding the character of the individual entries and their integration in the catalog are unaffected by the technology used and remain as valid for the optimum achievement of the objectives of the catalog as ever. I am coming to these ideals shortly, but I cannot forgo commenting first on Mr. Gorman's presentation because I think that it characterizes best the spirit of the present revision.

Mr. Gorman begins by emphasizing that the advent of the computer inaugurates "a new era in librarianship" and urges strongly a reconsideration of "our pre-computer systems" and, if need be, "the abandonment of cherished ideas of the past" in order to benefit fully from the potentialities of the new technology. As examples of these potentialities, he suggests the possible abandonment of the idea of the main entry—which certainly would greatly simplify and expedite the process of cataloging—and cites what he considers a conspicuous improvement in our filing system induced by its computerization. Together, these examples suggest that the promise of the computer is not only to mechanize and expedite operations, but to simplify and improve the quality of the systems themselves. I shall be discussing the question of the main entry later, but would now like you to look with me a little more closely at the filing exploit which Mr. Gorman urges upon us as an example to be followed "throughout the whole range of cataloging practices."

What happened in that case is that some of our filing rules proved rather inhospitable to the computer. One of the most vexatious of these rules was the requirement that a numeral be filed as if it were written out as a word in the language of the text—for example, the numeral *3* should be filed as *three,* or *drei,* or *trois,* etc.—something incongruous to the nature of the computer. However, a reconsideration of this rule, prompted by a desire to facilitate the use of the computer in filing, led to the conclusion that the filing of numerals as if they represented words was really "a manifest absurdity," a confusion of "elephants" and "oranges"—that numerals belong with numerals and words with words. This realization at once obviated the obstacle to computerization of filing and contributed clearly to the improvement of the filing system itself.

But is the filing of a numeral as if it represented a word really "a manifest absurdity"? A recourse to the catalog will readily reveal that numerals and the words expressing them are frequently interchangeably used in similar titles and names and sometimes in the titles of editions and translations of the same works. For example:

Four Greek Poets (Edmund Heeley, ed. & tr.)
4 Great Comedians (Donald W. McCaffrey)

Seven Years' Harvest (Henry Seidel Canby)
7 Years' Solitary (Edith Bone)

Seven Arts Press
7 Poets Press

The Seven Arts (serial)
7 Arts (serial)

Nineteen Eighty-Four (George Orwell)
1984 Revisited (Robert Paul Wolff)

Four Thousand Years of China's Art (Dagny Carter)
4000 Years of Chinese Art (Wadsworth Atheneum)

Twentieth Century America (David A. Shannon)
20th Century America. 3d ed. (David A. Shannon)
Twentieth Century America. 4th ed. (David A. Shannon)

One Thousand and One Nights
1001 Nights

Les Mille et Une Nuits
1001 Nuits

Tausend und Eine Nacht
1001 Nacht

Would separation of the names and titles beginning with numerals from those with the numbers expressed by words really facilitate the use of the catalog by those for whom it is made? And what about names and titles beginning with roman numerals? Mr. Gorman hails the "simplicity" of "the principle which states that one should file a character as it is and not as if it were something else;" how, then, is one to file a character which is at the same time an alphabetic letter and a roman numeral? The periodical titles *The Twentieth Century* and *The XXth Century* are alternate expressions of the same number; would it help the catalog user to have them separated in filings, and, if so, where would a reader be expected to look for the latter title in the catalog? What we have here is a situation where a number may be expressed in writing by words, numerals—arabic, roman, and others—or a combination of words and numerals, e.g.:

> *One Hundred Million Acres* (Kirke Kickinbird)
> *100,000,000 Guinea Pigs* (Arthur Kallet)
> *100 Million Lives* (Richard Fryklund)

The traditional filing rules are designed to cope with this situation; but the new principle "that one should file a character as it is and not as if it were something else" simply ignores it. And what this example really illustrates, it seems to me, is that in undertaking a change or revision of any rules one would be well advised to determine first the underlying problem or problems that may have given rise to those rules. Which brings me to the subject proper of my part in this discussion.

One of George Santayana's dicta, which is engraved as a guiding principle in my mind, is his admonition that "Those who [ignore] the past are condemned to repeat it." As custodians of the records of the past, we implicitly profess that an awareness of the work and thoughts of our predecessors is essential if we are to benefit from their experience and avoid repetition of their mistakes. It behooves us, therefore, in considering the revision of this Bicentennial, to recall the cataloging ideals promulgated in the first Centennial of this country and note the changes contemplated.

In 1876, on the occasion of the first Centennial, the Bureau of Education published its monumental "Special Report" entitled *Public Libraries in the United States of America: Their History, Condition, and Management*, which included a disproportionately lean-looking (89 p.) Part II representing a separate and quite distinct work entitled *Rules for a Printed Dictionary Catalogue*, by Charles A. Cutter. The inclusion of these rules as a part of the festive report expressed recognition of the importance of good cataloging to the quality of librarianship, and of Cutter's *Rules* as an eminent and fitting contribution to the commemoration of the Centennial by the library profession.

What are the basic characteristics of the catalog envisaged by Cutter that won for his rules the recognition accorded them? The answer may readily be observed on the pages of his *Catalogue of the Library of the Boston Atheneum, 1807-1871*, the second volume of which also appeared in 1876. That catalog, based on Cutter's rules, exhibits a deliberate brevity and clarity of the individual entries, and a pattern of integration of the entries designed to reveal to the user of the catalog the intrinsic relations of the materials in the library and thus help him/her to utilize the library's resources more fully .

Cutter, as if anticipating the *ISBD* a hundred years later, took pains to explain at length and emphatically the importance of brevity and clarity in catalog entries, and his explanation warrants extended quotation here:

> The more carefully and student-like the probable use of the library the fuller the title should be—*fuller, that is, of information, not of words*. Many a title a yard long does not convey as much meaning as two well chosen words. . . . The title must not be so much shortened that the book shall be confounded with any other book . . . , or that it shall convey a false or insufficient idea of the nature of the work. . . . On the other hand, it must not retain anything which could reasonably be inferred from the rest of the title *or from its position under a given heading*. [Italics added.]

This prescription is further supplemented by an explanatory footnote:

> It must make these omissions not only that the catalogue may be short but *that consulting it may be easy*. Other things being equal, *that title is best which can be taken in at a glance*. What has been said in defense of full titles may be true, that "it takes longer to abridge a title than to copy it in full," but it is also true that it takes longer for the printer to set the unabridged title, and *longer for the reader to ascertain its meaning*, and a long-title catalogue besides being more expensive is more bulky and therefore less convenient. [Italics added.]

In the course of the following quarter of a century Cutter continued to improve his rules, and issued three more editions embodying various additions and changes. But in all these years he apparently found no cause for changing a single word in the above statement—except in spelling: from *catalogue* to *catalog* and *defense* to *defence*. Nor did Cutter neglect the matter of punctuation and capitalization, but counseled "a minimum of capitals" and the simplest punctuation—foregoing even the use of ellipses to indicate omissions in the transcription of a title "unless by *etc.* when the sentence is manifestly unfinished." All of this was intended to clear for the reader his/her path in the catalog, to obviate anything that might distract his/her attention or otherwise retard his/her progress, and to facilitate in every way possible his/her search in the catalog.

Now, is this still a valid ideal of cataloging? The answer could hardly be in the negative. The catalog is an instrument of communication between the library and its users; and the clearer and more salient the relevant information is, the more readily will it be comprehended, and the more effective will be the use of the catalog—not only by the public but also by the library's own staff in their multifarious operations. But the present revision, incorporating *ISBD,* will literally clutter the entries with obtrusive redundancies and esoterics that will only obscure the content of the entries and obstruct the use of the catalog.

What is behind the redundant repetition of the author's name after the title when the same name is already given before that title, and behind the esoteric punctuation added to the normal punctuation of the entry? We are given a theoretical explanation and three practical reasons, none of which is, I think, tenable.

The repetition of the author's name, it is asserted, follows from a recognition that the heading of an entry and the description of an item are two distinct elements intended to serve separate purposes, and, to be complete in itself, the description must include the author's name appearing in the item cataloged. The author heading, it is argued, is not a part of the description but an "organizational factor" which may or may not agree with the name appearing in the publication. When the name in the author heading happens to coincide with that in the author statement there is an apparent redundancy, but that is merely a fortuitous result of circumstances, not one to be attributed to the requirements of *ISBD*. This theory might indeed be maintained if the catalog contemplated were to be one based on the idea of a title-unit entry, where the author heading is not an organic part of the entry but one of the added "organizational factors." However, if the catalog is to be based on the traditional main entry which normally begins with the author's name as the heading, and we recall that that name is normally to agree with that used by the author in his works, then *ISBD* is a prescription for wholesale redundancy in the catalog. The proceedings of a conference, for example, which heretofore have readily been located in our catalog under the name of the conference followed by the title, are, under *ISBD*, to have the full name of the conference gratuitously repeated after the title only to encumber the entry and obscure the significant elements of its content; e.g.:

> Conference on the Environmental Impact of Water Chlorination, Oak Ridge National Laboratory, 1975.
> The Environmental Impact of Water Chlorination: proceedings of the Conference on the Environmental Impact of Water Chlorination, Oak Ridge National Laboratory, Oak Ridge, Tennessee, October 22-24, 1975/Robert L. Jolley, editor . . .
>
> 76-602547
> MARC

Under certain circumstances, the author's name may be repeated thrice—in the heading, the title, and after the title; e.g.:

> International Computing Symposium, 4th Antibes, France, 1975.
> International Computing Symposium, 1975: proceedings of the International Computing Symposium, 1975, Antibes, France, 2-4 June 1975 . . .
>
> 75-38988
> MARC

I submit that a theory productive of such extravagant entries is hardly calculated to serve best the interests of the library or of the users of its catalogs.

As for the practical reasons, we are told that *ISBD* "is designed to meet three requirements"—in fact, requirements that could only miraculously be met. The first requirement is "that records produced in one country or by the users of one language can be easily understood in other countries and by the users of other languages." Does it really mean what it says—that an entry written in a given language will suddenly become "easily understood" by all who do not understand that language, presumably by the mere addition of the *ISBD* punctuation? The *ISBD* punctuation only tags, not very clearly and not very consistently, the anatomy of an entry and purveys no other information. All that one who will take the trouble to familiarize himself/herself with the symbols could tell from the *ISBD* punctuation is what part of the entry contains the title, what part the edition statement, and what part the imprint. There is, of course, the most conspicuous and frequently used slash (/) which marks the statement of responsibility, but whose absence may be misleading. When the title is not followed by the slash, it may appear as one without a statement of responsibility, when in fact there may be a clear statement of responsibility but one which grammatically forms a part of the title, in which case the slash is not used. This is about all the intelligence to be derived from the *ISBD* punctuation; is this to make an entry in a given language "easily understood" in all other countries where that language is not understood?

The second requirement to be met by *ISBD,* we are told, is "that the records produced in each country can be integrated into files or lists of various kinds containing also records from other countries." It should be clearly recognized, to begin with, that integrability of entries requires an agreement on the rules to be followed in their preparation, but not on any particular rules. The rules to be followed must be validated on their own merits. What can be said in favor of *ISBD* is that it represents an international agreement; but an agreement on inadequate rules is worse than a disagreement. The former serves to sanction and entrench methods detrimental to the quality of our catalogs, while the latter would at least serve to keep the issues alive for future reconsideration—as happened in the case of the British refusal to go along with the American compromises in the last revision. In one report on *ISBD,* Sumner Spalding relates about the ill-advised decision to restrict the use of square brackets in the entry to the title proper and the author statement, so that even the initiated could not tell from the entry whether the other information is from the title page or elsewhere in the book; and he sighs, "We lost the battle on this one."[1] Spalding's regret is quite understandable, for few of those seeking to identify particular editions 'in the catalog, including the library's own staff, will fail to be confused by the results of this decision. But would not the cause of cataloging have better been served if those who recognized the fallacy of this decision had refused to go along with it—and thus would have saved the library users of their own countries incalculable confusion? Beyond this, I think, the illusion is created that *ISBD* is crucial for integrability of the entries produced in various countries and that its adoption will usher in the day when the entries produced in any country will readily be integrable in the catalogs of any other country. The reality is that the primary and indispensable requirement for integrability of entries—on a local, regional, national, or international level—is an agreement on the rules of entry, not description. So far we have agreed only on the general principles of rules of entry, and there are yet the forbidding barriers of language and alphabet to overcome. The grand objective projected here will be little affected by *ISBD*. Meanwhile we are asked to accept encumbrances that will needlessly impair the effectiveness of our catalogs, and of all the operations and services of our libraries depending on them, for an indefinite time to come.

The third requirement which is to be met by *ISBD* is "that records in written or printed form can be converted into machine-readable form with the minimum of editing."[2] True, but this is accomplished by transferring part of the necessary editing for the computer from the editor to the cataloger. What is more important, however, is that the inclusion of the *ISBD* symbols lends the entry the character of a communication for the reader interspersed with asides to the computer. This may do well for the computer, but the reader cannot be programmed not to note these symbols and will inevitably be distracted by them.

To sum it up, *ISBD* stands in sharp contrast to the ideal of concise and clear entries followed by the founders of Anglo-American cataloging and reemphasized in the first phase of the last revision. The claims that *ISBD* will make the entries produced in any country "easily understood" in any other country and integrable with the entries produced in any other country are obviously and incredibly extravagant. There is nothing in *ISBD* to improve the quality of our catalogs, but much to impair their clarity, intelligibility, and effectiveness which the previous revision has sought to enhance. Therefore, I submit that the adoption of *ISBD* in the present revision does not constitute progress in cataloging but, on the contrary, retrogression.

The second basic characteristic of Cutter's catalog, as noted before, is the pattern of integration of the entries in it—that is, its structural character. Unlike most of the catalogs of his day, Cutter's catalog, like Panizzi's before him, was not merely a list of names and titles among which a book bearing a certain name and title might readily be located, but was intended to serve comprehensively as an informative guide to the library's resources. The idea of this guide was based on the premise that a reader in search of a particular *book* is in need of the *work* contained in it; that the reader may be unaware of the fact that the book sought by him/her is one edition of the work which may be found in the library in other editions or translations published under different names of the author or different titles; that there may also be other works, by the same author or other authors, that are closely related to the work wanted by him/her and that might therefore be of potential interest to the same reader; and, therefore, that to enable a reader to utilize adequately and fully the resources of the library the catalog must be designed to tell the reader not only whether or not the library has the particular book sought, but to display at once all the related materials in the library which might serve his/her interest. To accomplish this purpose, Cutter, following and improving on Panizzi, ruled, first, that a book is generally to be entered under the name of the author of the work contained in it; second, that an author is to be entered in the catalog under one particular name, with references from any other names under which that author might be looked for; and third, that the editions and translations of a given work, regardless of their individual titles, were to be "arranged" together under the original title to prevent their dispersal in the catalog. These entries were to be supplemented by references to call attention to related works entered elsewhere in the catalog—such as prologues, epilogues, continuations, supplements, adaptations, dramatizations, commentaries, criticisms, etc.—and references to assist the user of the catalog in the location of a given author or title. Thus, for example, a reader consulting Cutter's *Catalogue of the Library of the Boston Atheneum* for Washington's *Farewell Address* would find in the alphabetical place of this title, among the other titles under Washington's name, not the entry sought but a reference "See above, *Address*"; but on turning to the latter title, s/he would find there all the editions of the *Address* the library had, with titles ranging alphabetically from *Address to his Fellow Citizens . . . to Valedictory Address*, including, of course, the title *Farewell Address*, preceded by the word *Same* to indicate that those are all editions of the same work. This pattern of integration of the entries was to lend the catalog the character of a bibliographical landscape revealing to the inquirer at once what authors were represented in the library's collections, what works of each author the library had, what editions and translations the library had of each work, and, finally, the relation of each work to other works in the library. Now, the question is, again, whether this ideal of the catalog is still valid? Between Cutter's rules and the last revision completed a decade ago, the replacement of the book catalog by the card catalog, and the concomitant substitution of added entries for many of the former references, without a full awareness of the impact of these changes on the ideological character of the catalog have caused a grave erosion of the ideal catalog sought by Panizzi and Cutter. The effect of this erosion can still be observed in our catalogs where the titles of editions and translations of different works of an author are generally interfiled in one alphabetical arrangement, disregarding the identity of the different works represented by these entries. This practice has produced such incredible results as separation of *Farewell Address, George Washington's Farewell Address,* and *Washington's Farewell Address* and their alphabetical interfiling with the titles of editions and translations of other works of Washington. This situation was finally remedied in the last revision by the provision of "uniform titles" to be used, following the author's name, whenever required to keep the editions and translations of a given work together. This method, it should be noted, was not necessary in the book catalog where the editions and translations of a given work could simply be arranged in the desired order on the pages of the book, preceded by dashes or the word *Same* to indicate that they represented the same work—something inapplicable in a card catalog where each edition or translation is represented by an entry on a separate card. Now, however, we are told that the "main entry" evolved by Panizzi and Cutter to produce the catalog sought by them—the entry which was also recently confirmed by the International Conference on Cataloging Principles in Paris, in 1961, after a special discussion based on *three* working papers on "The Function of the Main Entry in the Alphabetical Catalog"—has been outdated for some time and is an anachronism in a day of computer technology.

There are those who claim that the idea of the main entry is a relic of the days of the printed book catalog where, for reasons of space and cost, an item was represented by one entry only, and has no place in a multiple-entry catalog where all entries are "of equal value." The main entry with all its attendant problems should therefore now be discarded, these individuals claim, in favor of a simple title-unit entry. These claimants, however, seem to be quite oblivious of the discussions of the function of the main entry and equally unconscious of the fact that a catalog based on a title-unit entry, which represents a book as a separate entity, will no longer have the character or serve the objectives of the catalog cultivated by Panizzi and Cutter and internationally endorsed. A catalog based on title-unit entry will revert in character to the primitive catalog representing essentially a list of names and titles among which a book bearing a certain name and title might be found—and nothing more. There are others who claim that in the coming computerized online catalog the main entry will not be needed to achieve any desirable integration of related materials in the library because this function could then be accomplished by an appropriate program. Mr. Gorman illustrates interestingly how this might be done. It seems to me, however, that what Mr. Gorman actually illustrates is not how the traditional main entry could be abandoned, but how its functions could be implemented in a computerized catalog. That does not change anything conceptually or procedurally in cataloging, but only technically, because of the nature of the new medium of the catalog. Despite the notions of some not-too-well-informed critics, the main entry has not been observed in cataloging as a fetish, but as a device to serve some well-considered functions; and it would be expected that in another technological environment the same functions might otherwise be carried out. But this does not constitute ideological or practical change. Meanwhile, the implication that what Mr. Gorman illustrates means abandonment of the main entry with, presumably, all its attending problems does injustice to Mr. Gorman himself, who obviously recognizes the importance of its functions, and contributes to the confusion of the meaning of the main entry, which more than any other aspect of cataloging has been misrepresented and misunderstood. Besides, the day of the exclusive use by libraries of the online catalog is not yet in the offing, and the heritage of our card and book catalogs is bound to continue to exist, or coexist, with the online catalog for an indefinite time to come. It should, therefore, be clearly understood that these catalogs will have to continue to be based on the traditional main entry if they are to serve the purposes they were intended to serve—that is, not merely as lists of the books in the library, but as informative guides to the library's resources.

The advent of the computer in the library is a proper occasion for a reconsideration of our cataloging goals and, more particularly, of our methods of reaching them, but not for a cavalier "abandonment of cherished ideas of the past." The adoption of the *ISBD* and the rush to abandon the traditional main entry in favor of a title-unit entry are an adventurous departure from the cataloging ideals advocated by the founders of our profession and sustained by the studies carried out in preparation of the last revision. They are not calculated to improve, but to degrade the quality of our catalogs and the vital role of these catalogs in the service of our libraries. The present revision was originally called for to continue the progress achieved in the last revision, but it is taking on the character, not of a continuation of that revision, but of a new adventure in Anglo-American cataloging.

REFERENCES

1. C. Sumner Spalding, "ISBD: It's Origin, Rationale, and Implications." *Library Journal* 98 (January 15, 1973):123.
2. International Federation of Library Associations, *ISBD (M)—International Standard Bibliographic Description for Monographic Publications*. 1st ed. (London: IFLA Committee on Cataloging, 1974), p. vii.

DISCUSSION

Paul Fasana: The organizers of the conference were very clever in providing the foil in the contrast of Mr. Lubetzky and Mr. Gorman. As I was listening it seemed that the significance is subtle, and I will be flat-footed and make it explicit. The difference in my mind is that between the deductive and inductive methods. With the deductive method, you begin with principles and ideals and proceed to apply them to reality. The result in terms of libraries are catalogs which are pejoratively called classical catalogs by people like Kilgour and are called catalogs with structure, integration, quality, and consistency by others. In contrast, with the inductive or scientific method, you analyze the individual occurrences and attempt to discover a pattern. It should be reemphasized that in the scientific method there is no guarantee that there is a pattern; an alternative to finding a pattern is being able to prove that there is no pattern.

If I were forced to choose between the strategy or the approach implied by these two speakers, I'm afraid my bias would lead me to Mr. Lubetzky. Only in his approach, which in effect will allow for an evolutionary, controlled way of changing, can we hope to come to grips with the future in a significant and meaningful manner. This morning Mr. Gorman said that he was for radical solutions. Such solutions are disruptive. They do not provide us with the continuity we need. The evolutionary approach Mr. Lubetzky exemplifies will allow us to worry about such important matters as the integrity of the record, the continuity of collections. As a librarian, I'm constantly concerned with being able to relate the past with the future. Mr. Lubetzky took as his text something that I find very, very important: "Those who cannot remember the past are condemned to repeat it." I would hope that we can avoid this.

One last comment. Mr. Gorman says that he has put *ISBD* aside, that he will not comment on it any further. Unfortunately, we will not have that luxury, because *ISBD* is the basis of *AACR*. In Mr. Lubetzky's preliminary comment something struck me very forcibly: that *AACR2* is an attempt to write a code for a catalog of the future. We're concerned with the present. However, we will be very concerned, come 1980—if we're to believe Mr. Remington of the Library of Congress—with implementing *AACR2* and trying to graft it on to our existing catalog. I think it was Ms. Richmond, in a speech that she gave at ALA during the centennial year, who said that we are really doing something sort of "ass-backwards" with *ISBD*. Rather than arguing that those who are promoting *ISBD* should be asked to show the benefits, it has been turned around so that its detractors are asked to prove its deficiencies. We who have been trying to defend our catalogs from *ISBD* are asked to prove that it will do some harm. The burden of proof should have been placed on the promoters of *ISBD*. We should ask them to prove empirically that it will be good, not necessarily that it will not do harm.

Edwin Buchinski: One has to listen very carefully to what Dr. Lubetzky says because he's a man with years of study, conviction, and something to tell us. One of the things he's telling us is to look at Cutter and to look very carefully at Cutter's perception of what the user wanted. I'm a little nervous when it comes to determining what the user wants. I have not studied the method that Cutter used to deduce user wants. And it seems to me, although I can't quote the particular title at the moment, that some researchers have shown—by what means I don't know— that the user doesn't see beyond the title. If the user does not read beyond the title, then the *ISBD* punctuation will not be distracting. Anyway, I think as I responded last time, that we need to be positive, as well as critical. If the controversy on the *ISBD* continues, it seems to me it would be nice to have some method of knowing whether the user does actually see beyond the title and is really distracted. The other concern is that the principles of Cutter are being sacrificed. Now, I guess all of you know that the code—*AACR2*—is not completely referenced as yet; we have not seen it. But I am afraid that I am not convinced that the code is sacrificing all of Cutter's principles.

Seymour Lubetzky: I agree that the question of what the catalog user is seeking is not as tangible as one could prescribe exactly. This is not the point. The point is whether the information contained and displayed on a catalog card entry is or is not of importance to the user; is or is not helpful; does or does not distract the attention of the reader. I don't know if this may not be a question of judgment. Cutter held that only those items which the user needs should be put on the entry. The repetition of the name of the author after the title, even if it is on the title page, is not necessary when the author is identified already in the heading. It seems to me that without any study it should be clear that as the eye moves over the page, the less matter there is, the faster and better the reader will comprehend. The presence of any other matter does affect the speed of reading the entry. If you have long names of corporate bodies involved in a short title such as *Profit*, then the title literally is drowned between the repetition of the name. I think it can be taken for granted that only those elements which are essential for the user's purposes should be presented on the entry to the reader and that other things should be eliminated. The same goes for the *ISBD* punctuation. Judging from my own experience—I've seen the *ISBD's* in the Library of Congress printed catalog, the *National Union*

Catalog—the presence of *ISBD* punctuation is *not* something that my eye can automatically skip over and ignore. Of necessity, I can't measure how much my eye has been retarded in moving, but I know that it has been retarded. I think that an experiment should be carried out by having at least two catalogs compared, one containing *ISBD*, the other containing entries as prescribed by Cutter. I would guess that the user of the Cutter-type catalog is much more comfortable; that it can be read much faster, and be more clearly understood, than the catalog using *ISBD* punctuation.

Joan Marshall: *ISBD*—this has been going on now, for what? Three years? And in the past, everytime this was discussed, it was asked why the punctuation, which is for the purpose of the machine, couldn't have simply been put on the tapes and suppressed or omitted from the printed record. It wouldn't have been that difficult. We were told it would be too expensive. It would have been a lot cheaper to suppress it and save three years of professional *angst* over whether or not it's going to disturb people. I don't think we're ever really going to find out. We won't even know the questions to ask.

I remember the first time I used a closed stack library—and I had been a library user for a long time. I couldn't get a call number and go to the shelf. I had an IBM card and I had to write down the title. It wasn't a book I was familiar with, and there was a long paragraph, all in capital letters and it looked almost like an analytic. I stood there and I thought, "I don't know what the title of the book is." But I took a chance on the title, and when I got the book, I thought, "That's the title." We're just never going to know what questions to ask. I still think that if we push for it, if we still feel strongly enough that it's worth doing, we can suppress the machine's punctuation in visible records. I don't think that's too much to ask.

I just wanted to comment, too, on this notion of title entry. I'm afraid that the whole notion of title entry comes about because people regard it as a way to save money. They figure that the catalogers sit down in their catalog rooms and spend an entire day trying to decide on the entry. As a cataloger, I would simply like to point out that it is not choice of entry that is so time-consuming in the catalog process. I can determine readily most of the time where I should have a title or author entry. It's deciding on the *form* of entry that's time-consuming. Unless we're not going to provide added entries, when the main entry is under title, we're still going to have the costly process of establishing the form of entry. I can decide if something should be entered under a corporate body; I can usually do that in two minutes. But then, I would have to sit down and establish the corporate entry, a task I would have to do no matter how the thing were entered. That's what takes money. So title entry is not going to save money for the administration.

Lubetzky: First, in regard to a program which would suppress the symbols for the computer which are not of any concern to the user of the catalog: The only reason I can offer as to why that has not been done is psychological, not technical. I was told by my colleagues in Los Angeles that to have the signal for the computer say "this is not to be printed" is one of the simplest tasks compared to the elaborate programs we will have to prepare to meet the requirement for the various packages that Mr. Gorman was talking about.

In regard to the title entry as a savings, there is no question that it is difficult to agree on the desirability of having a title-unit entry rather than an author entry. There is no question that there would be an enormous savings. But as Mr. Gorman again says, the computer will not search merely for line titles. If you are going to look for a title, the answer in the computer will present you with the whole package. In other words, the computer will do exactly what the main entry does now in the manual catalog.

But what of the manual catalog? What decisions will you make for identifying an author, or for identifying the work, and for linking them? There is one point that Mr. Gorman did not explain and I don't know whether it can be demonstrated successfully. I think that the linkages that he provided merely concern themselves with the identification of an author, which, of course, is part of the main entry. The identification of the work is important, but the decision concerning choice of entry—who or what is to be regard as the author—is really not the last decision; it should be the first. For example, if you have two or three authors, then a choice of author, and a decision on the identity of the author and the identity of the work must be made. This is to provide for organization under one particular place in the catalog. If you are not going to provide for the choice of author, then you will have to repeat the various entries under the different authors and to provide the linkages between them. Again, in an online catalog, this may be a question of involved but solvable problems. In a large manual catalog, it would be completely impractical. There is great importance in having a work in one place under one author: there may be a good continuation; there may be works in progress; there may be all kinds of adaptations, for the stage and movies; and there may perhaps be translations. If, therefore, you are not going to have a choice of author and identification of the work at the beginning, there will be no way to refer or relate all of the adaptations to the work, because the various manifestations of the work will be strewn in various places. To have title entry and be thus forced to provide the linkages in all these stages would not only enormously complicate a catalog. For the cataloger it would mean that every time a new work which related to this work appeared, it would have to be related not only to one place, but every other place this work appears. The number of references would become overwhelming. If there was a main entry for the original work, this would not be necessary of course, because all of the different versions would be organized under the main entry and efficiently related to each other.

Lisa Tiffer: Thus far the stress has been on the user, where I'm sure we all agree it should be. Could you recommend one or two published or unpublished, well-conducted studies of the library user's use of the card catalog or book catalog in academic libraries?

Lubetzky: I'm sorry, I cannot help you very much. I saw one or two and I would not recommend them because they were based on assumptions which have no relevance to the structure of the catalog. For example, one study with which I am familiar showed how many people have looked under this thing, and how many have looked under that thing, and whether they looked under the author or under the title, and what the user used. To me, this is of little value. People have different preferences. What is important is not how people approach the catalog, it's what they find at the end. And this, therefore, would have no bearing on the matter.

Connie Riverdale: Let's forget about *AACR2*; I have not seen it, and I don't know what it's going to look like. If you would give advice to the editors of the next revision, of *AACR3*, what advice would you give to them?

Lubetzky: My approach here, which would also be my approach for the next revision, is always to go back and see what objectives our predecessors have tried to accomplish. This is not the way for many wishy-washy persons who have never considered Cutter, probably one of the greatest librarians of his day, and some-times thought a sacred person. I could tell you many things about Cutter that you probably would find incredible. As an example, you probably would not believe that Cutter used the terms *books* and *works* alternately, without making a distinction between them. In his mind, he had a clear solution. All that he provided was that the editions and translations should be arranged together. It was not a problem of entry for a printed book catalog, it was a problem of arrangement. To just add a line, and then quote a different title is not entry, it's arrangement. But in his rules he used both terms—sometimes *book* and sometimes *work*—something that has been responsible to a very considerable extent for the confusion which exists from his day until the time of the next revision. Regarding *AACR3*, you have to study what has been done in order to benefit from the experience and thoughts of our predecessors.

Gorman: I think that there's a certain amount of heat, not light, being generated on the basis of misapprehension. It always seems to me that the kinds of things which I'm interested in doing are the same sorts of things that Professor Lubetzky is interested in doing. However inadequately, I do try to relate what we know of the past and what we've learned in the past to the modern situation. I think it is a little hard to be accused of abandoning the past, or of not knowing about it, which is even worse. I really don't think that there is the big divide. I think that we have the same kind of ailments. The kind of developed system that I talked about earlier is capable of presenting a work, its manifestations, of linking one work to another, of linking an author to his work, and a work to the physical items which make up the work. I didn't explain, and maybe I should have, that the links are capable of expressing all the relationships that Professor Lubetzky is asking for. In other words, you could link a name to a work, and say that this was the primary name, or a joint authorship, or any other kind of relationship that you wanted to.

There is enormous misapprehension about *ISBD*. *ISBD* is a way of describing things; it doesn't have any presuppositions about title main entry. I think this whole business about whether punctuation is obtrusive or not is quite honestly not worth discussing. All catalog entries are artificial constructs. Some use one system of punctuation; some use another. I don't see any evidence whatever that one system of punctuation is better or worse than another. It's almost a case of it doesn't matter what we do as long as we do it all the time, and as long as we all do the same thing. All these deductions that it somehow would structure the catalog are quite wrong. The lady who has suggested that the punctuation ought to be suppressed is also under a misapprehension because it wouldn't be suppressed; one would think she doesn't want the catalog entry to have any punctuation at all. It's just a matter of words not differentiated one from the other. As it happens, the way the Library of Congress automated the *ISBD* was different from the way we did it in Britain. In fact, we don't include the *ISBD* punctuation in the computer. Far from being a signal to the computer, it's something the computer creates because we think that we want it in the print-out. To be quite honest, I really do feel that there's a kind of artificial dichotomy here. I can't imagine why people want to engage in debate about this anymore, because there are so many more important issues; so many more far-reaching things. You say that, looking towards hard catalogs, switching your *ISBD* entry to another one is confusing.

Look at any printed volume of the *British National Bibliography* using the *ISBD*, and I defy anybody to say that the entries using full *ISBD* punctuation are in any way confusing, unattractive, unaesthetic, or whatever. I would like to get the point over that I don't think there is this big difference. I think we're working in slightly different areas, in a way. I'm thinking in terms of relating exactly the kinds of things that Professor Lubetzky talks about to a modern situation. I've always admired Professor Lubetzky's work. I admired his paper this morning, and I agreed with it, and I would really like to end this kind of false confrontation.

Lubetzky: I have never thought that Mr. Gorman and I were in disagreement. As a matter of fact, I have always felt that I have been indebted to him for the very many complimentary things he has said about me in his writing. And I don't feel that there is any division at all. I tried to say at the very beginning that what appears to be a division, if any, between us arises from the fact that Mr.Gorman has provided for a different type of catalog than the one I have. And as of the moment, we do not have the kind of catalog that Mr. Gorman describes, nor is it in the near future. I thought *AACR2* applied to our present catalog, and from this point of view feel that use of the *ISBD* and the advocacy of title entry are detrimental, at least in the context of our present catalogs. But it is not a disagreement on principles. If Mr. Gorman is going to provide for the same thing by means of a program in the computer, then we are completely agreed. I am not completely agreed with Mr. Gorman on the weight that can be assigned to the signals for the computer, the *ISBD*. I don't know how well we can measure it. To me they are definitely undesirable. Mr. Gorman asks, should we omit punctuation all together? This is not the point. We have punctuation. What we have here is double punctuation; one for the reader and another one for the computer. The latter should be suppressed if it is for the computer and not the reader. Any justification for punctuation is that it should be of value to the reader. If it isn't, then I think it is an undesirable element which should not be there.

Anne Lipow: I really hate to follow this great expression of solidarity. In regard to Dr. Lubetzky's point about user studies, I think that user studies are important. The point is *not* what the user finds at the end, but very much what they find at the beginning of their search. I think the problem is that the users are not finding enough at the beginning to lead them to the end. I think that's the point of this Institute.

Lubetzky: I don't think you can do anything about a person who goes to the catalog and doesn't know for what. If the user has something in mind, a name or a title or anything, then you have to provide help from that point of view. Our problem begins when the user comes to the catalog and begins at any point. If nothing is known about a book because it has a wrong citation and either the author or the title are known, I wouldn't know how the catalog could provide help. It can help if you know the name of the author. If you know the name of the author, but there are other authors with the same name, the only thing that you can do is tell the user to read through everything you have on all these authors.

I accept that the catalog user has to bring some information. And the question of the cataloger is, beginning with that point of view, where are you going to lead and what are you going to tell the user? If the user comes with the name of an author, but a title uncited in the catalog, you have to tell the user you do not have that particular citation, but that you will provide a survey of all the other editions or translations in the catalog by the author. They might even be of greater importance than the original title. That is what I mean when I say what the user finds at the end of the catalog search is most important.

Fasana: Each speaker today has agreed that we're in a period of transition or at a threshold; that's all they seem to have agreed upon. Mr. Lubetzky's thesis was that *AACR2* was to be a mechanism to help us in a period of transition. I would like to emphasize this point because it seems to me very, very important. Within this context it's interesting to compare the attitudes or strategies of Mr. Lubetzky and Mr. Gorman. With Mr. Lubetzky we have stress on continuity, consistency, imposing structure *a priori*, the creation of five data bases which are interrelated and integrated. With Mr. Gorman we have stress on the revolutionary use of the computer, a sharp break with the past. This is exemplified by his comment that we file things as they appear. What I'm trying to lead up to is the inescapable fact that card catalogs do exist. They exist with all of the characteristics that Mr. Lubetzky has identified and for the short-range future it's very clear to me that what we need is an evolutionary approach, a code, in effect, that will help us during this transition period.

At NYPL we closed our catalogs in 1972. If we were confronted with the alternatives that Mr. Gorman described this morning, it would have been a horrendous undertaking; as it was, it was just almost overwhelming. So I would suggest that for the short-term future what we have to adopt is the Lubetzky approach. For the long-term, I would like to pose a question: Is what Mr. Gorman described to us this morning the only alternative that should be considered? Is it the only approach to the development of an ideology or a theory of the future of the catalog? Or, is it as Ms. Richmond suggested, that we should approach this whole problem in terms of empirical research and attempt to see, after investigation, where it is that we should go?

Lubetzky: I can only express, of course, the way I see it. I read Mr. Gorman's paper with great interest and I spent a good deal of time talking with him. I really don't see much difference between my view and Mr. Gorman's. Strange as it may seem, the only places where we seem to disagree are (1) in terminology where we use a different terminology, and (2) about the online catalog which he thinks of as being different from our present catalog, whereas I see no difference in the ideology. His packages, or the name package, title package, or work package are the same packages we have now in our catalogs. The main entry is a package. It has the author associated with a work instead of associating it with various editions and translations of this work. Call them *packages* or call them by any other name. The way he describes the various packages and their use by the computer is very interesting and promises to me that the result will be one which will not be different from what we get now. I didn't find any other differences. As to whether there is a different way to accomplish those purposes, I am not aware of one. I have been a student of the history of cataloging; I have tried to find what was the underlying ideology and select from it what was good and omit what did not seem to be justified. That, I assume, must be the approach of the future. Constant revision of the ideology, I think, is important, but, to me, it still is the ideology which is the basis. The technology must be a means to accomplish the purposes which the ideology leads us to recognize.

Eleanor Crarey: It's always a privilege to hear Seymour Lubetzky enunciate and bring us back to the heart of the matter in this way. I was especially glad that he was saying that he and Michael Gorman are not that far apart. It did strike me that Cutter's ideals certainly can be better realized with a machine-manipulatable catalog than in a card file, because the idea of bringing everything together in one place is so much more possible in a machine file. I would suggest that Cutter had to set up some of his ideas before we were faced, as commonly as we are now, by many different widely scattered agencies inputting into a catalog which is then to be used by all those agencies. Therefore, we require a lot more standardization. *ISBD(M)* or *(G)* really acts in my mind as the framework upon which you then have to hang all the content of standardization; that it is foreign in many ways and yet not as foreign to our patrons as we worry about. I've noticed that our public library patrons are far less aware of it than librarians thought. I would also risk disagreeing with Mr. Lubetzky on one point and that is the idea of a title followed by the author statement even when it is identical to the main entry statement. If you have a microform catalog and if you have an author added entry, you are faced with an added entry author statement, the title and then, hopefully, an author statement. If you have not repeated that author statement after the title, when you look in the added entry it is very difficult to know who your main entry author is. That is one of the reasons why it is very helpful to have that statement repeated whether it is identical or not.

Lubetzky: We have here some slight misunderstanding that results from the fact that if we have the main entry, then the author's statement will always be there no matter what added entries you will make, because the added entries are based on the main entry. The main entry is used not only by itself as the main entry, but also as the unit entry comprising each added entry. Thus, you do not need the repetition of the name of the author.

Crarey: But some microform catalogs do not list the main entry with the added entries.

Freedman: I'm not aware of that; it depends upon how you organize that microform catalog. For the ones I've seen, the added entries are followed by the main entry and an abridged body of the record. There may be some that do it the way you're saying though, which would be a case in point. However, even with *ISBD*, there's no guarantee, regardless of the form of the catalog, that you will carry anything more than a short title and a call number, dropping even the subtitle and the balance of the title statement, including *ISBD*.

Unidentified Speaker: It seems to me we're talking about all kinds of catalogs: microform, online, card catalog, book catalog—and we're looking toward the wave of the future. I know that all these exist right now and that some libraries have multiple forms. My question is this: Assuming that we were to close the card catalog and the book catalog and possibly not have a microform catalog, and that all libraries were online—maybe in the year 5,000—would it really be necessary to worry about main entry? If you had multiple access points, couldn't you just key in these various items and call up the record and get a print-out? Maybe in the year 5,000 there'll be different kinds of print-outs. Maybe we won't be only printing out on paper or on tape. I have no idea what technology will be available, but we seem to be talking about all kinds of filing and worrying about whether we file one as o-n-e or the numeral 1, or we file 1984 as 1984 in Spanish, as one thousand nineteen hundred and eighty-four. It seems to me that it is quite possible in the future we won't even have to worry about this sort of thing.

Lubetzky: I tried to imply before that I don't care what method we use to achieve the end; what's important to me is what the end is. Whether you use main entry or you have the magic pronouncement: give me this. As long as you get what I think you ought to get, that's fine. And especially if you use a computer, the methods by which you accomplish this purpose will be different. The point is the purpose will be accomplished. You are referring to the fact that where we have multiple access points we can accomplish everything. I think that the phrase *multiple points of access* has been used to imply something which does not exist. There is no new situation that exists; we have always had multiple points of access. They took the form of references and added entries; these are multiple points of access. You didn't have as many as the computer makes possible; we can now have more, but it seems to me to imply that you have a specific point that you want to reach and the computer gives that particular point to you. But to me, the catalog has to tell you more than what you ask for. I illustrated this by the use of the *Farewell Address* of Washington. The answer of a good catalog is not to say yes or no, a binary answer, to whether we have this *Farewell Address*, but to tell the user whether the library has the *Farewell Address* in so many editions and translations, and to present the user with all of the alternatives from which to choose. Now this is not just a point of access, it is considerably more. If by *point of access* you mean that you ask for a *Farewell Address* and you get everything that the main entry now gives you, very well, then I'm completely satisfied. If it's not the same thing, then it doesn't accomplish these purposes. Did I answer your question or did I misunderstand it or misinterpret it?

Unidentified Speaker: When I said *multiple access* I meant, for instance, the International Standard Book Number (ISBN) or the various control numbers, too, but also Washington's *Farewell Address*, assuming you key-in the uniform title and whatever else the computer requires, as well as the other titles by which it's known. Then you'll be able to retrieve by alternate titles, uniform titles, various things, and your Washington's *Farewell Address* is going to print out. You're going to be able to see the list on every possible title, Washington's *Farewell Address* in every possible edition.

Lubetzky: That's what Mr. Gorman illustrated in his paper; is that correct? I fully agree with this. To me, however, that does not mean abolition by the title unit of the main entry; what it does is provide for the functions of the main entry by means appropriate to the computer. That's all right with me!

Joseph Rosenthal: I'd like to respond to the question raised because it's a fairly widely held perception that if you're online, filing rules don't matter any longer. I think that's not entirely true, that the arrangement or display of records must be considered at some level. Some concern must be paid to the situation where you want to address a fairly large body of records and where the way in which those records are presented either contribute to or inhibit the ease of the user in finding a particular record.

The Newest *Anglo-American Cataloging Rules*

by John D. Byrum, Jr.
and Frances Hinton

On March 29, 1974, delegates of the national library associations and national libraries of the United States, Canada, and Great Britain met at the headquarters of the American Library Association (ALA) in Chicago. The object of this tripartite meeting—to complete the planning of a project to prepare the second edition of the *Anglo-American Cataloging Rules (AACR)*—was a direct result of several significant developments affecting bibliographic control of library materials which have occurred since the *AACR* was published in 1967. First, sudden progress toward the formulation of international standards for the description of monographs, serials, and other media had been realized. This development clearly indicated the need to redraft the *AACR* provisions for bibliographic description so that the code would keep abreast with the effort to promote the international exchange of bibliographic data. Secondly, there had occurred in recent years a proliferation of cataloging rules for nonbook materials, reflecting dissatisfaction with the *AACR* in both its coverage and treatment of these resources. It had become apparent that only through a wholesale revision of its rules for nonprint media could the *AACR* provide the standardization which was lacking in this area. Thirdly, considerable success had been realized in reconciling points of divergence between the separate North American and British texts of *AACR*, leading to the prospect that the two versions might in fact be unified. In addition, it seemed that a single text of the *AACR* had potential for contributing to the development of a truly international cataloging code. Finally, the scores of amendments, which had been issued to change rules or clarify their meaning, had mounted to the point where catalogers' copies of the *AACR* were seriously out-of-date, if they were not bulging with tip-ins.

It was, therefore, not the purpose of the 1974 tripartite meeting to decide whether to undertake a revision of the *AACR* but rather settle the objectives and procedures for achieving such a revision. Toward this end, those present drafted a Memorandum of Agreement to govern the preparation of the second edition.

This document names five bodies as the authors of the revised edition: The American Library Association, the British Library, the Canadian Committee on Cataloguing, the (British) Library Association, and the Library of Congress. It

*The authors wish to acknowledge the contribution of Helen Schmierer who assisted them in preparing that part of the text which summarizes cataloging developments related to machine processing of bibliographic information.

provides that the content of the revised edition will be decided by negotiation among these authors.

The memorandum enumerates the aims of the revision as follows: First, the reconciliation in a single text of the present British and North American texts. Secondly, the incorporation in the single text of all amendments and changes agreed to and implemented since 1967. Thirdly, the consideration for inclusion of all work currently in process and all proposals for amendments by the authors and by national committees of other countries that use English versions of the *AACR* that have been put forward by a date not later than seven months from the commencement of editorial work on the revision. And finally, provision for international interests in the *AACR* and for its use in countries other than those in North America and the United Kingdom.

The agreement established a Joint Steering Committee (JSC) for revision of *AACR*. This body consists of one voting and one nonvoting representative of each author organization and functions to appoint an editor and associate editor, determine questions of policy for the editors, consider all proposals in relation to a stipulated timetable, ensure adequate communication among all persons and bodies concerned with the revision, assess for approval the rules framed by the editors, and present the revised text for publication. Thus, the ultimate authority for the production and content of the second edition rests with the Joint Steering Committee.

The Memorandum stipulates a two-year timetable for the project: commencement of editorial work on January 1, 1975, and publication of *AACR2* in 1977. This agreed schedule, constrained as it is for several reasons, has now had to be adjusted to accommodate an unanticipated development, a Draft Review Program. It now seems probable that the final text will be delivered to the publishers in fall 1977 and should therefore appear in print during 1978.

Within this framework, the American Library Association's Resources and Technical Services Division (RTSD) established an ad hoc Catalog Code Revision Committee (CCRC) and vested in it ALA's authority for proposing and approving modifications of the *AACR* until the second edition is published. CCRC includes 11 voting members who have been selected to achieve representation of various types of libraries as well as differing kinds of cataloging expertise.

In addition, efforts have been made to involve and inform other persons and groups which might be affected by the code revision project. Within ALA, all divisions and roundtables were invited to designate representatives to the committee. The RTSD sectional Executive Committees were asked to identify groups which ought to follow CCRC's activities, and one—the Serials Section—has set up a special *AACR* Revision Study Committee which attends CCRC meetings. CCRC has also established regular liaison with the Interdivisional Committee on Representation in Machine-Readable Form of Bibliographic Information (MARBI) which agreed to review all revision proposals to determine their effect on the MARC (Machine-Readable Cataloging) formats. At the same time, the ALA/RTSD Filing Committee has demonstrated interest in advising the committee on matters related to the organization of catalog records in both machine and manual environments. Because CCRC's role in code development is to revert to the Descriptive Cataloging Committee (DCC) after the current revision of the *AACR* has been completed, the entire membership of DCC participates in CCRC's work. As for groups outside ALA, nearly 30 organizations with an identifiable interest in the bibliographic control of library materials were asked to designate representatives to the committee; those which preferred not to could elect instead to receive its documentation for information and comment. And, finally, to maintain communications with the profession-at-large, CCRC regularly prepares summaries of its minutes for publication in *Library Resources and Technical Services (LRTS)* and through press releases advises other library-oriented periodicals of its major activities and concerns. As a further effort at encouraging participation by American librarians in the code revision project, the committee held open hearings during the ALA Midwinter Meeting in January 1975 and at the ALA Annual Conference in July 1976, thereby providing a forum for those attending the conferences to voice suggestions for improvement of the *AACR*.

As a further extension of its interest in widespread participation in the development of *AACR2*, the Catalog Code Revision Committee has advocated a program to involve groups that have assisted the revision in the review of the final draft of the second edition. The Joint Steering Committee has agreed with this approach and approved the proposed review with the understanding that it will concentrate on the comprehensiveness and adequacy with which the agreed principles and policies set out have been implemented. The library-related organizations in the United States and ALA units concerned have been contacted, and the Draft Review Program is now in progress.

To facilitate the consideration of suggestions that it has received, CCRC formed Rule Review and Revision Proposal Teams. Each team was responsible for a block of related rules. Their charge was to identify lacunae in the code and to determine which provisions entail problems of interpretation, suffer from insufficient examples, yield undesirable results, or otherwise seem defective. As an aid to this work, CCRC commissioned the preparation of an annotated bibliography covering publications that offer a critical assessment of the *AACR*. All comments and proposals submitted by individuals or groups were reviewed by one or more teams. After completing the process of generating and reviewing input, teams presented reports of their recommendations to the committee as a whole, and by July 1975, transmittal to the Joint Steering Committee of those which were approved had begun. At the beginning the teams served as a necessary filtering device. They examined and collected hundreds of proposals that often made repetitious or conflicting recommendations. Some of them were so generally accepted that there was little or no committee discussion when a team presented its report. Other team recommendations generated extended, even heated, discussion; on occasions, team positions were never accepted by CCRC as a whole.

By September 1976, the voting members of CCRC and the nonvoting representatives of ALA units and other organizations decided that the team structure had outlived its usefulness. One major problem had always been the amount of time required for team discussions, which sometimes left insufficient opportunity for the group as a whole to consider the same problems. Moreover, as CCRC's chief concern became consideration of draft texts submitted by the editors, it became apparent that the team discussions were to an extent repetitive of those of the committee as a whole. Therefore, during the concluding phase of the revision project, which is devoted to overall review of the final draft text, CCRC members, the representatives of ALA units, and other organizations will function as a single group.

In Great Britain and Canada similar efforts have been made to obtain comments, criticism, and recommendations for improvements from as many individuals and organized groups as possible. Given the opportunity to provide input, they have made many valuable contributions to the policy and practice prescribed by *AACR2*. Indeed it may be said that many, if not most, of the changes this text incorporates are the result of complaints about existing rules and proposals for their improvement. Stress is laid on this point to avoid any impression, should it exist, that the revisions reflected in the second edition are, in the words of one of my colleagues, "the brain children of an ivory tower group of theorists sitting around a table dreaming up work for themselves and catalogers throughout the world."

Another point which we hope these introductory remarks make clear is that *AACR2*, even more than the 1967 version, is the result of give and take, of compromise, of negotiation, of concessions made graciously or grudgingly. Overriding the development of the revision project has been an honest attempt exerted by all the authors and by both editors to achieve a code that can be applied with consistency and with relative ease in order to communicate bibliographic information clearly and understandably.

Looking to the future, the Catalog Code Revision Committee has developed a project proposal to introduce *AACR2* to librarians in the United States, Canada, and Great Britain. The aims of this project are:

1. To acquaint the library public to the second edition by familiarizing them with its major provisions and its implications for national and international bibliographic control and by assuring that the role of *AACR* in promoting national, regional, and local bibliographic interchange is recognized and understood;

2. To prepare, through a basic introductory workshop, a group of people who would subsequently lead regional institutes and workshops to transmit the introduction of *AACR2* to a wider audience; and

3. To produce a group of multimedia resources which can be marketed for use with library education programs and staff training sessions in which the revised *AACR* will be introduced to a still wider audience.

The Resources and Technical Services Division of ALA is currently seeking funding for this project, by means of which we hope to encourage an orderly transition from *AACR* to *AACR2*.

This then provides you with a general orientation to the objectives and operational framework of the current code revision project and to CCRC's role within it.

Since July 1974, the Joint Steering Committee has assembled seven times to consider matters of policy, proposals submitted by the author organizations, and position papers and draft texts prepared by the editors.

To guide CCRC as well as the other author organizations in originating revision proposals, the Joint Steering Committee announced in January 1975 certain underlying principles for the content of the second edition. First, it decided that the revised *AACR* will maintain general conformity with the Paris Principles on which the 1967 rules are based. Secondly, the Joint Steering Committee wants the second edition to take particular account of developments in the machine processing of bibliographic records. And, thirdly, it affirmed a commitment to conformity with the *ISBD(M)* as a basis for the bibliographic description of monographs and to the principles of standardization in the bibliographic description of all categories of materials.

The JSC reached early agreement on the necessity of providing for uniform treatment of all materials. Implementation of this decision as applied to bibliographic description led the Associate Editor to outline a standardized framework, based on *ISBD(M)* to which the Joint Steering Committee had committed itself, for use in revision of *AACR*. The JSC accepted the resulting proposal in principle, but became concerned that unilateral development of this framework might be viewed as an isolationist exercise, since the IFLA (International Federation of Library Associations and Institutions) Office for UBC (Universal Bibliographic Control) had already inaugurated efforts to promulgate several international standards for bibliographic description of particular materials. The JSC also recognized that the second edition could be outdated shortly after its appearance, if its prescriptions varied from those included in these emerging *ISBD*'s. Moreover, the likelihood of some incompatibility between these *ISBD*'s was viewed as a real obstacle to realization of UBC.

Consideration of these possibilities prompted the Joint Steering Committee to open negotiations which culminated in an international meeting held in October 1975 under the auspices of the IFLA Committee on Cataloging to consider the JSC's formal statement on the need for specifications of a generalized standard for bibliographic description. A second meeting was convened in March 1976 with the chairpersons of existing *ISBD* specialized working groups and representatives of the JSC as participants. At these meetings the framework and most details were agreed upon, and the Associate Editor was given the assignment of preparing the final draft of the preliminary edition of *ISBD(G)* for approval at the IFLA Annual Conference in August 1976.

In itself, *ISBD(G)* will never be used to describe à work. It merely provides a list of data elements that must be included, gives the order in which they are to be placed, and prescribes the punctuation that will tell the human being or the machine reading the description the exact nature of each element. This framework is intended to function as the basis for the future development of all specialized *ISBD*'s. The *ISBD(G)* has also served as the primary source for the revision of that part of the *AACR* which concerns bibliographic description. This section will precede the rules for choice and form of heading, since the cataloging process logically suggests development of the bibliographic description before the addition of the access points.

Part I, Bibliographic Description, begins with a general chapter which contains rules applicable to any form of material. Among its features is a section on "levels of detail in the description" which differentiates between and establishes the requirements of a minimum, standard, and full description. This chapter is followed by a series of chapters on specific categories of materials, covering: printed monographs; cartographic materials; manuscripts; music; sound recordings; motion pictures and videorecordings; graphic materials; machine-readable data files; three-dimensional artifacts and realia; microforms; and serials. Additionally, a chapter on analytical entries is provided. Both the general chapter and the chapter on a particular kind of material being described must be used together. Overall, there has occurred a deliberate reduction in the number of situations for which the *AACR* legislates with regard to bibliographic description in the second edition. Part I allows the optional incorporation of general material designators, e.g., sound recording, but refers the users of the code to an appendix which stipulates two lists of such terms—one reflecting British preferences, the other indicating North American usage.

The second part of the *AACR* will deal with organizational factors relevant to the selection of access points and collocation of bibliographic entries for all types of materials. The chapter covering choice of main and added entry headings is framed in terms of basic bibliographic conditions and progresses from works of single authorship through unknown, shared, changing, mixed and diffuse authorship, related works, and concludes with guidance in selection of uniform titles.

The second section treats matters pertaining to form of headings and uniform titles and includes rules for formulating references.

At its November 1975 meeting, the JSC identified the major issues which required resolution in order to enable the editors to complete the redrafting of that part of the *AACR* concerning choice of entry and form of heading. In February 1976, the JSC considered alternative positions and for the most part brought these matters to a conclusion. At its May and October 1976 meetings, JSC reviewed rule proposals based on its policy decisions and considered recommendations made by the author organizations concerning these rules.

Responding to demands for a narrower definition of authorship, including CCRC's proposals, the JSC has agreed to the following principles: A work is considered to be of personal authorship if a person is chiefly responsible for the creation of the intellectual or artistic content of the work. A work is deemed to require main entry under corporate body if it falls into one of four categories. These comprehend: (1) works of an administrative nature dealing with the corporate body itself, its internal policies, procedures, and operations; its finances; its officers and staff, or its resources; (2) legal and governmental works of the following types: laws; decrees of the chief executive having the force of law; administrative regulations; constitutions; charters; court rules; treaties, etc.; legislative hearings; (3) works which report the collective thought of the body; (4) works which report the collective activities of a named conference; of an expedition; of an event, such as an athletic contest, an exhibition, a fair, or a festival, which satisfies the definition of a corporate body. A work involving a corporate body and which names the person or persons preparing it is entered under the corporate body if it falls into one of these categories; otherwise, it is treated as if no corporate body were involved for purposes of main entry heading. (*AACR2*, of course, allows generously for representation of corporate body headings as added entries, since the rules for secondary entries have been liberalized.) Implicit in this approach are substantial limitations on the possibility of entering serial publications under corporate body headings, since it excludes all except those within the four categories; there is no separate rule for entry of serials in *AACR2*.

Within the context of personal authorship, the JSC has also agreed with the CCRC view that for cataloging purposes an artist is not the author of reproductions of this artistic work unless the originals were made for this purpose. Furthermore, it was decided to delete the statement, currently embodied in footnote 2 to Chapter 1 of the *AACR*, that "chess-players are the 'authors' of their recorded games." At the same time, the JSC did decide to extend the authorship principle to librettos, although in doing so it retained the "optional exception" appearing in the current British Text which permits entry of librettos for particular musical works under the composers of those works.

It was during the course of deliberation of the matter of authorship principle that the JSC was asked to consider the proposition of abandoning the main-entry concept and of adopting instead the unit-entry concept. One of the author organizations suggested that for each work a standard bibliographic description should be prepared to which would be added a record of access points deemed essential or desirable; the code would specify the most suitable form for recording the access points so as to collocate the works of an author and the editions of a work. However, this proposal was later withdrawn in recognition of the fact that the time frame for the current revision project is too constrained to permit sufficient consideration of a change of this magnitude. *AACR* will continue—at least through the second edition—to preserve the distinction of main-entry heading. Nevertheless, the rules mention the possibility of considering all access points as equal in importance.

In other actions related to authorship principles, the JSC has decided to define *shared authorship* as occurring when there are two or more persons or bodies performing the same function in relation to a work, such as joint writers, joint composers, and the like; to define *mixed authorship* as occurring when there are two or more persons or bodies performing different functions in relation to a work, such as a writer and a reviser; and to define *diffuse authorship* as occurring when in the case of shared authorship there are more than three persons or bodies, none of which is the principal author; or in the case of mixed authorship, there are more than three functions, none of which is regarded as the principal function.

Over the years, the *AACR* has been subjected to criticism for provisions that sanction the use of form subdivisions in headings for certain legal and religious publications. It is not surprising, therefore, that strong representation from several quarters, including CCRC, has come before the JSC to urge that this policy be abandoned in the second edition. At the same time, others have voiced opposition to his change, primarily on the grounds that it would have an adverse effect on existing catalogs. After careful consideration, the JSC agreed that the offending subheadings shall be dropped and that uniform titles based on the title of the work itself are to be substituted as a replacement for them. In a related action, the JSC accepted a recommendation that entry of materials such as laws (but not constitutions) should be under the promulgating jurisdiction rather than the jurisdiction which they govern. However, final decisions on these matters are awaiting consideration of a survey, undertaken at CCRC's request by C. Sumner Spalding, of various legal traditions to determine the extent to which authorship principles may generally apply to the category of legal materials.

In any case, the number of special rules to cover main-entry headings for religious and legal publications has been reduced as a result of a policy to make the general rules as fully comprehensible as possible and desirable. For example, the general rule for adaptations applies also to paraphrases of the Bible. The general rule for commentaries applies also to legal commentaries. The choice of entry for chiefs of state is the same as that for works by popes or other high ecclesiastical officials. The rule for concordants is a part of the general series of rules for treaties, intergovernmental agreements, and the like.

Concerning choice and form of headings for personal names, the JSC has had to answer two major questions. In settling both, it had to confront position statements that reflected fundamentally different philosophies.

The first of these questions was: What are the requirements of personal name headings in respect to their fullness? To this query, two diametrically opposed answers were put forth. The first advanced the view that the fullest form of name known should be chosen for headings in order to maintain the integrity of existing large catalogs and to promote international exchange of bibliographic data. The second, which CCRC supported, rested on the premise that, as a workable tool for the user rather than a bibliographical dictionary, the catalog should feature name entries in forms most likely to be known to the user—which normally would comprise forms most commonly appearing on title pages. This position is in agreement with the Paris Principles, and the JSC has accepted it.

At the same time, some of the author organizations (including CCRC) felt that information about the full name in catalog records would serve the catalog user as a means of identifying entries and also reduce the need for revision of headings in order to resolve conflicts. Ultimately, a compromise was developed that provided for the fully spelled-out form as a parenthetical addition in the heading if it is needed to differentiate names, and permits such an addition if the cataloging agency desires it. Consistent with this approach is the JSC's decision that *AACR2* should prescribe main-entry heading under initials or numerals whenever authors have preferred to represent themselves through these devices, and are rarely or never identified by their real or full names.

The second of the major questions concerning choice and form of personal name headings was: Should the heading for an author who writes under more than one name be the name by which the author is commonly identified, the author's real name, or the author's name as it appears on the title page? CCRC's initial position on the issue was that entry should be under the real name. However, a strong minority argued that entry should be under the form appearing on the title page on the grounds that it was in conformity with the Paris Principles and with the concept of the basic provision of entry under names by which authors are identified in their works. The JSC resolved the issue by agreeing that the editors should draft a revision based on the provisions of the CCRC proposal that entry should be under the predominant form if there is one, otherwise under the name as it appears in the work.

In respect to corporate body headings, the JSC has consistently taken the position that a corporate body should be entered under its name, even if the body is a part of some larger organization. It has also taken the position that the entry of government agencies should conform to the entry of other corporate bodies as closely as possible.

It has not proved feasible to develop a single rule for entry of subordinate corporate bodies and government agencies. However, the two rules are parallel in structure and wording. Subordinate entry of corporate bodies is confined to those bodies whose names imply that the body is a component of another body, or is an administrative subdivision of some higher body, or whose name requires the name of the higher body for complete identification. Subordinate entry of government bodies is similarly limited. In addition and in conformity with the Paris Principles, although in opposition to Eva Verona's recommendations, top echelon executive agencies (as defined in government manuals), legislative bodies, courts, etc., are specifically named as bodies to be entered subordinately. Although the rule for government agencies mixes the function of the agency with the structure of the name as criteria, it appears to be an easier rule to apply than the present rule, and one that should result in greater consistency of headings.

Other decisions have been directed toward achieving a consistent form of heading. These include the use of systematic romanization in headings for names in nonroman alphabets and optional methods of recording place name qualifiers for all corporate bodies. Moreover, it has been concluded that *AACR2* should provide for a pattern of standardized punctuation to set off any qualifiers added to headings after corporate names. In addition, the rules covering corporate body headings have been reorganized to eliminate special rules whenever possible and to relocate those that are required in proximity to the general rules to which they apply. Moreover, provisions treating geographic names have been pulled together to constitute a separate chapter.

In our view, the decisions taken by the JSC are consonant with the Paris Principles and have the effect of propelling the *AACR* into chosen alignment with them. Allowing for the ambiguity of articles 9.11 and 9.12 of those Principles, the approach to main-entry headings for corporate bodies does not depart significantly from the Paris agreement, even though *corporate authorship* as such is not a feature of *AACR2*. By giving up the provisions of the existing separate rule for entry of serial publications, the *AACR* gains greater compatibility with the prescript of footnote 7 to article 9.12. In discontinuing form subheadings for liturgical works and legal publications, the JSC has brought the second edition into conformity with article 9.5 of the Paris Principles, thereby eliminating one significant point of divergence between them and the *AACR*. Nor has the JSC taken any action to reinstate rules to allow for the entry of certain corporate bodies under the place names of their locales, thereby upholding the recent decision to eradicate what had been recognized as the most significant departure of the *AACR* (North American Text) from the Paris Principles. At the same time, it has also left undisturbed the recent revision of Rules 4 and 5 that sought to make compatible the *AACR*'s treatment of collections with the practices recommended by the Paris agreement. And, as already indicated, personal name headings as covered by *AACR2* represent yet another area where the code has been brought into better agreement with the Principles.

With regard to editorial matters, the JSC prefers that rule statements be expressed generally in the imperative mode and indicated in the positive rather than in the negative. Further, it has agreed that an effort should be made to avoid sexist terminology, such as the exclusive use of the masculine pronoun, and that the editors should bear in mind problems of translation so that the revised edition can be rendered more easily into other languages. The JSC has established the *Encyclopaedia Britannica* style manual together with *Webster's Third New International Dictionary* as the authorities to which the editors should refer in choosing between variant American and British spellings; thus, in the second edition the word *cataloging* will appear as *cataloguing*.

From the very outset of the code revision project, it has been clearly recognized that preparation of the second edition would be of interest to more than the library communities of North America and Great Britain. Provision for international involvement was one point in the Memorandum of Agreement which marked the inauguration of the current effort. Furthermore, the second edition, by the terms of the grant which is funding it, is to represent a contribution to the development of an international cataloging code.

In order to stimulate international input, the JSC obtained the cooperation of the IFLA Office for UBC which invited catalogers in unrepresented countries to recommend revisions of the *AACR* and to comment on the potential of the second edition as an international code. In response, comments and suggestions covering both broad concepts and specific rules were received from all over the world. All of these data were reviewed by the code revision committees of the author organizations, and recommendations forwarded to the JSC. Specific JSC decisions which relate to international concerns include the following:

1. That systematic romanization should be used in headings for personal and corporate names in nonroman alphabets. Examples will be romanized by the ISO (International Organization for Standardization) standard (if one exists) as the one completely neutral form.

2. That as a matter of policy and principle no reference will be made in the second edition to particular national library practices in relationship to code provisions.

3. That the editors should consider distribution of European languages among the examples when choosing examples.

4. That the IFLA publication *Names of Persons* should be indicated as a

source of information on names not treated by the *AACR*.

5. That a general instruction should appear at the beginning of the code to enable a cataloging agency using a language other than English to substitute that language throughout the rules wherever reference is made to the English form of the name and preference is given to the English form.

Finally, we would cite the promotion of international standardization resulting from the *ISBD(G)* as deriving to a measurable extent from activities related to production of *AACR2*.

The JSC has been pursuing negotiations with the American Library Association, the Canadian Library Association, and the Library Association concerning arrangements for the publication of the second edition. Although the parties involved have not yet reached final agreement on contractual details, certain matters have been agreed upon. For example, the second edition will appear in both cloth and paperback, and probably also in unbound copies for those users who prefer to maintain it in loose-leaf form. In addition, the JSC is seeking to arrange for publication of an abridged edition of the *AACR* with the goal of accomplishing it as soon as practicable after completion of work on the second edition.

Although publication of the second edition will mark the culmination of the current code revision project, it will not mean an end to code revision as such. Under the terms of the grant that finances the project, royalties from sales of *AACR2* will be used to establish a common Anglo-American Cataloging Rules Revision Fund. The JSC has forwarded to the author organizations detailed recommendations for the establishment of a successor body in order to provide a mechanism for regular future maintenance of the code.

Since the major theme of this Institute concerns The Catalog in the Age of Technological Change, it is appropriate to conclude these remarks by commenting specifically about those features of *AACR2* which, in the words of the JSC's policy statement, "take particular account of developments in the machine processing of bibliographic records."

During the last two years, the CCRC has addressed the concern expressed in this policy statement. As you will recall from earlier remarks, CCRC invited a number of ALA bodies and other interested parties to participate in the code revision exercise. At least three groups participating in the revision have special interests relating to machine-processing concerns. The Information Science and Automation Division (ISAD) appointed a representative to the CCRC. Liaison was established with the RTSD Filing Committee through its chairperson, and two-way communications have also been maintained throughout the project with the MARBI Committee, which also serves as an advisor to the Library of Congress in matters related to the LC/MARC communications format.

The ISAD representative and these two committees have received code revision documents and have regularly participated in code revision work through attendance at meetings or correspondence. In addition to these formal arrangements, CCRC has also discussed and acted upon submissions from others related to machine processing of bibliographic information.

In 1976, a team of CCRC members and representatives to CCRC was appointed to specifically address matters related to machine-readable bibliographic data and machine processing of bibliographic records. Accordingly, the team reviewed all pertinent documentation, the majority of which was submissions from the RTSD Filing Committee and the MARBI Committee, and reported its findings to the CCRC.

In its discussion of these matters, the CCRC has held:

First, that the cataloging rules should accommodate machine-readable considerations whenever possible; except when there is a bibliographic or linguistic warrant to be served, this warrant should take precedence over any machine-readable consideration.

Second, that cataloging rules should articulate the general presentation of bibliographic data in displays, whether these displays be on cathode-ray-tube terminals or appear in printed or other products such as printed cards, book catalogs, computer print-outs; but that the cataloging rules should not contain statements governing the representation of information in machine-readable form or statements about the content designation (tags, indicators, subfield codes) of data in machine-readable form.

And, third, that the principle of *file as is*—that is, filing on elements in exactly the form and order in which they appear—supported by the RTSD Filing Committee, should be followed and that entry forms should be so constructed to permit this principle to be followed.

The CCRC has forwarded to the JSC three broad recommendations that address machine-readable concerns: (1) Numerical Information in Titles in *ISBD* Areas; (2) Numerical Information in Headings and Filing Titles; and, (3) Transcription of Initialisms and Acronyms in Titles and Name Headings. These recommendations, in general accepted by the JSC in its Fall 1976 meeting, specify the presentation of numbers, acronyms, and initialisms in headings and references, and in description such that the principle of *file as is* is served and at the same time linguistic and bibliographic warrants are also served. In another significant action which pertains in part to technological aspects, the JSC has accepted CCRC's recommendation that a related work should be entered under its own author or title with an added entry for the work to which it is related.

The CCRC continues to direct attention to machine-readable concerns as the editors submit draft rules for CCRC consideration. In addition, as part of the draft review of *AACR2* that is currently under way, CCRC has submitted copies of the review draft to each member of the MARBI Committee.

The project to revise the *AACR* is nearing completion. No one who has participated in this undertaking suffers from the illusion that the ultimate, perfect code has been produced. Surely the Draft Review Program will reveal any significant shortcomings with regard to the consistency and comprehensiveness of the rules, the style and clarity of the presentation, and the adequacy of the examples; these deficiencies will be rectified before *AACR2* is published. But, we think it is not premature to venture our personal conviction that *AACR2* will be easier to apply, will result in greater consistency, and is better organized than its predecessor; in addition, it represents a triumph of international cooperation.

DISCUSSION

Paul Fasana: Any discussion of CCRC and its efforts puts in mind the Japanese story of Rashomon. For those of you who don't know the story, it concerns one set of facts as interpreted by several different people. At lunch I had a discussion which was quite different from what we've just heard from Ms. Hinton. I'd like to point out a few of the differences at this point.

Not all has been harmony as she has pointed out. This is reflected in the use, perhaps misuse, of several terms. At different times Ms. Hinton has used *revision, redraft, rewrite, new edition, revised edition,* and *second edition.* Which is it?

Each is different to some degree and this kind of muddled thinking is reflected in the rules we're preparing. For example, if we look carefully at some of the reactions to the draft that are beginning to emerge, I would submit that it was only in the past two months that 50 or so copies were sent out to be reviewed by people other than those on CCRC. However, look at some of the reactions: we have the United Nations threatening to write their own rules because they feel that they can't use the rules. We have law librarians threatening not to implement because of the subdivisions. We have the government documents librarians being terribly exercised by the restricted definition of corporate headings. And finally, we have the art librarians in a tizzy because they think the forms used for certain types of headings have been tampered with. I would suggest that these four groups reflect concerns about corporate headings. Perhaps the new code is deficient in this area, and greater time and effort should be spent looking at these rules before they're issued.

I would also like to make three comments and ask three questions of Ms. Hinton. First, concerning the scope of the effort: What was the intent of original aims? As she pointed out, in the Memo of Agreement the aims were laid out in this order of priority: First, there should be a single North American and British text. Second, changes since 1967 should be incorporated into a single text. Third, works in progress be considered. There was no reason to say that that had to be included. Fourth, international needs and changes should be considered. I would submit that during the course of two years or so, CCRC has considered radical things that don't seem to fit in with any of these aims, such as abandoning main entry and restricting corporate authorship by eliminating it entirely, and now euphemistically calling it corporate emanation. And then finally—fortunately it was defeated—it considered the arbitrary entry of serials under title. The question is: Does the original scope of effort as envisioned when the aims were written reflect what has been done as described by Ms. Hinton? Second, the purpose of the code was that it be used with existing catalogs. There is some question whether this can be done. What impact will the new code have? It's still too soon to know because, though Ms. Hinton praises the reorganization, I have some difficulty because I can't relate the new headings to the old rules. Therefore, though I've read the rules for many hours, I'm confused on many issues. At the New York Institute, Mr. Byrum was asked specifically what the impact of the code would be on existing catalogs. He stated that it will have the specific impact of forcing medium- to large-size libraries to close their catalogs. Now that was a personal opinion, but Mr. Byrum was Chairman of the Committee. Now I suggest to you that this is rather radical and rather important for us. LC has announced that it will close its catalogs by 1980. Informally, I'm told by LC people that the new code certainly is playing a significant part in this decision. The next question I would ask Ms. Hinton is: What is her opinion of the new code's impact on existing catalogs?

And finally, there are two new features in the code: levels of completeness, and choice of options. I would suggest that both of these features will cause a great deal of mischief in cataloging departments. There are more than 100 options in the code, many of which are trivial, but it gives the effect of having tinker toys, because you can pick and choose. Recently, the four national libraries of Australia, Canada, the United States, and Britain met and agreed that they would try to come to some agreement about the options. In a recent LC (Library of Congress) *Information Bulletin* there is a candid or cynical (I'm not sure which word best applies) long report on the meeting, and it was interesting to see that they all agreed to go contrary to the spirit of the new code with respect to personal names. They, in effect, said that they would consistently use the fullest form of name. The last question I raise is: What effect will these two options, two of several, have on cataloging departments throughout the nation?

Frances Hinton: I suspect that Mr. Byrum's personal opinion that *AACR2* will force libraries to close their catalogs is partly wishful thinking. As he said in New York, he felt that they should have closed them when the 1967 code came out. I also think it is hardly fair to imply that the Library of Congress is closing its catalog because of the forthcoming second edition of *AACR*. William Welsh has been talking for years about closing the Library of Congress' catalog. He's been promising it next year, next year, next year for 10 years now, long before *AACR2* was even thought of.

My own feeling about it is that it certainly will have effects on existing catalogs, because there are a number of changes in the forms of headings prescribed. The greatest impact of *AACR2* will be on catalogers all over the world, because it will be a much easier code to use. I think it's better organized and more systematic. It hasn't gone far enough, but it's certainly a step in the right direction.

As far as having gone further than the Memorandum of Agreement intended, I don't think so. We have gone further than anyone expected us to go, but, until the question was posed to catalogers all over the world about flaws in the *AACR* 1967, people were not aware of how widespread the dissatisfaction was with many of its provisions. Once you've got people coming at you from all directions saying that there is something wrong with this rule, there is a flaw here, this does not yield the results that we want, then you can hardly ignore them. There were many suggestions that have not been incorporated into *AACR2*. Those that have been incorporated have come into existence because the majority of members of the National Committee and of the JSC were convinced that this was the correct approach. It's not that we took every suggestion that came to us, threw it into a hopper, mixed it up, and produced a code. That is not at all the situation.

I'm going to ask Mr. Gorman to respond to the question about options. Whether Mr. Fasana is right about there being 100 options in the code, I don't know. I cannot see ones I am aware of creating any great problems. Can you?

Michael Gorman: I think the options are much more clearly marked in *AACR2*; whereas many of the rules in the present code imply that there is an option, because it uses words such as "may be used," and so on. I don't believe that there is a greatly increased number of options in this code. I did do a survey of them for the British Library on behalf of the group of four which was referred to. Our impression is that there aren't a great number more. It may be 100 as opposed to 80, but it certainly isn't 100 as opposed to none or as opposed to 10. I suspect that the JSC has probably laid a stick for its opponents to beat it with by marking the options very clearly, but one of the intentions of the code is to express things clearly.

Eleanor Crarey: The question of options struck me most forcefully when I had a chance to read through this fairly voluminous document. There are two things that happen: First, you have three levels of possible description. Within those three levels you have a variety of options that do not necessarily need to be consistently applied. Now, I have very mixed reactions to this, because, on the one hand, this opens up the possibility of any library cataloging according to the needs of its own clientele in a very specified way. On the other hand, it actually guarantees duplication in a cooperatively produced catalog unless you carefully define the options and the level of cataloging and specify where and when each applies. If you're using that catalog as an interlibrary loan tool, and you must attach location information to one of the items that is in the catalog three different ways, you have to be very careful how you attach the location information. So I feel rather divided on this point. I do think, however, that the way it's been specified in the new rules allows cooperating agencies to clearly define how they will proceed if they decide that they will cooperate. Of course, they have to decide which options they will apply and how.

Now as to the issue of closing catalogs, I think the present code fails to deal with the amendments that are in there already. Any catalog of long duration is already in a fair amount of chaos, and it is very difficult to locate things with any consistency, anyway. To continue in any kind of machine-readable situation, we are faced with the necessity of dealing with amendments whether or not we have a new code. The thing is, a new code allows us a fresh start.

I'm fascinated with what happens with some of these options. The rule for librettos, for instance, exactly reverses the present code, which would enter them under the composer with an added entry under the librettist. Also consider the use of choosing common names. AFL-CIO has now become the preferred entry rather than the added entry. So there will be some very interesting exact reversals.

I was a little startled in some ways by a statement that other decisions have been directed towards achieving a consistent form of heading. These include systematic romanization, headings for names in a nonroman alphabet, optional methods of recording place names, and qualifiers for corporate bodies. This epitomizes some of the problems that in one way we are systemizing, but in another way we are desystemizing. We are going to have to address these issues very carefully as we proceed.

Hinton: I'll take my turn at options, but without the text I'd hate to be pinned down on it. The national libraries are expected to record all of the details, insofar as it applies to the object being described. Any library can decide for itself that it does not need all of this information for all materials. It can decide that it will use the maximum level of description for some materials, and the minimum level of description for other materials. These are administrative decisions that are made by every library in this country, and always have been, without the options being stated. The only thing new in this is that it is spelled out as a possibility and that the elements that must be included are specified. Therefore, you should not get, even in shared cataloging, duplication of records just because one library includes more detail than another when describing the same object. They should be recognizable.

The "optional addition of places" was an unfortunate phrasing in my speech on the subject, and I apologize for that. I should have corrected it. The option there is very much the same as the optional method of recording the full forenames of authors who use only their initials. You would always add the place in the heading if that is necessary to differentiate two corporate bodies with the same name. If the libraries so desire, the addition of the place could be made to all corporate body headings. It's not an optional addition exactly; it's an optional method of recording the information. I don't think it's going to cause much trouble.

Jean Weihs: I would like to ask about the rule which states that the original painting is to be entered under the artist, but a reproduction will be entered under the title, unless the artist has decided that the painting was intended to be reproduced for the print. I have been the nonbook consultant to the Canadian Committee on Cataloging, so I have done some research on this. I asked all kinds of libraries what they thought about this rule. Unanimously, they were opposed to it. Even the Ontario College of Art, which is a special library and has many original paintings and reproductions, said that they would never use this rule. There were three reasons for this from all the libraries: First, they thought it would be a tremendous burden on catalogers to figure out whether or not an artist intended his/her work to be reproduced. Second, they thought that many works of art have nondistinctive titles. There are many, many paintings that are titled *Portrait of a Man, Portrait of a Woman, Mood Number Six;* some are even untitled. They felt that in many instances the title was the least interesting point of entry that they would want. And third, in multimedia catalogs which have a subject approach, or whose public uses a subject approach, it would mean that an artist's works would not stand together. For instance, in reproduction of Renoir's work under the subject IMPRESSIONISM, Renoir's works would not stand together in the catalog but be spread out according to their titles. I would appreciate it if you would tell us the rationale for this decision. I know everybody has been speaking against options, but I would like to know what the possibility is for making this an option for those libraries?

Hinton: I suspect that even without an option those libraries who do not accept this principle won't pay any attention to it. The rationale is that Renoir would probably spin wildly in his grave at the notion that a black and white photographic reproduction of one of his colored paintings was in any sense his responsibility. The rationale for paintings is that certain types of art prints, for example, are designed to be reproduced in multiple copies. Any of these prints are, in effect, the original object. But a black and white reproduction or even a color photograph of a painting which cannot possibly show the texture and so forth of the original is more an adaptation of the original work of art. It is an adaptation without an author; therefore it is to be entered under title. A photograph of a piece of sculpture is an adaptation which cannot possibly show the full roundness of the original work of art. These are adaptations rather than the work of the artist. I'll grant you that this has its impractical side, but philosophically it has convinced me.

Susan Martin: This is a somewhat frivolous question but I was just curious: Under *AACR2* what is going to be the main entry for *AACR2?*

Hinton: I'm not sure; I would say it is the work of diffuse authorship and entered under title. It has more than three authors.

Bethany Mendenholm: I'd like to point out the ARLIS (Art Library Society of North America) position on art reproductions if I remember correctly what it was. The position was that the artist is the subject of the reproduction. We didn't envisage there even being an added entry for the artist included in the code. We were recommending a return to the old dichotomy where the artist was, in most cases, the subject, unless we were talking about original work.

Maurice Freedman: Before going on to your next question, a point of clarification: Would you say the rule does or does not represent what ARLIS recommended?

Mendenholm: Only in part. The concept that a reproduction should not be entered under the artist's name was consonant with ARLIS's recommendation, but making an added entry under the artist was not. ARLIS's recommendation was that the coverage for the artist be a subject entry, which I gather is not included in *AACR2*.

Freedman: If I understand you, the reproduction of a painting entitled *Untitled* would appear under a subject entry for the artist whose original painting was called *Untitled*.

Mendenholm: You referred to the dissatisfaction with *AACR2* which you realized after you started fielding all the comments, that this was more widespread than was anticipated, and that it was necessary, therefore, for us to go beyond the original mandate. Given the current grumblings which Mr. Fasana referred to, and given the very real consequences to all of us in adopting this—closing catalogs, for example—why it is necessary to keep to a very narrow time construct in the promulgation of this? Why not give it more discussion time?

Hinton: Money, among other things. There is no more money to support the code revision project. The Council on Library Resources gave x-number of dollars to be used within a particular time and I don't think the Council on Library Resources is of any mind to go shelling out money for ten years the way it did before. Even if you kept on talking for ten years, I don't think you could fully be aware of the code's impact until you start using it. Some of the flaws in the 1967 code were not recognized until catalogers actually started trying to apply those rules.

I did not mean to say that the JSC has gone far beyond the original mandate. The original mandate was very clear: to consider for inclusion all proposals made.

Joseph Rosenthal: Since you brought up the subject of money, I'd like to speak for just a moment about the utilization of library resources in the 1970s and beyond, when we have less money in real terms than we used to. There was a grant of over $100,000 for the CCRC work, I believe, or the JSC work on the code revision. In addition, there has been a large expenditure of time and effort, and, implicitly, money, by the representatives from other organizations who worked with the CCRC and probably with the other authors, and by a great many people in a great many libraries who have reviewed draft documents emanating from the CCRC and other authors. But I would imagine that the greatest cost of the code is yet to come; it's in the training of the people who are going to work with the code and in the actual changes that result in our catalogs and displays of bibliographical data.

I'm quite concerned about the draft code as it now stands. I really was not all that aware of what preceded the 1967 code, but I have the feeling from the comments so far that there is a good deal more concern about the *AACR2* and a good deal more heat about the substance of the *AACR2* than there was about the 1967 code. In part I believe that the long genesis of the 1967 code and the opportunity for a widespread discussion helped temper the dissatisfactions that accrued before the 1967 code was issued. I'm not at all certain that this edition will meet with as favorable a reception as the 1967 code did. And I, for one, would urge that more time be given to try to fashion the best possible code since the greatest costs lie ahead of us.

Freedman: I'll add a couple of glosses of information, if you'll allow me. Prior to the *AACR* 1967, there was an extended discussion in the *Library Journal* among Professor Lubetzky and others about the draft of the *AACR*, which had been completed by C. Sumner Spalding. John Cronin, the Director of the Processing Department at that time, had directed Alice Toomey, who was a cataloging expert at LC and at the time Head of the Catalog Maintenance and Publication Division, to do a detailed, rule-by-rule analysis of the 1949 rules and the draft of the *AACR*. What that embodied was a rule-to-rule comparison of the 1949 rules with the concomitant *AACR* rules, with lines drawn between them so one could see exactly what had been done. This comparison had been sent out, because of Mr. Cronin's interest in the new rules, to the heads of technical services of all the members of the Association for Research Libraries and any others concerned with the new rules. A copy was made available to anyone who wished one. It was quite an expensive undertaking, but it maximized the dissemination of the new rules, and made maximum possible comment. Such a rule-by-rule comparison would not be unwelcomed in the current situation.

It always grieves me when I hear that money is the primary consideration as to whether a set of catalog rules will be written and how long the consideration of what the rules will be. The cost implications of ill-advised or hastily prepared rules for American libraries'catalogs would grossly transcend any short expenditures.Too many decisions are made primarily on terms of immediate out-of-pocket costs.

Hinton: I agree, a rule-by-rule comparison of the code is going to be very necessary for training purposes. That's an honest answer, though; there are economic limits beyond which no organization in the world can continue working on the code. Perhaps it is correct that we should have a longer period of discussion, but don't forget that the two things making the 1967 code palatable were superimposition and the incorporation in the North American Text of Rules 98 and 99, for example, which retained many of the old forms of headings. These did not particularly come from the open library field; these were from libraries like Mr. Rosenthal's and Mr. Fasana's, the ARL libraries which had the greatest stake. The vast size of their catalogs made them reluctant, for economic reasons, to make changes. If those changes had been made in 1967, they would not be suggested as changes today. You would have had fewer cards to change and fewer problems created. Some changes must come, not change for change's sake, but because the results are desirable. They cause trauma at the time; but the longer you put them off, the more traumatic the change is going to be.

Gorman: I'm perturbed about two or three aspects of what's going on. The first thing that's worrying me is that things are getting wrenched out of context. There seems to be an atmosphere of rumor and picking on one point, like this discussion about the art works. That rule resulted from consultation with people who are supposed to be experts in this field and from the general principles of authorship. Very clearly said, it is: It may be practical or it may be desirable in some ways to enter under the artist, but it sure isn't an author heading. It's ridiculous to assail people who are making a code, on the one hand, for abandoning all the principles which have been going strong for 100 years, and, on the other hand, for applying the principles; on the one hand, for not consulting with people, and, on the other hand, for taking advice.

The second thing I'm perturbed about is the attitude of people who are not going to go along with the code. All these people, as I understand it, had opportunities through the appropriate mechanism to argue their case, to avoid being just plain bad losers who in the end say, "Since you didn't do exactly what we wanted to do, we're not going to use the whole code."

The third thing I'm perturbed about is this general atmosphere of negativism which seems to be building up. I was accused this morning, I think unjustly, of thinking that all change was good and of equating it with progress. It seems to me that there are an awful lot of people around who think that any change is bad.

Karen Bendorf: First, while you are correct in stating that the increased clarity of the rules will reduce duplication in shared cataloging data bases, the introduction of three different levels of fullness for records will cause havoc for data bases that are shared by multiple users who commit themselves to different levels and who have an interest in using each other's records for their own libraries.

The second point has to do with rules for geographic names. *AACR2* states to to establish a geographic name you are to use the English form if one is in general use. If there is not one in general use, the name is to be established according to ''gazetteers and other reference sources published in English speaking countries.'' I can appreciate the problems caused by *AACR*'s current rule about requiring a very specific set of reference works that can be used for sources of names, but was there not some sort of compromise between that over-specified list and this over-generalization? This could also cause problems for shared catalog users.

Hinton: We decided in principle that we would not recommend reference sources or practices for a particular library. The *National Board of Geographic Names*, which the Library of Congress by law is required to use, could not stay in the code, but I'm not quite certain why ''gazetteers and reference tools in English'' is too vague.

Bendorf: Because they vary in the form in which they record names, particularly the countries that change names frequently, such as African countries. And different libraries may have different reference sources.

Hinton: Yes, they may, although presumably, if the country changes its name, you would change your heading and have two entries for it.

The *AACR*, Second Edition, What Next?

by Phyllis A. Richmond

The topic to be considered is "what should we do next in code revision?" My thesis is that this should be the last code revision based mainly on consensus. My basic assumption, for *purposes of argument only*, is that the second edition of the *Anglo-American Cataloging Rules (AACR2)* is the best that can be devised under present conditions, although this may or may not be the case.

So far, no code since 1940 has been satisfactory to the point where it will stand for any length of time. We have had virtually continuous code revisions since about 1938. By the time the next one is published, that will be a period of 40 years. This includes several drafts and two-and-one-half to three different codes (depending upon whether you view the present one as an edition or a new code).

The standard reasons given for code revisions, besides dissatisfaction, are changing times, computers, microtext, library automation, and so on. These are all valid, but a cataloging code is an intellectual thing, a construct of the mind, attempting to apply some order to a mass of documentary material in all kinds of formats. We have seen a kind of code where a legalistic approach was tried—a rule for almost every identifiable situation, and we have seen the opposite—a set of rules to be applied generally to a variety of situations.

The logical basis for code revision was outlined by Seymour Lubetzky.[1] A recent discussion by Eva Verona has pretty much identified arguments on the points where there are still major differences of opinion.[2] There is not too much that can be done at this time and for the next decade on improving upon the logic of these two librarians. The full verification of this logic and settling of differences now needs to be made by other means. Although much of the argument for this or that solution of a problem of entry or description seems valid, we shall not reach a greater degree of certainty over the general validity of our rules until we look more carefully at the sources producing the types of data which we use as a basis for rule-making. This careful look should help identify the variety of situations recognized by users of the library's collections and by noncatalog librarians, as well as by catalogers.

Rules have been changed by trial-and-error, by logical argument and counter-argument, and by fiat. None of these methods has been particularly enduring because none of them involved more than a token amount of research. What we need is a much better understanding of the materials to which our art is applied, with the possibility of interpretation by science.

PROBLEMS

To explain what this encompasses, the work of Thomas Kuhn in the history of science is enlightening. Kuhn, first of all, noted that science and technology were two separate fields before Francis Bacon joined them, in theory at least, in the early seventeenth century. Actually, in spite of Bacon, technologies, until the last third of the nineteenth century, were more properly classified as *arts*. Advances in technology did not follow scientific research until then. Nowadays whole industries are a result of laboratory discoveries such as how to split the atom or the invention of the transistor. Several new sciences arose in the seventeenth, eighteenth, and early nineteenth centuries because "critically important advances in the understanding of nature resulted from the decision of scientists to study what craftsmen had already learned to do."[3]

In other words, the art was explained in scientific terms. There was a joker in this. To quote Kuhn further:

> In all these cases [where scientists studied what craftsmen knew how to do] . . . the resulting benefits have accrued to science not to technology. . . . When Kepler studied the optimum dimensions of wine casks, the proportions which would yield maximum content for the least consumption of wood, he helped to invent the calculus of variations, but existing wine casks were, he found, already built to the dimensions he derived. When Sadi Carnot undertook to produce the theory of the steam engine, a prime mover to which, as he emphasized, science had contributed little or nothing, the result was an important step to thermodynamics; his prescription for engine improvement, however, had been embodied in engineering practice before his study began. With few exceptions, none of much significance, the scientists who turned to technology for their problems succeeded merely in validating and explaining, not improving techniques developed earlier and without science's aid.[4]

Which is to say, scientific study of a craftsman's art produced new methods which could be applied for better understanding of the natural world, but otherwise confirmed what the craftsmen had already discovered.

Information scientists refer to the arts of the librarian as *information technology*. The implication is that by studying the technology they may improve the art; the information scientist will show the technologist how to do the job better, whatever the job is. Kuhn, however, would say that this process would produce a science, but not improve the technology or art. There is no evidence from the history of science or the history of technology to show otherwise. Anything gained will accrue to information science rather than to library practice.

Recently I asked an operations research man why he and his colleagues spent their time on circulation. He said it was because this was an area where processes could be measured. If our *Rules* were coded so that a human being could assign them to works just as MARC (Machine-Readable Cataloging) codes are assigned, there is no reason cataloging results would not be readily amenable to measurement as well. Maybe we shall be operations-researched at some time in the future, but the person who undertakes such study will have to know both fields well. This kind of research, whether on processes of cataloging, acquisitions, or whatnot, should produce results to show that, with due respect to all the fancy mathematics, the specific arts of cataloging, acquisitions, or whatnot are being done as well as can be expected. (This will shake up library managers no end.) The point is that this is not the type of research that will necessarily help in devising future cataloging codes.

The transformations affecting cataloging in the past four decades have been as much socioeconomic as technical. We have come up against the extreme expense which change brings to an existing catalog. In some cases it has seemed better to close off and begin again because of the expense. We have begun to change forms of catalogs to make them more responsive to change. We have been playing around with the wording, expression, and emphasis of the rules. No matter what we do, there are certain things that have to be emphasized and whether we put them first, last, or in the middle does not affect what they are.

The thing we have not determined to any great degree is the conditions and forms under which our various clients expect to find these factors. Nor have we considered our obligations to the authors of the works being cataloged. We have been very cursory in our treatment of works according to intellectual level or content. As Lauren Doyle put it during the Great Relevance Rumpus:

> Perhaps the author has as much of a right to be served as the searcher, i.e., in order that his [or her] articles should be retrieved by "relevant readers." And perhaps in that same sense the information store is as interested in searching the searcher as the searcher is in searching the information.[5]

There is a very significant matter involved here. It has been recognized to some degree in the dialogue patterns used in online searching systems. The possibility of building such a dialogue capability into future catalog codes should at least be considered. It would be one way of allowing *main entry* to those who want it, and *no main entry* or *semi-main entry* to those who do not. And the user who wants to eliminate all that extra punctuation that comes with the *International Standard Bibliographic Description (ISBD)* or book numbers, class numbers, card numbers, notes of various types and so on, could specify what was to be omitted by some kind of a *delete* command. By the same token, an *add* instruction could be included for the user who wanted more information, such as reviews of a book, citation patterns, and so forth, available through connections to other multidisciplinary data bases, as well as to those that are discipline-, mission-, or problem-oriented, or interdisciplinary.

This brings up a possibility which has barely been considered in code revision: How should a multidisciplinary data base like MARC be interfaced with other kinds of data bases to give the user the best possible access to recorded information? Specifically, there are broad coverage indexing and abstracting services, citation indexes, and reviews. Full service with all these forms is not yet available except in part through other multidisciplinary data bases which themselves do not intercommunicate with each other or with MARC. Nevertheless, all of them could be tied in rather closely to almost any approach via cataloging. Right now we have each data base as a law unto itself. What about an Anglo-American code that would apply to every situation where there is a bibliographic citation (using *citation* in the sense of entry rather than reference)? Surely the time has come to start thinking about that. With further development of networks and data bases, it certainly will occur to users that they need a combination of online ready-access capabilities, preferably at one sitting and without having to switch mental gears to such a degree as is currently required.

Up to this point, the discussion has covered what kind of research is not needed, and a preliminary account of user expectations in terms of online bibliographic systems related to the possibility of an umbrella Anglo-American code. We stand squarely in a no-man's land between a rough technology and a vague science. Cataloging has been an art, a rather well-defined art and probably close to its zenith in its present form. Let us assume for the sake of argument and strictly tongue-in-cheek that the current cataloging rules are the best we can devise, that any further alterations are merely nitpicking and not worth the effort—like changing the dimensions of a wine cask by a few thousandths of an inch. This may seem a hazardous assumption, but the results are worth considering. One way or another we will need codes.

CODES

Before moving to consideration of socioeconomic and cultural factors affecting codes, a brief outline of the nature of codes is needed. A cataloging code or any code, as in the case of man-made laws or rules or customs, will be observed by the majority. This is a common feature of society and is enforced by social pressure or socially accepted legal measures. Most drivers stop at stop signs. Some do under duress—there may be a policeman concealed in nearby bushes, others as a matter of prudence—a fast car with the right of way can be injurious. The majority stop because they see sense to the process and consensus based on this perception produces the necessary social pressure for conformity. This is elementary behavioral science. The result is a typical distribution of pattern of behavior. It can be measured, predicted and, since the distribution has been applied in many different social systems, it has about 49 different names: Zipf's Law, Pareto's Law, Weber-Fechner psychophysical laws, Lotka's Law, and so on. The specific type of curve that goes with these distributions has the property of self-similarity, that is, each section has the same form as the whole, but on a different scale. The best known of these empirical hyperbolic distributions in library context is that of Bradford.[6]

The stop sign pattern also occurs in every cataloging code. Internally each code has a few basic rules which are widely used because they fit the majority of cases, plus a large number of more unique rules which are used more rarely. The rules themselves may differ, but the pattern of use is similar from code to code. Whether one set of rules is better than another requires a value judgment based on some set of criteria which would have to be defined very carefully. So far such value judgments with regard to rules have not been made with well-defined criteria or objectively. This is one area where research is badly needed. First we need to determine which parts of value theory[7] are applicable; then how to apply them to rules in an objective manner. So far, our changes have been made largely by more or less common subjectivities founded on individual perceptions and called *experience* or on unsystematic *observation* or even on fads of various types.

Since objective value analysis is still pretty much an unknown science and since the tenuous assumption is being made that the new set of rules is the best that can be devised under current conditions, let us then consider where we stand. We have a set of rules that can only be improved by some methodology other than that used to date. If we leave the application of these rules to people to be called *technologists*, because the *art* of cataloging has gone as far as it will go, we may now look in a totally different direction. We step outside our normal activities and we become scientists. What does this mean?

First of all it means that we have to begin to look at the world around us, not just at *us* leading *them* through the tremendous mass of bibliographic materials. We need to become patient and objective observers of the makers of the materials as well as the materials themselves. The materials reflect their makers and the makers created them to fill social needs. It behooves us to determine what these social needs are and why they have arisen. Fortunately, wc have help in this respect because the sociologists of science and the sociologists of knowledge and even some economists have made pioneering efforts in this direction.

THE REWARD SYSTEM

The work so far accomplished by sociologists of science and now spreading to knowledge in other areas has led to discovery of a process called "the reward system of science."[8] Probably this sytem is common to academic research in all subjects, although this has not yet been demonstrated, to my knowledge. The reward system functions on the basis that a person who makes a discovery trades his/her knowledge, makes it public, in exchange for the rewards of recognition. The rewards of recognition can run anywhere from a Nobel Prize or one's name on a major breakthrough (Einstein's Theory), to getting tenure on a faculty or a fellowship.

For example, suppose that I set up a theory and develop some projects that will run on a whole collection of microcomputers in my back room. After such brain-breaking thought, back-breaking toil, and burned fingers, I discover a systematic way to take any piece of writing, identify unique patterns in it, and determine exactly what theories, assumptions, hypotheses an author used; whose work led him/her to conclusions (whether this work was cited or not); what school of thought is there (whether stated or not); or if eclecticism is involved, where all the pieces of ideas and notions came from; and, finally, where in general this piece of work fits into the totality of knowledge. This kind of information would save some scholars a lifetime of work. It would replace citation indexing as a source of data for many studies. It could help in attribution of authorship for anonymous works. It might even have a spinoff in intelligence or detective work. I write up my theory, my designs, my programs, my data, and my results and make this ery available to all who can read—in exchange for recognition.

This is a straightforward case, whether the discovery is issued as a monograph or a journal article. The bibliographic tools would pick it up and disseminate it. Now supposing I compile a list of some kind of information that is hard to find. It takes ten years to put it together. Or I find a rare manuscript and I spend ten years editing and annotating it. In either case, I am creating something that did not exist before and it takes much work. When I publish the results, I shall receive recognition from scholars. But in either of these cases, with the *International Standard Bibliographic Description (ISBD)* interpreted by the standard bibliographic tools as entry under title, without necessarily an added entry for compiler or editor, my reward is going to be quite a lot longer in coming. The scholars are going to have a hard time finding it, especially if word of mouth or invisible college members pass the reference along as *Richmond's index* or *Richmond's edition of Suchandsuch*, which would be normal practice, even in library science.

In a similar vein, a most interesting study was completed by Nancy Williamson of the University of Toronto.[9] In the process of comparing cataloging and bibliography, which appear to have much in common, she needed specific data from bibliographies to use as a source for locating bibliographic principles and to find rules, if there were any, used by bibliographers in compiling the bibliographies. At the same time, she did not want to bias her study by using bibliographies compiled by librarians or those who said they had consulted librarians and thus were familiar with catalog codes. In other words, she wanted to find out how people who were not librarians and unfamiliar with the code would enter the various types of authorship or nonauthorship which are enumerated at such length and with such precision in the *Anglo-American Cataloging Rules*. For this, she eventually found 175 bibliographies in the field of English language and literature, carefully screened to be sure they passed the requirements. The data were analyzed by computer, using routines from the *Statistical Package for the Social Sciences*.[10] Special coding sheets were designed and the *code* book itself comprises 109 pages, covering some 33 different details examined in each bibliography.

The results revealed bibliographic practices which could only have been a result of using principles and some kind of unwritten rules. Though not formalized as a code, these were definite enough for purposes of comparison with cataloging equivalents. The most significant variation between cataloging and bibliography-making appeared in the matter of authorship. Bibliographers tended to prefer a name as entry point and were not particularly fussy as to what the *author* did to the work—compilers and editors were used as entry points—nor did they worry so much about multiple authorship. This was also true of style manuals in the same subject, which were checked to determine what would-be authors were being told to do.

Dr. Williamson wrote:

> In many instances it was clear that the bibliographers were not concerned with establishing intellectual responsibility for a work, but rather with identifying it and locating it. Furthermore, they assumed that a name is a better means of identification than a title. . . . there was little in the sample of bibliographies which suggested that bibliographers considered title entries an improvement over author entries. In truth, there seemed to be a strong preference for the use of some other feature of the work if possible, leaving title as the last possible choice. . . . [11]

In her conclusion, Williamson wrote that:

> [I]n the light of the bibliographers' approach to authorship, the definition of authorship should be reexamined. In this context some thought should be given to whether or not the present trend in cataloging rules toward greater use of title entry is valid. With specific reference to works prepared under editorial direction and collections prepared by a compiler, reconsideration should be given to the possibility of accepting the name of the editor or compiler named on the title page of a work as viable entry.[12]

This type of research needs to be extended to other subjects and verified or refuted. If the users are coming from bibliographies and style manuals expecting to find editors and compilers considered as authors, and their names are even one cross-reference away, we are inconveniencing our clientele. With the full use of the computer, multiple entry points will make the question academic, but our computerized catalogs are not that sophisticated yet and will not be for some time. Meanwhile, regardless of entry point, the reward system is still going to demand that the person who did the work receive the recognition. And users will expect this.

CITATION ANALYSIS

The reward system operates so that the scholar receives tangible and visible evidence of recognition in the form of references called *citations*. These are a kind of intellectual toll paid for the use of the discovery. It is an acknowledgement of intellectual debt. It is also recognized as a rough measure of quality. High quality work is cited for a long period of time. Herman Fussler has suggested that there should be some study of the relation of citation patterns to catalog rules, with a view to seriously considering whether the rules should fit citation practice.[13] There is much to recommend such an activity.

The tracing of citations backward in time creates a chain of relationships among documents, journals, scholars, and ideas. While there are varieties of citations, and not all are necessarily complimentary,[14] a citation indicates some influence of one author upon another. Networks of citations can make *invisible colleges* visible. Citations traced forward in time reveal the effects of seminal research. One can take citations from a single work and go backward for influence of predecessors, spread out currently for influence of an invisible college, and go forward for influence on later research. Sometimes a snowball effect will turn up with one piece of research affecting developments in many areas. Drawing lines to connect related documents may turn up patterns that look like stars with rays emanating in all directions, where a key study has been made.[15]

Citation analysis is still in its infancy. Besides *invisible colleges*, there are networks of coauthors, networks of papers, networks of journals, networks of cocitations, and probably networks of editors, networks of index entries and abstracts, and maybe even networks of reviewers. The reviewer's place in citation chains is an important one because conceivably a carefully done critical review could make or break a line of inquiry or alter the direction of a chain of citations. Authors' networks tend to be problem centered, with membership changing from time to time as interests of members change.[16] There are networks of subjects, naturally, but this aspect of citation analysis has been somewhat taken for granted.

Citation analysis is pursued as a research method in information science, psychology, and sociology because it is highly revealing of scholarly practices. For catalog code making, it would entail examination of how authors cite works. Eva Verona has suggested that establishment of the form of a name used by an author should be made by frequency—in other words, actual measurement by counting the occurrence of various forms in the author's works.[17] This could be supplemented by a similar measurement to find out under what form of name the author was most frequently cited. Conceivably, the author might use a form of name on the most cited work that was different from the most frequently used form on all his/her works. *Best known* could be reinterpreted as most-frequently-used-by-the-author or most-frequently-cited, either of which would be a more precise method than leaving the choice up to the individual cataloger. Using either method we advance from Lubetzky's logic to a relatively objective means of achieving that logic with a concrete means of measurement.

OTHER FACTORS

The process of looking for unobtrusive means of measurement needs to be extended to the process of rule-making. Citation indexing is one such methodology. There are others. One such case would be to look for empirical hyperbolic distributions in the behavioral patterns of users' searching activities. Finding such patterns means that one has discovered a situation where a practice involves an overwhelming majority. This kind of distribution is represented by a curve which shows a hugely lopsided frequency for the majority, then a dramatic drop, dribbling off into a long tail of mostly zeros and single instances. Wherever this kind of majority is found—in any subject—one may be certain that whatever the practice is that produces such a pattern, it will be satisfied by rules taking it into account. It may be that catalog rules will rest more securely on this kind of user habit than on any other. The problem is how to develop a satisfactory methodology for finding such practices among users.

A different kind of unobtrusive methodology has been found by Dr. Donald Cleveland. This was used to obtain entry points into a bibliography using data plus relationship-indicating equations based on probability theory.[18] This sophisticated method is computerized and gives results which essentially support a *logical* position on entry, such as that of Lubetzky. Like the calculus of variations, the methodology has wider application than for cataloging rules, though what it does so far applies to some parts of cataloging. If the equations are or could be made applicable, it would be both a step toward automatic cataloging and toward putting the further development of descriptive cataloging on a scientific basis. Conceivably, the *art* itself would then become a true technology and a candidate for technological improvements. The proposed change in name of the Information Science and Automation Division (ISAD) strongly suggests that if the scientific basis for cataloging rule-making proves out, there will be a home waiting for its technology.

CONCLUSION

These are by no means the only possible research methods leading to a new type of catalog code. Nor will the development of a science of bibliographic control or a lively technology occur quickly. All the subjects with which we deal are changing constantly. Methodologies in these subjects also change. We shall have to keep up with all of these changes—a process that at present we do very poorly. So our technology—if it comes to that—will have to have a built-in factor for keeping up with change without pulling down the whole edifice. Our science, if we reach one, should lead us in directions we do not even imagine as yet.

For the immediate future, let us assume this present code revision is the best possible under current conditions. Let us leave it completely alone for about a decade or even more. Meanwhile let us get busy on the research necessary for a new code much more responsive to the needs of our users and to the makers of the subject content of our records. We particularly need to study the expectations of our users, as well as their bibliographic habits. At the same time, we should consider the motivation of our authors, not stopping with what they call themselves or what intellectual responsibility they bear for a work. We need to find out *why* they presented their work the way they did and *why* this way is considered to be important. Then, with further developments in library technology, we can build a solid foundation for producing another code, substituting knowledge of the nature and variety of users' needs and approaches for what we now imagine those needs and approaches are.

As to the research that will produce this code of the future, it would be folly to say in advance what it will be like, where it will lead, or what it will reveal. I have suggested points of departure as a step toward sounder basis for the code, but they may not be the methods we finally will come to. We have come to the end of one methodology and must search for another. The next generation should not have to spend so much of its intellectual life in a haze of continual discussion of code revision.

REFERENCES

1. Seymour Lubetzky, *Cataloging Rules and Principles: A Critique of the ALA Rules for Entry and a Proposed Design for Their Revision* (Washington: Library of Congress, 1953); idem, *Code of Cataloging Rules: Bibliographic Entry and Description. A Partial and Tentative Draft* (n.p.: American Library Association, Resources and Technical Services Division, Cataloging and Classification Section, 1958); idem, *Code of Cataloging Rules: Author and Title Entry. An Unfinished Draft. . . . With an Explanatory Commentary by Paul Dunkin* (n.p.: American Library Association, 1960).

2. Eva Verona, *Corporate Headings: Their Use in Library Catalogues and National Bibliographies; A Comprehensive and Critical Study* (London: IFLA Committee on Cataloguing, 1975).

3. Thomas S. Kuhn, "The Relations between History and History of Science," *Daedalus* (Spring 1971), p. 285.

4. Ibid.

5. Lauren B. Doyle, "Is Relevance an Adequate Criterion in Retrieval System Evaluation?" *Automation and Scientific Communication. Short Papers* (Washington: American Documentation Institute, 1963), pt. II, pp. 199-200.

6. Robert A. Fairthorne, "Empirical Hyperbolic Distributions (Bradford-Zipf-Mandelbrot) for Bibliometric Description and Prediction," *Journal of Documentation* 25, no. 4 (December 1969): 319-43.

7. Nicholas Rescher, *Introduction to Value Theory* (Englewood Cliffs, NJ: Prentice-Hall, 1969).

8. Discussion of the *reward system* began in the mid-1950s. Probably the most easily obtained introduction to the field is through two works: Warren O. Hagstrom, *The Scientific Community* (New York: Basic Books, 1965) and Norman W. Storer, *The Social System of Science* (New York: Holt, Rinehart & Winston, 1966). For side effects, see Robert K. Merton, "The Matthew Effect in Science," *Science* 159, no. 3810 (January 5, 1968): 56-63. Other articles by Merton on the system may be found in his book, *The Sociology of Science: Theoretical and Empirical Investigations* (Chicago: University of Chicago Press, 1973), pt. 4, pp. 279-412.

9. Nancy Williamson, *Cataloguing and Bibliography: A Comparative Study of Their Interrelationships as Seen through Their Principles and Practices* (Ann Arbor, MI: University Microfilms International, 1977).

10. Norman Nie, Dale H. Bent, and C. Hadlai Hull, *SPSS: Statistical Package for the Social Sciences*, 2d ed. (New York: McGraw Hill, 1975).

11. Williamson, *Cataloging and Bibliography*, pp. 343-44.

12. Ibid., pp. 352-53.

13. Herman H. Fussler, Introduction to "Prospects for Change in Bibliographic Control." The Thirty-Eighth Annual Conference of the Graduate Library School, November 8-9, 1976.

14. Ben-Ami Lipetz, "Improvement of the Selectivity of Citation Indexes to Science Literature through the Inclusion of Citation Relationship Indicators," *American Documentation* 16 (1965): 81-90. A summary of the citation indexing phenomenon may be found in Sheila J. K. Bertram, *The Relationship between Intra-Document Citation Location and Citation Level* (Ann Arbor, MI: University Microfilms International, 1970), no. 70-20, 925, pp. 1-44.

15. Eugene Garfield, "Historiographs, Librarianship, and the History of Science," *Toward a Theory of Librarianship*, ed. Conrad Rawski (Metuchen, NJ: Scarecrow Press, 1973), pp. 380-402. This article is based on an earlier work: Eugene Garfield, Irving H. Sher, and Richard J. Torpie, *The Use of Citation Data in Writing the History of Science* (Philadelphia: Institute for Scientific Information, 1964).

16. Diana Crane, "Social Structure in a Group of Scientists: A Test of the 'Invisible College' Hypothesis," *American Sociological Review* 34, no. 3(1969): 335-52. The topic is covered in more detail in her *Invisible Colleges; Diffusion of Knowledge in Scientific Communities* (Chicago: University of Chicago Press, 1972).

17. Verona, *Corporate Headings*, p. 156, suggestion 4a.

18. Donald Cleveland, *A Geometrical Model for Information Retrieval* (Ann Arbor, MI: University Microfilms International, 1974), no. 74-10779.

DISCUSSION

Paul Fasana: I was intrigued by Ms. Richmond's inventory of the disciplines that can and probably should be applied to the problems that are familiar to libraries and information science. I would ask a question: Did she mean to emphasize user and creator only, because there are other functions in libraries that are vital and important? We're not only interested in the packages themselves. There are rare book libraries, for example. I would hope that your inventory was incomplete and simply meant to be illustrative, because I think these other aspects are equally important and also should be studied.

Ms. Richmond has now given us what we should do, but she hasn't given us how we should do it. How do we marshall these forces? It will require a battery of people from many disciplines. Where will we get the monies to actually support these people in their researches? To whom and how will the effort be directed? You just can't set off dozens of scientists going in several directions if the ultimate objective is to get something that is practical.

Finally, then, how do you synthesize all of this information or research into something that will be practical and can be translated into something that can be used by librarians? In terms of traditional librarianship, much of this research has been done in library schools, and there is great criticism as to the quality and the caliber of that kind of research. I would assume that you are not suggesting that library schools take on this responsibility.

You mentioned Mr. Fussler; I'm wondering if you're anticipating setting up a college of retired illustrious administrators who can give us the benefit of their experience. You also alluded to the American Library Association *ISAD*. What role do you see the professional association playing?

Edwin Buchinski: There's not much one can say on the topic although the approach that's been advocated is interesting. The motivation of our office recalls a story related to me by one of our catalogers. The catalogers were looking for a good example of how *AACR2* would treat nonbook materials. Someone came up with a multimedia serial; one issue may come out as a tape cassette, another one as a set of slides, etc. They tried to research the title to determine what its frequency was. Eventually, someone found a note which seemed to indicate that the author's sole objective was to make life miserable for librarians.

Phyllis Richmond: These kinds of questions are very hard to answer. My list, of course, is incomplete. If I made a complete list, we'd be here all night. As far as the practical is concerned, sometimes you have to avoid the practical and go for the impractical to try to figure out what is going on behind a situation. Eventually, what comes out as practical is not necessarily what you expected. I can't think of an exact example to give you right off the bat, but so far the type of research I mentioned has been started in certain library schools and in institutes where they undertake research projects.

I come from a place that is loaded with information scientists who regard practicing librarians as technologists in a derogatory sense. It's a constant battle there to demonstrate that librarians aren't technologists. On the other hand, I have to tell some librarians, "Let's get on the ball and do something else besides have our noses to the grindstone, and think of more fundamental aspects of librarianship." I've tried to indicate what some of these areas of potential research are in a couple of recent articles. I still am interested in trying some of these things when I get done with PRECIS (Preserved Context Index System). I can't do them all; it takes too many people. I would simply love to have people do dissertations on them, but, as I've tried to explain to people on the Cataloging Policy and Research Committee, the process of selecting a topic of a dissertation is up to the student and not the faculty member. The students don't always take the hints you give them. So you can't necessarily get them to do a beautiful problem, because they want to work on something else. I've gotten positively intellectual since I've gone into teaching.

Maurice Freedman: Any comments, questions, statements? Reactions?

Unidentified Speaker: Is it possible, starting from your initial example, that we actually have done the best that we can, that our technology reflects our various users, and that after you have done all this scientific research, the conclusion will be that there is no one code that can help everyone, and the same questions that we have right now will remain unanswered?

Richmond: Well, they would be answered to the extent that there was no code. This could happen; I don't know. The thing about research is that you never know where it's going to lead. You're going off into the unknown where nobody has been before and what you find may or may not be what you originally start out to find. One has students now and then who will start out with hypotheses, make assumptions, have everything going nicely for about a year, and then discover it doesn't work. That's always a great catastrophe. They come in and you say simply, "Well, that blocks off this alley. Let's look for another." So you look for another solution. This may be what we have to do if it turns out that the situation is as you suggested. It's perfectly possible that that may be the answer.

Seymour Lubetzky: I think in the course of the day several people have expressed themselves about the need for a user study. I addressed this point earlier, but I have a related point, which I would like to express. The reason I question the assumption made in user studies is that it is hard to determine how the user approaches the catalog. Does the user generally know precisely what s/he needs? I would like to make an analogy: One goes to a physician and says, "What have you got for sneezing and what is causing the sneeze?" Well, of course, there are very many reasons for sneezing, and there is a whole array of medicines for it, none perhaps to stop it because the sneeze itself is not the malady. It's not the sneeze that bothers the patient, there is something else that s/he does not know about. His/her sneeze is only a symptom—a single, particular manifestation—of his/her actual problem. The same is true of a catalog user. The particular *book* s/he is seeking might well be only a particular manifestation of the *work* s/he desires to have.

There are two problems in cataloging. One is how do people look for what they think they want and how can we give the answer best? The fact that you look for a title doesn't necessarily mean that that is what you want. For one thing, even if you were to make any number of studies on approaches to the catalog, you would find very divergent results depending on who the people being tested are, by what methods they are tested, and at what time they are tested. The book that was originally looked for without success by title may then be looked for by author for a variety of reasons. Perhaps the author's name is well known, although the book is published anonymously.

To me the first approach is not what we look for but what we find when we use the catalog. Let me give an example. If a person looks for *The American Scholar*— does it mean that he really wants *The American Scholar*? This actually happened when I was at the Library of Congress. A man came up to me and said he had been referred to me by the reference department. He was trying to find a list of editions of Emerson's *The American Scholar*. Beginning with the *National Union Catalog* at the Library of Congress and the card catalog he found under AMERICAN SCHOLAR a number of editions beginning with those published in 1890, but knew that it was a lecture read by Emerson in the 1830s. He was therefore quite sure there were earlier editions, but it appeared the Library of Congress didn't have them. He made a note to call this to the attention of the Library of Congress so that it might try to secure some earlier editions because the first edition is much more valuable than any of the editions published later on. Later on, as he proceeded from AMERICAN SCHOLAR, he found two entries under ORATION DELIVERED BEFORE THE PHI BETA KAPPA. Fortunately, one of the two entries made by the careful cataloger had a note which said, "Usually published under the title *American Scholar*." To that man there was something wrong with that catalog if he looks under *American Scholar* and can't find other editions of that work. That's exactly what he was looking for—earlier editions. There was an 1837 and an 1838 edition, but they could not easily be located under the title he had as a reference. Thus, the fact that this particular user approached the catalog with a seemingly precise citation is of little consequence. What is important is what he found or failed to find at the end of his search.

What I'm saying is we should study how a person approaches the catalog, but we are not to let the results we find lead us to think that that completely specifies the requirements the catalog is to satisy. What we have is something which may be entirely different from that which seems to satisfy the superficial requirements discovered in user studies. The history of cataloging, for example, has evolved along that line. We have the catalog, as I discussed it in 1975, based on the assumption that if a person looks under a name and title that is exactly what s/he wants and that it will fill his/her needs. This is not necessarily what s/he wants. It might be that what s/he wants is something else. It could have been under another name; or it could have been under another title. Access to particular books and the works they comprise are two different things. So let's not ignore the second when discussing the first. What kind of an answer will be most valuable and helpful to the user of the catalog? That is the criterion which determines the effectiveness of that instrument.

Richmond: I'm afraid that requires a psychiatrist to answer. I don't know; the user says he wants what he wants. There must be some way of getting at it, but I don't think we've found it yet.

Ruth Tighe: First I want to thank Dr. Richmond for what I thought was a very informative, thought-provoking, and stimulating presentation. Then I want to ask just one thing: Could you restate or summarize what led you to make the assumption that the present techniques for revising catalog codes are no longer applicable? Do you really feel that's been true for a long time or is it only true now?

Richmond: I feel that codes are pretty much based on consensus. We argue and we argue and we argue. My whole life as a librarian has been spent arguing about catalog codes, and it seems to me that it might be nice if we had a little more solid basis than somebody saying, "I think," somebody else saying, "I think." Some of the things we have heard today are similar to what was said at Stanford in 1958. I recently did a sketchy biography of Lucille Morsch and had to go back and read all the material on her career. How familiar everything was! Things go around in circles, and so I thought maybe we ought to break out of the circle. There might be some other way of revising codes, and one way might be by research, in order to get a better handle on things than we have now.

A Critique of the Draft *AACR*, 2nd Edition: Impact of the Rules on Documents Cataloging

by Bernadine E. Abbott Hoduski

Everything about government documents is fascinating and challenging! But nothing is more challenging than cataloging documents. Back in 1965, four of us just out of library school were hired by a state university. The director allowed us three days to get the lay of the land. On the fourth day, he sat us down and asked, "Well, what do you want to do for the library?" Before I could utter a word, the other three pointed at me and said, "She wants documents and we don't." And I did and still do.

I decided in library school that documents were the only real challenge left in librarianship and, besides that, they looked like a lot of fun. This particular university collection presented a challenge indeed. The library staff found it difficult getting the user and the documents together. They had the most problems with documents which had been cataloged and classed under Dewey. A standard answer to a student's request for a census publication was "come back in a few hours and we will have it for you."

There was a separate documents collection but it had been gutted of most of the choice reference tools and *important* documents. These documents were shelved in reference or throughout the regular collection. The documents collection itself was housed in a dark, dank, sublevel basement, a good block's walk from my desk in the Reference Department.

Those documents not classed in Dewey were classed in the Superintendent of Documents (SuDoc) system. The majority of the collection was not cataloged. The documents shelflist consisted of unintelligible check-in cards.

Something drastic had to be done to make this collection accessible and usable. Among other things a separate documents department was established, the over 70,000 volumes were moved to the new wing next to the Reference Department, all documents, reference tools, bibliographies (government and other), guides, and so on were pulled from reference and documents stacks and put into a documents room reference corner. A catch-up bindery program was instituted, adding immensely to the colorfulness and usefulness of the collection, as anyone familiar with the thousands of green, white, and brown congressional publications will testify.

In order to help the user, we decided to catalog as many documents as possible and include these cards in both the main card catalog and a documents room catalog. Because the regular cataloging staff was overwhelmed with the conversion from Dewey to LC (Library of Congress) project, I was assigned to catalog documents along with my regular acquisition and reference duties as head of the Documents Department. This suited me just fine because I felt that the one who has to answer questions based on a catalog should help construct that catalog.

I learned a lot about cataloging documents between 1965 and 1969. I began with the cataloging of serials, since so many documents fit into that category. From there it was a natural step to catalog each monograph within certain series. The congressional hearings were tackled first because LC had started to catalog most of the hearings and was consistently choosing as the main entry: UNITED STATES, CONGRESS, NAME OF THE COMMITTEE and, if needed, the NAME OF THE SUBCOMMITTEE. This congressional material was vastly underused because at that time there were no good access tools. This was long before CIS (Congressional Information Service) hit the scene. From there I went to executive branch large series.

Our Acquisitions Department was receiving the LC proof slips. It seemed easy enough at first to sort out all the documents cards. The only easy part about it was sorting out those cards with the main entry U.S.————. All the other cards had to be looked at individually since often there was no clue as to the real identity of the publication. If it did not say "printed by GPO" or give a documents series title or number, it was impossible to recognize unless you worked with documents every day.

The next solution was a standing order with LC for every item in every series. This worked well only for the series where LC cataloged everything in the series and the LC catalogers recognized that the document was part of a series.

Using the obvious source for verifying the existence of cataloging information, the *National Union Catalog (NUC)*, was a frustrating and time-consuming experience. Since I was cataloging the collection from scratch, I was cataloging series by series. It was impossible to outguess *NUC* (in other words, ALA and the *Anglo-American Cataloging Rules [AACR]*) as to the main entry. Sure as I looked under personal author, the entry would be under title or corporate author. No matter what I looked under, it was cataloged the other way. I found the best source to be Andriot's serials listing. Andriot had done all the work of finding LC order card numbers for series and his work was arranged by SuDoc class number. I also used *The Monthly Catalog of Government Publications* and some specialized bibliographies. Unfortunately a number of these cards never appeared because even though LC had assigned a number, the publication had never actually been cataloged. In about 1971 LC changed its policy in this area and was no longer preassigning LC order card numbers to documents unless they were sure that they were going to be cataloged.

At the same time, I was constructing a shelflist which was arranged by the SuDoc class number. The headings were not *AACR*, but traditional documents style. Each card had U.S. parent agency, and any subagencies down to the agency actually responsible for the document. Since all the documents were U.S., it was basically an alphabetical file by the main word of the parent agencies (e.g., Department of Agriculture, Department of Commerce). Arranging the file by SuDoc number eliminated the problems of department since the SuDoc number is cuttered on the main word of the agency (e.g., U.S. Secretary's Office. General Publications: individual title = HE 1.2:Ag2). The shelflist was open to the students and faculty and was heavily used.

Four years of attempting to catalog everything in a depository collection taught me that it was easier to do all the original cataloging than to try to outguess the rules in order to find cataloging data, which often as not, was not adequate to serve the documents searcher.

In 1970, I set up a library for the Environmental Protection Agency (EPA) Region VII. I decided to catalog all the documents issued by EPA, no matter what its previous name (e.g., U.S. HEW, Public Health Service, Air Pollution Office, U.S. Interior, Federal Water Quality Administration, etc.) by *AACR,* and class them under the SuDoc class system. I used many of the techniques for obtaining catalog data that I had used before, but I found that most of EPA's documents had never been cataloged. Those that were cataloged were entered under such a variety of headings that I spent most of my time making added entries and see references. The added entries were made because half the time, the document was entered under personal author or contract firm and no added entry was made for EPA. The see references were made because most of our laboratories were entered under their own names and no clue was given that they were part of EPA (e.g., Robert S. Kerr Laboratory). For that matter I had to add information to the basic record itself so that our own EPA users would know that this card referred to an EPA document.

I also served on an EPA-wide library committee which established its own machine-readable catalogs. The arguments about how books and documents or reports should be treated were so divisive that we decided to produce several catalogs—books, EPA reports, technical reports, and journals. In 1977, EPA assessed the problems of multiple format and rule governed catalogs and gone to one catalog for everything, using the COSATI rules. Not only EPA libraries but information centers are cooperating in this new effort. The *Anglo-American Cataloging Rules (AACR)* simply do not meet the needs of the scientific and technical community and that takes in a lot of documents. EPA is just the latest in a string of large cataloging agencies and libraries to go to COSATI.

In an attempt to get cataloging data, I sent a copy of most of the publications issued by EPA since 1949 to the Library of Congress.[1] This was done only after checking to see if there was LC copy. Over half of those publications were rejected as being outside the scope of LC's cataloging policy. I and other EPA librarians also sent a copy of every publication to the GPO's (Government Printing Office) *Monthly Catalog* and the NTIS's (National Technical Information Service) *Government Reports Announcements*. The majority of them were accepted and cataloged by GPO and NTIS.

All during the time that I was building card catalogs for documents, I relied heavily upon other tools such as the *Monthly Catalog of Government Publications*, agency catalogs, *Government Reports Announcements*, and commercial services for actual access. Even though these tools lacked complete coverage and often duplicated each other, they were much easier and faster to use than the catalog that I had slaved over. Many documents librarians would never trade these access tools for an *AACR* constructed catalog.

Documents librarians are hoping that changes in *AACR* and the decision by GPO and some state libraries to use *AACR* and the MARC (Machine-Readable Cataloging) format will make it possible for them to use standard cataloging and integrate this cataloging into central card and data bases. The Government Documents Round Table (GODORT) sent me to represent them on the Catalog Code Revision Committee (CCRC). GODORT also has a committee following the work of revising *AACR*.

Documents people are quite discouraged at this point. We turned out at the CCRC public hearing asking for greater recognition of documents as a unique group of material deserving a special chapter like movies or microforms—deserving uniform entry under corporate body, more added entries, consideration of the needs of fully identifying contract and grant reports, and so on. Instead we find ourselves battling to maintain the status quo and not end up with a worse mess than *AACR1* and superimposition.

Documents people, and by that I mean particularly members of GODORT, feel that the rules will result in the same chaos for government documents under the new rules as exists under the old. In fact, the decisions on corporate authorship and form and entry of corporate names are a regression rather than an improvement.

The basic concern, of course, is corporate authorship. The decision of CCRC and the Joint Steering Committee (JSC) to limit corporate authorship and get as many works as possible under title and personal authorship violated the authorship principle. Sumner Spalding, former head of LC Descriptive Cataloging and resource person to CCRC, reflects our concerns in his January 1977 memo to CCRC:

> The Joint Steering Committee made certain decisions in May of 1976 that resulted in the text of RR 1A/4 which, in the light of the JSC decisions, was approved by CCRC in July, with suggestions for some minor modifications. These decisions involved two significant changes, one theoretical (the discontinuance of the concept of corporate authorship) and the other substantive (the restriction of corporate headings for works representing the product of the collective activity of bodies to only the publications of conferences, expeditions, etc.).
>
> Whereas rule revision procedures on all other matters have started with extensive and even exhaustive study and discussion on the part of CCRC and its teams, continued with a determination of a committee recommendation to be forwarded to JSC, and ended with a JSC decision, the matter of discontinuing the concept of corporate authorship began and ended at the top and came down to CCRC as a fait accompli. As a result, this proposition has never been considered by CCRC on its merits and hence none can say what the committee's position is on the matter.
>
> Inasmuch as the JSC decision in its theoretical aspect is contrary to the American generalized theory of authorship and is contrary to Eva Verona's proposal for an internationally acceptable definition of corporate authorship—and in its substantive aspect is contrary to American practice, and to the Paris Statement of Principles, and to Verona—, it seems to me that the committee and its constituency, ALA, ought to know unequivocally where CCRC stands on the merits of these questions.[2]

CCRC voted at its January 1977 meeting to accept these changes. As one of the CCRC members put it, these changes are not part of a British plot. GODORT continues to oppose these basic changes in *AACR*. It is unfortunate for documents people and librarianship that Spalding resigned at this same January meeting before discussion of these issues took place.

CCRC fought for over two years about the concept of authorship. Now there is no such thing as corporate authorship, only corporate emanatorship. Footnote 2 from *AACR*, chapter 21, partially explains emanatorship. "Consider a work to have emanated from a corporate body if it is issued by that body *or* has been caused to be issued by that body *or* if it originated with that body."

If we are no longer going to base the rules on authorship principles then we should be just as pragmatic with documents as we have been with movies and legal publications. Movies are to be entered under title, and legal publications will be entered according to their own special characteristics. The committee gave in to art librarians in agreeing that the artist is not necessarily the author of the reproductions of his or her own works.[3] Why not give in to the documents people who at least believe in the authorship principle, particularly the American principle that a corporate body can be, and is, responsible for the authoring and creating of its own works?

Because documents librarians have traditionally believed that a government agency is responsible for its own works, they have come up with their own cataloging schemes based upon the government body as author. This is true not only in the U.S., but in Canada and Great Britain as well. The major government cataloging agencies such as the Government Printing Office (GPO) and Her Majesty's Stationery Office (HMSO) have until very recently used the same procedures. Both GPO and HMSO have started using *AACR* rules and are receiving a lot of unfavorable feedback. Documents people around the world never really believed that the cataloging agencies they depended upon so much would go to *AACR*. Many of these librarians never bothered to learn anything about regular library cataloging except that they did not like it.

The rules for choice of main and added entries in *AACR2* (numbers 21.1B to 21.1B4, *Entry under corporate body*) are so limiting that many works will be entered under personal author or title, that should be entered under corporate body. The main-entry guessing game for documents will be further complicated even if the main entry is a corporate body, because you won't know whether the parent or the subordinate body has been chosen. The differences of opinion among catalogers will lead to confusion and inconsistency. The same title will probably appear both ways in many shared cataloging data bases. Tracking down an agency's publications will be no easier under the new rules than under the combination of *AACR1* and superimposition. It is not for nothing that those using OCLC (Ohio College Library Center) asked GPO to publish the OCLC call numbers in the *Monthly Catalog*. That is also why documents catalogers and reference people are asking for a search key in OCLC on the SuDoc class number.

In order to understand the full impact of these rules on documents cataloging I would like to quote them in full:

21.1B. Entry under corporate body
21.1B1. Definition. A corporate body is an organization or a group of persons that is identified by a particular name and that acts, or may act, as an entity. Consider a corporate body to have a name if the words referring to it are a specific appellation rather than a general description. If, in a script and language using capital letters for proper nouns, the initial letters of the words referring to a corporate body are consistently capitalized, and/or if, in a language using articles, the words are always associated with a definite article, consider the body to have a name. Typical examples of corporate bodies are associations, institutions, business firms, nonprofit enterprises, governments, government agencies, projects and programs, religious bodies, local churches and conferences.[a]

Note that some corporate bodies are subordinate to other bodies (e.g., the Peabody Museum of Natural history is subordinate to Yale University).

Consider *ad hoc* events (such as athletic contests, exhibitions, expeditions, fairs, and festivals) and vessels (e.g., ships and spacecraft) to be corporate bodies.

21.1B2. General rule. Enter a work emanating[b] from one or more corporate bodies

---

a. Conferences are meetings of individuals or representatives of various bodies for the purpose of discussing and acting on topics of common interest, or meetings of representatives of a corporate body that constitute its legislative or governing body.

b. Consider a work to have emanated from a corporate body if it is issued by that body *or* has been caused to be issued by that body *or* if it originated with that body.

under the heading for the appropriate corporate body if it falls into one or more of the following categories:

    a) those of an administrative nature dealing with the corporate body itself
        or its internal policies, procedures, and/or operations
        or its finances
        or its officers and/or staff
        or its resources (e.g., catalogues, inventories, membership directories);
    b) some legal and governmental works of the following types[c]:
        laws (see 21.31)
        decrees of the chief executive which have the force of law
        (see 21.31)
        administrative regulations (see 21.32)
        treaties, etc. (see 21.35)
        court decisions (see 21.36)
        legislative hearings;
    c) those that record the collective thought of the body (e.g., reports of commissions, committes, etc.; official statements of position on external policies);
    d) those that report the collective activity of a conference (proceedings, collected papers, etc.); of an expedition (results of exploration, investigation, etc.); or of an event (an exhibition, fair, festival, etc.) falling within the definition of a corporate body (see 21.1B1), provided that the conference, expedition, or event is openly named in the item being catalogued;
    e) sound recordings, films, and videorecordings resulting from the collective activity of a performing group as a whole where the responsibility of the group goes beyond that of mere performance, execution, etc. (see also 21.23).

In some cases of shared responsibility (see 21.6) and mixed responsibility (see 21.8-21.27), enter such a work under the first named corporate body. Make added entries as instructed in 21.29-21.30.

In case of doubt as to whether a work falls into one or more of these categories, treat it as if it did not.

21.1B3. When determining the main entry heading for works that emanate from one or more corporate bodies but that fall outside the categories given in 21.1B2, treat them as if no corporate body were involved. Make added entries under the headings for prominently named corporate bodies as instructed in 21.30E.

21.1B4. If a work falls into one or more of the categories given in 21.1B2 and a subordinate unit of a corporate body is responsible for it, apply the following provisions:

    a) if the responsibility of the named subordinate unit is stated prominently, enter the work under the heading for the subordinate unit;
    b) if the responsibility of the named subordinate unit is not stated prominently, or if the parent body is named in the chief source of information and the subordinate unit is not, or if the subordinate unit has no name, enter the work under the heading for the parent body.[4]

Even if the corporate body is used as an added entry, it may not help since the form of the corporate body will be the same as the main entry. An entry is useless, if it does not clearly identify the body.

Documents (foreign, international, federal, state and local) frequently carry agency names which are highly similar. Without identification of the hierarchical relationship or organizational affiliation, the user cannot safely rely upon the specificity of the bibliographic information which appears on a card or a computer display, nor can one

---

    c. Some legal and governmental works are entered under bodies other than the body from which they emanate (see rules 21.34-21.36).

accept the place of publication as a reliable discriminating element to resolve the confusion.[5]

GODORT has made several suggestions to solve the problems with the rules. One suggestion is an alternative rule for an added entry which includes the complete heirarchy of the body. Another suggestion is a rule for modifying the name of an agency with additions that clearly identify the agency. There are also suggestions for rules for structuring corporate body names.

Including an added entry with the complete hierarchy of the body's name would permit any library or information agency accessing the data the option of manipulating the data to suit themselves. Those who provide search services would be able to go to any element of the entry which served their needs. For example, one may wish to search for every EPA Air Pollution Office publication. This would be impossible if the Air Pollution Office publications were sometimes cataloged under EPA, sometimes under Air Pollution Office, and sometimes under a subottice of the Air Pollution Office.

Those who oppose an added entry with the complete hierarchy claim that the automated authority files of the future will solve the problem. This pie in the sky solution is a long way off and I am doubtful that it will really solve the problem of tieing individual records into the authority file. If you don't give all the information in the individual bibliographic record, how can you tie it into the authority file? For example, if the publication says EPA Air Pollution Office and you only put down EPA, how would the authority file lead you to Air Pollution Office? There is also no other place in the bibliographic record where you give the complete hierarchy in a standard progression from government down to subordinate body. Neither in the statement of responsibility nor the imprint can you consistently give the complete hierarchy for identification or searching purposes. It is difficult to construct a search key on an element that jumps all over the record.

There are tools such as government manuals and agency handbooks which show the major parts of an agency. Understanding the structure of the government is essential in cataloging documents. Too often administrators believe that a document is just like any other work and fail to assign documents cataloging to a specialist. That has been a major philosophical problem at the Library of Congress. The late James Bennet Childs, one-time head of Descriptive Cataloging at LC and long-time documents specialist, has often pointed out how the quality of documents cataloging went downhill after the special cataloging unit was abolished.

The general rule in chapter 24, number 24.17 *Headings for Corporate Names* for government bodies and officials is vague and subject to multiple interpretation. The rule reads:

GOVERNMENT BODIES AND OFFICIALS
24.17. General rule
Enter a body created or controlled by a government under its own name (see 24.1-24.3) unless it belongs to one or more of the types listed in 24.18. However, if a body is subordinate to a higher body that is entered under its own name, formulate the heading for the subordinate body according to 24.12-24.14. Refer to the name of a government agency entered independently from its name in the form of a subheading of the government (see 26.3A7).[6]

AMERICAN BATTLE MONUMENTS COMMISSION
x UNITED STATES. *American Battle Monuments Commission*

ARTS COUNCIL OF GREAT BRITAIN
   x UNITED KINGDOM. *Arts Council*
BOUNDARY COMMISSION FOR ENGLAND
   x UNITED KINGDOM. *Boundary Commission for England*
CANADA INSTITUTE FOR SCIENTIFIC AND TECHNICAL INFORMATION
   x CANADA. *Institute for Scientific and Technical Information*
CANADIAN NATIONAL RAILWAYS
   x CANADA. *Canadian National Railways*
CONSEJO SUPERIOR DE INVESTIGACIONES CIENTIFICAS
   x SPAIN. *Consejo Superior de Investigaciones Científicas*
COUNCIL ON INTERNATIONAL ECONOMIC POLICY
   x UNITED STATES. *Council on International Economic Policy*
DUNDEE HARBOUR TRUST
   x UNITED KINGDOM. *Dundee Harbour Trust*
UNIVERSITY OF BRITISH COLUMBIA
   x BRITISH COLUMBIA. *University*

The various ways of entering government works whether under the general rule or the special government rules prompted GODORT to submit the following proposal:

To: CCRC   1976
From: GODORT (Hoduski)
Subject: AACR revision—comments

24.20A and 24.20B

When a government agency, office or bureau is entered under its own name and that name does not include the name of the government or the name of the highest unit in the hierarchy (parent body) confusion often results. The agency is confused with an agency with a similar name in other governments (local, state, federal, international) and private laboratories, research centers, organizations and businesses.

A good example is when the name of an agency begins with the term national such as National Center for Disease Control and National Heart and Lung Institute. Most federal agencies whose names begin with national are part of another agency. If these agencies or offices are to be entered directly under their own names then they should be modified with the addition (Government— parent agency - United States. Department of Health, Education and Welfare or DHEW). If they are entered under Government and name of agency they should be modified with the parent agency (parent agency = DHEW).

Examples: NATIONAL HEART AND LUNG INSTITUTE (United States. Department of Health, Education and Welfare)
          UNITED STATES. NATIONAL CENTER FOR DISEASE CONTROL (Department of Health, Education and Welfare)

          or

          NATIONAL HEART AND LUNG INSTITUTE (U.S. DHEW) UNITED STATES. NATIONAL CENTER FOR DISEASE CONTROL (DHEW)

GODORT proposes that the following rule be included in the section *24.10 Additions and modifications. Governments*, or in *24.20 B Direct or indirect subheading*.

RULE:

1. When a government agency, office or bureau is entered under its own name and that name does not include the name of the government, or the name of the highest unit in the hierarchy (parent body) the following additions should be made.

1.a. If the name of the government is not used and the highest unit in the heirarchy (parent agency) is used, the addition should be that of the government (e.g., United States)

AMERICAN BATTLE MONUMENTS COMMISSION (United States)
BOUNDARY COMMISSION FOR ENGLAND (Great Britain)

1.b. If the name of the government is used and the name of the highest unit in the heirarchy (parent agency) is not used, the addition should be that of the highest unit of the hierarchy (e.g., Department of Health, Education and Welfare)

CANADA. IMMIGRATION DIVISION (Department of Manpower and Immigration)
CALIFORNIA. (U.S.) EMPLOYMENT DATA AND RESEARCH DIVISION (Health and Welfare Agency)

1.c. If the government name and the name of the highest unit of the hierarchy are not used in the heading, both the name of the government and the name of the highest unit of the hierarchy (parent agency) should be added (e.g., United States. Department of Health, Education and Welfare)

INDIAN HEALTH SERVICE. INPATIENT CARE BRANCH (United States. Department of Health, Education and Welfare)
COUNCIL ON INTERNATIONAL ECONOMIC POLICY (United States. Executive Office of the President)
NATIONAL HEART AND LUNG INSTITUTE (United States. Department of Health, Education and Welfare)
NATIONAL INSTITUTE OF LAW ENFORCEMENT AND CRIMINAL JUSTICE (United States. Department of Justice)

The rules in chapter 24, rules 24.18 *Government agencies entered subordinately*, types one through ten, are particularly disturbing to documents catalogers, not only because they limit the types of agencies to be entered subordinately but because they are hard to understand and consistently interpret. I will cite all the types but will just discuss a few of them at length.[7]

24.18. Government agencies entered subordinately
Enter a government agency as a subheading of the government if it belongs to one or more of the following types. Make it a direct or indirect subheading as instructed in 24.19. Omit from the subheading the name or abbreviation of the name of the government in noun form.
Type 1. An agency with a name that contains a term that by definition implies that the body is part of another, e.g., "department," "division," "section," "branch."
ILLINOIS *(U.S.). Dept. of Education*
OTTAWA *(Ont., Canada). Engineering Dept.*
UNITED STATES. *Division of Wildlife Services*

Problems of interpretation of this rule occur unless the examples are very good. The example UNITED STATES. *Division of Wildlife Services* is confusing. What is the Division of Wildlife Services a division of? In the federal government, the only departments which can be entered directly under UNITED STATES are executive departments which are covered by type four. Other departments, divisions, sections, and branches must be entered as a subheading under another agency. In this case rule 26.2 (direct or indirect subheading) also applies. The example in 26.2 of INDIAN HEALTH SERVICE. INPATIENT CARE BRANCH illustrates the problem of interpretation: whether to enter under its own name, or under the government.

Assume the hierarchy for Division of Wildlife Services is as follows:

> United States
> Department of the Interior
> Fish and Wildlife Service
> Division of Wildlife Services

Should we enter it as a subheading under the Department of Interior, in which case there would be entry under the name of the government (UNITED STATES. *Department of Interior. Division of Wildlife Services*)? Or should we enter it as a subheading under Fish and Wildlife Service which presumably would be entered under its own name (FISH AND WILDLIFE SERVICE. *Division of Wildlife Services*)? However, the cataloger may have a reasonable doubt whether Fish and Wildlife Service should be entered under its own name or under the government. The functions of this federal service are also performed by many comparable state agencies, which have the same or similar names. Thus, a cataloger may use type three and enter under government as UNITED STATES. *Fish and Wildlife Service. Division of Wildlife Services*.[8]

> *Type 2*. An agency with a name that contains a word normally implying administrative subordination (e.g., "committee," "commission") providing the name of the government is required for the identification of the agency. Do not enter subordinately when the name of the agency contains the name or abbreviation of the name of the government.

> CANADA. *Royal Commission on Banking and Finance*
> GREAT BRITAIN. *Royal Commission on the Press*
> UNITED STATES. *Commission on Civil Rights*
> UNITED STATES. *Committee on Retirement Policy for Federal Personnel*
> UNITED STATES. *Interstate Commerce Commission*

A report listing all federal advisory committees is submitted to Congress each year by the President.[9] Advisory committees are established by statute, executive order or memorandum, or agency authority. In 1975 there were 1,267 committees. Of these, 272 were new. Another 233 were terminated. These advisory committees counsel executive branch departments and independent agencies (including those in the Executive Office of the President and the Congress). They are established in relationship to these bodies and receive money and personnel support from them. In most cases they can not even call a meeting of their own group. The agency establishing them must call the meeting. They must report to the bodies creating them. Committees established by Congress may report directly to Congress or to an agency designated by Congress.

A study showed that the most common terms used to describe advisory committees are: committee, advisory committee, review committee, council,

council on, advisory council, board, board of, advisory board, panel, panel on, panel on review of, advisory panel, working group, commission, and study section.

There is confusion between commissions, councils, and committees established by Congress as independent agencies (such as Federal Communications Commission, U.S. Commission on Civil Rights, Railroad Retirement Board) and those established primarily to advise. The same terms are sometimes used to describe both types of bodies. Advisory committees under the Federal Advisory Committee Act, Public Law 92-463 can only exist two years and then they must be reestablished. They must also be listed in the advisory committee report; therefore catalogers can easily establish their status as committee or independent agency.

A good example of the same term used for both types of commission is:

Example. The Radio Technical Commission for Aeronautics advises the Federal Communications Commission.	Hierarchy: United States Federal Communications Commissions Radio Technical Commission for Aeronautics

Other examples of advisory committees:

Example: Citizens Advisory Committee on Environmental Quality advises the Council on Environmental Quality (an office established by the Executive Office of the President),	Hierarchy: United States Executive Office of the President Council on Environmental Quality Citizens Advisory Committee on Environmental Quality
Example: Merit Review Board for Hematology advises the Veterans Administration.	Hierarchy: United States Veterans Administration Merit Review Board for Hematology
Example: National Study Commission on Records and Documents of Federal Officials advises Congress.	Hierarchy: United States Congress National Study Commission on Records and Documents of Federal Officials
Example: Council on International Economic Policy, created by Presidential memorandum. It is part of the Executive Office of the President just like OMB.	Hierarchy: United States Executive Office of President Council on International Economic Policy[10]

The examples listed under type two are misleading. UNITED STATES. *Commission on Civil Rights* is not a good example. If you enter it under its name, as stated in 26.1, it will be under U.S. COMMISSION ON CIVIL RIGHTS since that is its name and it is cited that way in most references and manuals.

UNITED STATES. *Committee on Retirement Policy for Federal Personnel* could be in any agency. I searched advisory committee report, *Government Organization Manual and Congressional Directory* and still could not find it. We need hierarchy to see if it should be entered directly under UNITED STATES without some intervening hierarchy.

The examples listed under 24. 17, *Council on International Economic Policy* and *Consejo Superior de Investigaciones Cientificas* should be kept under their respective countries. We have already seen that the Council advises the President and the Consejo could reasonably be expected, as part of Mexico or some South American government, to do the same.

If advisory committees can not all be listed under their establishing agencies, then perhaps a compromise could be reached whereas the following entry would appear:

UNITED STATES. *Merit Review Board for Hematology*. (Veterans Administration)

> *Type 3*. An agency with a name that is so general that it requires the name of the government for its identification.
> FRANCE. *Bibliotheque national*
> GREATER LONDON COUNCIL. *Research and Intelligence Unit*[11]

This is a rule with which documents people can live. How many times we have pointed out the problems of similar names between state, local, and federal agencies. Getting a print-out of all the Environmental Protection Agencies in the country can be expensive when all you want is the federal one.

> *Type 4*. An agency that is a ministry or similar major or top echelon executive agency as defined by official government publications.
> GREAT BRITAIN. *Home Office*
> GREAT BRITAIN. *Ministry of Transport*
> HUNGARY. *Közellàtàsügyi Minisztèrium*
> ITALY. *Ministero della cultura popolare*
> UNITED STATES. *National Aeronautics and Space Administration*

What about legislative branch agencies such as General Accounting Office, Library of Congress, Congressional Budget Office, Office of Technology Assessment, Government Printing Office, or Office of the Architect which act as executive departments within the legislative branch. This rule should be expanded to include them or a footnote should indicate that they are included.

Examples:
UNITED STATES. *Government Printing Office*
    Hierarchy: United States
             Congress
             Government Printing Office
UNITED STATES. *General Accounting Office*
    Hierarchy: United States
             Congress
             General Accounting Office[12]

> *Type 5*. Legislative bodies (see also 24.21).
> GREENWICH *(London, England: London Borough)*. *Council*
> FRANCE. *Assemblèe nationale*
> GREAT BRITAIN. *Parliament*
> UNITED STATES. *Congress*

Type 6. Courts (see also 24.23).
>   ONTARIO *(Canada). High Court of Justice.*
>   UNITED STATES. *Supreme Court*

Type 7. Principal armed services (see also 24.24).
>   CANADA. *Royal Canadian Air Force*
>   GERMANY. *Heer*
>   GREAT BRITAIN. *Army*
>   UNITED STATES. *Navy*

Type 8. Chiefs of state and heads of government (see also 24.20).
>   GREAT BRITAIN. *Sovereign*
>   MONTREAL *(Que., Canada). Mayor*
>   UNITED STATES. *Presidents*
>   VIRGINIA *(U.S.). Governor*

Type 9. Embassies, consulates, etc. (see also 24.25).
>   CANADA. *Embassy (U.S.)*
>   GREAT BRITAIN. *Consulate (New York, N.Y., U.S.)*

Type 10. Delegations to international and intergovernmental bodies (see also 24.26).
>   GREAT BRITAIN. *Delegation to the United Nations*[13]

The rule covering entry of government agencies as direct or indirect subheadings will simply add to the confusion.

24.19 Direct or indirect subheading
Enter an agency belonging to one or more of the types listed in 24.18 as a subheading of the lowest element in the hierarchy that is entered under its own name. Omit intervening elements in the hierarchy unless the name of the agency has been, or is likely to be, used by another agency entered under the same higher body. In that case, interpose the lowest element in the hierarchy that will distinguish between the agencies.

UNITED STATES. *Dept. of Health, Education, and Welfare. Office of Education*
>   Hierarchy: United States
>   Department of Health, Education, and Welfare
>   Office of Education

GREAT BRITAIN. *Dept. of the Environment. Headquarters Library*
>   Hierarchy: Great Britain
>   Department of the Environment
>   Headquarters Library

Refer from the name in the form of a subheading of its immediately superior body when the heading does not include the name of that superior body.

INDIAN HEALTH SERVICE. *Inpatient Care Branch*
>   Hierarchy: United States
>   Department of Health, Education, and Welfare
>   Public Health Service
>   Health Services Administration
>   Indian Health Service
>   Division of Resource Coordination
>   Office of Program Statistics
>   Inpatient Care Branch

x INDIAN HEALTH SERVICE. *Office of Program Statistics. Inpatient Care Branch.*
CANADA. Immigration Division
>   Hierarchy: Canada
>   Department of Manpower and Immigration
>   Immigration Division

x CANADA. *Dept. of Manpower and Immigration. Immigration Division*
CALIFORNIA *(U.S.). Employment Development Dept.*
    Hierarchy: California
            Health and Welfare Agency
            Employment Development Department
x CALIFORNIA *(U.S.). Health and Welfare Agency. Employment Development Dept.*
CALIFORNIA *(U.S.). Employment Data and Research Division*
    Hierarchy: California
            Employment Development Department
            Employment Data and Research Division
x CALIFORNIA *(U.S.). Employment Development Dept. Employment Data and Research Division*[14]

The example of INDIAN HEALTH SERVICE. *Inpatient Care Branch* is a very poor example although typical of the kind of headings you will get under this rule. There are Indian Health Services in many of our states and this rule will cause them to be filed together with little to distinguish one service from the other. The latest version (as of early 1978) decided by mail vote of the Joint Steering Committee is:

24.19 Direct or indirect subheading
Enter an agency belonging to one or more of the types listed in 24.18 as a subheading of the government. Omit intervening elements in the hierarchy unless the name has been, or is likely to be used by another agency entered under the same government heading. Add between government heading and name of agency the name of the lowest element in the hierarchy that will distinguish between the agencies.
Examples: UNITED STATES. *Federal Bureau of Investigation*
        UNITED STATES. *Division of Chronic Diseases*
        x U.S. HEW. *Public Health Service. Division of Chronic Diseases*

but

UNITED KINGDOM. *Department of Employment. Solicitors Office*

Liberal use of added entries is essential to accessing documents. This will be particularly true with the new rules since the rules will force so many documents under personal author and title. Even with the difference of opinion as to where users look for documents, it is obvious that users approach them from many ways, corporate and personal author, title, series, report numbers, etc. The added entry rules should be liberalized rather than restricted. Formalizing the rule of three will be detrimental to good documents reference.

21.34A. Two or more persons or bodies involved
If the following subrules refer to only one person or corporate body and two or three persons or bodies are involved in a particular instance, make added entries under the headings for each. If four or more persons or bodies are involved in a particular instance, make an added entry under the heading for the first named in the source from which the names are taken. This will eliminate added entries for many government and technical reports.[15]

Scientific users want more corporate and personal authors cited per technical and scientific report. The rule should be changed to use up to four names rather than reverting to the rule of one. Why limit rather than increase service just to save the cataloger a little work? This rule is important now, because GPO is cataloging thousands of technical reports into *AACR*.

Of course, the cataloging agency can always revert to the rule 21.33D. ''If in the context of a given catalogue, added entries are required under headings and titles other than those prescribed in rule 21.34, make them.'' But why legislate the minimum?

The next rule which bothers documents reference folk is 21.34E *Corporate body*, ''Make an added entry under the heading for an openly named corporate body, unless it functions solely as publisher, distributor, or manufacturer. In case of doubt make an added entry.''[16]

A MARC format for technical reports is desperately needed. It is very difficult for national cataloging agencies like GPO, NTIS, DDC (Defense Documentation Center), ERIC (Educational Resources Information Center), NAL (National Agriculture Library), and NLM (National Library of Medicine) to exchange cataloging data when there is no common format. Of course, they can take data in other formats and use them but that is time consuming and costly. Since these agencies are not all using the same cataloging rules, there is no guarantee that they are even collecting the same data. It is impossible to exchange data that has not been collected.

AACR should be expanded to include chapters on cataloging scientific and technical reports and journal articles. If we can have separate chapters for motion pictures, microforms, cartographic materials, etc., we should recognize the uniqueness of the technical report literature. A whole cataloging world has developed using the COSATI rules, and CCRC and JSC continue to ignore them and their needs. Documents people can not ignore this other world because our feet are in both worlds and we are charged with bringing both together under the library roof.

Documents people are not happy and will not be happy with *AACR* for documents unless drastic changes are made. They are willing to accept the shortcomings of *AACR* in order to get documents into the mainstream of library cataloging. They hope that getting documents into the system will help eliminate duplicate cataloging of documents between government agencies and libraries around the world. They also hope that it will encourage more complete bibliographic records.

Problems of quality and consistency in cataloging decisions will be alleviated when GPO takes over the cataloging of most federal documents. A cooperative program between GPO and LC allowing GPO to become the authority for establishing federal headings is being worked out. LC and GPO are asking for a grant from the Council on Library Resources to make such a program a reality.[17]

GPO would do the work of establishing authority records for federal government names and other corporate bodies, such as research, management firms, laboratories, etc., under contract to the federal government. LC would verify and input these records into their name authority files. This information would become available to the rest of the library community.

GPO will soon get online access to the LC/MARC data base.[18] This will enable GPO to learn of LC's documents cataloging weeks or sometimes months before it goes into the OCLC data base. This way the final GPO product appearing in OCLC will be as close to LC as possible. LC can also take advantage of GPO's cataloging in OCLC. The LC Gift and Exchange Division, Federal Documents Section can access OCLC when a document comes in, print-out GPO catalog copy, attach it to the book and send it on to LC Descriptive Cataloging. The LC catalogers then will be sure to add the Superintendent of Documents Classification numbers, stock numbers and other information that only GPO can provide for the record. Then, if and when an LC/MARC record bumps the GPO record in a data base, the LC record will be complete. OCLC has promised GPO and the Federal Library Committee that GPO's record will be the authoritative record and that the LC record will not bump the GPO record.[19]

The ideal LC/GPO cooperation will happen in a few years when GPO can access LC's in-process cataloging file and input records directly into the MARC system. Then the problem of duplicate records between GPO and LC and even duplicate records within LC, between CRS (Congressional Research Service) and LC Processing will be partially solved. It will never be completely solved as long as libraries in the networks insist on inputting poor or duplicative documents cataloging. These records will also become part of the SCORPIO system and be available online to the offices of the members of Congress.

LC and GPO working together can provide some innovative and useful services. For example, the standing order services for documents series cards could be based upon GPO item numbers. These item numbers are assigned to classes of documents. Most of the classes are legitimate library *AACR*-blessed series. Others are made up of classes or series such as general publications, handbooks, regulations, etc. The cataloging for these made up series would be ordered by depositories who receive everything in these series.

LC is going to sell the GPO/MARC tapes. LC is also doing a market survey to see if there is a big enough demand for MARC/GPO cards on demand. The cards could be arranged by SuDoc number, subjects, personal and corporate author, and so on.[20]

I want to end this talk by quoting the GODORT letter to Paul Fasana, President of RTSD in full. This letter presents GODORT's position on *AACR*.

Dear Mr. Fasana:

The revision of the *Anglo-American Cataloging Rules* in a manner to insure reasonable and easy access to users of government documents is of crucial interest to the Government Documents Round Table. Most documents librarians have traditionally avoided cataloging documents by *AACR* because of the difficulties in applying the rules in a consistent manner to serve the needs of the user. Documents librarians have come up with their own schemes for cataloging documents, most of these schemes based upon the government body as author. They had hoped that changes in the rules and the decision of GPO to use *AACR* and the MARC format would make it possible for them to use standard cataloging.

Instead we see some of the librarians who have been following the progress of *AACR* revision consider alternatives to the rules. The United Nations and other international organizations librarians have formed a working group to write their own rules for the cataloging of UN and other international documents. They have opted for Unit entry under title. Each agency will catalog its own documents and share this cataloging via a computerized network.

State and local documents librarians are talking about writing their own code. COSLA has asked GODORT to establish standards for inputting their state documents into OCLC because it is already obvious that inputting them under *AACR* 67 and superimposition is creating chaos.

The '67 rules and now the proposed new ones, make it difficult not only to input documents into network catalogs but to retrieve them. The cataloger wastes immeasurable time deciding under which entry the document is entered and often due to frustration, simply adds a new record, according to the cataloging standards of the inputting library. Studying the *Monthly Catalog of U.S. Government Publications* shows how diverse the decisions of catalogers are when based upon the '67 rules.

GODORT has made a series of proposals, both written and verbal, offering solutions for these problems. We feel that CCRC has not devoted sufficient time to discussing and solving the problems of choice of entry and form of entry for corporate bodies. We feel that the rules for choice and form of entry should be discussed as thoroughly as those for description have been.

GODORT is also deeply concerned about the resignation of three CCRC members and one resource person. These are people who understand corporate authorship and choice of entry. We will especially miss Sumner Spalding who wrote so many resource papers enabling the committee to make basic decisions. Mr. Spalding's memo of January 23, 1977 to CCRC supports the belief by GODORT that the new *AACR* will not meet the needs of documents users. Two serious changes affecting corporate authorship have been adopted without adequate discussion by the American cataloging community.

The changes are in Sumner's words:

These decisions involved two significant changes, one theoretical (the discontinuance of the concept of corporate authorship) and the other substantive (the restriction of corporate headings for works representing the product of the collective activity of bodies to only the publications of conferences, expeditions, etc.)

Inasmuch as the JSC decision in its theoretical aspect is contrary to the American generalized theory of authorship and is contrary to Eva Verona's proposal for an internationally acceptable definition of corporate authorship—and in its substantive aspect is contrary to American practice, and to the Paris Statement of Principles, and to Verona—, it seems to me that the committee and its constituency, ALA, ought to know unequivocally where CCRC stands on the merits of these questions.

CCRC voted at its January meeting to accept these changes. GODORT continues to oppose these basic changes in *AACR*.

GODORT is pleased that *AACR* will undergo a review process by all interested groups. GODORT believes that a code which is useful and acceptable internationally is essential to the exchange of bibliographic information. How can the library community benefit from shared cataloging of government publications if the code itself is repudiated by the librarians of the issuing agencies?

To summarize, GODORT is opposed to the revised *AACR* rules on choice of entry and form of entry for corporate authors since these will only generate confusion for users of the bibliographic data created or generated by cataloging librarians. Document materials (foreign, international, federal, state, local) frequently carry agency names which are highly similar. Without indication of the heirarchical relationship or organizational affiliation, the user cannot safely rely upon the specificity of the bibliographic information which appears on a card or a computer display, nor can one accept place of publication as the reliable discriminating element to resolve the confusion.

GODORT therefore urges that RTSD specifically charge the CCRC to carefully deliberate this matter so that the resultant rules, whatever the final format, are clearly the intent of the full CCRC and are not just the implementation of an idea set forth from the JSC. These rules need to be consistent and, in their development, the widest possible range of input from practicing librarians should be sought. In realizing that the implications of these revised rules will be costly to the library and information community, the end users should be assured that full discussion and investigation were carried out by the CCRC before any rules were finalized.

Sincerely,

Nancy M. Cline

Editor's Note: Since the tape of the discussion period was defective, no transcription was possible of the discussion following Ms. Hoduski's presentation.

NOTES

1. It was about this time that EPA (Environmental Protection Agency) also received a letter asking that the agency send copies of everything published by us to LC. So since we had never complied with the law in the past we decided to rectify our past mistakes. Of course we also naively thought that anything sent to LC would be kept and treasured.

2. Memo to John D. Byrum, Jr., Chairman, Catalog Code Revision Committee from Sumner Spalding, Resource Person. Subject: Committee position on the merits of (1) discontinuing the concept of corporate authorship and (2) the text of category r of RR 1A/4. January 23, 1977.

3. The final version of *AACR2* reverses this decision because many other librarians said they would not be able to find the art works. The same argument on the part of documents librarians met deaf ears.

> 21.16B Enter a reproduction of an art work (e.g., a photograph, a photochemical reproduction, or a reproduction of sculpture), under the heading for the original work. Make an added entry under the heading for the person or body responsible for the reproduction.

4. This is quoted from the final draft version. There is very little difference between the last two drafts.

5. Letter to Paul Fasana, President, Resources and Technical Services Division, ALA from Nancy Cline, Chairperson, Government Documents Round Table, March 17, 1977.

6. Since this paper was presented at the Institute, the rule numbers have changed and some of the wording. The end result is the same.

7. The final draft version of each type is given as a footnote. The discussions after each rule were presented as a proposal to CCRC, before and after this paper was presented.

8. *Type 1.* An agency with a name that contains a term that by definition implies that the body is part of another, e.g., "department," "division," "section," "branch," and their equivalents in other languages.

> VERMONT. *Agency of Environmental Conservation. Department of Water Resources*
> OTTAWA. *Department of Community Development*
> UNITED STATES. *Department of the Interior. Division of Wildlife Services*

9. Federal Advisory Committees, Fourth Annual Report of the President, 1975, U.S. General Services Administration, 1976 (no. 040-000-00345-2).

10. *Type 2.* An agency with a name that contains a word normally implying administrative subordination (e.g., "committee," "commission") providing the name of the government is required for the identification of the agency.

> AUSTRALIA. *Department of Commerce and Agriculture. Bureau of Agricultural Economics*
> CANADA. *Royal Commission on Banking and Finance*
> UNITED KINGDOM. *Royal Commission on the Press*
> UNITED KINGDOM. *Central Office of Information*
> UNITED STATES. *Commission on Civil Rights*
> UNITED STATES. *Committee on Retirement Policy for Federal Personnel*
> but
> ROYAL COMMISSION ON HIGHER EDUCATION IN NEW BRUNSWICK

11. *Type 3*. An agency with a name that has been, or is likely to be, used as the name of another agency, providing the name of the government is required for the identification of the agency.

ILLINOIS. *Environmental Protection Agency*
UNITED STATES. *Environmental Protection Agency*
BEZIERS. *Museè des beaux arts*.
   Name: Musee des beaux arts
GREATER LONDON COUNCIL. *Research and Intelligence Unit*
   Name: Research and Intelligence Unit
but
MUSEE DE POITIERS

12. *Type 4*. An agency that is a ministry or similar major executive agency (i.e., one that has no other agency above it) as defined by official publications of the government in question.

UNITED KINGDOM. *Home Office*
UNITED KINGDOM. *Department of Transport*
ITALY. *Ministero del bilancio e della programmaziones economica*
UNITED STATES. *National Aeronautics and Space Administration*.

13. *Type 5*. Legislative bodies (see also 24.21).

GREENWICH. *Council*
FRANCE. *Assembleè nationale*
UNITED KINGDOM. *Parliament*
UNITED STATES. *Congress*

Type 6. Courts (see also 24.23).
ONTARIO. *High Court of Justice*
UNITED STATES. *Supreme Court*

Type 7. Principal armed services (see also 24.24).
CANADA. *Canadian Armed Forces*
Germany. *Heer*
UNITED KINGDOM. *Army*
UNITED STATES. *Navy*

Type 8. Chiefs of state and heads of government (see also 24.20).
UNITED KINGDOM. *Sovereign*
MONTREAL. *Mayor*
UNITED STATES. *President*
VIRGINIA. *Governor*

Type 9. Embassies, consulates, etc. (see also 24.25).
CANADA. *Embassy (U.S.)*
UNITED KINGDOM. *Consulate (New York)*

Type 10. Delegations to international and intergovernmental bodies (see also 24.26).
UNITED KINGDOM. *Delegation to the United Nations*

14. Since my speech this rule has undergone two drastic revisions. The second revision being more palatable to documents people than the final—but neither rule being the answer.

At an August 1977 meeting of the Joint Steering Committee on suggestion of Canada the rule was changed to:

> 24.19 Direct or indirect subheading
> Enter an agency belonging to one or more of the types listed in 24.18 as a subheading of the government. If the body is not entered as a direct subheading of the

name of the government according to 24.20-24.26 and belongs to a hierarchy that includes a ministry or similar major executive agency (see 24.18, Type 4), including the name of the ministry, etc., in the heading. Omit other intervening elements in the hierarchy unless the name of the agency has been, or is likely to be, used by another agency entered under the same higher body. In that case, interpose the lowest element in the hierarchy that will distinguish between the agencies.

UNITED STATES. *Department of Health, Education, and Welfare.*
   Office of Education
      Hierarchy: United States
                Department of Health, Education, and Welfare
                Office of Education

UNITED KINGDOM. *Department of the Environment. Headquarters Library.*
      Hierarchy: Great Britain
                Department of the Environment
                Headquarters Library

CANADA. *Department of Manpower and Immigration. Immigration Division.*
      Hierarchy: Canada
                Department of Manpower and Immigration
                Immigration Division

Refer from the name in the form of a subheading of its immediately superior body when the heading does not include the name of that superior body.

CALIFORNIA. *Health and Welfare Agency. Employment Data and Research Division*
      Hierarchy: California
                Health and Welfare Agency
                Employment Development Department
                Employment Data and Research Division
   x CALIFORNIA. *Health and Welfare Agency. Employment Development Department. Employment Data and Research Division*

QUEBEC *(Province). Ministére des richesses naturelles.*
Service de l'exploration gèologique
      Hierarchy: Quèbec
                Ministére des richesses naturelles
                Direction gènèrale des mines
                Direction de la gèologie
                Service de l'exploration gèologique
x QUEBEC *(Province). Ministére des richesses naturelles.*
Direction de la gèologie. Service de l'exploration gèologique

15. 21.30A. Two or more persons or bodies involved
      If the following subrules refer to only one person or corporate body and two or three persons or bodies are involved in a particular instance, make added entries under the headings for each. If four or more persons or bodies are involved in a particular instance, make an added entry under the heading for the first named in the source from which the names are taken.

16. The final version of *AACR2* rule 21.30E *Corporate body* states ''Make an added entry under the heading for a prominently named corporate body, unless it functions solely as distributor or manufacturer. Make an added entry under a prominently named publisher if the responsibility for the work extends beyond that of merely publishing it. In case of doubt, make an added entry.''

17. LC and GPO did not get the grant. They considered the project so important that they went ahead with it anyway in late 1977.

18. GPO started using the LC/MARC data base and SCORPIO files in late 1977. As of April 1978 GPO found that they were cataloging the congressional hearings so fast that the data were not yet available in the MARC files.

19. As of April 1978 this has not occurred. LC still has not installed an OCLC terminal in Gift and Exchange Division to search for GPO records. LC cites a lack of resources as the reasons for not getting a terminal.

20. As of April 1978 there is still not a big enough demand for such a service. OCLC also failed to get enough people interested in such a service to justify providing it. OCLC wanted libraries to get everything cataloged by GPO rather than individual titles, as LC is proposing. The evidence seems to indicate that libraries are going for computer tapes, the *Monthly Catalog* itself, and individual records generated from the OCLC data base.

Sample entries and page follow on next three pages:

SAMPLE ENTRY

Monthly Catalog of U.S. Government Publications

76-1435   A 1.9:2148/6

Reid, William J.

Aphids on leafy vegetables: how to control them / [by W. J. Reid, Jr., and F. P. Cuthbert, Jr.] — [Rev. Feb. 1976] [Washington]: U.S. Dept. of Agriculture, Agricultural Research Service: for sale by the Supt. of Docs., U.S. Govt. Print. Off., [1967]

14 p.: ill.; 24 cm. — (Farmers' bulletin; no. 2148)

"This publication is intended for the commercial grower of those vegetables whose leafy or flowering parts are marketed."

Item 9

S/N 001-000-03478-1

pbk.: $0.35

1. Plant lice — Control. 2. Insecticides I. Cuthbert, Frank P., joint author. II. United States. Agricultural Research Service. III. Title. IV. Series: United States. Dept. of Agriculture. Farmers' bulletin; no. 2148.

S21.A6 rev. no. 2148 1969   72-604400

632/.7/52   OCLC 0084699

SUPT. OF DOCS. CLASS NO.—This is the number assigned by the GPO Library to identify the document cataloged.

EDITION—The edition is recorded from information in the document.

SERIES STATEMENT—This appears in parentheses and includes the phrase identifying the document as one of a series.

NOTES—Notes include miscellaneous information about the physical makeup of a publication or about the information contained in it.

ITEM NO.—This document was distributed to depository libraries requesting this item number.

STOCK NO.—This is a Government Printing Office sales stock number. It is used only in ordering from the Superintendent of Documents.

PRICE—Price, GPO or other, is included if known.

ADDED ENTRIES (Roman numerals)—When the Government author is not a main entry, it is included with added entries.

LIBRARY OF CONGRESS CARD NO.—Included for libraries ordering printed cards from the Library of Congress.

OCLC NO.—This is the number assigned by the Ohio College Library Center to identify this record in the data base.

MONTHLY CATALOG ENTRY NO.—The entry number is assigned after the records are arranged alphanumerically by the Superintendent of Documents classification number. The first two digits establish the year; the last four digits locate the record in the Catalog.

MAIN ENTRY—A main entry may be a personal author, a corporate author, a conference, uniform title, or the document title, as established by Anglo-American cataloging rules.

TITLE PHRASE/AUTHOR STATEMENT—Title phrase and author statement are recorded from the title page, cover or first page of the publication cataloged. Material in brackets is supplied from other sources.

IMPRINT—The imprint contains place of publication, issuing agency, and date of issue. Includes name of sales agent, if any.

COLLATION—Collation notes pages, illustrations, and size.

SUBJECT HEADINGS (Arabic numerals)—Headings are selected from Library of Congress subject headings. Some local and NLM subjects will be used. Local subjects will be indicated by a star (★). NLM will be indicated by an asterisk (*).

LIBRARY OF CONGRESS CLASS NO.—This is given when it appears in the publication or the OCLC data base.

DEWEY CLASS NO.—Dewey class is recorded if it appears in the Ohio College Library data base.

SERIALS SUPPLEMENT SAMPLE ENTRY
Monthly Catalog of U.S. Government Publications

77-6213   HE 20.2459: (v. nos. & nos.)

Children today. [Washington] U.S. Dept. of Health, Education, and Welfare, Office of Child Development, Children's Bureau; for sale by the Supt. of Docs., U.S. Govt. Print. Off.
20402
ill. 27 cm. (DHEW publication; no. (OHD)
$6.10 (U.S.) $7.65 (foreign) $1.00 (single copy)
index varies in price
v. 1-   Jan./Feb. 1972-
Indexed by: Education index ISSN 0013-1385
Indexed by: Nursing literature index ISSN 0550-3957
Indexed by: Hospital literature index ISSN 0018-5736
Vols. for (Mar./Apr. 1973-) for sale by the Supt. of Docs. U.S. Govt. Print. Off. Bimonthly.
Item 449
ISSN 0361-4336: CODEN: CHTDA
Supersedes: Children
Main series: United States. Dept. of Health, Education, and Welfare. DHEW publication; no. (OHD)
1. Child welfare—United States Periodicals. 2. Children—Care and hygiene—Periodicals. I. United States. Children's Bureau.
HV741.C5362   362.7/05
OCLC 1159272
72-620933

Callout descriptions:

SUPT. OF DOCS. CLASS NO.—This is the number assigned by the GPO Library to identify the document cataloged.

TITLE PHRASE—Title phrase is recorded from the title page, cover, or first page of the publication cataloged.

IMPRINT—The imprint contains place of publication, issuing agency, and name of sales agent.

SERIES STATEMENT—This appears in parentheses and includes the phrase identifying the document as one of a series.

NOTES.—Notes include miscellaneous information about the physical makeup of a publication or about the information contained in it.

LINKING ENTRIES—Provide bibliographic and historical information as well as allowing internal machine linkage between related records in a computer file.

SUBJECT HEADINGS (Arabic numerals)—Headings are selected from Library of Congress subject headings. Some local and NLM subjects will be used. Local subjects will be indicated by a star (★). NLM will be indicated by an asterisk (*).

ADDED ENTRIES (Roman numerals)—When the Government author is not a main entry, it is included with added entries.

LIBRARY OF CONGRESS CARD NO.—Included for libraries ordering printed cards from the Library of Congress.

DEWEY CLASS NO.—Dewey class is recorded if it appears in the Ohio College Library Center data base.

MONTHLY CATALOG ENTRY NO.—The entry number is assigned after the records are arranged alphanumerically by the Superintendent of Documents classification number. The first two digits establish the year; the last four digits locate the record in the Catalog.

MAIN ENTRY—A main entry may be a corporate author, or the document title, as established by Anglo-American cataloging rules.

SUBSCRIPTION ADDRESS—May include street address, city, country, and zip code of sales agent.

COLLATION—Collation notes, illustrations, and size.

PRICE—Price, GPO or other, is included if known.

DATE—Beginning date of publication and/or volume designation.

PERIODICITY—Current frequency of publication.

ITEM NO.—This document was distributed to depository libraries requesting this item number.

ISSN—International standard serial number, assigned or authenticated by the National Serials Data Program. Each number is unique to a title and is part of the international effort for uniform control of serials.

LIBRARY OF CONGRESS CLASS NO.—This is given when it appears in the publication or the OCLC data base.

OCLC NO.—This is the number assigned by the Ohio College Library Center to identify this record in the data base.

SAMPLE PAGE
The ERIC Source Directory

Page 128

Health Resources Administration   BBB12752
(DHEW/PHS),Bethesda, Md. Bureau of Health Manpower.
SN   Department of Health, Education and Welfare,
     Washington, D.C. Bureau of Health Manpower.

Health Resources Administration   BBB11075
(DHEW/PHS), Bethesda, Md. Bureau of Health Re-
sources Development.
NOTE Name changed to Bureau of Health Manpower
     (1975)

Health Resources Administration   BBB10776
(DHEW/PHS), Bethesda, Md. Bureau of Health
Services Research

Health Resources Administration   BBB10787
(DHEW/PHS), Bethesda, Md. Div. of Associated
Health Professions.
NOTE Unit of Bureau of Health Manpower.

Heatlh Resources Administration   BBB08755
(DHEW/PHS), Bethesda, Md. Div. of Manpower
Intelligence.
NOTE Formerly a unit of Bureau of Health Resources
Development.; Dissolved as of March 1974.

Health Resources Administration   BBB12388
(DHEW/PHS), Bethesda, MD. Div. of Medicine.
NOTE Unit of Bureau of Health Manpower.

Health Resources Administration   BBB11011
(DHEW/PHS), Bethesda, Md. Div. of Nursing.
NOTE Unit of Bureau of Health Manpower.

Health Resources Administration   BBB11650
(DHEW/PHS), Rockville, Md. Div. of Comprehensive
Health Planning.
NOTE Unit of Bureau of Health Resources Develop-
ment.

Health Services Administration   BBB12672
(DHEW/PHS), Rockville, Md.

Health Services Administration   BBB11393
(DHEW/PHS), Rockville, Md. Bureau of Community
Health Services.

Health Services Administration   BBB13340
(DHEW/PHS), Tucson, Ariz. Indian Health Service.

Health Services and Mental Health   BBB01632
Administration (DHEW), Bethesda, Md.
SN   Public Health Service (DHEW), Washington,
     D.C.
     Health Services and Mental Health Administration.

Health Services and Mental Health Administration
(DHEW), Bethesda, Md. Community Health Service.
USE   Community Health Service (DHE/PHS),
      Bethesda, Md.

Health Services and Mental Health   BBB07638
Administration (DHEW), Bethesda, Md. Office of
Communications and Public Affairs.

Health Services and Mental Health   BBB04741
Administration (DHEW), Bethesda, Md. Regional
Medical Program Service.
SN   Regional Medical Programs Service, Bethesda,
     Md.

Health Services and Mental Health Administration
(DHEW), Cincinnati, Ohio.
USE   Public Health Service (DHEW), Cincinnati,
      Ohio.

Health Services and Mental   BBB07314
Health Administration (DHEW), Rockville, Md.
Bureau of Community Environmental Management.

Health Services and Mental   BBB06263
Health Administration (DHEW), Rockville, Md. Div.
of Emergency Health Services.

Health Services and Mental Health   BBB07753
Administration (DHEW), Rockville, Md. Federal
Health Programs Service.
SW   Federal Health Programs Service, Rockville,
     Md.

Health Service and Mental Health   BBB05741
Administration (DHEW), Rockville, Md. Maternal and
Child Health Service.

Health Services and Mental Health Administration
(DHEW), Rockville, MD. National Center for Health
Services Research and Development.
USE   National Center for Health Services Research
      and Development (DHEW/PHS), Rockville, MD.

Health Services Mobility Study   BBB09745
New York, N.Y.

Hearst (William Randolph) Foundation,
Los Angeles, Calif.
USE   William Randolph Hearst Foundation, Los
      Angeles, Calif.

Heartland Education Agency,   BBB13017
Ankeny, Iowa.

Heath City School District,   BUB63361
Ohio.

Hebrew Univ. of Jerusalem   KPF31817
(Israel).

Hebrew Univ. of Jerusalem   BBB00789
(Israel). Dept. of Psychology

Heffner (Richard) Associates,   BBB08954
Inc., New York, N.Y.

Cataloging for Public Libraries

by Sanford Berman

To begin with a vulgarism: The public libraries have definitely *not* got their shit together. Our clientele is no less than the whole population. And that clientele is voluntary, not captive nor coerced. Moreover, it spans all ages and classes and education-levels and faiths and ethnic backgrounds. That clientele uses the public library equally for fun; for practical, nitty-gritty information; and for enlightenment. In all these regards, the public library is distinctly unlike the school, academic, or research library. Unsurprisingly, its collection development reflects this, too. Generally, we buy from an annual universe of perhaps 35,000 to 40,000 English-language, American published trade titles. A middle-sized library like Hennepin adds approximately 9,000 new book and A/V titles yearly, many in multiple copies. Few of these are in foreign languages. And few are highly technical. Many, however, are children's titles. A lot is fiction. And a growing percentage is in the form of slides, tapes, films, kits, and records. Also, public library collections are literally dynamic. They turn over rapidly. They are *now*-oriented.

The catalog presumably facilitates access *to* the public library's stock *by* the public library's clientele and staff. *Presumably*, that is. In fact, it doesn't work quite that way. And a large part of the problem is that major cataloging codes and practices have been designed by and for the research and academic libraries. Public libraries, even though they represent the *majority* clientele, have been pitifully *underrepresented* in our highest policy-making councils. And, what's worse, they have themselves failed to aggressively lobby for their own interests.

What are those *interests*? Well, they flow from what I'd like to posit as the three fundamental principles or objectives that ought to underly both descriptive and subject cataloging:

1. *Intelligibility*. Bibliographic data—i.e., the substance and format of catalog entries—should be helpful to catalog users. And should make sense.

2. *Findability*. That is, access. It should be quick and fullsome. This involves the use of contemporary, familiar language; entering works under the author's title-page name; and assigning enough added entries—for titles, subtitles, collaborators, and subjects—to make the material findable where people are likely to look for it.

3. *Fairness*. That is, fairness to the material being cataloged and—in terms of subject cataloging in particular—to the topics themselves. For instance, it's *not* fair to the whole category of materials we call *audiovisual* or *nonprint* to either not catalog them at all (which is extremely common) or to treat them in a second-class

way vis-à-vis books. And, as another instance, it's not fair to employ rubrics for ethnic groups that are not their *own*, preferred names.

Now let's apply these principles or objectives to descriptive and subject cataloging, as well as to classification.

First: Descriptive Cataloging. For a profession that's increasingly so economy-minded, it's remarkable how much unnecessary and often unintelligible junk we insist on *keeping* in our catalog entries. Or wantonly *adding* to them. In the public library context, I submit that we don't need:

—secret punctuation, such as slashes, dashes, and equal-signs, that only the divinely ordained can understand.

—compulsory author-statements following titles when the name is identical to the main entry and thus redundant.

—brackets (they're insignificant to everyone but library-types and actually insulting to catalogers).

—unhelpful, space-wasting *1st ed.* statements.

—mysterious Latin ciphers, such as *s.l.* and *s.n.* (in brackets, of course), that could well make ordinary plebes feel like dummies.

—Roman pagination, which in most of our materials is seldom extensive nor of any tangible value to users.

—centimeter spine-sizes; when a book's too tall to fit on the regular shelves, the odd size is ordinarily indicated in the call-number itself by something like a *folio* prefix.

—ISBN numbers and prices; the numbers because nobody outside of the Acquisitions Department gives a damn, and the prices because they're likely to have risen considerably even before the cards get filed.

For reasons of intelligibility, it would also be wiser to use fewer abbreviations: for instance, spelling out *pages, edition, illustrations, folded, color*, and *volumes*.

Still dealing with descriptive cataloging, what *do* we need?

—Perhaps more important than anything else, *all* pseudonyms should be legitimized. If an author chooses to write a book as *Jean Plaidy*, and the publisher not only prints *Jean Plaidy* on the title page but also advertises and markets the book that way, and reviewers review it that way, and bookstores sell it that way, and patrons expect to find it shelved that way, how does it serve either findability or common sense to catalog it under HIBBERT? And accordingly shelve it under *H*? (The same applies to works written by *Philippa Carr* and *Victoria Holt*, two other pen names for the same person.)

—To promote greater access, more added entries, especially for subtitles and catch-titles, need to be assigned. For example: Peter Schickele has so far produced six or seven records and one book in which the key words *P. D. Q. Bach* appear in the titles, but not as the *first* words. For none of these works has LC made a *P. D. Q. Bach* added entry. Similarly, *Planets of Wonder: A Treasury of Space Opera* deserved an added-title entry for *Space Opera Treasury*. And *Your Erroneous Zones*, a current bestseller, should be findable by way of *Erroneous Zones*. (But in a library that uncritically accepted the MARC [Machine-Readable Cataloging] record, it's not.)

—It would also be a good thing to make added entries for small, noncommercial presses, the kind cited in Len Fulton's annual *International Directory of Little Magazines and Small Presses* and SRRT's *Alternatives in Print*. (The rationale is much the same as for tracing the agencies associated with government documents.)

Second: Subject Cataloging. There's a mammoth *findability* problem that divides into at least two categories.

In the first, access is impaired by archaic, awkward, or simply strange nomenclature that most normal persons would never look for on their first try. It only contributes to user-frustration and a very poor library image when material on minnows is cataloged under FUNDULUS HETEROCLITUS, on Tay-Sachs disease under AMAUROTIC FAMILY IDIOCY, or on smoking and health under TOBACCO—PHYSIOLOGICAL EFFECT.

In the second category, access is seriously reduced by neglecting to create and to use descriptors for many topics—especially ethnic, alternative, sexual, and age-related subjects—for which there's *ample literary warrant*. Works on such themes are typically subject-traced under nonspecific, much-too-broad headings, which in effect buries the material. Incredibly, for instance, there are still no direct and specific LC headings for FAMILY PLANNING (which is *not* synonymous with *Birth control*), COUNTER-CULTURE, ALTERNATIVE ENERGY SOURCES, RHYTHM AND BLUES MUSIC, REGGAE MUSIC, FOOD CO-OPS, PATIENTS' RIGHTS, MEN'S LIBERATION, DISCOTHEQUE DANCES, CLONES AND CLONING, ALTERNATIVE LIFE-STYLES, AGEISM, FIRST DAY IN SCHOOL, NEW BABY IN FAMILY, CHILD ADVOCACY, DEPROGRAMMING (now a major civil liberties issue), INNER CITY, VITAMIN B-17 (or LAETRILE), SENIOR CENTERS, NATIONAL LIBERATION MOVEMENTS, HOMOPHOBIA, APPROPRIATE TECHNOLOGY, and THIRD WORLD LITERATURE (an anthology of recent Third World writings is most likely to be subject-traced under LITERATURE, MODERN—20TH CENTURY).

Despite all the written and spoken words, and the charge that to even raise the issue now is *to beat a dead horse*, there are, regrettably, a host of continuing problems in the area of *fairness*. While there have been some praiseworthy improvements over the past few years, many biased headings persist, headings that disparage or distort the topic itself, prejudice the user against the material cited, and reinforce damaging stereotypes, many of them demeaning the very people who *use* the catalog. Some examples:

(1) *Sexist.* These are most commonly masculine, subsuming terms that exclude women from certain occupations and historical groups—in fact, from humanity itself. These descriptors are still alive: BOATMEN, CITY COUNCIL-MEN, FIREMEN, FOREMEN, LONGSHOREMEN, STUNT MEN, STATES-MEN, WATCHMEN, MAN and MANPOWER. (All of these can be painlessly transmuted into natural, androgynous forms, e.g., CITY COUNCILMEN becoming CITY COUNCIL MEMBERS; FIREMEN: FIRE FIGHTERS; LONG-SHOREMEN: LONGSHORE WORKERS; STATEMEN: POLITICIANS and WORLD LEADERS; and MAN: HUMANS (which would place the *man* entries where they logically belong, adjacent to such already-established forms as HUMAN BIOLOGY, HUMAN ECOLOGY, HUMAN EVOLUTION, and HUMAN GENETICS).

(2) *Racist and ethnocentric terms.* For instance, TRIBE in glosses or phrases (like IBO TRIBE) and the many *primitive* constructions that are tantamount to labeling Third World peoples and their cultures as *savage* or *barbaric*; INDIANS OF NORTH AMERICA—LAND TRANSFERS (when what's *really* meant is *forced removals*); *Question* forms like JEWISH QUESTION and RACE QUESTION that actually don't handle the material well—and make *victims* seem to be responsible for their own victimization; and the ludicrous ENGLISH LAN-

GUAGE—TEXTBOOKS FOR FOREIGNERS—SPANISH (that's what Chicanos and Puerto Rican Americans must look under for materials on *English as a second language*.

(3) Headings that accord Christianity *first place*. Numero uno. They are legion. And probably violate the *Establishment Clause* of the First Amendment.

(4) Agcist forms like CHILDREN—MANAGEMENT (instead of the familiar and nonjudgmental CHILD-REARING) and AGED (instead of SENIORS or SENIOR CITIZENS).

(5) A number of wretched, insensitive cross-references, like from *Dumb* to DEAF, and from *Feeble minded, Imbecility,* and *Morons* to MENTALLY HANDICAPPED.

Again in the realm of *findability*, an average 1.3 subject tracings per title is too low to maximize subject-access to materials especially in small- and medium-sized collections. What's required is a somewhat more generous policy, together with the assignment of subject headings to certain whole categories, such as adult fiction and drama, that have been almost totally uncataloged to date. Also, even juvenile fiction, although more liberally subject-traced, could be better accessed by applying more specific descriptors when possible; for example, TEDDY BEARS instead of TOYS, or SINGLE-PARENT FAMILY instead of the catch-all FAMILY.

Pursuing *findability* for another instant, it would be nice for central cataloging sources or individual libraries themselves:

—to practice more creative cross-referencing, for instance introducing cross-references from *Flapjacks* and *Hotcakes* to the primary heading, PANCAKES, WAFFLES, ETC.; from *"Coke"* and *"Snow"* to COCAINE; from OSHA (the acronym) to UNITED STATES. OCCUPATIONAL HEALTH AND SAFETY ADMINISTRATION; and from deliberately misspelled names to their correct homonyms: such as *Rogers, Mary* to *Rodgers, Mary*.

—to create and apply subject headings for literary and media genres, if they're likely to interest users, e.g., GOTHIC FICTION, TALL TALES, SUSPENSE STORIES, BEAT POETRY, HISTORICAL ROMANCES, PIXILLATION FILMS, EPIC FILMS, and CAUTIONARY TALES AND VERSE (which nicely fits a lot of things by Hilaire Belloc and Heinrich Hoffmann, for example).

—to create and apply subject heads for consumer, personal-finance, and other people-helping topics, e.g., FRAUD IN DOOR-TO-DOOR SELLING; DRUG ABUSE COUNSELING; DRUG ABUSE PROJECTS AND SERVICES; JOB HUNTING (the nearest rubric at present is APPLICATIONS FOR POSITIONS); MONEY-SAVING COOKING; LOW-COST TRAVEL; *Choice of* forms for insurance, surgeons, nursing homes, shoes, etc.; WOMEN'S PROJECTS AND SERVICES; HANDICAPPED—PROJECTS AND SERVICES; and the subhead, —FUNDING SOURCES, under some of those *Projects and services* heads to cover material on grant-making bodies in those areas.

—to create and apply headings for themes of special ethnic or local interest, e.g., BAGELS, ROSEMALING, MEXICAN-AMERICAN DETECTIVES, CHINESE-AMERICAN FAMILIES, GHETTOES, KWANZA, KIBBUTZ, SHTETL, INDIAN RESISTANCE AND REVOLTS, and KUBBESTOLS (the latter being Norwegian log chairs, still made by some wood-carvers in Minnesota).

—to create and apply headings for popular fictional characters, places, and things, like: MR. SPOCK; NARNIA; the illustrious trio of SHERLOCK

HOLMES, DR. WATSON, and PROFESSOR MORIARTY (preferably with-
out death-dates, since there's much dispute on that delicate matter); MISS
MARPLE; MARY POPPINS; INSPECTOR MAIGRET; STEVE AUSTIN
(cross-referenced, of course from "Six-Million Dollar Man"); BUGS
BUNNY; ANANSI; and WINNIE-THE-POOH.
—to create headings for major literary and media awards, and then apply them
to the winning titles actually in your collection; e.g., ACADEMY AWARD
FILMS, LAMONT POETRY SELECTIONS, HUGO AWARD WINNERS,
GAY BOOK AWARDS, ARMSTRONG AWARDS IN FM BROADCAST-
ING, and CORETTA SCOTT KING AWARDS.
—to drop from public library headings such subdivisions as —POPULAR
WORKS and —ADDRESSES, ESSAYS, LECTURES that only create artifi-
cial divisions in the catalog. And for the same reason to limit the use of the
—UNITED STATES and —HANDBOOKS, MANUALS, ETC. subheads.

   Third: Classification. From the standpoint of most public libraries, *classification* means Dewey. And three basic points seem appropriate:
   (1) Just as with subject headings, contemporary and even *old* subjects are not
adequately nor quickly accommodated by DDC. Where, for instance, do *femi-
nism, workers' control, abortion,* and *homesteading* belong?
   (2) Catalogers would hugely benefit from a comprehensive index to DDC that
swiftly and directly links topics and numbers. (Try finding *prison reform, wife
beating, intellectual freedom,* or *vasectomy* in the 18th edition index.)
   (3) Almost no public libraries can afford to completely reclassify entire
sequences when a new Dewey edition appears. But if they *don't*, the practical
result of those burn-'em-down-build-'em-up *Phoenix* schedules is to destroy
call-number integrity and make browsing more than a little difficult. Even if less
intellectually satisfying to librarians, patrons—i.e., browsers—would be better
served by updating and reforming Dewey through expanding the scope of existing
notations, extending others numerically, and giving life to some of those many
unused digits.

   From the overall cataloging perspective, there are several more things we
need:
   —LC catalog cards *and* MARC records for AV titles: records, slides, kits,
films, etc. (At present, public—and also school—libraries may spend up to 15
percent or more of their materials budget on media, but find no *outside copy* for
new titles, and so elect to either undercatalog the material or perform totally
original cataloging, which can be costly.)
   —More accurate and usable CIP (Cataloging in Publication) data, which might
be achieved if the Library of Congress just plain refused to prepare CIP entries
when publishers furnish too little information to permit correct, responsibile
cataloging.
   —And a final, two-part need: First, to convince rightly cost-conscious administrators that good, quality cataloging is, in fact, economical because it
promotes the use of those very materials that they've spent so much money on
picking, getting, labeling, packaging, and shelving. And second: Catalogers
themselves need more independence and encouragement to change *outside
copy*, to introduce helpful cross-references, and otherwise to make cataloging
truly responsive to the library's users. (Cataloging should certainly *not* be a
joyless, irrelevant, and zombielike process. But in too many libraries I fear
that it is the case.)

If my public library colleagues agree that at least some of these needs and suggestions are valid, how do we get them recognized and implemented? Frankly, I'm not sure. But I *am* convinced that it's high time to start talking about them.

DISCUSSION

Paul Fasana: Mr. Berman has given us a lot to think about. I guess I would begin by disagreeing with everything he says for my library. Librarians have an unnerving habit of assuming that all libraries and all patrons are the same. They go even further and assume that all patrons are academic patrons. Therefore, the typical view of a user is a student or a researcher, and the typical evaluation of a user's need is usually phrased in terms of a captive audience, i.e., a student. The New York Public Library (NYPL), an independent research library on 42nd Street (apart from branch libraries) does not have an academic community, so we have many of the same problems that Mr. Berman was referring to.

Unfortunately, we tend to enshrine this thought and it's led us to at least four things. First, a single code: Is this a reasonable consideration at this point in time? Can we in fact have a code and provide records that are usable for all kinds of patrons? We're trying, it seems, in *AACR2* to provide for this through options. Mr. Berman has mentioned cross-references. However, I don't think these are adequate; they are patches. We should perhaps analyze whether or not a single code for different kinds of libraries is a reasonable consideration.

Secondly, we have been beaten with the idea for years now that we should catalog a work once and only once. Tied in with this is the fact that we have one and only one source of data. We're told that this is cheaper. However, we all know that it's often cheaper to do original cataloging than to try to find and fashion an LC card to fit into our catalog. Perhaps we should question this premise again. Let's look at the problem of a single source. In fact, can we expect a single source—in this instance, LC—to be able to provide a record that can meet all of these needs? Several years ago LC very graciously took on and began to add children's headings, but they were just grafted on. How effective, how useful are they, in fact? Maybe we should look at this matter again.

My third and fourth points concern two things that go into the future that will either tend to enforce these premises or cause us to think freshly. One is technology. We keep asking the technologists: Can, in fact, the computer provide us with solutions? Can the bibliographic records store all variations and possibilities? Through proper manipulation, can we get out records that will be useful for a public library and an academic library? I think the questions have been asked, but I don't think they've been adequately answered.

There is a great deal of talk now of creating all kinds of interconnecting networks on a national and international level. Most of those talking are attempting to gloss over the differences that exist, rather than to look at them intelligently. What I would like to suggest is that Mr. Berman has provided us with a very vivid picture of a community that does not fit easily into *AACR*, which is expressly made for our academic, research libraries.

Edwin Buchinski: I suppose that it is probably not very widely known that *AACR* starts out by providing for three levels of descriptions called *minimum, standard,* and *full.* It seems to me that the minimum description would adequately serve Mr. Berman's needs. Perhaps a more critical presentation of that would provide very useful input to the review process previously mentioned.

In the course of the discussions there has been a theme of change. A change is needed to discard outdated cataloging practices and to provide for new materials and for special interest groups. An attempt was made in Michael Gorman's paper to illustrate a new concept of a record. He didn't carry his concept far enough, though. He just didn't elaborate on the concept that the standard packet could be user-group specific, as perhaps the public library's need for children's literature. I said "perhaps"; I'm dead certain it could be accommodated out of the file which has a series of names. It's possible to take in the kind of structure that Mr. Gorman outlined yesterday and to identify what is needed by the public libraries, the university libraries, the medical libraries, etc.

I hope I'm not disclosing any secret information, but in the past three months I've had the opportunity to work with LC and an evaluation team specifically appointed to look at the role of authority files in the national bibliographic network. The report is soon going to be available, but I would like to emphasize that the idea that there is only one structure meant to tie everybody together is probably a misconception. We haven't got LC's okay that they're going to design the network in any particular way, but at least at that level the concept is being looked at. How do the requirements of special groups, such as public libraries, medical libraries, and other specialty groups, link together?

Sanford Berman: In direct response to Mr. Buchinski concerning the business about levels, I'd like to be charitable, but I can only characterize that as rubbish. It would, of course, be one of the lower levels of description that we were accorded. And that would be merely a matter of saying, "Hey, if you want to deviate, you have our permission to do so. But we're not going to do it for you in terms of what appears on the outside copy that you're securing from us, either directly in the form of cards, through vendors, or off the tube as MARC records." So I'm not personally satisfied with that kind of response. The public library people and some others have needs that have long been unmet, but jolly well ought to be as soon as possible. I think what's utterly crucial is the matter of mechanics, of how to go about it.

In connection with that, I think it's the greater part of wisdom in a situation like this to bow to those who know more about the matter than I do. There's been no foreplanning—they have no foreknowledge of this—but I would like to invite our chairperson, Mr. Freedman, and also Dave Remington, who directs the LC Catalog Distribution Service, to comment on what the network and LC cataloging distribution potentialities are to begin to accommodate those unmet needs, particularly public library needs. In many regards I would also associate the school and community college libraries in the same bundle of similar kinds of needs.

Let me preface this further, if Mr. Freedman doesn't mind. He delivered an excellent paper that we're going to reprint with pleasure in the June 1st *Hennepin County Library Cataloging Bulletin* on precisely this topic, "Public Libraries, LC and the National Bibliographic Network." I think he outlined what might be indeed the feasible way in the network fashion to go about meeting our needs without doing in anybody else in the process, and hence my suggesting that he say a couple of words.

David Remington: I think the critical thing at this point, since Mr. Berman probably has articulated his views as well as anyone has and has done a great deal to focus on some of the weaker points and some of the more difficult problems with subject headings, is to ask how we implement this. I believe that Mr. Freedman is interested in taking a systematic and total view of the public library's needs in terms of bibliographic control, particularly descriptive and subject cataloging. I think that's critical.

The first thing we have to establish is the kind of support we have for the kinds of things Mr. Berman is talking about. Do we sit here and do we listen and do we laugh? Where do we really begin to support implementation of this? We need more than Mr. Buchinski's suggestion, but it's a good start. And having called it rubbish, Mr. Berman, it might be helpful starting from there to take up the charge which the Children's Literature Committee made at the Cataloging and Classification Section at Midwinter. It was a suggestion that we have both an alternative catalog card and an alternative approach to the display of cataloging data.

It can't be said too often that we're now at a point where having full cataloging detail, having the kinds of things that are being planned and worked out by people like Mr. Gorman and so forth, we can select from the various approaches and options that we never had before. We think in terms of the unit card today but it's as obsolete as it could be, because we simply have technology that allows us to be selective—if a couple of things happen.

One, we need to have a code, and it needs to be a code that is not mandated by the Library of Congress but is mandated by the major type of library, in this case possibly just public libraries, that says this is what we want. That's absolutely essential. It may be in *AACR2*; I don't know.

The second thing we need is something Mr. Berman has provided, although as former Assistant Chief of Subject Cataloging, I'd have to say I have differences as to how feasible it is for LC to do. He has created a computer output microfilm authority file that surprisingly almost no major library journal in the country has picked up or even considered. I know they know about it. It is for us to look for what we should be doing in subject analysis for public libraries. When I say "public libraries," I am not excluding academic libraries necessarily. Academic libraries have people—people who are not scholars and researchers in every incarnation of their use of the library. They are generalists; they are people looking for recreational reading; they are human beings looking for information, even if they're the best chemists or the best sociologists in the world. That is one of the other things we need: a subject authority file. If Mr. Freedman comes up with something that relates to shared cataloging for public libraries, then we in effect have to have authorities that all of us would look at and that all of us would use in that shared catalog for the public libraries.

I'd also like you to know that the Children's Literature Section at LC is preparing a draft list of its headings which could be examined outside of LC, not on a card-by-card basis, but on a systematic basis. After you have those two authorities and perhaps a few public libraries doing the cataloging and applying those authorities outside of LC or in conjunction with a network, it's not inconceivable that commercial card producers—if they had a MARC record that carried these authorities—could distribute that cataloging.

It's clearly in the plans of the Library of Congress' Catalog Distribution Service to handle not just LC's cataloging and not just unit cards. We are presently launching into the distribution of someone else's cataloging. Naturally it's following the *AACR*, using LC subject headings and attempting to use LC main entries; but the Government Printing Office's *Documents Catalog*, which appears in the *Monthly Catalog*, is being distributed in the MARC II format. We're planning a card service that makes sense and that uses our rather elaborate, but not online, access system in the LC Cataloging Distribution Service.

So we're very much interested in these problems. Hopefully, in a year or so not only will we not go out of business, but we may be able to handle catalog cards for other than just single-entry unit cards.

Maurice Freedman: Mr. Berman referred to a speech I gave in Chicago that I'd do better justice to by having you read than by trying to hit the high points. It will be in the *Hennepin County Library Cataloging Bulletin* (#28), in the *Journal of Library Automation* (June 1977) as part of the proceedings of the Networks Institute, and in the November 1, 1977, issue of *Library Journal*. If you're interested, that will give a more coherent discussion of it. However, the HCL version of that speech will be illustrated by the fine artist, Inese Jansons.

In response to Mr. Berman's question, there is now an awareness, a willing-ness and an openness at LC that is very hopeful. The people who have been critical of LC or who have been asking for more or wanting more, have been doing it for many years; it's not a new thing. But the response that we're receiving is relatively new, and gratifying.

Two days ago I spoke at the Connecticut Library Association. I gave a version of that network speech. It was amazing talking to people who are in these smaller libraries. The response they gave was tremendous. Talking to large groups composed mainly of academic librarians, technical services librarians, research librarians, and automation people is extraordinarily frustrating, because they think people making these kinds of requests for responsive, contemporaneous headings, and for different cataloging practices are sort of kooky, unrealistic, oddballs.

But going out and getting the responses of these other people who don't go to ISAD institutes, MARC user group meetings, etc., and who are working at the grass roots in medium and small public libraries with the kinds of problems we're addressing, is completely different. It's good to hear their attitudes and opinions and the kind of positive feedback they give. They were virtually unanimous in their dissatisfaction with current rules and practices.

David Remington's expression of LC's interest is good to hear. One of the things I would ask, though, is that there be some legitimization of people like Sanford Berman. When the committees get appointed by LC, CLR (Council on Library Resources), and ALA (American Library Association), when the con-sultants are brought in, the people who have been pleading, asking, or declaiming don't seem to be the people who are invited to participate in the actual planning; they aren't brought in to discuss the delineation of plans. So I hope that there will also be another kind of change—the participation of the dissidents and critics in the planning and decision making.

The kind of thing I talked about was really a network model that would allow for a more complex MARC structure, one that would allow for alternate au-thorities. LC has already done this, anyway. The MARC format, for those of you who have worked with it, has provisions for juvenile headings and for NLM (National Library of Medicine) headings. On a more systematic basis, it has a provision for—let's call it for the time being—public library headings. That's the input side of it. The output side would be to develop a range of products that would extract from that more complex or rich MARC record the elements that are needed for the given library public. In one sense, from a product end, this is the kind of thing Michael Gorman's conception of a bibliographic record would include. Now, I see LC as the most likely place to manage all this since it has by far the greatest staff and resources. It would be in many respects a minor effort for them to speedily catalog American trade publications. The effort they put into the shared cataloging program of the National Program of Acquisitions and Cataloging (NPAC) where preliminary cataloging information was air freighted from various countries around the world and rushed through the special new catalog division that was set up to specially handle this. This is an example of the forces LC can bring to bear to solve a pressing problem. The kind of resources LC applied to handling the publishing output of France or Germany would be more than what's needed to rush catalog and provide richer catalog records for the American trade publications sought by public and school libraries. I say this in the article. Organizing it and doing it and putting out some kind of plan that's workable is a big job, but can be done if the commitment is there. It would just take a lot of work.

Unidentified Speaker: I wish to speak for my employer, Brodart. Mr. Berman, who is a very personable and enthusiastic librarian, certainly comes across. We need more leaders, first of all, who can inject that personality and excitement into the profession. One of Mr. Berman's points was how to accomplish some of the things that he mentioned this morning. One of the ways, of course, is by hearing people like himself get up, talk, expound, and publish in the journals, and by having librarians read those articles and get excited about them. Tell your administrators about them. That's how things get changed, because at the cataloging level we cannot change things. We do not have this independence that Mr. Berman mentioned. One of the problems, of course, is that it costs money to enhance your subject headings and points of access. Administrators, always concerned with cost, perhaps cannot see the benefit that is going to come to the public.

Recently, Brodart experimented with *in-depth subject headings*. We took a basic list of school titles from one of the Wilson publications, examined these works, and enhanced it with additional subject headings—as many as 50, but with an average of 13 subject headings per title. In addition we used current language to assign subjects to these words, some of which Mr. Berman mentioned. REGGAE MUSIC was one I remember distinctly. We were not locked into the established subject heading authorities. But, it does cost money to do this and we did *not* have a response from the public to pay for it. Actually, we're in business to make money and we do need a mandate to do this kind of thing. So, you have to get it going and get us the mandate for the service.

Freedman: That's the kind of thing I did address in the paper. It has to be a national service, it has to be a standardized product. It's impossible for a given vendor or library to try to do this kind of work on their own and disseminate it or universalize it. What I have in mind is the contribution of cataloging data from libraries such as Hennepin County to a national authority base that would reside at LC. The cataloging data would then be integrated into MARC records which, with this enriched data, could be distributed by LC's Cataloging Distribution Service to commercial vendors, to processing centers, to anyone who wanted to use it in additional ways, as well as the same way they're using the MARC tapes now. I would think that the commercial people would have no problem at all accepting that product, especially since it takes off their back the encumbrance of having to do original cataloging with the concomitant increase in the cost of service.

Berman: I would only suggest that the gentleman's anterior point is extremely well taken although I don't choose to belabor it. I think he's right from the producer's end—and I don't often sympathize with commercial producers—but it's certainly something to be said. I tried to say at the very outset of my remarks that there probably has not been sufficient consumer-like and assertive, much less aggressive, input and leverage exerted upon our chief cataloging copy producers.

Now the ultimate producer is, of course, LC. I don't really want to beat the same horse, but LC happens to be the only horse, if you're going to beat one, in the corral that counts. It's not altogether its fault because the critics (I'm surely one of them and happy to be one) have been so far, not necessarily deliberately, more or less characterized as freaks and flakes who are not to be taken seriously. That's partly because the foolishness or disasters that we as catalogers face daily are seldom translated into letters to LC.

I am almost inclined to agree with the vendor or LC administrator that these people don't really know what they want, and that they behave like sheep. Now let me make a little analogy; this is a cheap one but it actually fits. You walk into your neighborhood supermarket and buy a loaf of crumby packaged bread and you take it home after having paid good money for it. You open it and discover that it is rotten inside. What's the ordinary response if you're a red-blooded American consumer? I mean, you scream like hell and run to the store and demand your money back. You do it either politely or otherwise, but you *do* something and you let them now that you've done it.

How many of you do it when you get wretched cataloging copy at the library? Do you send notes to Mr. Custer at the Decimal Classification Division? A work that we got lately—maybe you know it, *Jody* is its title—is really all about a woman, an adopted child, trying to trace her identity. When it was subject-traced with only her name and classified, believe it or not, in *973*, did you do anything about that? I don't think most of you did. *973* is general American history; that's where you put something on American civilization. It's utterly boggling and that's not an isolated incident. I can cite you several more from last week.

Elizabeth Weidenmann: I used to wonder too about repeating the author in *ISBD* and, as somebody who works with African materials, I've come to the conclusion that it's just a wonderful idea because African authors in particular frequently change their names. When you get pre-*ISBD* records, and have to go back and change to the author's new name, you have to annotate your card. When I wrote to LC about this they said that they change the main entry all right, but they don't make an annotation or change the body of the entry. So you end up with a record that doesn't match the book. I wonder what Mr. Berman has to say about that. Also, is it ethnocentric to eliminate U.S. as a subject subdivision?

Berman: No, I don't think it is. Remember I was speaking from the public library's context, and when I said it creates artificial divisions I meant precisely that. Let me take an absolutely incontrovertible example. First, if you've got anything under AFFIRMATIVE ACTION in your catalog, by definition that heading only applies to the U.S., so it's foolish to add a subheading. But more particularly, for material on income tax, we have nothing on and are unlikely ever to get anything on income tax in Brazil or Venezuela or even Great Britain.

On the other matter, I would prefer simply to repeat what Marvin Scilken often quotes as a maxim for such matters. Namely, it frequently is the case that what is a convenience for the librarian often proves an inconvenience to the library user.

Freedman: I'd like to comment briefly, too, since this is one aspect that Ms. Weidenmann discussed a long time ago regarding *ISBD*. It's really a practical problem with respect to the kind of services available from the Library of Congress. If there was some kind of authority service that would highlight or indicate changes, it wouldn't be necessary to construct these kinds of local practices to keep track of name changes.

Marie Griffin: I'd like to question using pseudonyms for entries, particularly in AV. For example, you have Charlie Parker, who recorded under some 30 pseudonyms. Now perhaps your users would know Yardbird Parker of The Birds, but then you get the record, *Jazz at Massey Hall*, which Parker recorded under the name Charlie Chan. I doubt very much if many of your users looking for Charlie Parker would look under CHAN, CHARLIE, rather than PARKER, CHARLES CHRISTOPHER. Would they find the record?

Berman: What I omitted was this. We're really talking about a person with more than one legitimate pseudonym, otherwise it's rather well provided for in the upcoming code. When you maintain your files in cases like these, and do legitimize each one of those pseudonyms, then you must use the alternative rule, which LC doesn't. It is an alternative that exists now in *AACR* and specifies that you compose, according to your own situation, very simple but appropriate linking notes. For instance, under HOLT and HIBBERT and so on, there would be the appropriate short statement: "For works written by this author under the pseudonym such and such, see such and such."

Bonnie Stone: My question concerns the author statement and the *ISBD* rules. We have been working under the assumption and from the literature that if the author's name is fully spelled out on the title page, and if there is just one author, it is optional to include it. Is it true that you do not have to repeat it in the author statement?

Freedman: I'm going to ask the author of the *ISBD* to answer.

Gorman: I think there's confusion between what the *ISBD* says, and how it has been used, and how it's been interpreted in our cataloging rules. A lot of attacks that have been made on *ISBD* are, in fact, attacks on either the American edition of the revision of Chapter 6 or on LC's interpretation of *ISBD*. What the *ISBD* says is that the elements which are not marked as optional in the *ISBD* must be recorded by the national bibliographic agency in the country from which the document emanates. In other words, somewhere in each country, somebody should make the full entry. It goes on specifically to say, "All other agencies may select the elements which they include in their description." Then it says that those elements which you do include must be presented in the prescribed order with the prescribed punctuation.

Now it may be that because of the technology by which catalog entries are distributed, that definitive entry is the only one which is made available. That is a purely temporary thing.

If I may on this point make another comment: What Mr. Buchinski said was not rubbish. What he said was that the code is now providing for various levels. Technologically, there's no reason why these levels of description should not be made available. If the public librarians, after having asked for a shorter entry, choose to think that because it's short the entry is somehow inferior, then I'm afraid I'm at a loss to follow the logic of it.

Griffin: Mr. Berman, you might want to add to your list that in *LC Subject Headings*, the 8th edition, we do have FEMALE DELINQUENTS.

Berman: I think they did undo that one. That's one of the praiseworthy improvements, and, if I'm not mistaken, it's now FEMALE OFFENDERS, or WOMEN OFFENDERS. It really eliminates the delinquent problem.

Griffin: Yes, but WOMEN OFFENDERS would not be much of an improvement.

Berman: At least it's a moderate improvement over the delinquent. Rather than take a whole lot of time on this, let me utter a brief commercial on behalf of a book which addresses precisely this area of women-related headings, Joan Marshall's *On Equal Terms* (Neal-Schuman Publishers, 1977).

One of the arguments among people who were making recommendations for drafts of Ms. Marshall's work was whether to specify women with respect to particular occupations or conditions, such as criminals. There are very good points on both sides for doing this, and for not doing it. What we started doing a long time ago at Hennepin was to show WOMEN and to use cross-referencing. If we use WOMEN OFFENDERS, then we cross-reference from OFFENDERS and WOMEN. We thought that we were responding to a real demand and need on the part of a great many people, young people and older people, who desired access to materials that were deliberately produced for and by women, and for which we provided the direct route. In every case where we made a special women's heading, we also made a special heading for men if the collection warranted it.

Griffin: That brings me to my next point on the 8th edition: The subject heading WOMAN was out. WOMAN has to be changed to WOMEN, so that there is no subject heading in LC for just WOMAN, which is a very basic concept. There's a man, there's a woman, and even today it takes one of each to beget another one. It seems to me that the deletion of that was maybe a little bit too hasty.

Berman: This is another case where LC was right, even if perhaps 40 or 50 years too late. It uses MAN in essence not to mean *men*, because that already exists as a heading to cover the gender. It means MAN strictly for *humanity*, or what I suggested is more appropriate and easily represented, *humans*, and it proves to be so in our catalog where that's the way it appears. The MEN and the WOMEN handle better individually the matter of each gender as a whole gender. MAN remains wrong just as WOMAN alone representing generic *women* was wrong.

Dorothy Puryear: I felt yesterday that I was one of the only public librarians here. I just wanted to express my complete enthusiasm for you and your point of view, Mr. Berman. Public libraries, especially in New York City, are feeling severe budget crunches, because we really haven't been relevant to people and, therefore, nobody uses us. The most optimistic studies have shown that only 20 percent of the adult population uses the public library once a month. Concerning my experience with the information and referral service for Queens Borough Public Library, we were thought of as freaks because our subject headings had to be an alternative list of subject headings within the public library. We made the list because the kinds of things that people needed to know and came in to find out were not findable in the LC subject headings. I can't agree with you more, and I only wish I knew how to be a voice to help change things for public libraries. I think it would really make a difference.

Berman: Let me point out that, precisely as my colleague suggests, there have been necessarily alternative lists developing. I can cite two that are rather extensive and certainly dynamic: those of the Detroit Public Library and the San Diego Public Library.

Judith Hopkins: I have one brief comment on author statements. I think there may be some confusion as to the requirement of *ISBD* proper, and the requirements of Chapter 6 of *AACR*, which is an American implementation of *ISBD*. In the vicinity of Rule 1340, it says you have to have an author statement with certain exceptions, one exception being if the author's name is a generative part of the title, such as *Shakespeare's Works*, for example. You cannot make that plain *Works*, so you simply don't have an author statement. Except for a few exceptions of that kind, Chapter 6 does require an author statement.

Freedman: Mr. Berman did not respond to Mr. Gorman's remark about public libraries asking for short entries and then complaining about the three levels. I think Mr. Berman's point was that there is no national distribution service that provides brief entries. He wasn't necessarily quarreling with the notion of three levels. If public libraries want to implement a third level, it's their own problem to do it locally. That's basically been the problem. They are always free to do it themselves, but unlike the nation's research libraries, which get what they need from LC, they must do it on their own, and it is very, very expensive.

Berman: In that regard I'd say that we also definitely qualify as a disadvantaged majority.

Eleanor Crarey: I've long admired and tremendously envied the kind of cataloging that's done at Hennepin, and I think most of you have seen Hennepin's materials, especially the subject authority file which is available on fiche at 42x reduction.

One of the things that encouraged me very much about *AACR2* was that it certainly allows a lot more title page cataloging and a lot more use of real pseudonyms. John Creasey finally appears in all his multitudinous forms. I can't agree more with the situation that public libraries cataloging is *now* cataloging. I do recognize that LC's subject headings are based on actual works even when they're in insulting terms. If that is the term an author has used to typify his work, they are stuck with it. I would like to see some way to formalize a better channel of communication from public libraries to the Library of Congress for cataloging of current, rapidly changing, socially relevant material. Public libraries are the ones that are able to, and must, respond more quickly than research libraries are able to, and do.

One question for Mr. Berman about AV cataloging from LC. I agree we need it from a central source but not based on the research level that I rather fear might occur.

Berman: I couldn't agree more; I would have hoped that it was implicit in my remarks that the availability of AV cataloging records on MARC would be within the context of what I envisage as the appropriate public, school, and community libraries package. In other words, I envisage a total approach toward better, more appropriate cataloging for our kinds of situations and for our kinds of users.

Fasana: I was happy that Mr. Berman emphasized that there are different kinds of libraries with different objectives and different needs. Within this context I'd like to pose two questions. First, can we expect a single code to meet all these needs? Is this technically feasible? In *AACR2*, for example, we have three levels of cataloging. Someone mentioned to me that the minimal level was intended to accommodate public libraries. Unfortunately, the minimal level of cataloging for the text concerns minor works and distinguishes it from the full level for important works. I would ask, can one code satisfy all needs? Or are we fooling ourselves? Should we in fact make up several codes?

Second question. Mr. Howard of the Library of Congress stressed a future wherein we have a centralized source for all information. It was based in terms of machine capabilities. I wonder if a single machine record for a title can really satisfy the kinds of needs that Mr. Berman has outlined. For example, can the machine delete the offensive *ISBD* from a record? Can a record include all the special kinds of headings and special kinds of cross-references that Mr. Berman feels he needs in his catalog? What I'm really asking is: Are we fooling ourselves into thinking that we can have one national system in one code?

Berman: I don't know if I can respond to this; it's such a gigantic question. We may be fooling ourselves and I would caution public libraries, school libraries, and libraries in general, whose needs are quantitatively different from the requirements of the super libraries like Yale, NYPL's research libraries, and Harvard, that indeed one code might not satisfy all our needs. I think it's been suggested by previous speakers that there are options and alternatives. But while the options at all different levels might be nice, the reality is that unless there is some special bibliographic center for creating and distributing cataloging for public and other nonresearch libraries, three levels of description or any other optional routes place the burden squarely on the individual libraries.

The Catalog in a Research Library and Alternatives to It

by Anne Grodzins Lipow

My talk today about the catalog in a research library and alternatives to it will center heavily around problems users confront at the place where I work, in the hopes that my institution is representative enough in size, types of users, and types of material to be a typical research library. The institution where I work is the University of California comma Berkeley (formerly known as *California period University comma Berkeley*; now known the same way by those, such as my campus, who cannot keep up with all of the national rule changes; known as *University of California comma Berkeley* by those who can; and known both ways by those who can start doing things *right* today but who are unable to go back in time to change what was already done).

At this University, where the faculty and student body have Ph.D.'s, M.A.'s, B.A.'s, B.S.'s, and Phi Beta Kappa keys, many if not most of the people who use the library suffer from a severe handicap: They tend to think that they would be exposing ignorance such smart people are not supposed to have if they ask a question of the reference staff. They therefore tend not to ask for help when they cannot find what they are looking for.

Some go away suspecting there are alternative ways to search but are too shy to ask. Others, rather than attributing their failure to a lack of knowledge, decide the system is so bad, so complex, so chaotic, that there is no way it can produce the wanted material. Or still others think they have the library figured out; they know they have exhausted all avenues and go away certain their material is not obtainable—probably because of recent cuts in the book budget they read about in the campus newspaper.

Thus, the library acquires its reputation for "never having anything I want," "never having the book available when I want it." Then, of course, there are those who always ask because that's easier than looking up anything in that unfathomable catalog.

No librarian is surprised, however, at the ignorance about using the library on the part of perfectly normal, intelligent people. How were they ever to learn? If we think back to when we were in library school, how many of us, after we took our first courses in reference and cataloging, thought (with some resentment), "If only I had known about this goldmine when I was writing term papers."

Wouldn't it be a wonderful world, then, if a user were self-sufficient in locating most items bibliographically, leaving the tough job of assistance with special verification problems, information retrieval, instruction in the resources of the library, finding related works the catalog has not pulled together, and the like, to the reference staff. I think this is a reachable goal, but to attain it we must first understand where and why the library user goes wrong under our present system. I will describe to you actual problems faculty at the UC Berkeley campus experienced using the catalog, taken from the library's BAKER delivery service, which I oversee. (B-A-K-E-R is the telephone number a UCB person, usually faculty, dials to request material. All who use the service give their citation information exactly as they know it—usually from bibliographies, publisher's ads, word of mouth, book reviews. Many use the service only as a last resort (there is a modest charge for it), when they themselves have searched in vain but feel in their bones that the library has it.

And that is a wise assumption since our statistics show that over the three years the service has been operating, the library owns between 88 and 90 percent of material requested. A study, still in progress, of a random sampling of 20,000 BAKER requests is showing that of the items the library owns, 22 percent were not accessible directly given the bibliographic information in hand. That is, 22 percent of the time, the item was determined to be in our collection only after further information about that item was obtained from a source other than the catalog. This figure does not include the many times a user may have missed a cross-reference card. It does include citations with lack of information about such significant elements as main entry or series information or periodical abbreviation; it also includes slightly wrong titles and misspelled authors.

Bear in mind, too, that the figure of 22 percent is low: sophisticated searchers were starting at the beginning with these requests and did not get discouraged, as regular patrons might, when they did not find it in the catalog at the first look-up. If they did not find it in the catalog under a second or third alternative known at the time of initial searching, it was not counted as ''not accessible directly.'' In other words, probably *more* than 22 percent of the time a user believes the library does not have an item when in fact it does.

The examples I have chosen are not the exotic sleuthing problems we have had or the horror stories, but the everyday, garden-variety request that one can expect from people using a research collection of nearly five million volumes. By a research collection I mean, for our purposes today, a collection with two important characteristics:

(1) It consists of a considerable amount of material that is bibliographically complex. In addition to personal authors and simple, unique titles, the material is known by its corporate or governmental authorship, editor, translator. It contains a goodly share of proceedings of meetings, congresses, symposia, conferences; Festschriften, manuscripts, and maps; a large body of material in other than the English language and in languages in other than the roman alphabet.

(2) The material in the collection must be preserved and made accessible, regardless of how old it is or how infrequently it is used.

By these examples, I hope to make the following points:

First, any research library, in trying to provide good access to the user, deals with a variety of rules: nationally promulgated rules, local rules to handle such situations as in-depth subject collections or nonbook materials; temporary rules to take care of special conditions such as a backlog.

Second, the rules, regardless of where they originate, become out of date: What was correct and reasonable to do 30 years ago was wrong to do 10 years ago, and what was right 10 years ago may be wrong today. Concerning national rules, for example, most academic research libraries continue to operate under parts of all three generations of rules—1908, 1949, and 1967. Ever-changing rules, then, are a fact of a catalog's life.

Third, any research library must and does attempt to keep up with changes in bibliographic description: changes in corporate body names, geographic names; changes in subject terms in accordance with new words in the language as well as words more appropriate to the times.

And finally (in fact, a summing up of the first three points), it has become virtually impossible to maintain the catalog system as the dynamic finding tool it is meant to be.

I shall show, however, that the situation is not hopeless. There are solutions—not magic ones or easy ones or even inexpensive ones—but they are realistic and workable.

For my first example, let me take the problem of midstream changes in series, using as the guinea pig the series *Advances in Experimental Social Psychology*. Volumes 1 through 8 of this series look alike. The bindings are all blue and the title pages read "Advances in Experimental Social Psychology, edited by Leonard Berkowitz." It is an annual publication, published by Academic Press since 1964.

But there is something different about Volume 9. The cover is still blue, but there are now two title pages, one which reads exactly the same as the previous volumes, the other: "Equity Theory—Toward a General Theory of Social Interaction, edited by Leonard Berkowitz." The one which the publicity tells my professor about is the different one, and the way the professor remembers it is by title only. He forgot the name of the editor. (One sometimes wonders if there is a conspiracy by the publishers to sell libraries two copies by representing a book two different ways. It is certainly the case that in a large library there is so much material to be processed, the library assistant checking in the items cannot be expected to search every title page in anticipation of change.)

In order to find Volume 9 in our collection, then, one must first learn through another source that it is part of a series for which the library has a standing order. The unsuspecting patron might give up thinking the library did not have it.

Remember the patrons I described who were sure they knew the rules? This one knew that the library restores an abbreviation to its whole term. He knew, for example, that the *MIT Research Monograph* is entered under MASSACHUSETTS INSTITUTE OF TECHNOLOGY, with the next line of print being RESEARCH MONOGRAPH. So when he went to the Massachusetts drawer to find the MIT Symposium on American Women in Science and Engineering (which had a distinctive title unknown to the patron: *Women and the Scientific Professions*), and it was not there, he assumed we did not own it. He didn't know what we know: its main entry is under the abbreviation M.I.T. because that is what the symposium calls itself.

Or take the person who happened to be in the vicinity of the library so took the opportunity to come in and renew a book that was sitting at home. She knew the author, Erik Ask-Upmark; she knew the Norwegian title, which begins *Resa genom* . . . ; but she did not know the one thing she needed to renew the book: the call number.

Looking under the title, she turned up nothing. And not understanding our filing rules, she found nothing under the author. That is, she expected to find him after the last *Ask* author, but when she came to that card—ASK, LARS—she found the next card to be ASK ANYBODY IN THE NEIGHBORHOOD.

She then thought the place to look was after all the *Ask*'s, but when she got there (ASK WHAT YOU WILL . . .), the next card was the author ASKA, J. And when she finally went through the A-S-K-plus items to *Asku* . . . and still did not find it, she threw up her hands in frustration.

What she learned later was that our library files word-by-word, ignoring hyphens and all other punctuation, except that single surnames precede all other entries beginning with the same word. Thus, ASK-UPMARK falls between the titles ASK THE DUST and ASK VERONICA. The reason it was important to know filing rules in this case was that this book was one of a category of books which for a few years we put into a temporary cataloging pool in order to provide at least one point of access until full cataloging could be accomplished. For several thousand books, then, we provide only an author entry with a temporarily assigned call number that has no relation to the book's subject or author.

Another problem was caused by our decision, some 30 years ago, to change our catalog structure from a dictionary catalog which contained all authors, titles, and subjects in one alphabet, to two separate catalogs, one by author and title, the other by subject. The two catalogs are in separate rooms. In the old days of the dictionary catalog, we saved ourselves the trouble of making a title card when the title was exactly the same as the subject.

So you can imagine what happened when our patron looked for Alexander Wiener's *Blood Groups and Blood Transfusion*, 3rd edition (1943) under its well-known title (not knowing the editor) and did not find it. It's an old book," he thought. "That's why the library doesn't have it." Patrons, you realize, have a marvelous capacity to rationalize the world around them. They construct logical-sounding reasons to explain their failures, which serve the function of maintaining order out of chaotic situations.

How do we explain to a patron that we catalog Boston's Museum of Fine Arts under BOSTON. MUSEUM OF FINE ARTS—but New York's Guggenheim Museum under JOHN SOLOMON GUGGENHEIM MUSEUM, NEW YORK. In fact, the naive patron asks, why under John Solomon, which no one knows? Why not under Guggenheim, with a cross-reference the other way?

We all know that cross-references, though an absolute necessity and a wonderful invention, are too easily missed, especially when the mind is set to see half a drawer full of cards but the eye finds nothing. Or worse, when the library is living by two rules simultaneously—one for past cataloging and one for cataloging from now on—the patron gets to the point in the file where his/her card should be, but it isn't because it is in with the cards reflecting the other rule. The patron does not then think to look for a note either at the beginning of the file or at the end explaining the matter.

We won't even go into the problem of the user who has bad information. Such as the one who assumed without another thought that his citation *JAOS* was the abbreviation for *Journal of Asian and Oriental Studies*, and searched the catalog in vain. That's because the correct name is *Journal of the American Oriental Society*.

A most common problem and one of the toughest to solve is the choice of main entry. *Main entry* to us at UC Berkeley has several implications. It is the place where one finds the most complete information about the locations in our 22-branch library system that house the material. It is also the card that is filed first, with the added entries filed as soon as possible afterward—but that sometimes can mean quite a delay. Also, for two of our branches, and they are major ones, the central union catalog has *only* a main entry card.

So when the patron was holding a publisher's blurb that gave editors (David Like, Jr. and Martin A. Paul), title (*Critical Evaluation of Chemical and Physical Structural Information*), publisher (National Academy of Sciences), sponsoring organization (National Research Council), and suborganizations (Committee on Chemical Crystallography, Division of Chemistry and Chemical Technology)—and looked to no avail under all of these entries, he understandably concluded the library did not own the volume. You can imagine his thoughts as he shook his head when he discovered we had it. It was listed under CONFERENCE ON CRITICAL EVALUATION OF CHEMICAL AND PHYSICAL STRUCTURAL INFOR-MATION, DARTMOUTH COLLEGE, 1973.

Going back to the *University of California* problem I touched on earlier, I want to reraise it in connection with cross-references. As I implied, at UC Berkeley we are not yet cataloging according to the 1967 *AACR* rules that call for it to be listed under UNIVERSITY OF CALIFORNIA. But since we do have many entries under that form—for example, title entries, such as *University of California Magazine, University of California Notes to Schools and Colleges*—the patron looking for *University of California Publications in English Studies* was misled into thinking we did not have it. She found two cross-references, neither of which was specifically hers:

> *University of California Publications in Automatic Computation*
> See:
> CALIFORNIA. UNIVERSITY.
> *Publications in Automatic Computation*

and another card:

> *University of California Publications in Culture and Society*
> See:
> CALIFORNIA. UNIVERSITY.
> *University of California Publications in Culture and Society*

By giving these two examples, it was hoped that patrons would generalize about similar titles; in fact we know they do not.

Besides the BAKER service, another way our library has of learning about how our patrons use (or misuse) the catalog is through a suggestion box for patrons who have problems finding their subject heading—a practice followed in many libraries. In addition to prominently displayed signs inviting users to tell us their problems, on the suggestion box itself is a further note:

> When you can't find a subject listed in the catalog, please write down the terms and phrases under which you searched. The Catalog Department will consider using the information as a basis for making cross-references and information cards for the subject catalog. For example, PEOPLE'S PARK. See BERKELEY, CALIF.—RIOTS, 1969 or BERKELEY, CALIF.—PARKS.

Then answers to these problems are prepared by our Catalog Department and posted on a bulletin board which has become a popular stopping place for good reading material for both patrons and librarians. Let me cite a couple of examples from that bulletin board:

One patron wrote: "I couldn't find *The Delaware Indians, a History*, by C.A. Weslager. I looked under INDIANS OF NORTH AMERICA—DELAWARE." What was wrong? Our answer was, "The rule is to look under the most specific heading possible to begin with. Indians of North America is too general. The subject heading on this is DELAWARE INDIANS—HISTORY." So, the patron learns s/he was "too general."

Yet another patron was not general enough. "How do I find material about the California Water Project (a proper name)? I don't find it under that name." Our reply was: "You should look under the following: WATER RESOURCES DEVELOPMENT—CALIFORNIA; WATER SUPPLY—CALIFORNIA; (plus a good list of other possible headings)" and a note: "If the project is a specific one, like TVA, the proper name might be used in the subject catalog; otherwise you must look under the broader terms." In this case, then, the patron was too specific.

An example which shows different headings for the same subject reflecting changing language is the one where the user was looking for material under GAY LIBERATION MOVEMENT. We informed the patron: "This is a new subject heading and will be used for new books received. For books already in our collection, look under the subject heading HOMOSEXUALITY."

Obviously, I could go on with these examples, but I'd better move on to a discussion of ways of eliminating these problems. Before that, however, let us step back for a moment and look at the total picture from the user's point of view.

Users who experience these situations with any frequency might get the idea that librarians stay awake nights dreaming up ways to frustrate their efforts to find material in the library, thereby making us indispensable and guaranteeing our continued employment.

In fact, you and I know that is not the case. And when we have the opportunity to explain to patrons the reasons we do what we do, they not only become better library users, they understand and accept that our predicament is largely caused by factors external to the library—such as changing language and changing bibliographic data. This was surely the feeling of those faculty members at my campus who attended a series of in-depth seminars on How to Use the Library, offered last June and again in September and taught by us librarians. In their written evaluations of the sessions, they repeatedly remarked that they, who had considered themselves knowledgeable users of the library, were amazed at what they hadn't known.

In sum, I would not want you to get the idea from my examples that I am assigning any blame for the situation we are in. In point of fact, I am well aware that catalogers, as a group, resist with every cell in their bodies, any attempt to erode or degrade or compromise the catalog. Nor am I criticizing any rule per se. I hope I have shown that all rules, regardless of how good they are, can become bad. I also don't want to give the impression that my own catalog at UCB is fraught with irrationalities. On the contrary, I regard it as a remarkable and ingenious tool, and to the extent it is insufficient, it is only one example in a universal state of affairs.

Now, what about solutions? In a nutshell, I believe we must support all efforts to provide online computer access to bibliographic information. I think this for four major reasons:

First—and this is somewhat oversimplified, but I will qualify it shortly—there would no longer be a need for choosing a main entry.

Second, problems resulting from arbitrary filing rules could be eliminated.

Third, the library could respond to changes as they occur.

Fourth, cross-references would not have to be discoverd by the patron; they could be automatically displayed in response to a user's input.

About the main entry question. In a discussion about computerized cataloging, I admit to being baffled by any argument that we must have a main entry or we must not have a main entry. The concept of main entry implies the existence of a selection of added entries, all of which provide the user access points for finding a specific item or group of items. The question of which access points to provide is relevant in a card catalog, but not at all relevant (or at least shouldn't be) in a computerized version where the item is entered once, one way, as one record, but may be retrieved by any significant part or combination of parts.

The present systems for retrieving journal articles demonstrate this capability. To transpose, say, Lockheed's DIALOG system or that of the new literature search vendor, Bibliographic Retrieval Service (BRS), to our situation for the moment, I could enter *Roots* into my computerized catalog system, assuming I forgot the author's name, and the system might respond, ''There are 242 titles with the word *Roots* somewhere in them.'' I might then instruct the computer to arrange them in alphabetical order and display only those titles whose first word is *Roots*.

Up to this point the system is parallel to the card catalog. I can now browse through all of the items, which may be considerable if my *Roots* has a subtitle. Or I might save myself this effort by instructing the system to link *Roots* with *Kinte* or display only those *Roots* titles published in the U.S. from 1976 on, thereby narrowing the number of possibilities to perhaps one or two. At this point I'm ahead of the game with the computer. In other words, *main entry*, referring to one of several points of entry, becomes meaningless when talking about computer access.

I feel much less strongly that the choice of entry should reflect the seat of intellectual responsibility, except in a common sense way. For example, under consideration in the revised *AACR* code is the proposal that such material as the constitution of a country be entered under that country unless another jurisdiction wrote it (as Great Britain did for Canada in 1867). The overriding guideline in tough cases should be: If the material were accessible only one way—as in, say, a printed bibliography, which is the one the patron is most likely to use? If that cannot be determined, it hardly makes a difference which you use as main entry.

On the other hand, I am much more concerned about the form which one would use to look for people, places, organizations, etc. In my opinion, it is highly desirable to have consistency in form—almost any reasonable form would do—in order that we may be able to talk to one another, library to library, library to printed bibliography, reader to friend, thereby assuring that we are talking about the same item.

I appreciate the debates over *AACR* code revisions trying to come to some agreement about such matters as determinants of personal authorship vs. organizational authorship. These discussions contribute to the important job of formulating *standards for bibliographic representation*. The idea of *main entry* as *primary point of access* is a relevant consideration in card catalogs, book catalogs, and microform catalogs (in varying degrees). It is not an issue at all, or so little an issue it is not worth talking about, in online catalogs.

We need to be reminded that discussions about whether or not to have a standard form of entry originated out of considerations of cost. We couldn't afford to do everything we used to, so standardized entry would be one of the casualties in any budget squeeze. So, for example, if you wrote one book under your full name, and another using initials instead of your given name, and a third under a pseudonym, we could no longer afford to do the authority work required to inform the patron that all three are the same author. It was recognized to be a step backward in service.

Those who now say we don't need standards, or that it's a waste of time, remind me of those who say that high school education is no longer needed for all children. Many even benefit, so the argument goes, by not having it! Isn't it clear that such people are rationalizing an unfortunate economic situation?

Also, *main entry* meaning *the nucleus around which all forms of a work are associated* must not be abandoned. Whether for a card catalog or an online catalog, that will require judgment, intellectual effort—in other words, human intervention—to achieve. I am not convinced that we must insist on calling that nucleus *main entry* since *main entry* has meant so much else that could be abandoned. What must be insisted upon, however, is that the function of providing linkages be maintained. A computer is quite capable of accepting extra points of linkage not included in the information provided on the title page. It is we who must decide to do it.

On the second point of the computer's capacity to eliminate filing problems. Let's go back to the case of *Ask-Upmark*. Again drawing from an existing system, this time the New York Times Information Bank, we coud key in *Ask*, limited to authors only, and displayed before us would be a numbered list of all authors whose last names began *A-S-K*. We would then pick the one we wanted simply by keying in the associated number.

Or, another commercial service, Systems Development Corporation's (SDC) ORBIT, allows us to truncate words at the left. So we could get all the UPMARK authors, including those who have letters preceding the *U*. Or, we could ask to see all records with the word ASK adjacent to the word UPMARK.

On the third point, enabling the library to keep abreast of change, you should be aware that *by a system of authority control*, it is possible to make a particular change to all relevant records with just one computer instruction. I'd like to give as an example a subject heading I read about in Sanford Berman's wonderful, award-winning, *Hennepin County Library Cataloging Bulletin*. His library is using the subject heading CHILDREN'S LITERATURE, NONSEXIST in two ways: one applied to material on the subject of nonsexist books—about which I have no quarrel. The other serves as a kind of form heading, applied to material deemed by someone to meet nonsexist standards.

If I could convince Sandy that his library is wrong to use this heading in the latter way (it opens to door to labeling Oliver Twist as anti-Semitic or Huckleberry Finn as racist), he could rid the file of that subject heading by a simple *delete* instruction. At any rate, even if I couldn't convince him, he will want to eliminate it in the year 2080 when no more sexist books will be written and people are no longer interested in finding nonsexist books.

If we had such capability today, we could change so many headings that are bad—such as INDIANS OF NORTH AMERICA—ALCOHOL PROBLEM, and all of the others Sandy Berman has educated us so well about.

As for the fourth point about automatic cross-references, let me again draw from the Information Bank. When you enter the subject heading SCHOOL INTEGRATION into the Bank, you are informed that this heading is not one used in the data base; the system automatically displays a note such as: "For material on this subject conjoin EDUCATION and DISCRIMINATION and SCHOOL BUS-SING [not the actual note]."

In other cases it might automatically place you in the correct portion of the file. So, for example, a user keying in MARK TWAIN could automatically be placed in the SAMUEL CLEMENS portion of the file.

Still another possibility which most of these systems provide is notification that there are cross-references, related terms, broader terms, narrower terms, or scope notes (STREET PEOPLE: This term covers material published since 1974; for previously published material use ALTERNATIVE LIFE STYLES) — all available to look at if you wish—the choice is yours.

For the record I must state that this new technology does not come without problems of its own—some correctable, some not, or at least not easily. One big shortcoming, for example, which must be worked on is the special language and grammar one needs to know to properly manipulate the systems. That will have to be changed to be more *conversational* and to require less training than is now needed.

Another problem stems from the requirement that the user know how to type to be able to look something up. No doubt staff will be available to help, as they are now. Of course, no computer system can do anything about the problem of insufficient information in the data base, as in the example I discussed earlier of the series *Advances in Experimental Social Psychology*, where a volume suddenly appears with a unique title. Somewhere along the line a human being has to enter the new or changed information into the data base. Also, I am not convinced that drudge work for library staff will have been eliminated. There is some evidence already that the computer may be replacing one kind of drudgery with another.

However, the benefits are clear: Through the use of computer technology we have the capability to (1) provide more access points, (2) provide simultaneously combined access points according to the *user's* choices (e.g., "I want everything on Brazil having to do with Electronic Calculators, published after 1973"), (3) change terminology throughout the files with ease according to today's needs, and (4) provide links to different versions of a work in ways unthinkable before.

This could come about not by each library going it alone, but by a national effort directed by a national library system. The Library of Congress (LC) makes a valiant and remarkable attempt at responding to pressures that it be that national library, but it doesn't fit the bill—nor does it have the mandate to do so. As reliable and energetic a source as it is, it does not have the governing structure of a national library.

I would accept as a beginning—but only as a beginning—the views expressed by John Knapp and others at the ISAD Institute in Chicago last February that a future online catalog could be the sum of all the local network holdings records. That is, begin with what we have now: several networks developing (Research Libraries Group, BALLOTS users, OCLC [Ohio College Library Center] users, LC) with the aim of working out one national uniform set of standards for format and representation of the records, and other standards for retrieval of those records. The input standards would be the same nationwide; the retrieval standards may differ depending on the kind of library retrieving. Or there may be one set of retrieval standards with a variety of options for retrieving depending on how much of a record the user wants to see.

This is an important distinction to make: input standards vs. retrieval standards. Cast in this light, it would be possible once standards were set, to assign categories of input to libraries across the country, thereby sharing that part of the burden to the point that each library could be cataloging far less of the nationally available material than it is now.

Rather than catalog departments going out of business, they could turn their attention once again to cataloging special local materials, eating away at storerooms of uncataloged materials, and making their collections as a whole more responsive to their local constituency. In fact, I believe that in order to do proper, user-oriented cataloging, the distinctions between catalogers and reference workers may well disappear. Catalogers would and should do reference work, and reference workers would and should do cataloging.

Also, in planning for national, user-oriented computer-based cataloging, it is imperative that all reasonable bibliographic information be entered into the record. Thus, the proposed *AACR* rule that governmental agencies as author entries not necessarily include the parent organization is a bad one. It would not allow a patron who knew, say, the subject of the publication and the primary agency (e.g., HEW), but not which of the many subdivisions of that agency issued the publication, to combine terms with success. Remember, the system can respond positively only if the data are entered to begin with. In preparation for computerization, let us not toss out old standards that were good.

I would reject any argument that called for less input because of costs. We must view the use of computer technology not merely as a substitute for what we are having trouble doing now, or certainly not as a way of saving money, but as a means to provide better access by the user. In many ways, as we have seen, the new technology frees us from the limitations of the old technology. It allows us to think about our libraries not just as buildings that house materials for a particular type of clientele or our catalogs as a tool to analyze a particular collection, but also allows us—with the help of devices such as telefacsimile machines, or fast delivery systems such as UPS—to see our libraries as nodes in a national network of resource libraries and our catalogs as providing access to those nodes.

If such a national system could be accomplished, I think we would see a blurring of the differences between the public library user and the research library user. That is, for a public library patron who wants more than a good mystery story or more than the best popular treatment of the subject of the DNA controversy, the *more* is accessible.

I want to end with a further word about costs. I'm hearing more and more: "Aren't we coming to the day when the costs are so great we will have to pass them on to the user?" As I said earlier, converting to online catalog access should not be viewed as a way of saving money but rather as a way of providing better access to the user. Providing better access is our job. That's our profession. That is what we are in business to do. I join with those who see the solution to the high costs as lying in a national library system, government subsidized, and tax supported.

To those of you who think that goal is unwinnable or that the costs are still too great, I must ask, "compared to what?" Where does the cost of a national, online bibliographic retrieval system line up compared to, say, the $4 million it takes the State of California to provide a mathematics textbook to the fourth grade children of California. As expensive? As important? More expensive? How much more expensive? As much as it costs to build a B-1 bomber? As important?

It may take a lot of our energies to realign the values of those making decisions on a national level, to remind them that public libraries and publicly-supported libraries (such as my land-grant school) were founded on the fundamental principle that free access to information is a prerequisite to a democratic society.

In 20 or 30 years it should be possible to see a terminal in everyone's home by their telephones with the capability of accessing the library—your library, my library, a national library system. We must reject all attempts to introduce user fees to access these online catalogs, just as we must work against user fees in relation to journal article search systems. We must be a vocal, vigorous force to use this marvelous technology not to limit access to information to those who can pay, but to provide access to anyone who needs it.

DISCUSSION

Paul Fasana: I guess Ms. Lipow should be admired for coming into the lion's den and baiting it, but I find some of her arguments facile and superficial. I don't mean to talk against what she is intending to convey but simply against some of the points that she's made. Let me begin with the catalog.

The catalog is a very complex tool; therefore, it requires study. Since it requires a great deal of effort to construct, we should require, perhaps, that reference librarians know as much about it. I recently had the unfortunate privilege of having to add several public service librarians because of cutbacks in the library. They came into cataloging and began to learn about cataloging and catalogs. Several had worked in public service for a number of years. I spoke with one of them one day, and he admitted that he was rather overwhelmed by the fact that the catalog was as rich and subtle as it was. This reference librarian had worked for a number of years without bothering to learn one of the main tools that he was using. I would suggest that in addition to sending catalogers out to the public service desk we might send reference librarians into the catalog room to learn what's going on.

I would also suggest that looking to the computer is too simple. The panacea isn't really there. If you go to the computer you have problems such as, what do you do with the retrospective information not in the computer? You inevitably come to the conclusion that you can't convert all of the retrospective bibliographic data. Therefore, you end up with systems where you have retrospective and prospective information. Looking, however, to what Ms. Lipow referred to as online, and assuming that you are getting over the problem of retrospective and prospective, is it really fair to compare indexing services to catalogs? Because Ms. Lipow was comparing some very facile and very good functions in an indexing environment where every word can be indexed. However, I would submit that perhaps the catalog, at least traditionally, has had certain other functions. I think it was Panizzi who said a function of the catalog is to reflect the total resources available from a collection or library, not simply to retrieve a single instance of an item. We should look at this problem more carefully. The computer can search rapidly. It can retrieve a record that perhaps will have the term that you're looking for, but is this in fact the same as getting all of the particular manifestations of a particular work? I would suggest that we shouldn't lose track of a tool that reflects the resources of our libraries, nor the fact that this is an essential function of the catalog.

Anne Lipow: Are you saying that before we can go to online cataloging we've got a lot of studies to do? There are many of them going on already regarding online cataloging. It's not an academic problem; it's not a problem for ten years down the road; it's a problem that people are struggling with now. The computer has demonstrated its capability to serve us and we want it to be super-responsive to our needs.

As regards standards, we don't want to let one person or two people or five people tell us what to do; we want to participate in the standards. I want to be sure

Mr. Fasana is there representing me when the discussions about those standards are taking place. I also want to be sure that Mr. Lubetzky is there representing me.

Getting back to studies, I don't know what you mean by study, but I'm leery of stalls in the name of study. We've gone beyond that point. I'm also against blindly going ahead. I'm for knowing what we're doing, and I think we know a lot more than we think we know.

Are you also saying that before a user can go on to use this new technology he'd better learn the old system first and how to get through the old catalog? I don't understand that. I am not for having to learn how to use the horse and buggy before you can use a car. We've gone beyond the horse and buggy.

I absolutely agree with you that catalogers should do reference work. The distinction between reference workers and catalogers is going to blur. Catalogers must do reference work and reference workers must do cataloging; no question about that. To know how your cataloging and the catalog is being used is essential. To do good reference work, one must know how to catalog—it is absolutely essential. They are twin sides of one coin and I didn't mean to separate them.

Edwin Buchinski: It seems that "manifestation of the work" has been used time and time again. There is also much concern for main entry. I'm not scared of the computer, nor do I believe *AACR* has done any injustice to traditional cataloging practice. I think that what the library has done in the past, and what is being talked about for the future, can be input into the machine and nothing will necessarily have to be sacrificed. At least where I am, we're talking about linking one record to another, various manifestations of the work. Some people wish to retain main entry and others title-unit entry, while still others talk about this as the identification of an item. I don't believe that any of this is being sacrificed.

I was very impressed with our last speaker's sincere call for standards. I share her feelings that we do know a lot and we can proceed. Maybe what is not required immediately is a huge financial scheme or all kinds of studies before taking initial steps. Some models could be built to test our theories. Perhaps when there is a model, the people that have reservations could better explain what the reservations are, so that the people designing the systems will not overlook important considerations.

In dealing with costs, I might point out that probably there is one other factor that was overlooked. That is the compensation for the author, which was an important aspect previously raised by Dr. Richmond.

Seymour Lubetzky: The point that I'm concerned with is the distinction between the computerized catalog and the visible catalog with regard to the main entry. That's where we disagree for the simple reason that the question is not how one looks for, and how one has to find things in a book catalog, or even how a manual catalog is different from a computerized catalog. I understand that in the computerized catalog you can do many things that make it easier to find what you want. Then you go on to speak about the approach of the user and whether it makes a difference to him or her whether you call the record a main entry or another entry. I think you missed the point that I tried to clarify yesterday. The point is not what the user asks for that you want to help him with, but what it is that the main entry helps you to find. If you do not use a main entry in the computerized catalog you will not find what you find now in the book catalog; there's no difference in that.

Lipow: Give me an example.

Lubetzky: Washington's *Farewell Address* was published under a number of titles ranging from *A* to *T*. Even those that have used the title *Farewell Address* have used it in variations such as *George Washington's Farewell Address* (under *G*), *Farewell Address* (under *F*), and *Washington's Farewell Address* (under *W*). If you look at the Library of Congress catalog or the *National Union Catalog (NUC)*, you might find another publication and you will never know whether it is or is not Washington's *Farewell Address*. Each edition has to be related in some way to all others. The main entry serves not only to relate editions of a work that appear under different titles, it also relates those works that have appeared under different names of the same author. What you are going to do with the computer is to provide another method for accomplishing this. You can call the author *X* and you can call the title *Y* and you can call a particular work *Z* to bring it together. That to me is not a question of abolishing or dismissing the main entry. That to me is not a question of needing a main entry or not needing one. You have it there—it's just in another form.

Judith Hopkins: I agree wholeheartedly with Ms. Lipow on the idea of the need for reference librarians to know cataloging, and catalogers to know reference. I had the good fortune as a beginning cataloger to work part time in the reference department. I try to teach my students that they're going to be the best users of the reference department that the library has.

As for the question of main entry, I think we're hung up on the terminology. We can think of it in terms of a citation entry. Let us just say, for example, we are looking not for a text of *Roots* but for a book about it, some hypothetical work entitled *Haley's Book and the Growth of Interest in Genealogy*. The word *roots* never appears in this title and you have given the assumption that one couldn't remember that Alex Haley wrote *Roots*. Unless we have a citation heading HALEY, ALEX—*Roots*, we cannot find this book. That is the equivalent of a main entry used as a citation. One other example is *The Life and Novels of Victoria Holt*. What is the subject heading going to be? That particular pseudonym? Her real name?

Lipow: I think that not being a cataloger is my real problem. I came into this discussion having used a system that doesn't talk about headings in the same way. Most of these computerized systems would assign Haley's *Roots* to the hypothetical title under something called an identifer, or a descriptor or a field. Whether it's a main entry field or not, let's just call it a field.

Marie Griffin: I'd like to support Ms. Lipow to the extent that when we consider an entry we consider it in the form of a catalog card that's three inches by five inches, and when we think of a record in a machine we have to think of access points. Maybe the two are not the same. When we input the author into the computer, for example, why do we have to repeat it? The printing of the material in the computer can be handled by a print program. The print program can put in the *ISBD* when you want to mail it someplace. For the computer itself what you need are the access points. You don't need to list in the notes all the performers—I'm used to doing sound recordings—and then list them again as points of access. All that really has to be listed in the computer is all the performers or all the authors of one work. If there are four authors to one work, you wouldn't have to list in the computer this work by A, B, C and D authors. All you'd have to list in the computer are all the authors and titles. Link them up and then you could find them under any one of those places. If we begin to think about the new technology as different from the three-by-five card perhaps then we can have some meeting of the minds. The computer points of access are essential, because we're going to have some kind of formatting of those points of access.

If we agree on standardization—to which I say "cheers"—then this problem of standardization plus authority will eliminate the question of pseudonyms. If you look for CHAN, CHARLIE and the cataloger who entered the material into the computer has made a reference that says "CHAN, CHARLES, Musician, see PARKER, CHARLIE," you're in. But if all you get in a card catalog or in a computerized catalog is CHAN, CHARLIE and nothing except one record, you're lost.

Unidentified Speaker: How do we get from here to there? That's my first question. My second question is: What sort of obstacles, such as financial and political, do you see in achieving total online access?

Lipow: On the first question, about transition, I don't think we've reached this point yet. If we can regard the card catalog as a tool that has been terrific and one about which our grandchildren going to the Smithsonian Institution will say, "That's what my grandmother used in the olden days," then we're on our way to letting it die with dignity. I feel that's what we have to do; let it die with dignity, and not keep patching it up with money and people. If we look at it that way we can pour reference personnel into helping with troubles with the catalog for a transitional period.

On the question about the obstacles, if we run into what we've run into here, you can multiply that by a factor of ten and you'll begin to understand.

Buchinski: I left out something which may be an item of information, and the documents that I'm going to refer to prove useful in calming all of us down a little. I believe we are all very familiar with what I'm going to call the *Anglo MARC format*. To a large extent it reflects three-by-five cards in a machine form based on cataloging rules that haven't given up the main entry. I would like to refer you to the German MARC format. They've done something very different, and if you could get a look at that format you will see that there is an attempt at analyzing access points. There is another major departure from the Anglo-MARC format, and that's an attempt to analyze the relationship of different works. I believe Ms Lipow referred to the series problem and linking it to a particular work. If you look at the structure in the MARBI (Representation in Machine-Readable Form of Bibliographic Information) format, the series has a separate record and is linked to separate descriptions for particular monographs. There are all kinds of ways of looking at the complete collection with the information that you have in store. This is just something that people may be interested in looking at as further study.

Eleanor Crarey: I'm very struck by the networking implications of Ms. Lipow's speech. I'd like to recall again what she's saying about the difference between input and retrieval standards. This is something I hope we will really keep in mind as we look at *AACR2* and the standards for networking. This is something that sometimes we had some confusion on. I see that there is also this suggestion about the catalogers being able to spend their time working on materials that are endemic to their own situations; I'm struck by the fact that as you expand your interlibrary loan you do discover pretty important things buried in some public library, in a small town somewhere; this is the sort of thing that public libraries should be contributing at the full standard that makes it accessible to any library anywhere.

Lipow: Thanks very much. I just wanted to say that in the journal retrieval systems, the retrieval works by having one of six or seven or eight standards depending on what you, the user, want; if you want everything, you use format 5 in Lockheed, and if you want very little, you use format 2; you get a list of titles. So that is a system where the retrieval depends on the user and not what library the user is in.

Fasana: After such an inspiring speech I'm reluctant to get up and say anything. However, I would like to take a few cracks at Ms. Lipow. I find her enthusiasm very encouraging. I find, however, that her ideal world isn't the world that I know. I come from a private institution supported by an endowment. Therefore, I find it interesting that she would claim that there should be public support for this, and free access. There is free access at the New York Public Library, but the federal government has not very willingly come forth with help to provide the support that's needed by many of the major research libraries in the nation today.

What I would really like to fault her on is not her views on the role of the federal government but on her simplistic view of the online catalog. The computer can offer some wonderful capabilities. They are not magical, however, and I frequently had the feeling that Ms. Lipow was confusing magical qualities and computer functions. The computer is very fast, but it's speed is degraded as you increase the size of its storage. Therefore, eventually, you have things working against each other. More access points greatly increase the amount of storage needed, and eventually, it greatly decreases the speed. The search capability is quite powerful and quite wonderful, but it's based on precise character matching. If you miss a key, you are not going to be able to find things that easily in the computer.

As for the complex and wonderful sort of Boolean search you described, I would point out to you that it is based on a very complex and costly input analysis and keying. The computer by itself doesn't sort, analyze, and set up data in nice little compartments that allow you to look at Boolean features, such as date of publication, language of publication, etc. All of these elements have to be analyzed before they're put into the computer, so that the computer can understand them.

Finally, I'd like to comment on the ability to change items in the computer. Granted the seemingly simple-minded examples that have been used, such as changing NEGROES to AFRO-AMERICANS and BLACKS, appear fairly straightforward. Changing from one concept to a mixed concept requires that you review every item in the store of the computer and make a decision. Catalogers tend to call it recataloging.

If you're complaining that we haven't been able to keep up necessarily with the world output in terms of cataloging, your view of the future perhaps will give us more work to do, more recataloging. The computer can be a great boon to cataloging, but I don't think that we should rush at it in an overly simplistic way. I think your attitude tends toward that overly simplistic view.

Lipow: I think that what I was trying to say was that some of our problems have already been solved. I don't think they were solved in a simplistic way. I drew on examples that we're using now, systems that are working, that are constantly changing, that are full of problems such as journal retrieval search systems. How they developed, I'm sure, was not simplistically, and I know that how we develop them further will not be simple. If I gave the impression that I thought it was easy, I want to correct that. It will not be easy. It will be at least as difficult as it would be to correct the situation we are living with now. If Mr. Fasana can give me a formula for keeping alive the card catalog that would solve the problems that we are trying to solve, not the least of which are the changes that need to be made, I will be very happy to listen to him. I think everybody is here because they are confronting problems with their card catalogs that are unsolvable within our budgets today. We cannot solve them, all of the changes that need to be made, all of the added entries that need to be made. For instance, to make the kind of entries that Mr. Berman suggests, such as making *Erroneous Zone* an added title entry for *Your Erroneous Zones*; making second word entries for all the possibilities—I think that can be done. We could employ all of the unemployed people of the world to do that, and if that's what Mr. Fasana has in mind and that's a realistic solution, that may be a better one.

A lot of us are living with computerized systems right now. We have here a decent enough percentage of OCLC and BALLOTS users. Although these systems are having certain troubles, *turn back* would be a bad message. We cannot turn back and those who have not yet come on to these systems are certainly thinking hard about it and are planning one way or another to improve them.

Unidentified Speaker: I think the use of the computer for cataloging is a fantastic idea. I know that if someone had asked me a year and a half ago, before we used the computer, what I thought of this, I probably would have fought it. Now I'm delighted that we're using it, but it has brought many problems which have not been solved. The thing that I'm angry with is that I see OCLC—I'm sorry for using OCLC, but it's the only system I know—expanding by leaps and bounds and at the same time we who use OCLC aren't getting trained as we should be trained. You have records in the system that you cannot retrieve. My point is that before everybody enters into the computer world, someone, please, help us clean up what already exists.

Michael Malinconico: I frankly confess to being bewildered by questions related to main entry and the computerized environment. Nonetheless, perhaps I might solicit an opinion from you. Are you sanguine that an online, interactive catalog in the foreseeable future will achieve a level of sophistication where the end result of a search will be one or two unambiguous responses? Or if you don't believe that, what would you do in the case where a significant number of choices are returned, and you fail to make a choice of main entry, that is, you fail to give a name to the works that are returned? How do you propose to organize them for the user, on a cathode-ray tube or on a print-out? Also, are you convinced that library users are always interested in a particular title or a particular work? Are they not perhaps on occasion concerned with getting a sequence which they might want to review? How would you sequence that list? If you have not given a name to the work, you have not chosen a main entry.

Lipow: I have to take a live example and again draw from systems I know. Let us say that there are 562 editions of *Aesop's Fables* in my library; some have *Aesop's Fables* in the title; some begin *Aesop's Fables;* some say *Fables of Aesop;* some say other things. Some don't even say anything in the title about Aesop. Let's call one *Legends of One Man's Time.* No *fable*, no *Aesop.* All are edited by different people.

Depending upon the user's need, if I know of a recently published *Aesop's Fables*, let us say by Harold Brown, I would go into my system and combine *Harold Brown* as an author field and *Aesop* as a title field and hopefully come up with one hit, or two hits, or five hits. In my good system it will say, "By the way, there are also a lot of other editions of *Aesop's Fables* and to see those enter number 27452." That means that somebody has to tag it along the way as *Aesop's Fables*. Now you take Thurber's *Fables of Modern Times*. That's only tangentially related to *Aesop's Fables*, but a cataloger may want to direct people to that by using a field that might be called an identifier, relator or descriptor—not main entry. This would show it's relationship to *Aesop's Fables* so that anybody wanting everything related to *Aesop's Fables* could do that.

How do I want it displayed? Display it anyway you want. I can have many display options: alphabetically by titles, alphabetically by author, alphabetically by editor, chronologically, and if the prices were in there I could even do it by price, I suppose. But in this case, if I had a bunch of Browns and Aesops, maybe I'd want to display all 1976s. Am I getting anywhere near your question concerning the problem of displaying or sequencing?

Malinconico: The problem is not with displaying. As near as I can make out from your response you are saying that there will be only one, two, five or six hits in the end. Which author?

Lipow: Well, what do you do now in the author-title catalog if you go into *Aesop's Fables*? The problem would be no different. If you don't know what you want and your field is 5,000 records, you're going to have to figure out how to narrow it in a card catalog. You go to the subject catalog under POLITICAL CORRUPTION or CORRUPTION—POLITICAL, and now-a-days that's a very large file. You have to decide how you want to deal with that. In the card catalog you'll find only one way, the author. I may want a different way and I have that option to exclude all books on Watergate. I may be sick of Watergate. I have the capability in Boolean logic of using the operator *not* to eliminate what I don't want.

The Library of Congress as the National Bibliographic Service

by Joseph H. Howard

Recently, the Library of Congress (LC) received a letter addressed to a *Miss Libby O. Congress*. We opened the envelope to read in it a letter that started with a salutation to "Dear Miss Congress" and went on for two pages to tell in extensive detail just why she should resubscribe to a particular serial. The most beautiful part of the letter was the personalized directive at the bottom of the first page. The words read: "Please turn over, Miss Congress."

Well, to my knowledge, Congress has not turned over. Miss Libby O. Congress may turn over slowly sometimes; in fact, I know from the frequent comments on the speed of our cataloging that we can turn very slowly indeed. Nevertheless, we occasionally feel that we are sometimes turning *faster* than we think we should in our efforts to serve as a *national library*.

Our library patrons need access to enormous amounts of material, and although we at LC may be improving in providing access to this material, we still have far to go. There is no one institution, in my estimation, that can provide all the bibliographic coverage needed by our patrons; certainly LC can't, although we catalog some 235,000 titles a year. Unfortunately, that is no more than the tip of the iceberg.

We are, however, living in very exciting times that provide us with the opportunity and the means to reconsider some of our present ways of doing things. We have the tremendous advantage of technological advances that help us to control and manipulate our bibliographic information. It is up to us to make sure that we use them wisely. We must, for example, be concerned not only with the publishing explosion, but with severe strains on our budgets. To use our money wisely we must do more than take advantage of the availability of these technological advances. We must also—and this is my very strong conviction—work together in cooperative efforts to control this material.

At present, we at the Library of Congress do very badly in covering certain types of materials, for example, government documents—local, county, state, national, and international. Nor do we cover microforms as we should. We don't catalog enough audiovisual materials—sound recordings, films—or a great number of other materials that librarians need to work with. I will outline what we are planning and try to support my conviction that if we are to cover all that material we need your input, your suggestions, your creative thinking in this venture so that we do things once and do them right.

Let me start with a brief review of past and current efforts at the Library of Congress. One of these, the cooperative cataloging program in which librarians cooperated by sending copy to the Library of Congress, was a good program, but it was not true cooperation. Moreover, it was enormously expensive. Thus the program was discontinued about 1967. I remember that date because I was the one to finally kill it.

In the meantime, we had taken a great step in cooperative cataloging in 1965 with the shared cataloging effort. This is a program whereby we share the descriptive part of the cataloging with other foreign libraries after having studied their bibliographies and so forth. As an example of the kinds of accord we arrived at: We agreed to accept and to share the description provided cooperatively by catalogers, expert in their native languages, at such great foreign libraries as the Bibliotheque National, The British Library, the German National Library, and so forth. This program of foreign and American cooperation was a great step forward. One of the most significant steps that we have made in cooperative cataloging is our present CONSER (Conversion of Serials) program, an online system with enormous potential. Although the data base that is to be created through CONSER will itself be quite remarkable, the spirit in which that program was conceived and the methods developed through our present coperative efforts have even more significance than the data base because they constitute a system on which we can build, working out whatever agreements and disagreements may arise as we proceed.

To take an example from the descriptive portion of the catalog entry: For the first time we at the Library of Congress and other participants have accepted each other's descriptions. We have suddenly decided that Cornell's descriptive cataloging is acceptable for needs throughout the country. All the participants have made a commitment to follow standards.

However, accepting *descriptions* from American libraries and from the National Library of Canada was only a first step, albeit a major step. The next big step was to accept the *choice of entry* of the participating libraries. Sophisticated catalogers will understand how radical a decision this was. Catalogers who use the existing Rule 6 know that the serials rule for entry is such a problem that no one can determine who's right and who's wrong. We in this project recognize that intelligent people can derive different solutions for choice of entry, and we have decided that whoever gets in first determines the choice. The rules, of course, are followed, but in cases of doubt the participant's choice of entry is the one that everyone else follows. Thus, accepting other people's choice of entry was our second major step.

The third major step has been to accept the National Library of Canada's form. Form of entry can be accepted for Canadian corporate names only if the authority files of the National Library of Canada are available. We do get such copies periodically from the National Library of Canada and we are always interacting with that file. Remember, too, that the ability to accept other people's form of entry depends on our interacting with a file so that we know what's going on. With that in mind, CONSER established certain agreements on subject classification and subject headings. This agreement is described in the *Cataloging Service Bulletin* 115 (Fall 1975).

Having reviewed LC's progress to date in cooperative cataloging, I would like to hypothesize on a way in which we may cooperate further. We are not ready for it yet, but we are getting closer every day. Before any such venture can begin we will have to assume what I have been stressing all along—that the Library of

Congress is online to other libraries. Not directly to every library in the U.S., of course, but available to and through networks to those who agree to accept bibliographic conventions, standards, etc. One of the provisos is that we will be online to certain other libraries in a cooperative cataloging arrangement. We need to assume (in fact, it is essential) that our name and subject authorities are also online and interactive with the bibliographic records—very much in the way Mr. Gorman previously outlined. The CONSER agreements, although not published, are available through the representative libraries and should be studied with a view to understanding the concept and significance of a bibliographic convention.

To illustrate the importance of these conventions, let me say that the University of Arizona, for example, has received an Arizona document. It queries the data base online and if by some miracle LC has already cataloged it they accept our form, adding their location or whatever local information they need that we have not provided. Basically, the accord or mutual trust means that they accept the LC record without change, though perhaps with additions. If, however, in its normal activities the Library of Congress has *not* yet cataloged the document, the University of Arizona, following the bibliographic conventions that we have agreed upon, will provide the description that *we* at the Library of Congress will accept and you, we hope, will also accept. They will provide the choice of entry and also the form of entry, if it is in the name authority file. If they have our form of name online, they can then follow that form of name at the time. If that name, however, is not in the data base, which is very likely even in this hypothetical case, there is a great deal of work still to be done. The University of Arizona will provide the input. That is, it will decide what the form of name for that body should be, provide its references, and then perhaps query or send a surrogate to the Library of Congress to validate and confirm that this indeed is the form, a process called *authentication*. Once it is locked in, that form will be used by everyone for that heading on Arizona documents. The same procedure will hold for any other headings established by the University of Arizona, in this hypothetical case, or by any other cooperating library.

We are now trying to work out ways in which to cooperate on choice of form. We are hoping to work out arrangements to accept input from libraries that follow or agree to accept LC classification. They would accept, perhaps not the Cutter, but certainly the basic class number and the Dewey number if we agreed to follow the same edition and the same rules. The same thing can be done for LC subject headings.

The example I have just described provides a major and very exciting indication of what we can do. Let's now go a little further to clarify the way LC sees its role in this. When we get the above-mentioned Arizona document, we will accept that quality record for description, for choice of entry, and for form of entry if the form has already been established. If it has not been established, we may want to work with the University of Arizona to ensure that when it establishes a form of name we will be able to use it too. What I've outlined for LC would, I hope, also be true for your library—that is, you would accept the University of Arizona's cataloging on the basis of conventions that ensure quality standards.

I would now like to review a few tasks that we have undertaken and are working on and to outline some new projects. This is in no way meant to be a comprehensive survey, either of what is being done or what needs to be done.

First, we need to get all our cataloging in machine-readable form. We must be sure that our name authorities are in machine-readable form, at least for all those names in the various MARC (Machine-Readable Cataloging) bibliographic data bases, and that those forms are interactive with bibliographic records. The same is true of the subject authorities. We need a national and international system for online cooperative cataloging, including the agreed upon bibliographic conventions ensuring quality control. We must also guarantee continued assistance to those libraries without access to online systems. For instance, we must continue our *National Union Catalog (NUC)* reporting, but for those without access to a machine input, we would hope that LC could take on the task of inputting for them. We do this manually now and we hope to be able to expand that operation to machine-readable records. The same holds true for serial titles. We need to distribute all this online or ontape bibliographic information, on top of our other services. We are not discontinuing our card service or the *National Union Catalog*, but we need to be able to produce our books and catalogs entirely by automated methods and provide these additional services.

Those are a few of our current projects or—in a very literal sense—projected efforts. Speaking more practically, where are we now with these projects? For the past several years, we have put into machine-readable form all of our map cataloging, our audiovisual cataloging, and our serial cataloging. In those three data bases, all languages are represented, and the nonroman alphabets are romanized. If a Russian serial is in the data base, it is in romanized form only. We also have put all our LC subject headings into machine-readable form. In January, 1978, we expanded our language coverage for monographs, so that all roman alphabet langauges are being put into machine-readable form. We have begun to put most of our name authorities into machine-readable form. We still lack MARC in areas such as music and phonorecords and all nonroman alphabet languages.

RETROSPECTIVE CATALOGING

So far I have been discussing current cataloging only. You realize that there are still millions of titles we have cataloged over the years that will not be in machine-readable form for a while. However, you are perhaps aware of the COMARC program through which certain libraries take LC records that have not been input in MARC and key them. We have been taking those tapes, validating them, and updating them from our official catalog. We are now making that information available. The continuation of that project will depend on the results of a report in midsummer.

That is one effort at retrospective cataloging. We have another possibility that is exciting, though still tenuous. Ten or fifteen years ago the Library of Congress, through Henriette Avram's office, sent out a deck of LC catalog cards to an OCR (Optical Character Recogniton) company—a company that has machines which can read certain records optically. We sent the deck out to see if the machines could read our catalog cards, which would then be automatically put into machine-readable form. The results were disappointing. The machines were capable of doing certain things, but there were so many mistakes that it would have been easier to start all over again than to correct the errors. Recently, another OCR company has maintained—and correctly, we think—that great strides have been made in the capacity to read records optically and put them into machine-readable form. We sent another deck of cards recently but, unfortunately, sent the instructions much later so that the results are not yet available. If, however, the various type fonts that we have had throughout the years can be read optically and put into machine-readable form, we can make great strides in working on our retrospective cataloging. A great deal of human intervention will still be necessary in the cataloging process, even with a format recognition program. Throughout its history, the Library of Congress has used various cataloging rules—*AACR1, ALA,* etc.—and format recognition programs do not recognize all the differences. Thus, after we run our cards through the format recognition programs, there will still be many corrections to make at immense cost.

I'd like to discuss name authorities in slightly greater detail and describe our progress in that area, because name authorities are vital in maintaining a data base with quality controls. Beginning in April, 1978, the Library of Congress began the input in machine-readable form of all the names originating in certain cataloging sections. We are still in the testing period but should be distributing the names in machine-readable form in the future. A record will include the personal and corporate names, as well as uniform headings and uniform titles, plus all the references that we would assign to that heading. Moreover, each heading and reference will be tagged for the rules used. The Library of Congress will have to rethink each heading to determine whether it was an *ALA* heading, an *AACR* heading, and if it is an *ALA* heading, the catalogers will have to provide the *AACR* form as well. The same procedure will also have to apply to *AACR* if there are major problems and if we do not adopt superimposition, which we hope not to do. The process, however, will make it possible when we close our catalogs to desuperimpose from *ALA* to *AACR* by machine. That is a highly oversimplified statement, of course; much more than punching a button will be involved. However, one of the things that will make it possible to desuperimpose will be the tagging of the name authority to identify it as *AACR* or *ALA*. In addition to the heading, the references, and these tags, the sources used to find that heading will also be identified, at least at first. If Congress does not move as fast as we would like, we may have to rethink the process.

What is the schedule for input? Our first schedule will be to input all new headings in all languages. We hope to phase this in first with all new headings that come up for the new books that we catalog. The next schedule will be for all old headings related to new books being cataloged. This is something we hope to do within two years, but that again is a most provisional and perhaps ambitious projection. We then need to have in the name authority file all headings that have already been used in any MARC bibliographic data base. Our estimation is that we have 845,000 nonunique names in the MARC data base. We don't expect to be able to perform that input without help, but we plan to apply for grant support for that purpose. That project needs to be completed by 1980 when the rest of our cataloging is expected to be in machine-readable form, providing things go well. One exciting grant request that we have made—mentioned by Bernadine Hoduski earlier during this conference—is for a cooperative effort between the Government Printing Office (GPO) and the Library of Congress to start building the name authority data base. The series authority file, however, is a problem not yet covered by the name authority project.

On the international front, we have started to work out cooperative efforts with the National Library of Australia, the National Library of Canada, the British Library, and the Library of Congress. (The minutes of those meetings were published in the *Library of Congress Information Bulletin (LCIB)* for April 8, 1977.) The intent of everything we do with these national libraries is to work closely with them so that their machine-readable cataloging can be part of LC's system, and so that the cataloging data generated by the shared cataloging program can be used with as little human intervention as possible. This would release some of LC's catalogers to catalog other important materials like the documents mentioned earlier. We have started first with the Anglo-American libraries, whose rules most resemble ours, but we are also working most fruitfully with other national libraries and appreciate their work and cooperation. We are trying to arrange it so that when a British or Canadian or Australian book comes into our library, we will have it online and will be able to catalog it with as little human intervention as possible. The procedure will help you by freeing us to catalog other materials. These four national libraries have also concurred on the matter of fullness of personal name. We have agreed to provide the form of name as the rules require and to take the option of adding, in separate fields, the fuller form of the name and anything else we can do. But we have done that only with the criterion of reasonable search.

I would like to discuss briefly what we call the register index formats for book catalogs. We are working on the idea and plan to publicize what LC sees as the probable developments in its book catalog program over the next few years, so that the library community can study and comment on them. An announcement should have been made by the time these words are published so that we will all have several years to work out the details.

LC's intention to move toward a register index was announced in the *LCIB* on June 27, 1976. We all recognize that the *National Union Catalog* is a fantastically helpful publication. We also know that it could be much better still.

When we have everything in machine-readable form, we plan to publish a register that will be a numerical listing of all the cards we produce, much like what we produce now except that it will not be an alphabetical arrangement but arranged by number. The index will consist of access points by all main or added entries. You will go to the index and find out what the main entry is, but you will also know a lot more from each access point. It won't be an index saying, "see the register." It will be an index that tells you the call number, the card number, and enough brief information, we hope, to take care of at least 80 percent of our patrons' needs through the index alone. We have not yet defined the elements in that index and will need your help on that. We will be able to do many marvelous things. We can, perhaps, publish a U.S. bibliography, taking all the U.S. titles out of the *NUC*, and issue it as part of the *NUC*. We can even construct it so that the Arabic titles are in one numerical sequence, or so that all phonorecords are in one sequence. We can mix it up and turn it around. We can also make sure the index corresponds to the portions that are being published. We may be able to sell the index in parts—for example, to provide public libraries with only English language titles or with all the Spanish language titles. The *NUC*, as we all recognize, is an expensive tool. It's very possible that we could offer sort of a customized service in COM (Computer Output Microform). If, for example, you wanted a list of all Spanish language titles, we might offer a service providing all the Spanish titles and the index to them.

These are some of the projects we're discussing. We still aim at closing the Library of Congress catalog in 1980; however, we still have many questions to answer.

What we will do with the old catalog has not been decided. We want to engrave it in stone and use it as a tremendously valuable resource tool, but we hope not to use it for current cataloging. We do plan—and this is not necessarily facetious—to put our catalog in alphabetical order before we publish it. Right now it would not win any great prize for alphabetization.

In summary, may I say, at the risk of being nationalistic, that I think that American libraries give as good service to their patrons as any that I know in the world; but we have far to go before we can give our patrons the excellent service that they deserve. With your help we can do it. Let's do it right, and let's do it as quickly as possible.

DISCUSSION

Paul Fasana: Mr. Howard has identified a great many things for us. I would like to comment on only two. First, Mr. Howard, you said that in a cooperative environment, rules had to be simple enough to be interpreted by everyone. I fear, however, that if you oversimplify to this extent you reduce everything to the lowest common denominator, at the expense of quality. I would hope that in advocating local input and international input you're not promoting the idea that all rules should be so simple that they are no longer standard. Granted, *standard* is an ambiguous term, because it can mean either quality or simply prescription. I hope, however, that in the Library of Congress, *standard* will always connote quality— quality cataloging, consistent cataloging, accurate cataloging. I hope that cooperative cataloging will not lower the standards that we have come to associate with, and become accustomed to, from the Library of Congress.

Secondly, you mentioned in passing a number of factors that will affect closing the catalog. I would like to attempt to list them and ask if these are the factors that will prompt you to consider closing the catalog. They include, firstly, an online system; secondly, *AACR2*, a catalog code that will be implemented. You talked also about inclusion of all current cataloging in MARC and then the authorities for that cataloging. You also threw a curve at us when you opened up the prospect of OCR, as perhaps another way out. Do you now see OCR as a possible way to avoid closing your catalog? Do you see OCR as a way of converting your retrospective records so that we can avoid the traumatic thought of closing the catalog? If that's not the case, I would like to ask one last question. A year or so ago, a paper was issued on closing the catalog that described what was called the *Rather Strategy*. Briefly, it was one of catalog containment: LC would close its catalog, would make the MARC data base completely self-sufficient and, in fact, would have linkages between the prospective and the retrospective catalog.

As a summary, several factors impinge on the catalog. Anything you do with your catalog will have great impact on what we do in the field. It is extremely critical that we know your thinking and your priorities relative to the factors causing you to reach these important decisions.

Joseph Howard: The choice of entry in this new system becomes less important if you have your access points in the machine. If you don't know what the choice is, but have other accesses, you can use them. This is true also of form of entry. If you have your form of entry as well as your reference structure—if you've done your reference structure right, which holds for manual processes, too—then when you query the machine, you're going to get a hit no matter what. I feel that we do not have a great problem with choice and form of entry. I think there has to be some sort of choice of entry, but I don't think it need be so complicated that the patron doesn't understand it—or that we don't understand it. I don't think the OCR equipment is a means of not closing the catalog because OCR can read that catalog, put it in machine-readable form, and go through our format recognition program so it becomes part of the automated data base. Thus you can more quickly divorce yourself from the manual catalog. I feel that we're going to have that manual catalog around for a long time. But whether you keep your whole file interactive and whether you keep the record structure between the two linked—that is, you spend the money to reconcile the two different sets of rules and so forth—I think that may also be moot with the name authority file because you're going to have all of those accesses. The only possible requirement may be that the cataloger will have to make sure that there is a reference at least from *AACR* or from the *ALA* form in the name authority file to the *AACR1* form; but the essential is that you can get a hit on any form of that name, whether it's Charlie Chan or Charlie Byrd.

Edwin Buchinski: I think there are several points to which attention should be drawn. Joe has mentioned the fact that we at the National Library of Canada are cooperating in the CONSER project and that there's been agreement on the form of name and on subject headings. Another significant aspect of this agreement is that only a small number of headings are involved. The project is being undertaken with caution. I think this approach underlines what is happening in the effort to move from the manual base to a machine system to network cooperation. I see the cooperation as cautious, as a low-key approach. This approach has made it a pleasure for me to be involved with the project, and I think I speak for other members of the National Library of Canada who have been working closely with LC, with Joe, and with members of his staff.

Judith Hopkins: I have two or three related questions. The online system that relates the Library of Congress to the library community sounds fascinating, but how do you intend to insure quality control with all this diversity in cataloging? Granted you're going to have online authority files, various access points, and other items, but I'm thinking more in terms of description than access points. Say some library as a matter of policy has never felt it necessary to include place of publication in its description, and it provides some records for the Library of Congress that lack place of publication. Then what do you do?

Howard: We hope to build upon the system that CONSER had developed and thus to have actual bibliographic conventions. The thing to do is to make sure that the conventions are accepted and adhered to. If there are alternatives in the rules, then we will have to agree on which ones are permissible.

Michael Malinconico: I'd like to expand on the point that Paul Fasana raised and ask you to speculate a bit. Let's assume the OCR conversion project you discussed is successful. Would you then see the resultant machine-readable data base as becoming an *integral* part of the post-1980 prospective catalog? And if so, could you speculate a little further as to what impact this will have? Will it perpetuate the current practices found in the LC catalog, for example, subject headings, superimposition, and so on? Or do you think machine assistance will help to convert those retrospective records—to desuperimpose, change subject headings, etc.?

Howard: Desuperimposing will be handled through the name authority file. For the retrospective records you can change the whole file when the name authority file is interactive with the bibliographic file. Now, added to the problem of the existing catalog with all its warts, there is the very practical limitation that at LC we cannot go back and recatalog any or all titles. Thus, as far as description goes, we will continue to have many different working rules for description and choice of entry. I don't think we would redo the old ones into *ISBD*. I don't see how we can afford to go back and recatalog. But I think we can clean up some things like form of entry. Not *choice* of entry, but form of entry.

Malinconico: To summarize, you're saying that the retrospective file, if converted, will become an integral part of the prospective catalog. Might this not have the effect of perpetuating some of the practices found in the current manual catalog?

Howard: That's true. But you must recognize that in the MARC bibliographic data base you have several rules already. In essence I am saying that I hope you would be able to integrate it. Moreover, the cataloging done then, though it may not have been perfect, was good.

Jessica Harris: I'm asking about a subject that, in my opinion, has been skipped in this workshop—subject headings. I believe that subject analysis needs study, to put it mildly, preferably before LC closes its catalogs in 1980. A proposal has been made by RTSD (Resources and Technical Services) that LC study the feasibility of applying PRECIS (Preserved Context Index System) to the catalog. Is there any responsiveness at LC to the need for a general study of alphabetical subject analysis—not a study of a particular *system*, but a close and open-minded examination of the problem?

Howard: Let me tell you what we are doing now, though I may not be answering you satisfactorily. Since the recent *LCIB (Library of Congress Information Bulletin)* discussion of cooperation among the four national libraries was written up, one person from the British Library has been assigned to come over to work with us to look at PRECIS and to see how it can fit in with the LC subject headings. We certainly are open-minded. We do not have the staff to study whether we need to throw out LC subject headings and start a new system like PRECIS. We have also been talking to Pauline Atherton about the subject of her presentation at ALA in Detroit, 1977, a system that can be added on the LC subject heading system to provide more access points. It is based upon terms that are taken from a book's index and table of contents, and used to augment the traditional access points.

Arlene Dowell: Is the COMARC program still on going? If so, are those records becoming a part of the online MARC data base?

Howard: The COMARC project got off to a very slow start because we had people who were willing to cooperate but who had huge work loads to discharge before they could send in their records. Between our staff waiting to work on the records and other libraries having no chance to do the work they had to do, the program was delayed. We expect to have a report soon and are now working inside LC to make sure that the COMARC data base can be used by us at LC as well. Whether it will be distributed as part of the MARC data base I don't know, but we hope at least to be able to say that it is at the level that we expect for our records. Whether it's two data bases or one I don't think makes much difference. What is important is that it will meet the standards we feel are necessary.

Donald Leach: Assuming that you do get the optical scanning equipment, won't you still have to tag everything manually in order to access it?

Howard: We have format recognition programs, and we would somehow run the data through them. It would do an awful lot of tagging for us. However, this is not *ISBD* format, and there would be many more mistakes needing human intervention in the tagging. Still, we wouldn't have to do it all. We would just have to correct and check it.

Eleanor Crarey: That is a marvelous display of goodies. Those of us who deal with cooperatively produced catalogs and buy MARC tapes from a vendor will certainly feel the effects of all this keenly. I had a couple of questions that you may have covered regarding the changing over of the back files when you eventually work on them. You talked about your name forms, the many rules that have generated those name forms, and the possibility of machine desuperimposition. Could you expand a bit? The changing name form problem is one that plagues us as our catalogs get older. Also, I didn't hear an exact date for the register index. By my calculations it seems to be 1983, or something like that. I also had a question about COMARC and those who are now participating in that program. At the time that they add titles that they have found in *NUC*, what do they do? Do they simply give a name as it was generated in the rules that existed at the time the name was cataloged, or do they update those names and upgrade the descriptive cataloging to fit present practice? What is actually happening on that?

Howard: By 1980 we hoped to have all current cataloging in machine-readable form, as well as every name that has been used with it and the rule under which it was cataloged. If we use the OCR equipment and go back and do the retrospective material, assuming it works we will also have to make sure that those names, too, are put into machine-readable form. The names going into MARC authority data bases would have to be coordinated with the bibliographic records. As for the dates of the register index, the year 1983 sounds like a good estimate. We're doing our publication on audiovisual material by machine now. In the case of COMARC records, we take the records coming in, check them against our official catalog to see what changes have been made in the official record, and check only certain access points to be sure they are right. But we do not recheck the pagination and similar details. We check the access points and make sure they fit in with LC's catalog.

Fasana: I was much impressed to hear Mr. Howard and especially gratified to hear him qualify the word *standards*. We generally use that term rather loosely to mean many things, but I'm happy to hear from him that it's standards of excellence he is striving for.

I'd like to ask three sets of questions. First: Will the future system as you envision it be a single system with a single data base? Will we interact-react with it in the same way that we do with OCLC? And then the obvious: What of OCLC in this new system? How will it affect other services that are now available? Some commercial services were mentioned; I would specifically mention OCLC, since it's such a widely used system.

Second: I'm confused about the scheduling and coordination of *AACR2* implementation and the closing of the catalog. If all these things don't come off on schedule and if you're confronted in 1980 with implementation of *AACR2*—and I think by international agreement with the four national libraries you are committed to implement by 1980 even if you're not in a position to close your catalogs—will you implement *AACR2* and interfile those records in the retrospective catalog? If you do, how will you treat superimposition?

Finally, your comments about OCR. I know that it's still premature, but let me pose a possibility. If OCR proves effective and you can, in fact, look to retrospective conversion of catalogs, will this drastically or radically alter your thinking with respect to closing your retrospective catalog? In effect, will machine capability of converting all these retrospective records change your attitude, your strategy, with respect to the retrospective catalogs?

Howard: Single system with a single data base? This is a technical networking problem that Henriette Avram is working on. The important thing to me is that when we call the record up we have *access* to the total thing. Whether part of it is in Ohio and part in the mid-Pacific and part someplace else is secondary. I don't know where the data base will reside; the essential thing—I've been assured of this—is that as a user of that screen I won't know the difference. That's an oversimplification, but the important thing to me is that the total file is accessible.

How will it affect the existing data base and OCLC? We would still have a distribution service of the MARC data bases, which would then be made available through purchase to anyone who wanted to buy it and use it in their system. BALLOTS or OCLC could use it if they wanted to buy it. We don't plan to change our existing services—book catalogs, card catalogs—as long as there's a need and they are financially feasible. We're going to have to consider other alternatives, such as COM (Computer Output Microform) as backups. By the way, we don't plan to get rid of our card catalog and have nothing but the machine-readable files. We plan to have backup on those—either book catalogs or COM—but we do not plan to do away with existing services unless it becomes financially impossible to continue them.

If we don't come off on schedule, what will we do? It means that things will be postponed. However, there are certain things that can be thought about. For instance, we could decide to publish the book catalogs for the materials that are in machine-readable form, and then have a hybrid system for nonroman alphabets.

What will we do when we close the catalog and have to worry about the question of superimposition? We are now working on a draft, trying to identify the factors that will affect our catalog. We already know some of them, and we think we have some ways out so that we will not have to have another superimposition.

As for the OCR equipment, and the closing of our catalogs: I don't think it will produce any change at all, we still want to close them.

Karen Bendorf: Will the format be updated to new languages?

Howard: We are looking at the code, and the way it affects us. We will have to look and see how it affects the MARC format. This is absolutely imperative and there are certain things that may have to be done to these formats. Lucia Rather, Assistant Director of Cataloging, will be supervising that work.

Les Walsteck: I'd like to know what changes you have in mind for subject catalogs. Since you're planning to close the catalog, it seems an ideal time to make some changes in that area.

Howard: That's true, and we do have some plans. We have already made many of the changes that have been suggested. We keep lists of headings that we think need to be changed, based both on our estimation and your letters. We are not, however, making a comprehensive study of LC subject headings. The American Library Association has asked us to look into PRECIS to see if there is some way that we can study its feasibility. The British Library will be sending someone later this year to work with us on PRECIS. Our staff has gone to several conferences. We are also keeping track of Pauline Atherton's work, which is conducted under a grant from the Council on Library Resources (CLR). It's meant to supplement the Library of Congress subject headings.

Unidentified Speaker: GPO is cataloging the documents, but they do not have the LC classification number in the documents that they are cataloging and classifying, and this makes it very difficult for people like myself who must go back to the *NUC* to find the classification number. I wish that someone would ask them to include the LC classification number, and I'm sure the Dewey people would like to have the Dewey number in as well.

Howard: What I'm postulating is a system that will be able to interact online with GPO. It's a matter of money and time. We will have that some day, but it's going to have to wait until we are totally interactive with them.

Unidentified Speaker: One of the problems that arises is that a lot of these records are in MARC but a lot of the MARC records in OCLC are bumped or deferred; so when you come up with a GPO number, you're just backtracking.

Howard: I know the problem. All I can say is that we're working on it. But it will have to wait until we are online.

Hugh Kirkendorff: I have four questions. First, I understand that LC either is, or is considering, going to an unformatted data storage system. Second, if we go to an international authority file, in terms of cooperation with other countries, what happens to those rules in the current *AACR1* and, I assume, in the *AACR2* that provide for entry of name on the basis of where the author is from, so that the name can be entered in one country in one way and in another country in another way? Question number three: My understanding is that LC is now experimenting with some printing of cards using a computer data base for nonroman alphabets, such as the Oriental. That is, my understanding is that the printing office of LC is using an automated system for printing nonroman alphabet materials on cards.

The last question is one that was implied in an earlier comment. Will LC cooperate with organizations like OCLC, BALLOTS, and others around the country as they would with an individual library, so that the cataloging that's done, perhaps within a system, could be fed into this central system we're all talking about, which we feel is going to be a national bibliography?

Howard: May I take the last one first? I'm not sure whether we could work something out with a system that has many libraries inputting. I think the important thing initially is that we work on cooperative efforts on the basis of language or subject. For instance, we might designate the University of Texas for Spanish and the University of California for documents, etc. But I have not thought about the idea of cooperative cataloging with a big system of many libraries.

As for nonroman printing, we are printing them manually, not by machine. The Catalog Distribution Service is using a system that will be able to output nonroman alphabets. We are now looking into input devices that will be able to input them, but we do not have any such device yet.

About an international authority file: first we'll work with those libraries, like the four national libraries that met in November (1977), to ensure that we're following the same rules. There is no great problem with form of name between these four countries, but we think that the answer to the problem of different forms of name can be handled through the name authority system that allows each country to have its own form of heading, if properly tagged. We would be able to take others' tapes and run them through our name authority file to pull out the form that we would use.

About formatted data storage, I have no idea. I am not an expert on that, but if you want to give me your name and address, I'll see if I can't have somebody call you about that.

Sue Martin: I have one question that is more in the way of clarification. Do I understand correctly that when LC closes its catalog internally in the future, it will make the catalog available to anyone who wishes to purchase it? If other libraries begin using or continue to use utilities like OCLC or BALLOTS when the national bibliographic network really gets going, might not the register index be used chiefly within LC and not be a widely dispersed product?

Howard: First of all, we plan to continue something like the *NUC* in addition to our online system. We plan to use register index for ours as well as others. It could be COM, it could be hard copy, or it could be both.

Martin: The question I have is about the problem I see in such programs as CONSER and COMARC; there is a discrepancy between the inputting library's record and the record as it finally appears when LC has made its changes. This is more of a problem, I think, from the inputting library's point of view. What you may get back is a record that has the main entry changed or, perhaps more likely, a tracing change from the original record so that it no longer corresponds exactly to your record.

Howard: We check every COMARC record against our official catalog. There are some things that participating libraries are allowed to change as a result of a recent meeting. We hope, for example, that they would change DOMESTIC SCIENCE to HOME ECONOMICS. If they don't, however, we will.

Martin: You change the heading, but if the library has their original input in its catalog, it's going to be different in that catalog from the way that it finally appears.

Howard: Right. They have the option to do what they want for their record. We're not telling them what they need to use; what we have assumed is that other people who are following LC would want the LC form of name.

Martin: That seems to me to be a problem. If you're using these data bases for interlibrary loans, and somebody comes along with a citation that has been generated on a national basis, and the library doesn't have it in that form because that's not the form that they originally submitted, how are they going to find it?

Howard: I agree with you totally, but I don't know the answer until we can drop superimposition and do things as perfectly as we would like to see them.

Soon Juhnge: I think we should reconsider the term *closing the catalog* because we cannot close the catalog unless we close our collection. When I move, my shadow moves. The collection is active, never static, so we cannot close our catalog as long as our collection is active. You at LC are not closing your catalog; you are transforming it.

Howard: Feel free to call it what you wish. Maybe my term is wrong.

Juhnge: I have another question. Do you have any group or program planning to establish closer cooperation with the National Library of Medicine, your closest neighbors?

Howard: We have some examples of cooperation with the National Library of Medicine (NLM). The National Agricultural Library (NAL) is also pretty close. But we have not as yet defined certain libraries who will be in a cooperative effort with us in the national online system.

Fay Johnson: I have one comment about some of the networking and OCLC. It is conceivable that if the Library of Congress had a cooperative arrangement for cataloging with one of the libraries that was already an OCLC participant, that library would still input their records through OCLC, and the records would then be transmitted to the Library of Congress. This is similar to what is currently being done with the COMARC tape where the libraries input and we then send the tapes to the Library of Congress.

Westermeyer: My question is partially answered by Ms. Johnson, but only partially. I work with medical books, and it seems that half the records come through with NLM information on them. Is it not possible to get together so that all the NLM is input on the LC/MARC tapes?

Howard: I think that it's possible, and I hope that's what will happen in the future. Right now there are different standards. We have made progress with the NLM and the NAL in relation to serials and we hope to continue to do that for monographs.

Unidentified Speaker: Do you think that the International Standard Book Numbers (ISBNs) will be extended to older books, and if so, is it possible to replace the LC number with the ISBN to identify a record?

Howard: For older books I think it's very doubtful, because the ISBN for monographs is meant as a sales number; it is assigned to new titles by publishers, and what you would do about titles published in 1830 and 1840, I don't know. We do know that one of the problems with the ISBN, from the LC viewpoint, is that it is a sales number; it does not necessarily relate to a bibliographic entry. If a publisher wishes to sell volume 3, they number all the volumes separately and have as many numbers as volumes for something that catalogers may catalog only once. That's a very simple example, but it indicates the problems involved in trying to substitute one for the other.

Stevens: But what purpose does it serve to record it on the catalog cards if it cannot be ordered by the number?

Howard: The book can be ordered by the ISBN, but the ISBN does not necessarily relate to the card number.

Freedman: I've been involved with the ISBN people. The book trade is very interested in the ISBN for obvious purposes, inventory control and order fulfillment. So it's to your advantage, at least from their standpoint, to order by ISBN so that they can more expeditiously fulfill your order. The problem with ISBN replacing LC card numbers is that ISBN refers to specific items published by the publisher, as opposed to *works* in the sense that Seymour Lubetzky talks about. There are many editions of one work; there are many versions of a work—paperbacks, hardbound, and each different binding that a publisher may put on a given work—and even if they used identical printing plates, each version would have a different ISBN. But there's usually only one LC record or card number. I think the ISBN people have proposed an ISBN bibliographic number, which would seem to be what is used for an LC number. One of the problems is that there may be several ISBNs for one LC card number or there may be cases where there are several LC card numbers for a single ISBN. It's very complicated, but the problems of substituting one for the other still remain to be solved.

Howard: The ISBN is completely different from the ISSN. The serial number is geared toward a bibliographic entry; the ISBN is not.

Freedman: The ISBN people have all kinds of publicity arrangements, and further questions should be taken up directly with them at ALA.

One written question was submitted from the floor. More detail is requested on LC's plans for subject headings. Do they intend to change the kinds of formats? Would it be a hierarchical display or a permuted display? Would there be more consistency in the content of the subject headings?

Howard: We don't plan anything like that now.

Freedman: I have two points I was going to raise. One takes off from the last one. I'm concerned about a PRECIS bandwagon. Everybody's excited about it; the ALA recommended that LC do a pilot project to investigate adopting it. I would hope that LC would consider not just PRECIS but alternative subject control systems, and that it would not study PRECIS with the predefined goal of *what* do we have to do to implement it and adopt it, but rather study it in a more objective way, asking, "Does this meet our needs? What alternative subject headings or subject control systems also should be considered with respect to meeting our needs?"

That's more of a comment than a question. The other relates to your point about technical services that are being established at LC. I worked there long ago, and one thing that seemed to be good was the way of communicating and providing help. LC has such a vast wealth of human resources, people with so much expertise in a great variety of areas; sharing this expertise with the country is marvelous and good to hear about. But the one thing that I thought of, as someone who has left LC and has gotten on the other end of it, is that LC should establish some mechanism whereby people who are outside LC would be formally funded to provide advice to LC so that the communication process works both ways. The Cataloging-in-Publication (CIP) program at LC is really commendable, but I would hope that there would be more formal mechanisms, some advisory group to advise LC of libraries' needs, rather than the present hit-and-miss basis for response.

Howard: We welcome comments. We do have the ALA as a channel. We also have comments from many, many people via letters and via phone calls. We certainly always welcome any kind of comments, and it's especially vital that we solicit them when we're on the threshold of tremendously exciting programs. Yes, we do want this two-way input. Whether we can set up another whole program to do this, I don't know, but meanwhile, we'll talk to anybody.

Problems and Prospects in Nonbook Cataloging

by Jean Riddle Weihs

When Mitch Freedman invited me to speak about the problems associated with the cataloging of nonbook materials, I asked the usual questions. How long a talk? Who will be the audience? Is the content to be historical, theoretical, or practical? He told me that for the purposes of this paper I was to assume that the audience knows a lot about book cataloging and nothing about nonbook cataloging. He asked for a discussion of the practical problems which face practicing librarians and media specialists and urged me to state my opinions on all matters. So you are about to hear a practical, opinionated speech.

My remarks will apply to circulating, multimedia collections rather than archival or specialized ones composed of one medium. The latter have their own problems which I do not intend to explore today. I will not be giving you a prescription for cataloging nonbook materials, but rather a discussion of some problems which require major policy decisions.

Many catalogers have related a sad tale, which more or less follows the same story line. Their center has acquired a few items, such as a dozen filmstrips or a few roles of microfilm. In the context of a large book collection, the cataloging of these items seems unimportant and the idea that these are but the forerunners of a large collection of nonbook materials is not considered. These items are cataloged in a nonstandard way with no attempt made to relate them to the general collection. A few more items appear and they are treated in the same manner. Over the next few years the nonbook collection grows and at one point the staff has to start recataloging it all beause the materials cannot be retrieved easily by the catalog record which now exists. The moral of this tale is that you should catalog the first nonbook item with the same care you will devote to the ten thousandth and recognize the possibility that your library may become a media center.

Before you catalog this first item, or recatalog many items, there are decisions to be made. This paper will touch on the basic ones: interfiling, intershelving, terminology, subject analysis, the importance of following a rigid hierarchy for sources of cataloging information, and finally what and how much to catalog.

INTERFILING

Cataloging policies cannot be structured without consideration of the use which will be made of the final product. My first strongly held opinion is that all entries for all items in a collection should be filed in one catalog. There should not be one file for books and another file or files for nonbook materials. An integrated all-media catalog, either dictionary or divided, provides the patron with the best service. It is a dedicated researcher who is willing to look through many files for the information s/he seeks. It is a knowledgeable and rare patron who knows that there are other files and where they are located. Most patrons check in the first file they see and go no further because of ignorance or lethargy. Good public service helps a patron to find his/her needs quickly and easily and an all-media catalog does just this. From time to time the accusation is made that libraries are run for the convenience of the staff. Even in this type of library an all-media catalog is an asset. It is less work for the staff to look in one file than many.

An effective all-media catalog requires all items to be entered following the same rules. For some years now an argument has raged over author versus title entry for nonbook materials. Despite the annotation on my speech published in the Institute's brochure, I do not intend to discuss this controversy at any length, because it is my understanding, although I have not yet seen the rules, that the *Anglo-American Cataloging Rules* 2nd edition *(AACR2)* will prescribe the same entry rules for all materials. I agree heartily with this, and to belabor past arguments which will not apply to future problems seems a waste of time. Figures 1 and 2 demonstrate rather simplistically one of the reasons that applying the same rules of entry to all media makes a more effective catalog.[1] You will note how much easier it is for a patron to understand when searching the subject file that the collection includes both the book and the filmstrip of *The First Book of World War II*, by L. L. Snyder. It is sensible that these two catalog records should stand together.

INTERSHELVING

My second strongly held opinion is that as many items as possible in a browsing collection should be intershelved. It is also good public service to have easy patron access to all materials. Intershelving is a big subject which does not have a place in the Institute's program. I have mentioned it because my paper is based on the assumption that the catalog copy I will be discussing is destined for an all-media catalog and that some type of intershelving of book and nonbook materials is anticipated. Some media centers interfile the catalog without intershelving the collection; others have an all-media catalog and intershelve certain media only.

In the present climate of economic retrenchment some media centers may be experiencing staff cutbacks. Interfiling and intershelving allow a more economic use of professional time because patrons find it convenient to do the initial search for materials on their own.

TERMINOLOGY

We started to investigate the problems associated with the cataloging of nonbook materials with the publication of *Nonbook Materials: The Organization of Integrated Collections* (1977). The biggest problem during these years and the biggest problem today is how to identify on the catalog records the format of a particular item. An early method was the color coding of cards. Everytime I speak in public about nonbook cataloging, someone in the audience asks about color coding, and my advice always has been, and still is, *don't*. If a media center has

FIGURE 1

CATALOGED ACCORDING TO AACR1

WORLD WAR, 1939-1945.
World War II in headlines. Toronto, Board of
   Education [1963]
3 sheets. 9 x 12 cm.

Microfiche.

   WORLD WAR, 1939-1945.
World War II (Filmstrip) Time-Life Books,
   [c1968]
   2 filmstrips color. 35 mm. and phonodisc:
2s. 12 in. 33 1/3 rpm, 23 min. (Time capsule
classroom research unit)

   Supplemented by 4 books, various charts,
maps and documents, and teacher's guide.

   WORLD WAR, 1939-1945.
World War II (Filmstrip) McGraw, c1962.
   38 fr. color. 35 mm. (American history
series)

   WORLD WAR, 1939-1945.
World War II. Benn, c1967.
   8 reproductions color. 63.5 x 93.98 cm.

Study prints with text on verso.

   WORLD WAR, 1939-1945.
Snyder, Louis Leo.
   The First book of World War II. New York,
F. Watts, c1958.
   96 p. illus., maps. (The First books)

   WORLD WAR, 1939-1945.
Smith, John George.
   Diary, October 10, 1940 - November 12, 1944.
Berne, English Press, 1945.
   126 p.

   Microfilm. New York, Reprint Corp., 1967.
1 reel. 35 mm.

FIGURE 1 (continued)

WORLD WAR, 1939-1945.
Shayon, Robert Louis.
    Historic voices and music from World War II
(Phonodisc) American Heritage Pub. Co.

    RB 408-409, 1966.
        2s. 12 in. 33 1/3 rpm.

        WORLD WAR, 1939-1945.
    The First book of World War II (Filmstrip)
        Brown Bros. Films, 1966.
            68 fr. b&w. 35 mm. (The First book
    filmstrip series)

        A slightly abridged version of the book by
    Louis Leo Snyder.

FIGURE 2

CATALOGED ACCORDING TO AACR2 DRAFT

        WORLD WAR, 1939-1945.
    World War II in headlines [Microform]. --
        Toronto: Toronto Board of Education, [1963]
        3 fiche: 9 x 12 cm.

            WORLD WAR, 1939-1945.
        World War II [Picture]. -- London: Benn, c1967.
        6 study prints: col. ; 34 x 47 cm.

            WORLD WAR, 1939-1945.
        World War II [Multimedia]. -- Chicago: Time-Life
            Books, c1968.
            4 books, 3 charts, 2 facsimiles, 2 filmstrips,
        1 sound disc + teacher's guide. -- (Time capsule
        classroom research unit)

FIGURE 2 (continued)

WORLD WAR, 1939-1945.
World War II [Filmstrip]. -- New York: McGraw-
Hill, 1962.
 1 filmstrip (42 frames): col. ; 35 mm. +
teacher's guide. -- (American history series;
set 4)

WORLD WAR, 1939-1945.
Snyder, Louis Leo.
 The first book of World War II [Filmstrip] / by
Louis L. Snyder. -- Toronto: Brown Bros. Films,
1966.
 1 filmstrip (68 frames): b.&w.; 35 mm. -- (The
First book filmstrip series)

WORLD WAR, 1939-1945.
Snyder, Louis Leo.
 The first book of World War II [Book] / by

Louis L. Snyder. -- New York : F. Watts, 1958.
 96 p. : ill., maps ; 23 cm. -- (The First books)

WORLD WAR, 1939-1945.
Smith, John George.
 Diary, October 10, 1940 - November 12, 1944
[Microform] / John George Smith. -- New York:
Reprint Corp., 1967.
 1 film reel; 35 mm.

 Original published: Berne: English Press, 1945;
126 p.

WORLD WAR, 1939-1945.
Shayon, Robert Louis.
 Historic voices and music from World War II
[Sound recording] / by Robert L. Shayon; narrated
by Luis Van Rosten. -- New York: American
Heritage Pub. Co., 1966.
 1 disc (40 min.): 33 1/3 rpm., mono.; 12 in.

more formats of media than there are distinctive colors, it will run into difficulties with shadings and the maintenance of the quality of color on the card stock. For example, how difficult is it to distinguish aqua from green? For *AACR2*, 23 or 24 general material designations (GMD's) are being proposed and there are not this number of distinctive colors. Color coding only works in a collection with a limited number of different formats and a card catalog. As media centers move into the age of technological change, more and more catalogs will be computer-produced, either book, COM (Computer Output Microform), or online. None of these is likely to use color coding.

Another early method of indicating type of material was the use of a media code as part of the call number. This can be used reasonably successfully by media centers which have segregated shelving because the call number separates the collection into format groupings. However, the segregation of formats can lead to an uneconomic use of space since many media are produced in widely divergent sizes. A wiser use of storage space is made when the media code is abandoned and all materials are intershelved. Oversized nonbook materials are then treated in the same manner as oversized books, specialized materials in the same manner as reference books.

The word *code* suggests some sort of translation to make it intelligible. The patron will need help by means of signs or personal contact with media center staff to understand the code. If public service and/or self-service is the goal, a media center will not complicate the call number by making it more mysterious than it already is to the average patron.

The most reasonable method of indicating type of material is to use words which the public can understand. This brings us to a consideration of what has been called until now *media designations* and what *AACR2* will be labelling *general material designations* (GMD's). Terminology has been the most contentious problem which we have encountered in the last ten years. As an example you will note that I have used the term *nonbook* throughout this paper. By this term I mean any material which is not in a booklike format. *Standards for Cataloging Nonprint Materials*, published by the Association for Educational Communications and Technology (AECT),[2] covers the same media as does *Nonbook Materials: The Organization of Integrated Collections*.[3] However, it uses the term *nonprint*. I do not think that the term *nonprint* can be applied to many microforms and some charts and kits. AECT obviously disagrees. The American Library Association (ALA) applies the term *audiovisual* to those items AECT would call *nonprint* and the Joint Advisory Committee on Nonbook Materials (JAC)[4] *nonbook*. I don't think *audiovisual* applies very well to microforms and machine-readable data files. In the *Anglo-American Cataloging Rules*, 1st edition, microforms are treated as books; JAC and AECT do not agree with this. Brian Enright coined the term *metabooks*[5] and Malcolm Shifrin suggested *materium/materia*[6] in attempts to solve this problem, but the terms did not find wide acceptance.

The difficulty of constructing a list of terms is great. Not only are there different interpretations of terminology, but particular words, such as *kit*, have different meanings on each side of the Atlantic Ocean. Trade names must be eschewed.

Generic terms have to be used if we are to avoid a proliferation of GMD's as new products appear on the market. Therefore, the list must be hospitable to new formats. Commercial catalogers advised us that their products could be sold more cheaply if generic terms were used. This would allow them to list the various formats of a particular item in one collation. For example, some producers market the same recording in disc, reel-to-reel tape, cassette, and cartridge format. Generic GMD's allow the same catalog copy to be used for all these formats and four collations to be listed. Individual libraries would then delete the collation lines which were not applicable. This economy can also be adopted by media centers doing original cataloging; two or more formats of an item can be listed in the collation provided the appropriate call numbers are indicated clearly.

Librarians and media specialists are becoming wary of the changing terminology. In the last ten years *phonotape* and *phonodisc* have combined to become *audiorecord* and now *sound recording*. Catalogers are reluctant to adopt new terminology unless they can see justification for the changes and can be assured that new terms will remain in effect for the forseeable future. With the publication of *AACR2*, librarians and media specialists are faced with a new list of GMD's. Not all of the terms on this list have been agreed to as yet, but it is likely that the list will include three new terms for materials which were not cataloged previously with media designations and a possible two or three changes from those terms listed in *AACR Chapter 12* (revised) and *Nonbook Materials: The Organization of Integrated Collections*. This means that there will be a maximum of six GMD's, the implementation of which will require decisions.

Media centers which are part of a larger cataloging group will have to abide by the policy decisions made elsewhere, so I will address these remarks to those who are in a position to make policy. Decisions will be particularly pressing for those people who have a new collection to organize or are able to have a new program written which could be applied to entries already stored in data banks.

If you are the policymaker for a well-established large media collection, which is cataloged with traditional media designations, you are not going to start recataloging. How many changes are you going to make? The answer to this will depend, of course, on available staff and budget, the size of the cataloged collection, and policies with regard to shelving. If I were the policymaker, I would change the GMD's where I had a small number of items in a particular medium. For a large collection I would consider whether the proposed changes in terminology would increase public service. For instance, I would have adopted the change which was effected in *AACR Chapter 14* (revised) from *phonodisc* and *phonotape* to *sound recording*, a term more easily understood by the public.

AACR2 raises some problems which decision makers have not had to face previously. It provides a GMD for every item in the collection including books and it makes the application of any or all GMD's optional. My advice to media center staff is to use all of the GMD's or none of them.

Let us consider the validity of these two options: first, the assignment of a GMD to every item in the collection. North American librarians and media specialists say that patrons do not read a catalog beyond the title, and the lack of an early warning GMD would cause confusion. If this is your experience, apply a GMD to every item. A GMD is also needed in online catalogs which suppress the collation.

Up until now it has been the practice for catalogers to assign media designations to some or all nonbook materials and not to books or, in some cases, to microforms. To give a GMD to an author reading his work on a sound recording and not to his book suggests that books are normal and the reading a departure from this norm. This idea should be discouraged. Nonbook materials are not second class stock. The two transparencies (Figures 1 and 2) I used to illustrate author versus title entry can also serve to demonstrate the more meaningful catalog produced with the application of GMD's to every item. Then consider what the entries would look like if the collation were suppressed, and you will see how necessary GMD's can be in an abbreviated online catalog.

Now let us consider the opposite option, that of the omission of the GMD from any catalog copy. The British have advocated this position for years and have been responsible for the option which allows for the elimination of GMD's in *AACR2*. I must admit that the British position has always held some attraction for me because the elimination of the GMD would solve the terminology problem. The last ten years have taught me that there can be no list of terms which will find general acceptance among the profession. In addition, some terms will always be confusing to the public and need interpretation. We as a profession should ask ourselves whether the need for an early warning signal is as pressing today. Is the public becoming more sophisticated about library collections and no longer surprised to find that nonbook materials can be borrowed? I would be interested in talking to anyone who has an opinion on this matter.

SUBJECT ANALYSIS

A problem which only surfaced to any appreciable extent with the advent of the all-media cataog is the subject analysis of nonbook materials. If all entries are to be filed in one catalog, either dictionary or divided, the same subject heading system must be used for both book and nonbook materials. If some or all items are to be intershelved, the same classification schemes must be applied. The standard subject analysis systems were devised for books. Some reworking of these systems appears to be needed in order to adapt them to media cataloging. In 1975 the American Library Association, Resources and Technical Services Division (RTSD), Cataloging and Classification Section set up an Ad Hoc Subcommittee on the subject analysis of audiovisual materials "to investigate and to identify any differences in the subject analysis and control requirements of nonbook materials and books."[7] A preliminary report was published in several professional journals in late 1976 and early 1977. The final report was prepared by the chairperson, Liz Bishott, in the latter half of 1977.

I was appointed to this committee to investigate the problems encountered in Canadian media centers. I have no reason to suppose that Canada differs from the United States with regard to these kinds of problems and so I shall summarize the main points in my findings which were reported in the *Canadian Library Journal* (October 1976).[8] The following remarks apply to the subject analysis systems most frequently used in Canada—*Dewey Decimal Classification, Sears List of Subject Headings,* Library of Congress classification and subject headings.

Currency in subject analysis is a more pressing problem for nonbook materials than it is for books because new subject matter frequently appears first in a nonbook format. Videotapes and sound tapes can create the need for a new subject heading long before the same content is produced in book form.

Many subject headings and subdivisions are book oriented. Media specialists feel it is ludicrous to apply such headings as COUNTING BOOKS or ALPHABET BOOKS to a filmstrip, and CONVERSATION AND PHRASE BOOKS to the many multimedia language packages now on the market. ENGLISH AS A SEC-OND LANGUAGE could replace TEXTBOOKS FOR FOREIGNERS, solving two problems at once—the book orientation of the latter and its discriminatory connotation mentioned earlier by Mr. Berman.

There are certain types of subject matter better suited to the nonbook format for which no subject heading exists, such as kits designed to develop orienteering, or for which the subject heading is inadequate, such as recording intended to promote creative movement. There is also no adequate Dewey number for the latter. It is difficult to classify the new interdisciplinary materials being produced.

It was the subject analysis of music recording that caused the most concern. Many librarians expressed the opinion that for the most part the systems had been devised for printed music and were inadequate for recorded sound. Public libraries want headings and classification which will meet the needs of nonsophisticated borrowers.

Catalogers have complained that the subject heading systems are not precise enough to deal with the very specific subject content which can be found in some media, such as filmstrips, motion picture loops, and transparencies. Some nonbook materials are less browsable than books and so their subject cataloging needs to be more precise as well.

How do catalogers cope with the problems outlined above? For those who use *Sears List of Subject Headings*, some solutions are in view. Barbara Westby, who has attended most meetings of the Subcommittee on the Subject Analysis of Audiovisual Materials, reported at the January 1977 meeting that she has incorporated into the forthcoming 11th edition of *Sears* many of the suggestions discussed at the Subcommittee's meetings. She has removed book-oriented as well as sexist and racist terms and has devoted one section of the introduction to the particular problems involved in applying subject headings to nonbook materials.

Ed Blume, who was chief of LC's Subject Cataloging Division, also attended many of the Subcommittee's meetings. In a letter to me dated March 10, 1977 he said that the Library of Congress (LC) would refrain from making any changes until the Subcommittee's final report was published.

The people involved in the construction of subject analysis systems are interested in your problems and suggestions for improvement of these systems. Write to them. If enough people are concerned about a particular problem, it will be studied and a solution sought. Figure 3 lists the people to contact and their addresses.

FIGURE 3

Suggestions concerning Library of Congress subject headings and classification should be addressed to:	Chief, Subject Cataloging Division Library of Congress Washington, DC 20540
Suggestions concerning the Dewey Decimal Classification should be addressed to:	Chief, Decimal Classification Division Library of Congress Washington, DC 20540
Suggestions concerning Sears subject headings should be addressed to:	Editor, Sears List of Subject Headings H.W. Wilson Co. 950 University Avenue Bronx, NY 10452

Study other published lists of subject headings. If you are unhappy about the academic approach to music in the Library of Congress subject headings, look at those in the *Hennepin County Library's Cataloging Bulletin*. I note that the Hennepin County Library's authority file is available on fiche at a reasonable price.

A controversy has arisen over whether to use GMD's as media form subdivisions, e.g., BATIK—MOTION PICTURE. The two sides of this question are firmly aligned by their differing concepts of the role of nonbook materials in a collection. Those who wish to use such subdivisions argue that they want all the various formats in a given subject field to stand together in the catalog because patrons ask for materials in this manner, e.g., for a motion picture loop on batik. These libraries generally have a divided collection.

Those who oppose media form subdivisions think that such subdivisions would reinforce the idea that books are normal and nonbook materials abnormal. They want to encourage the public to understand that information can be found in many different formats. These media centers generally integrate their collections. It will be obvious to you by now that I agree with the latter position. I would not use media form subdivisions.

If you have an automated file, you do not need to worry about this controversy because the file can be searched by GMD. To add a media form subdivision would duplicate information and, therefore, raise costs.

SOURCES OF INFORMATION

More than ten years ago one of the problems which was brought to our attention concerned the interloan of nonbook materials. Producers had cursed the media world with a plethora of titles for many items making the identification of a particular item difficult in some instances. Many media lack the equivalent of a title page, so that it is necessary to follow rigidly the hierarchy of sources of information set out in *AACR2* if interloan is to run smoothly. Media centers must agree on what is the identifying title in order to exchange a particular item. Several years ago I cataloged an inconsequential filmstrip which has remained in my memory because it was a perfect example of the title problem. The cannister label title was *The Big Red Barn*, the leader frame title *The Big Barn*, the title frame title *The Red Barn*, and the manual title *John and Mary Visit Grandfather's Farm*.

Most nonbook materials lack the equivalent of an ISBN (International Standard Book Number). Therefore, the proper identification of title assumes additional importance in shared cataloging.

HOW MUCH CATALOGING?

Frequently I am asked: What should be cataloged? Should each item be cataloged separately or as a set? How much of the collection should be cataloged? Ideally everything should be cataloged. However, I am aware that budget considerations often impose restrictions which force compromises. Therefore, I am going to discuss some things which you could consider when making decisions.

From time to time when visiting a media center I am told that few of the patrons ever use, for example, slides. Upon further questioning I find that the slides are uncataloged and stored in the work room. Patrons cannot use media which they do not know exists. If you have a similar situation in your library, catalog a section, such as all slides about American art, put them on open shelving, and see what happens. The chances are that you will be convinced of the necessity of cataloging all media. There is no point in owning materials of which the public is unaware. What is acquired should be cataloged; otherwise money has been wasted.

There are libraries and media centers with restricted budgets where money cannot be found for any extra service. A possible, but definitely second best, alternative in these situations is to treat nonbook materials in the same manner as many libraries deal with paperback books, that is, the materials are not cataloged, but put on easily accessible shelves for circulation. Put them in pamphlet boxes or Princeton files by classification. For example, have all the nonbook materials on the moon in a box or files labelled 523.3 and placed at the end of the books with the same classification.

The cry is sometimes heard that it is impossible to put nonbook materials on open shelves because they will be stolen. I have never seen any statistics showing that nonbook materials are more subject to theft than books. If a library expects a certain loss in its book collection, it should not be upset by a similar loss in its nonbook materials.

Another objection sometimes made is that nonbook materials cost more than books so their loss is more significant financially. I don't think that this is true for many media. A filmstrip, transparency, slide, chart, map, microform, microscope slide, sound disc, and many pictures cost less than the average book. The more expensive media such as kits, models, and games are too large for someone to sneak past a vigilant charge out system. Motion pictures, videorecordings, and machine-readable data files may require special storage. Motion picture loops can be expensive and small enough to secrete. Sound tape cassettes appear to attract thieves in some libraries. If the disappearance of these latter two media are a problem, use dummies on the shelf and store the item at the circulation desk.

A third alternative to cataloging is to place in the catalog, card, book, or online, guide cards or similar references such as are shown in Figure 4.

FIGURE 4

VOLCANOES

    Additional material on this subject will be found in the vertical file under the above heading.

VOLCANOES

    Additional material on this subject will be found in the vertical file under 551.21.

VOLCANOES

    Additional material on the above subject will be found in the special collections indicated below.

☐ Vertical file   ☐ Picture file   ☐ Art collection

☐ Map drawer   ☐ Slide trays

At the beginning of this speech I said that I would not discuss shelving, but I have found it impossible to ignore it entirely. People cannot use what they do not know exists. If an item is worth purchasing, it is worth cataloging. If for some reason cataloging is not possible, patrons must be made aware in some other manner of the media center's resources. I know I am repeating myself. I have encountered the *List No Media, See No Media, Use No Media* phenomenon enough times that I think the point must be made forcibly.

Producers are very fond of packaging varieties of media together and selling them as kits. Many of these kits are carefully constructed into a meaningful unit and these should be fully cataloged with analytics for those parts of the kit which can be physically and intellectually separated for independent use. However, if a producer has created an instant kit by throwing everything s/he has on a given subject into a box, it may be more useful to break up the kit and catalog each item separately.

Many items are sold in sets, e.g., a set of six filmstrips. These can be cataloged in one of two ways: either cataloged as a set and analytics made for the parts or each part cataloged separately and the whole linked by means of series added entries. The following generalization works well for a browsing collection. If each unit within a set would have significantly different classification numbers and subject headings, catalog each part of the set separately. If, on the other hand, each unit within a set would have the same classification and subject headings, catalog the set as a unit.

During this paper I have touched on the problems which are brought to my attention most frequently. In the given time span it is impossible to discuss all the nonbook cataloging problems. If when you are working you come across a problem which perplexes you, you should write to someone in the field who may be able to help you. The authors of *Nonbook Materials* receive letters frequently asking for opinions on cataloging problems. We are happy to help you and we find that these letters help us as well to improve our own work by pointing out areas which could be strengthened or expanded. We are rewriting our book to bring it in line with *AACR2*. Your suggestions would be welcomed.

NOTES

1. Rather than spend hours looking for the perfect examples to illustrate a point, I have invented some of these items.

2. Alma M. Tillin, and William J. Quinly, *Standards for Cataloging Nonprint Materials; an Interpretation and Practical Application*, 4th ed. (Washington, DC: Association for Educational Communications and Technology, 1976).

3. Jean Riddle Weihs; Shirley Lewis; and Janet MacDonald, *Nonbook Materials: The Organization of Integrated Collections*, 1st ed. (Ottawa: Canadian Library Association, 1973).

4. The Joint Advisory Committee on Nonbook Materials was the body which decided the terminology to be used in *Nonbook Materials: The Organization of Integrated Collections*.

5. B. J. Enright, "Non-Book/Media Materials and the Library: A Note," *Library Association Record* 72 (December 1970): 368-69.

6. Malcolm Shifrin, *Information in the School Library; an Introduction to the Organization of Non-Book Materials* (London: C. Bingley, 1973).

7. *ALA Handbook of Organization 1976-1977* (Chicago: American Library Association, 1976), p. 56.
8. Jean Riddle Weihs, ''Problems of Subject Analysis for Audio/Visual Materials in Canadian Libraries,'' *Canadian Library Journal* 33 (October 1976): 435, 455.

DISCUSSION

Paul Fasana: I find very little to differ with in Ms. Weihs' presentation, although I would like to pose one or two questions. You mentioned that intershelving is your prime objective, but you also mentioned that mainly with respect to media centers. I wonder if you'd be willing to comment on intershelving in terms of a typical academic library or a library that would be more conventional. Perhaps there are certain considerations in an academic library that might dictate separate shelving. It's very wasteful, for example, to try and put some of the nonbook media on shelves. There is a preservation problem. If you try to put small boxes of microfilm next to even standard-sized books, there will be problems with books wobbling back and forth which has a detrimental effect on the construction of the book. This would be a very serious preservation problem in academic type libraries.

The second point concerns nonbook cataloging and the *AACR*. *AACR* is rather radical with respect to nonbook materials, especially with respect to entries. Most media centers have not used *AACR* in the past but have followed their own home-grown rules. Will many media centers or nonbook collections be persuaded to adopt *AACR*? In what kind of time frame will they do it? What will they have to do in their catalogs other than revise the general media designators? Will, in fact, cataloging done for nonbook materials in *AACR2*, be interfilable with cataloging previously done?

Jean Weihs: Certainly I don't think that a research library whose main objective is to preserve material will intershelve. Most university libraries wanting to keep their collections almost forever should be much more careful of book storage and materials than a circulating dynamic collection. The kinds of collections I am talking about are public school libraries where the collection is weeded at frequent intervals, and where a book is not expected to last for fifty years or more. In these situations intershelving increases circulation considerably.

I did two informal studies in two libraries. One was an elementary school library and one was a junior high school library in which the librarians were extraordinarily cooperative. They allowed us to rearrange their collection. We discovered that in both libraries when the media was intershelved the circulation of all the materials rose—books included. Now, of course, schools have very many nonreaders in the library who really don't want to be there, and these people were very attracted to the media. They would first see beautiful study prints on motorcycles, then they'd look at film loops on one, and eventually they would be so fascinated they would be reading the book. The school librarians were very intrigued by this, and I have since been told by many school librarians who have used intershelving that this is true generally. As I say, there are no formal studies on this at all. These are informal studies.

Public libraries have used intershelving of materials and they have found the same thing applies. People are positively delighted to find that there are motion picture loops on how to throw a ball properly, art slides, and all this sort of thing. They have gotten very good reactions putting media on the shelves.

I don't think that intershelving is necessarily very wasteful. I talked about putting oversized materials with the oversized books. Take out anything that doesn't go on the normal shelf and put it somewhere else. Another way that this could be done, for example, is to put all the nonbook materials on gardening on the gardening shelf.

As I say, I could talk another two hours on intershelving. My experience has been that it has been successful. I have had no experience whatsoever with academic collections. Therefore, I cannot speak about those collections. As I am associated with the Seneca College in Toronto—which you would call a community college in the States—we intershelve things. Most community college libraries in Toronto intershelve and have dynamic collections. They are not going to be keeping things forever. They have found that weeding is useful and that people use all the media a great deal.

Will media centers accept *AACR*? I don't know. After discussing and working on the list of general material designators, I feel material designators seem sensible to the people who use the media. We can't set up artificial terms that aren't meaningful to the media specialists. The rules I've seen are sensible. I have disagreements with some of them and have reported them to the Canadian Committee on Cataloging; but in general, I think they're a vast improvement on the first edition of *AACR*. I think the sensible media centers will accept them. With the old rules it was impossible to interfile cards.

Edwin Buchinski: With *AACR2* there is a very conscious attempt to eliminate the book bias. Ms. Weihs mentioned that she has been reviewing the descriptive parts and shortly she'll be getting the entry parts. I hope that she will agree that a successful attempt has been made. Ms. Weihs is a liaison member of the CCT and used the phrase *catalog no media, see no media, use no media*. The CCT certainly hasn't been cataloging or using media as yet, but we weren't prepared to see no media. In one of Ms. Weihs' presentations to the committee about the problems of media she came in and said, "See this? What is it?" After some explanation, it was something called the *talking page*.

Suzine Nicolescu: AV materials are really a pain in the neck. For example, you said that we should catalog AV materials the same as we do books, providing the same subject headings, interfiling in the catalog, and intershelving material as much as possible. Libraries, particularly academic libraries, do not seem to have enough personnel to take care of these things. For example, City College has an art department which owns 80,000 art slides. How could you integrate such things? I may believe that everything *should* be intershelved, but many kits are a conglomeration of media and require money for someone to show how to use them and hardware for playback or viewing. How do you cope with that?

Weihs: If you don't have the money I suggested that you catalog these things like paperback books and put them on the shelves. You can organize slides in subject areas. You could take all the slides by Whistler, for instance, and put them in one box. Put on the outside AMERICAN ART—WHISTLER, catalog them, and then give a contents note so that at least somebody can find them under WHISTLER and AMERICAN ART. This is not as good as cataloging every slide, but I realize it's a great job to catalog 80,000 slides. On the question about kits with different media, I think you have to have a staff who can train people to use these things. If you're hiring library technicians, it's their job to show people how to use the equipment.

Pat Stevens: I'd like to ask for a comment on the widespread practice of cataloging nonprint materials without viewing or listening to them. The Library of

Congress has done this for motion pictures.

Weihs: Frankly, I have no idea how somebody can catalog an item without viewing it. I think that this leads to very bad cataloging practices. Some places catalog from producer's sheets. One of the things that the other two authors and I have done, as we produced these things, was to find out who filled out these sheets. Sometimes the producer of the particular media does it. But sometimes the person will look at me and say, ''I think Mary. She's on the switchboard.'' I become very dubious of this. I am also dubious about the *AACR2* prescribing the source of the title as the label. Some of the labeling on media is very bad, and I do think that you have to look at a thing to make sure your cataloging matches the label.

Barbara Johnson: You asked for some comments about tagging things so that you know whether or not it is nonbook material. I run a medical library where a great many requests have to be mediated. The equipment is stored in the library and has to be lent from the library in order for the materials to be heard or shown. Because of this we indicate the medium in the integrated catalog so that people using it have an idea that they have to ask for some more information, instruction, or equipment. I think this is a legitimate reason for media designation in a situation of this kind.

Charles Ralston: I suggest that in future editions some consideration be given to materials used by the handicapped, those that have impairments with hearing, vision or other handicaps. There are materials that are expressly designed for these people and I think they need some kind of form designation and perhaps directions on use and packaging.

Nancy Williamson: Ms. Weihs, would you care to comment on *AACR2*'s impact on cataloging nonbook materials, specifically the rules which will not permit the artist to be the author except when the item is the original?

Weihs: I have violently disagreed with this to the Canadian Committee on Cataloging. I think this is a ridiculous rule. It may be fine for art collections, but I called the Ontario College of Art, which has a large art collection, and asked their opinion. They said they would not want to use this rule either. For the kinds of collections that I'm used to dealing with, most people would not care to distinguish or would not even know enough to distinguish whether the print was a reproduction of a picture or not. All they care about is that it was by Picasso. Much modern art has nondistinctive titles like *Mood Number Four, Picture Number Eight, Untitled,* which makes title entry really ludicrous.

Sanford Berman: To continue briefly with information exchange only, I suspect that one of the great impediments to intershelving, as you rightly propose, is packaging, particularly for cassettes and for the small filmstrip and other combinations. Most of the packaging provided by commercial vendors that are known nationwide is pretty bad. It is lousy, falls apart, looks bad, and so on. In the Twin Cities our library and some others have prevailed upon a local producer to prepare good looking, durable packaging for these smaller items. I think this makes them perfectly accommodative to the ordinary bookshelves.

Weihs: Almost every week I get brochures and letters from producers about the latest thing that they plan to bring on the market. I'm very surprised by the large number of containers and packages there are for nonbook materials, and certainly I think it would be very interesting for somebody to do a study of the whole question of storage. It's a whole area that nobody has investigated, other than little bits done here and there.

Nicolescu: Recently our university put into the computer about 3,000 titles of 16mm film. Now it has come time to decide what kind of subject headings to use.

All nonlibrary media specialists want to use descriptors. All librarians want to use LC subject headings because all of our books carry those headings. If you were in my position, would you think LC subject headings are worth fighting for? I need moral support.

Weihs: I would certainly use LC subject headings if you used them for your books. Otherwise you can't integrate.

Eleanor Crarey: I'm a little puzzled about one thing. Did you say you didn't have a chance to read *AACR2?* There was a question that came up yesterday from Ms. Hoduski's speech when she had said that she understood that motion pictures were going to be entered under titles. I read the whole draft through and I did not find anything saying that, and I was looking for that specifically. So I hope that you'll have a chance to look at this more. It is of some concern when we do buy motion pictures more and more in our system and feel that it is almost useless to catalog them under anything but titles. Your points about integration—ideally, yes, of course, we wish we could integrate all of our cataloging for AV material into the regular catalog. If the patron comes and wants subject access on an item, s/he should have a full spectrum of what's available; but at this point, the terms used by LC that are pertinent to AV materials are very far apart from book terms, and certainly in any contemporary music scene they are unfortunately far apart. So I'd be interested in what we can do *right now;* we have a microform catalog, film format. I also have to take exception to the idea of open and integrated shelving. I feel exactly the opposite; I think you lose shelving space by trying to integrate unless you can box things. The shelving and sizes and shapes are so incredibly different. You seem to think this saves shelving. I think you lose shelving this way, and also I think your patrons must be more honest in Canada than they are here because it's so easy to get things in the pocket and go out the door. I think the dummy idea is a good one.

Weihs: I wasn't quite sure what you meant by terminology; were you referring to the general material designations or media designations; or were you talking about subject headings?

Crarey: No, the actual subject terms applied to specific items.

Weihs: Well, this is true. As I said in the study I did on the subject analysis of nonbook materials, the problem that librarians and media specialists felt most depressed about was the cataloging of music recordings. The suggestion I was making, of course, is that you use another list, such as the Hennepin County list, for instance, which I think is quite good in this regard, and just abandon the other lists. For instance, one of the things that we found is that practically no *Sears* users used the *Sears* subject headings for music; I mean they simply just avoided that section of *Sears;* if they came to music they simply didn't use it, and used something else because the headings were so inadequate. Lots of people were sticking to the LC subject headings because they felt they couldn't develop their own lists, but I certainly didn't.

I just don't know where to start on the subject of intershelving. The subject just goes on. So many people have intershelved their materials and found it the most exciting experience, as far as library work goes. We were given a grant of money (I don't know whether you realize the writing of books is a very expensive proposition and this grant of money was helpful.) To us at first it seemed very large, but as we got into the research we found it was very small, so we did unofficial studies. Librarians cooperated with us and as long as we did their work and went in and reshuffled their shelving and things, they were very happy. We had one librarian who was an amateur carpenter who made all kinds of shelves of his own trying to experiment with things. What we did find, and what was quoted to us constantly by people mostly in the United States and Canada, is that intershelving raises circulation of not only nonbook materials but the book collection as well. This is what surprised people.

I want to make absolutely clear that I am not talking about academic or research libraries, but about public and school libraries where the patrons are nonsophisticated. They aren't going in with a definite title and author who they absolutely have to have, the fourth edition, or a certain translation; in other words, they've been given an assignment on the monarch butterfly. Whatever you have on the monarch butterfly is just fine with them. We particularly found that the circulation rose in school libraries where you have, of course, a lot of people coming to a library that don't want to be there and a lot of nonreaders. We found that the nonreaders were very attracted by the media. For instance, boys would be terribly attracted to find gorgeous study prints on motorcycles. They'd advance from the study prints to the film loops and that excited them. Then they went to another media and eventually we found that these boys would be reading the books that were standing on the same shelves as the media. They got so involved in learning about a subject that they loved, that the schools found there was an advance in the reading that these students were doing. As I say, I could go on forever on this subject.

Fasana: You sounded rather paranoid about nonbook materials being considered second class citizens, yet you want to consider anything other than a media center as a second class citizen when it comes to nonbook materials. I would submit that libraries are acquiring and storing nonbook materials more and more. In my library, for example, of twenty million pieces organized for use, three-quarters are nonbook materials. So we do have very strong needs in large academic, research libraries for this kind of thing.

I know that in nonbook libraries there have been a wide variety of standards and codes in the past. The new code has been introduced. Granted you don't know exactly what's in it, but will libraries adopt it? And if they do adopt it, what will they do with the expensive catalogs they have? Obviously, the home-grown rules treated entry in a very different way from what the new rules will do. Will they, in fact, recatalog? Will they abandon their catalogs, close them, and start fresh?

Weihs: I have been working on the rules for description. I haven't seen the rules for entry. Therefore, Mr. Fasana, I can't say. The last set of rules, *AACR1*, was unusable for integrated collections. You had one set of rules for entry for one thing and another set of rules for another. For instance, if you have a picture reproduced as a slide, you had a media designation and it was entered under title. If you had the same picture as a poster, it didn't have a media designation and it was entered under the artist. I think the new rules will be respected if they are sensible.

To go back to the *AACR2* rule regarding artists and reproductions. I think that media centers will not find that sensible. They have bought that copy of a Renoir painting because it is Renoir, and because a teacher asked for some of his prints. I would expect that most of the media centers I know would not use a rule like that. Because I haven't seen the rest of the rules, I don't know, and we have not settled quite a few of the problems of nonbook materials. They simply have not come up for discussion in the Joint Steering Committee. I hope that there will not be a great change in the terminology used. I think that if there is a great change that that may put a lot of people off.

Unidentified Speaker: Is the classification you suggested the same as for books because of shelving purposes, or just because some people know a field of interest is classified in certain numbers? Also, why do we subdivide book materials differently from audiovisual materials?

Weihs: Answering your first question, I would classify material because I would intershelve it. Therefore, if you're going to intershelve it you have to have it classified. Even if you have decided to segregate your material it is wise to classify it; if you're going to go into a machine system, classification is one of the ways you can call up a bibliography.

Secondly, the whole subject of subdivisions is a big problem. When we were writing our book we had to give great consideration to the subdivision *Pictures, illustrations, etc.* As you think about that subdivision you will realize that about 95 percent of audiovisual materials could have this subdivision. You could have drawers full of this subdivision and it becomes meaningless. That's just one illustration. All the subdivisions were meant for a book-oriented cataloging system. When you introduce nonbook materials into the cataloging system in any quantity, you have to start rethinking that subdivision problem.

Ellen Lang: You were discussing the use of subject headings. It's been my experience that many schools are tied to using audiovisual materials as the actual materials for a course. It's hard for them to realize the concept of having true subject headings for these materials in the same way they would have them for books. What is your thought on this?

Weihs: That is a case of public relations. One of the problems with school libraries is that principals quite frequently don't see any use for them at all, or very little use. Or they just put the kids there to keep them quiet. It's a matter of public relations to explain why it's absolutely necessary to give good cataloging to nonbook materials.

Berman: In your opinion, how well will the new *AACR* handle AV items or packaging that holds more than one form of media?

Weihs: This is an area of *AACR2* that has not yet come up for discussion. I do not agree with the way the rules are constituted now. At the moment, if you have an item that has two different media, there are two ways of cataloging it. The first way is to decide whether one of the media is dominant. If one is dominant, you would catalog the item by that medium and put the other in the collation. If, on the other hand, you consider that neither of the media is dominant, you would use a double, general material designation. For example, you would have *filmstrip* plus *sound recordings* after the title. If you have more than two items, you would catalog it under the general material designation *multimedia*. This means that there is no place for the items which have been considered kits before. Another example is one in which there are boxes of cards with which students work on math, English, and various problems on their own. If you're going to go down the list of general material designations, you might give the term *book* to it, but I think there are very few of you who would want to catalog it as a book.

When we put out the limited edition, we had all items composed of two different media designated as kits. Then, when we wrote the first edition, the Joint Advisory Committee on Nonbook Materials advised us that the proper way to catalog a kit was by the dominant medium. The feedback that we have gotten in the last four years since the book has been published shows that people dislike the concept of dominant medium very much. One of the reasons is that it takes a great deal of cataloging time to try and establish which is the dominant medium. It is also causing a problem in networking, because somebody decides the filmstrip is dominant and another library decides that the sound recording is dominant. When they are sharing the cataloging, they don't recognize that it is the same item. This is something that people in this room should consider.

Berman: A couple of years ago when we got involved greatly in this domination issue at our place, we resolved not to play Solomon's game to determine which was dominant or recessive, and used the designator "kit." I think the result was quite satisfactory.

Index

Compiled by Sanford Berman